Language: The Social Mirror
Third Edition

Elaine Chaika
Providence College

Heinle & Heinle Publishers
A Division of Wadsworth, Inc.
Boston, Massachusetts 02116 USA

The publication of *Language: The Social Mirror, Third Edition* was directed by the members of the Heinle & Heinle ESL Publishing Team:

David C. Lee, Editorial Director
Kristin Thalheimer, Production Editor

Also participating in the publication of this program were:

Publisher: Stanley J. Galek
Editorial Production Manager: Elizabeth Holthaus
Project Manager: Judy Keith
Assistant Editor: Kenneth Mattsson
Production Assistant: Maryellen Eschmann
Associate Marketing Manager: Donna Hamilton
Manufacturing Coordinator: Mary Beth Lynch
Book Designer: Laurel Roth Patton
Illustrator: Aliona Katz
Illustrator, map, page 281: Leslie Genser
Cover Artist: Frances Middendorf
Cover Designer: Bortman Design Group

Library of Congress Cataloging-in-Publication Data

Chaika, Elaine, 1934-
    Language, the social mirror / by Elaine Chaika.—3rd Ed.
        p. cm.
    ISBN 0-8384-4731-7
    1. Sociolinguistics.   I. Title
P40.C45 1994
306.4 ' 4—dc20

Heinle & Heinle Publishers is a division of Wadsworth, Inc.

Manufactured in the United States of America

ISBN: 0-8384-4731-7

To Lee, Adrian, and Alex

Acknowledgements

I would like to thank the following language professionals who gave helpful comments during the development of this revision.

Nancy Burkhalter, University of Wyoming
Ann Calhoun-Sauls, Belmont Abbey College
Marvin K. L. Ching, Memphis State University
Joan Kelly Hall, University of Georgia
Sarah Hudelson, Arizona State University
André M. Kapanga, University of Nebraska at Lincoln
James Kohn, San Francisco State University
Ines Senna Shaw, North Dakota State University
May Shih, San Francisco State University
William Spence, Western Maryland College
Gerald J. Tullai, Central Connecticut State University
Hanna K. Ulatowska, University of Texas at Dallas
Jessica Williams, University of Illinois at Chicago

I would also like to thank my students, who are the source of my continuing education.

Table of Contents

91143

Phonetic Symbols Used in this Book

[ ] =   phonetic symbol for actually pronounced sound
/ / =   phoneme, sound hearer thinks has been made
< > =   conventional spelling

Note: all values of sounds are as most American English speakers pronounce them. Native French speakers, for instance, would not pronounce the [pʰ], [tʰ] and [kʰ] with the puff of air represented by the superscripted [h].

CONSONANTS:

[p] =   <p> in apple, soap
[pʰ] =   <p> in put
[b] =   <b> in boot
[t] =   <t> in atlas, boot
[tʰ] =   <t> in toy
[d] =   <d> in dog
[k] =   <c> in Mac, <k> in look, <ck> in back
[kʰ]=   <c> in cut, <k> in kill
[g] =   <g> in go
[ǰ] =   <g> in rage, <j> in joy
[m]=   <m> in me
[n] =   <n> in not
[ŋ] =   <ng> in sing, doing
[θ] =   <th> in thigh
[ð] =   <th> in thy
[s] =   <s> in so, <c> in city
[z] =   <z> in zoo, <s> in is, lose
[š] =   <sh> in shall, <su> in sure, <ch> in machine, <ti> in nation
[ž] =   <si> in persuasion, <su> in pleasure
[č] =   <ch> in church
[r] =   <r> in rat, <l>[1] in colonel
[ɚ]=   vowel + <r> in word, bird, nerd, curd
[l] =   <l> in lady
[w]=   [w] in win
[y] =   <y> in yet, <u> in use

VOWELS:

Note: Dialects of English[2] differ greatly in the pronunciation of vowels. Therefore, it is difficult to impossible to find words as examples that will reflect the value of each vowel for all speakers. For instance, some dialects pronounce *talk* and *coffee*[3], with an [ɔ], but others use an [a]. The grid below represents the human mouth, and the vowel symbols on it represent the approximate position of the tongue when it makes those vowels. A good way to get a feel for the values of these sounds is to start at the high front [i] (as in *seat*) and gradually move the tongue down, keeping it forward. Then start with the high back [u] as in *boot* and move down, keeping the tongue back. The [ə] is the mid central vowel, and the other central vowels are higher or lower. To approximate the [ɨ], Wolfram and Johnson (1982) start at the high front vowel and move the tongue backward, but not all the way to the high back vowel [u]. Alternatively, start at [ə] and move the tongue up and forward. There is also a difference in tenseness between certain pairs, so that when you say [i], you feel a tightness in the tongue and jaw, but when you lower it to [I], you feel the relaxation of both. The higher of each mid and high vowel is always tense (try them), and the lower one is lax (try them).

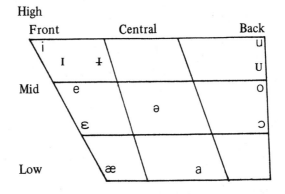

Position of the tongue for vowels

[i] = <ee> in *beet,* <ea> as in *beat*
[I] = <I> in *bit*
[e] = <a> in *bait,* <ea> in *great,* <ei> in *weight,* <ai> in *wait*
[ɛ]= <e> in *bet,* <ea> in *head*
[æ] = <a> in *bat*
[ɨ] = <a> in *can,* <u> in *just* (unstressed[4] and said rapidly as in *jus' a minute)*;

(also, some Southern pronunciations) of <i> in *sister, dinner*[5]. Some Americans have this as the vowel before /r/ in *ear, deer*, and *beer.* Eastern New England uses this vowel even though the /r/ is dropped. This vowel may be tense or lax. In Eastern New England and New York City, the tensed version is highly stigmatized.

[ə] = first <a> in *above*, final <a> in *sofa*. Word final <-er> in /r/-less dialects in *farmer* (always unstressed)

[ʌ] = <u> in *but*, <o> in *son*

[a] = <a> in *father*, <o> in *not*, <al> in *palm*, <au> in *aunt* (Eastern New England, Black, and most British dialects)

[u] = <oo> in *boot*

[U] = <oo> in *soot*, <u> in *put*

[o] = <o> in *not* (British English only)[6]

[ɔ] = <ou> in *bought*, <o> in *coffee*, <al> in *talk*, <aw> in *saw*, <or> in *orange* (Some dialects have this sound only before [r]). Elsewhere, they use [a]. If you say *talk* and *tock* differently, chances are that you are using [ɔ] in *talk*.

DIPHTHONGS:

[aⁱ] = <i> in *ride*

[ʌⁱ] = <i> in *rite, right*

[eⁱ] = <ai> in *raid*, <a_e> in *made*

[oⁱ] = <oy> in *Joyce*

[ɔⁱ] = <oy> in *joy*

[æᵘ] or [aᵘ] = <ow> in *now*, <ou> in *lousy*

[ʌᵘ] = <ou> in *louse*

[oᵘ] = <ow> in *know*, <oa> in *road*, <o_e> in *rode* [7]

Notes

1 The first <l> is pronounced as an [r], not the second
2 This seems to be true of many languages. Apparently, vowels are not so important in deciphering words, so that they can be used as social or regional markers.
3 The first vowel in *coffee*. Most dialects do pronounce the final vowel similarly, although there are differences in how high or low that is, and how long it is held.
4 Phonologists in the 1930s and 1940s reported this only in unstressed syllables, but it occurs in stressed syllables in many dialects of American English.
5 Wolfram and Johnson (1982, p. 29). Additionally, many speakers in New England and the Great Lakes cities increasingly have this vowel in stressed syllables spelled with <a> and pronounced [æ] in older American English. New England and New York City quite regularly use this [ɨ] before nasals as in *camera* and *dance*.
6 American English does not use the true [o] sound anymore. The true [o] is in most of the European languages, as in Spanish *loco*, Italian *ricotta*. However, most American linguists have adopted this symbol for the vowel sound in *boat*, which is actually a diphthong composed of [o] and [u].
7 Many American linguists have adopted the Trager-Smith system of recording English diphthongs: [ay] for the vowel in *ride* and [aw] for the vowel in *now*, but this is confusing, as in these combinations in ordinary spellings, such as *say* and *saw* stand for very different sounds. Following older IPA practice, and Wolfram and Johnson (1982), I represent the diphthongs with the superscripted vowel showing the direction the tongue moves after making the nucleus of the diphthong [o] or [a].

References

Wolfram, W., & Johnson, R. (1982). *Phonological analysis: Focus on American English*. Washington, DC: Center for Applied Linguistics.

Introduction

In a sense, every discipline asks and tries to answer questions. The sociology of language asks questions about our most basic human behavior, talking. The sociolinguist asks questions, perhaps some you have asked yourself, such as:

Have you ever wanted desperately to voice an opinion but had the words "stick in your throat"? Have you ever had the opposite experience of being compelled to speak when you didn't want to? Do you sometimes find yourself forcing "small talk" with someone you either don't know or don't much care for? Are there people who never seem to leave you room to "put your two cents in"? And others whom you feel you have to drag every word out of? Do members of some ethnic groups seem pushy to you, and others seem cold?

Have you ever noticed how some people, without giving you any overt commands, can make you do things you don't want to? Do you ever find that you want to flee when someone heaps praise on you, and yet you don't get angry at all when someone else insults you, for instance, by calling you "cheap"? Yet, at other times, even when no derogatory labels are used, you feel very insulted? What is the difference, anyway, between teasing, joking, and real insults?

Has anyone ever accused you of having an accent? Do you notice that other people have accents? Is there any one correct accent? How come there are different accents at all, especially since we all watch the same TV shows and go to the same movies?

Why have some immigrant groups lost the languages that their fore-bears spoke, whereas others have retained the languages of theirs? Do you ever feel uncomfortable talking to people from cultures different from your own? Do they seem to stare too much, or, conversely, never to look you in the eye? Have you ever noticed how some people smile too much, and others are stony-faced? Why is it that you always seem to be talking at cross-purposes with some people, whereas with others you find yourself right "in tune"? Do women and men really speak different languages?

These are the kinds of questions that interest people who study the sociology of language, the field also known as **sociolinguistics**. The reason that these are answerable in terms of sociology is that differences in speaking practices can most often be correlated with the practices of socially defined groups within a society or across societies. There are regional, ethnic, social class, occupational, and even age differences in modes of speaking and there is no way to understand members of any society without understanding these differences. In fact, we find that every social division within a society relates to some facet of speech, or, to put it another way, when people identify with each other socially, their speech will reflect that identification.

Speech here refers to the entire complex of language, regional and social accent, social conditions under which one feels one can or must speak or be silent, body motion, facial expression, the amount of personal space one requires in an interaction, one's choice of vocabulary items, the entire situation of communication. There is another side to communication as well. Not only do we use sociolinguistic rules to produce speech, but we also use them to make judgments about other people, and they, of course, judge us by the way we speak. In fact, much of what we understand people to be saying, the actual meaning that we retrieve, is governed by our sociolinguistic rules. It is not too much to say that without an understanding of ordinary speech practices, we cannot understand any society. Teachers, psychiatrists, social workers, lawyers, physicians, all need to understand the variation in communication practices among the people they deal with. Much of this book will show that without such knowledge, these professionals are hampered in doing their work effectively.

Some scholars try to maintain a distinction between the labels **sociolinguistics** and **sociology of language**. Hudson (1980, pp. 3–5) defines *sociolinguistics* as 'the study of language in relation to society,' and *sociology of language* as 'the study of society in relation to language.' He, however, admits there is a great deal of overlap between the two. Earlier, Joshua Fishman (1970 p.1) says that "sociology of language examines the interaction between . . . the use of language and the social organization of behavior." He then, rightly I think, uses the term *sociolinguistic* to refer to the same concerns. There is no way to draw a demarcation between the two, as they are two halves of one coin. For instance, in much of the English-speaking world, an [r] is dropped if the next sound is a consonant. That is a matter of the structure of those varieties of English which are [r]-dropping. However, in Eastern New England and New York City, there is variation in dropping the [r]. Some speakers do it more than others, and social facts explain which speakers will do it. We must talk about [r]-dropping both as a rule of language and a fact of social structure. As we shall see, because of their marking function, such speaking practices help to maintain social organization. As Fishman (1970, p. 1) says, "sociology of language focuses on the entire gamut of topics related to the social organization of language behavior . . . including language use . . . language attitudes . . . overt behaviors towards language and [its] users." This book will demonstrate that language structure and language use at any given time, and language change over time, reflect the social conditions within a society. Language and society are so intertwined that it is impossible to understand one without the other. There is no human society that does not depend upon, is not shaped by, and does not itself shape language. Every social institution is maintained by language. Law, religion, government, education, and the family are all set in place and carried out with language. We use language to reveal or conceal our personal identities, our characters, and our background, often wholly unconscious that we are doing so. Almost all of our contact with family and friends, and much of our contact with strangers involves speaking. And, much of that speaking is strongly governed by rules, rules that dictate not only what we should say but also how we say it. We manipulate others with language, and they manipulate us, often without either party being at all aware of the manipulation.

Sociolinguistics is the study of the ways people use language in social interactions of all kinds. The sociolinguist is concerned with the stuff of everyday life: how people talk with their friends, families, and teachers, as well as to storekeepers, doctors, and enemies. Sociolinguistics is concerned with apparently trivial matters, with the talk on street corners and in bars as well as in the classroom or on the stage. It is concerned with the behaviors people aren't usually aware of, such as when you say "so anyway" or "well" before you make a statement, how often you pause and say "like" or whether or not people look others "in the eye" as they talk, and, even if it's true that women talk a lot and men don't. Sociolinguists even study matters such as where people choose to sit in a cafeteria or at a meeting, or the amount of space they want between themselves and someone else while they are talking.

Such everyday matters are highly revealing, showing how a given society is stratified. Often people think of social stratification as a matter of money, but it actually entails any kind of identity grouping in society. Often money or lack of it cuts across social stratification. By **stratification,** I mean, the different groups which make up the society, those who are considered upper class or lower, those who consider themselves as belonging to one ethnic or racial group rather than another, and even those who feel it is worthwhile to work hard in school, and those who do not. As we shall see, this is often not a matter of laziness or stupidity, but of different child-rearing practices, unconscious loyalty to one group, or alienation from another.

Moreover, as Fairclough (1989) and Lakoff (1990) have so persuasively shown, such apparently diverse matters as politeness rules in society, the way we ordinarily converse, and the words that newspapers use to report incidents are all effective ways of maintaining power relations within society. Even the selection of a standard accent, dialect, or language is a strong force in determining who will and who will not have power in any modern nation. Since our language and social learning are typically relegated below everyday awareness, people typically do not realize how social and political structures are maintained through everyday speaking practices. People are largely unaware of what they actually do when they speak and of how they unconsciously "fill in the blanks" when others speak (Fairclough 1989:77, 233–247; Lakoff 1990:1–6).

Most people find that an academic course in the sociology of language is both interesting and exciting, a true consciousness-raising experience. Students become more conscious of their own behaviors, how they are responding to other people, and how others behave and respond. Typically, everyday language behaviors are ignored in education at all levels. Despite the intense interdependence of language and society and language and knowledge, it is still possible for students to study such fields as politics, sociology, and psychology without ever examining the daily, unself-conscious language through which all of these are mediated. It has become increasingly evident that, without such examination, there can be no social or political emancipation.

Moreover, such inquiry heightens one's sensitivity not only to one's own speech behavior, but to the speech of others, to sources of misunderstanding, to deeper understanding, to the sharpening of one's "intuitions" about people, and even to matters like how rock songs are sung and why, and the dialogue of soap operas, novels, and movies. Sociolinguists (e.g., Tannen 1981; Scollon and Scollon 1981) have increasingly found that serious misunderstandings occur between members of different groups simply because they do not share the same rules for politeness, or because their ideas of what it is permissible to joke about differ.

Examining the speech activities of different social groups also casts light on the conditions, values, and beliefs that have helped shape the groups. Conversely, it also shows how social situations determine what kinds of speech will be used and how speech develops to meet social needs.

Perhaps most importantly, sociolinguistics tells us what messages we are really giving when we speak, messages that are not put into actual words. It shows how and why we feel uncomfortable, even hostile, to some people, especially those who do not share the rules of speech behavior that we abide by, rules so thoroughly learned that we are not even aware of them.

Students of sociolinguistics should gain new respect for all peoples, more than any number of lectures on brotherhood or sisterhood could ever give them. This is because the sociology of language shows the true genius involved in all language activities. This genius can often be seen even when people use language considered incorrect or vulgar or it is spoken by people whom we might otherwise view as primitive or technologically backward.

Reference

Fairclough, N. (1989). *Language and Power.* Language in Social Life Series. New York: Longman.

Fishman, J. (1970). *The Sociology of Language: An Interdisciplinary Social Science Approach to Language in Society.* Rowley, Mass: Newbury House Publishers.

Hudson, R. A. (1980). *Sociolinguistics.* New York: Cambridge University Press.

Lakoff, R. T. (1990). *Talking Power: The Politics of Language.* New York: Basic Books.

Scollon, R., & Scollon, S. B. K. (1981). *Narrative Literacy and Face in Interethnic Communication.* Norwood, N.J.: Ablex.

Tannen, D. (1981). Indirection in discourse: Ethnicity as conversational style. *Discourse Processes,* 4, 221–238.

Chapter 1

What is Language?

We take language very much for granted. It is just something that we do without thinking much about it. Children are not taught their native language. They figure it out for themselves from social interaction. Language is multilayered and does not show a one-to-one correspondence between message and meaning as animal languages do. For this reason, every meaning can be expressed in more than one way and there are many ways to express any meaning. Languages differ from each other, but all seem suited for the tasks they are used for. Languages change with changing social conditions.

THE COMPLEXITY OF LANGUAGE

We so take our ability to speak and understand for granted that we usually don't stop to consider what is involved when we say even the simplest things. We certainly cannot articulate the complex sets of rules we use for pronunciation, for sentence construction, and for discourse production. Nor can we explain what we actually do when we understand another speaker. In fact, this knowledge lies below the level of conscious awareness. If it did not, if we were conscious of everything that goes into speaking, oral communication would be considerably slowed down.

Stop one second. Pretend you are telling a friend what you did last night. How did you decide what words to use? There is almost always more than one word or phrase to express a message. There is always more than one grammatical form that can be used to express the same thought. How and why do you choose the one you do? There are even different ways of pronouncing the same words. Did you say something like "wontcha" rather than "won't you"? Why would you expect your friend to know that "wontcha" really stands for 'won't you'? Or that "meetcha" means 'meet you'? And why choose one pronunciation over another?

Such questions are far from trivial, for the answers to them tell us not only about our society, but as we shall see, they tell us vital things about what it is to be human, what it means to be able to utilize language to give and receive messages. Since we use language to learn and to remember, there isn't really any way to understand how the human mind functions without understanding language, any more than we can understand human societies without understanding their languages.

It is essential, then, to learn what all human languages have in common as well as how they differ. Understanding what they have in common helps us to define what a human being is, but so does understanding how they may differ. We find that languages vary, but they don't vary randomly. They vary in certain respects only. In others, they are alike. However, most of this book will be concerned with the variations, for these are what constitute the sociology of language. This chapter will attempt to delimit what language itself is, how it is constructed, and how it is learned. Certainly, this does not substitute for an in–depth study of language, as in an introductory linguistics course, but it should give the reader a glimmering at least of the incredible complexity of language, at some of the issues that are at stake in sociology which are not so evident if one doesn't appreciate how language is constructed. For instance, we can iterate the proposition that all dialects are equally complex, and we will, but if the reader doesn't perceive the true complexity of even the most nonstandard of speech, this will appear to be merely an idealistic proposition.

Linguistics is the academic discipline that deals with the structure of human language and its varieties. Throughout most of this book, dialects rather than language as a whole will concern us. **Dialects** are varieties of a language, usually, but not always, mutually intelligible to their speakers. Laypersons often call them **accents.** Strictly speaking, however, **accents** refer only to differences in the way words are pronounced, whereas dialects encompass differences in grammar as well as word choice. Here we talk about language itself and whatever we say about it also pertains to dialects.

THE LEVELS OF LANGUAGE

Human language is multilayered. It is composed of a system of meaningless elements that combine by rules into meaningful structures. Sounds, meaningless in themselves, form meaningful words or parts of words. These words combine by rules into sentences, and the sentences combine into discourses, which include conversation, books, speeches, essays, and other connected sentences. Each level has its own elements and rules for use and each also relates to the other levels, also by rule.

As a consequence of being multilayered, human language is not **isomorphic** with its message. This means that there is no necessary one-to-one correspondence between message and meaning at any level.

In contrast, animal communication systems, so far as we can tell, are isomorphic in message and meaning, and there is no breakdown into separate layers of sound, words, or syntax. Both the mulilayered character of language, and its lack of isomorphism create its potential complexity both in message production and in sociological significance, as we shall see.

Human language seems to be the only communication system that combines meaningless elements into meaningful structures. For most speakers, but not all, the meaningless elements are sounds. Languages of the hearing–impaired such as Ameslan (American Sign Language) substitute elements of gesture that are combined into larger units (Bellugi and Fischer 1972).

As far as we know, other animal communication systems are not multilayered and use only meaningful elements. That is, every sound, gesture, or posture used in a nonhuman communication system means something in and of itself. Furthermore, the order in which the sounds and movements of nonhuman communication appear does not affect their meaning. If a monkey emits a call for 'food' and one for 'follow me,' it will mean 'follow me food' no matter which comes first. In nonhuman communication systems, the sum of the message always equals its parts.

In contrast, in human language the message does not necessarily equal its parts. *A Venetian Blind* is not the same as *a blind Venetian,* nor does *count the savings* mean the same thing as *the savings count.* Meaning in language can be more than the sum of its parts, as in *Gwen ordered pizza; Fred, chop suey, and Alex, a hot dog.* We know that Fred ordered chop suey, and that Alex ordered a hot dog, even though the verb *ordered* is not repeated.

Meaning may as easily be less than the sum of its parts, as in *Max is a good kid.* There is no referential meaning to *is.* Many languages, like Russian and Chinese, leave the *is* out, saying the equivalent to 'Max a good kid.' Even to an English speaker, 'Max a good kid' has the same referential meaning as 'Max is a good kid.' Because there are some American speakers who do leave out the *is* in this kind of sentence, however, a distinctly social message is conveyed about the speaker's ethnicity and social class if he or she omits the *is.* Saying "Max is a good kid" and "Max a good kid" will convey the same message about Max, but quite different messages about the speakers of each utterance in English. Thus any utterance might convey both referential and social meanings, and these are not necessarily equal to the sum of the parts used.

Those languages—and dialects—which require the insertion of *is* do so because of arbitrary rules of language, not because of its meaning. That is, *is* and its counterparts *am, are, was, were, be, being,* and *been* do not refer to any action or emotion, nor even to a state, as do verbs like *run, hate,* and *live*. One cannot define *is* as one can such other verbs. In sentences like *Max is a good kid, is* has the major function of filling the slot reserved for verbs in the English sentence. Therefore, the use of *is* belongs to the level of **syntax**, the technical term for **grammar**.

Because elements of language, notably individual sounds, have no meaning in and of themselves, they can be divorced from meaning. Thus, human languages can multiply meanings far beyond those of other communication systems. The essentially meaningless elements of sound and syntax can be combined by rules into a multitude of words, sentences, and discourses. Humans are not confined to a repertoire of inborn messages, as are, for instance, birds, dogs, or elephants. Instead, humans can take the elements of their languages and use them to create new sentences, sentences that they have never heard before, sentences that can be understood by others who know the same language. For instance, look back to the beginning of this chapter, and see how many of the sentences (if any) that you have either heard or read before, sentences which you, nevertheless, had no difficulty understanding.

In contrast, every other creature that we know of is limited to messages that are inextricably tied to meaning, so for them meaning can never be changed. This means that they can never express a new thought or convey a new message of any kind. To a dog, for instance, a growl is a growl. True, it can be used for play, but then it is still a growl, as when a dog is pretending to kill by worrying an old rag. The growl, even in play, cannot mean 'I love you.' or 'I want to go with you.' The dog does have ways of "saying" those things, but he cannot make a growl carry those messages.[1]

A human, on the other hand, can say "I love you" sarcastically so that it conveys the meaning 'I hate you.' Then, too, the human can use the individual sounds in *I love you* in very different messages. For instance, the l and v in *love* can also be used in *villify,* a word that has quite a different meaning from *love.* Humans can even take sounds of their languages and combine them anew to make up new words, so long as they follow the rules of their particular language for combining sounds correctly. In English, for instance, one could use the *l* and the *v* to make up the word *cluvy* if there was a need for a new word to designate a thing, a quality, or an action for which there was no existing word. Alternatively, one could take an existing word, say *silly,* and make it mean something new. In fact, English *silly* once meant 'holy.' Apparently because people used it ironically often enough, it eventually took on its present meaning. Thus old elements, be they sounds, words, or sentences can be used in new ways. This allows human languages to change over time, even within the lifespan of individuals, and these changes are sensitive to societal conditions.

Although there are built-in rules for word and sentence formation in human language, these rules are constructed so that an infinite number of new words and sentences can be created in any human language (Chomsky 1959, 1965, 1972). So far as we know, no other animal, no matter how intelligent, has such versatile options in its communication system. Therefore, other animals are not able to change their communications to fit new circumstances as humans can and do.

The Sounds of Language

The actual sounds that any language uses to form words have no referential meaning in and of themselves. The *b*'s in *baby, but, bad, bill* or any other word in English—or any other language—have no inherent meaning. Words representing those meanings do not have to have *b*'s in them at all. In French, for instance, *baby* is *enfant* and *bad* is *mal.* So far as we know, the fact that English and French use different sounds in words meaning approximately the same thing makes no difference whatsoever. The sounds that a language uses are arbitrary. Out of the whole universe of sounds that humans can make, no language uses more than a small subset, and one subset of sounds is as good as another for "doing" language.

However, because individual sounds have no referential meaning in and of themselves, this doesn't mean that some of them can't have sociological meaning. That is, one pronunciation of a word might mark a speaker as being educated or hip or an outsider and another will mark him or her as being uneducated, nerdy, or very much part of a given group. The person who says "cayunt" [kʰeyənt] for *can't* is giving social and regional information quite different from that of the person who says "cahn't" [kʰant] for *can't.* Similarly, saying "pinny" [pʰIni] for *penny* may signal either regional or racial feelings of identity or both.

In terms of evolution of language, there must have come a time when sound was divorced from meaning for hominids, and that, in itself, must have been a major breakthrough. Once individual sounds were no longer inherently attached to meaning as in animal languages, then they could be combined and recombined into innumerable meaningful words, thus increasing the possible messages logarithmically. It is linguistically more economical to have *b, m, a, d* mean nothing in and of themselves individually than if *b* always had to mean one thing, *a* another, and *d* still another. By meaning nothing in themselves, sounds are then available to create a plethora of words like *ad, am, ma, bam, bad, mad, dam* and *dab,* as well as, potentially, *bamd, mbad, mab, ab, ba, damb, amb, amd, dma,* and so on.

Each language uses only some of the hundreds of possible sounds that human beings can hear and utter. Then, each has its own rules for combining these sounds into syllables. Even if two languages use the same sounds, the rules may not allow them to be combined in the same ways. For instance, both English and Swahili use the sounds [ŋ], [g], [w], and [e]. However, Swahili allows the [ŋ] to appear at the start of words, whereas English can use it only at the end. Therefore, Swahili has a word [ŋgwe], which means 'strings', but English does not. And, of course, there are combinations of sounds that English allows but Swahili does not, such as the combination of [gd] in *ragged* ("They ragged on Marge mercilessly.")

Phonemes

Not only does each language use its own subset of sounds, but what is even heard as a different sound differs from language to language. We are all familiar with the fact that the Japanese have difficulty with the sounds [r] and [l] in English, so they may pronounce *baseball* as "basebaru." The reason for the final [u] is that, in Japanese, words must end in a vowel, and the reason that [r] replaces English [l] is because [r] and [l] are one **phoneme** in Japanese. That is, the Japanese have both sounds, but they do not hear the difference between them because, in Japanese, an [l] automatically becomes an [r] between vowels. The fact that *Sally* is an old diminutive of *Sarah,* and *Molly* was originally a form of *Mary* shows that even English speakers do process the similarity of [l] and [r], but in English, these are considered separate phonemes. Hence, we hear the difference between *rice* and *lice*. Languages like Japanese which automatically convert [l] to [r] between vowels[2] are using these sounds as **allophones** of each other. That is, speakers don't even hear that they are using what to us are different sounds. They perceive [l] and [r] as one sound composed of the allophones [l] and [r].

Sometimes it is English which perceives two sounds as one. For instance, if you hold your finger to your lips and say "pit" and "spit," you will feel a strong puff of air when you make the first [p], but not when you make the [p] after [s]. This puff of air is called aspiration. In many languages, the aspirated [p] and the unaspirated one are two distinctly different sounds. For instance, in both Korean and Hindi, a [p] and a [pʰ] are heard as being two clearly separate sounds, so [pal] and [pʰal] are two different words. In English, since we do not consciously distinguish between these sounds, we hear [pal] as a funny way of saying [pʰal]. Think of how a French, Spanish, or Italian speaker pronounces *pill,* for instance. That is the unaspirated [p] in [pal], but in English, the phoneme /p/ consists of two sounds with the aspirated one always occurring before a stressed vowel. In French, there is no aspirated [p] at all; hence, the French fail to put that puff of air in English words. (And English speakers automatically and erroneously do put the puff on words like French *peau.*) When trying to speak a language which has both the aspirated and unaspirated [p]'s as separate phonemes, English speakers do the equivalent of what the Japanese do with [l]'s and [r]'s. That is, they treat them as one sound, and simply use each as an allophone according to the rules of English. A foreign accent is partially a matter of using the wrong allophones of phonemes or not even distinguishing between phonemes in the foreign language.

No two languages divide the phonetic universe up into the same sounds. Each language uses a subset of all the possible sounds humans can produce, as noted above, but each language groups several sounds into one sound. The sound we think we hear is the phoneme. The several sounds that we hear as that one sound is the allophone. Apparently, the reason for this complexity is that we subconsciously notice the allophone and this tells us where the sound is in the word. For instance, when we hear the [p] in *spit,* even if we missed the [s], the very fact that there is no aspiration tells us an [s] probably occurred before it. By the same token, when we hear the [pʰ] in *pit,* we know that the sound occurred at the start of the word. Because languages group their sounds into phonemes composed of allophones which occur in specific positions in words, this means that humans need only hear about 50 percent of every message and can still decode it reasonably accurately. This enables spoken language to be produced at a much greater rate than if each and every sound in the stream of speech had to be heard distinctly. When the Japanese speaker hears the [r], it tells him or her that the sound came between two vowels. When the English speaker hears the [pʰ], it tells him or her that a new word has started. One reason that foreign accents can be difficult to understand is that we are not hearing the allophones, which are so important in decoding.

Morphemes

Technically, some whole words, as well as the parts of words are called **morphemes.**[3] The word *renewed,* for instance, is composed of three morphemes: *re-, new,* and *-ed.* These are considered morphemes in English because we recognize the *re-* as a prefix that is attached to many words to convey the meaning 'again.' *New* is a morpheme that is also a word in itself. That is, it can stand alone with no other morphemes attached to it. The ending *-ed* is an English morpheme for past tense. This is required by the grammar of English in certain contexts. The word *renewed* thus illustrates the different kinds of morphemes that appear in languages: those used to add meaning to a given word; words in themselves; and affixes required by the grammar of a language. **Affixes** are morphemes that appear at the beginning or end of words, and, in a few languages, that are inserted in the middle of them. Morphemes can be defined as the smallest unit in a language which gives meaning or has a grammatical function.

We are so used to what our language or family of languages does in regards to word formation that we don't think of the many other ways there are to "do" a language. What we are used to seems natural and inevitable, but languages may achieve the same ends quite differently. This is readily seen in the use of morphemes. In English and other European languages, typically, morphemes required by grammar are put at the end of words as **suffixes,** but other languages have them at the beginning. That is, the grammatical information occurs in the **prefix.** We see this in Swahili.

faw 'break'	nfaw 'is breaking'
law 'go'	nlaw 'is going'
sun 'sleep'	nsun 'is sleeping'
ǰo 'fight'	nǰo 'is fighting'

What English does by the combining of the word *be*[4] and the morpheme *-ing* as a suffix, Swahili does by adding an *n* before the root word itself. This *n* is not merely a sound in Swahili. It is an entire morpheme and gives the Swahili speaker similar meaning to the English speaker's "is —ing." Whether it is a single sound with meaning used as a prefix, as in Swahili, or a combination of a word with a suffix on the next word, as in English, the same effect is achieved and one way of doing the verb is as efficient and sensible as the other.

To give an idea of how varied languages may be in how they convey messages, consider the plural in Samoan, a Polynesian language. It seems evident to English speakers that to indicate that one person has done something, one adds an -s at the end of the verb, as in "He goes," as opposed to "They go." Samoan does this quite differently. It repeats the next to the last syllable of the verb to indicate plural. This is an example of an **infix** rather than a prefix or suffix.

manao 'he wishes'	manao 'they wish'
matua 'he is old'	matutua 'they are old'
malosi 'he is strong'	malolosi 'they are strong'
punou 'he bends'	punonou 'they bend'
	(data from Gleason 1955)

Notice also that words that would be considered adjectives in European languages are verbs in Samoan. Again, different languages have different ways of conveying the same messages, and even parts of speech are not inviolable across languages. This matter will arise again when we consider different dialects of English (Chapter 8). No one way of forming plurals (or any other grammatical category) is inherently better than another, nor is one "part of speech" necessarily superior than another for conveying ideas. Different languages do different things for the same purposes with no apparent difference in communicability.

The actual intricacies of morphemes can be a course in itself, but this discussion should give some notion of the kinds of variety one may expect from language to language—or even dialect to dialect.

Words

We think of words as being basic in language, but as the foregoing shows, words themselves are created from phonemes and morphemes. We also think of words as containing a specific meaning, but, in fact, most words carry many meanings. For instance, the word *energy* in English refers to a human being's physical or mental energy or electrical or fossil fuel power, but it doesn't refer to animals. That is, it seems odd for me to say, "My new puppy has a lot of energy." Yet, in other languages, English *energy* would refer both to humans and animals, but not fuels, or it would refer to animals and fuels, but not humans, or one would need three separate words for the separate notions. Every word subsumes a different complex of meanings in different languages—or even different dialects of one language.

SYNTAX AND DISCOURSE

Words themselves combine by rules of syntax into sentences. Sentences, in turn, combine into discourse. This can be either oral, as in conversation, or written, as in texts. Although we usually think of sentences as having rules of grammar, we shall see that discourse also has rules. These determine the order in which sentences may be arranged, as well as what can be left out of a sentence and what must be included. Even the forms sentences take are often determined by their position in a discourse. For instance, whether or not one can make a noun like *children* into the corresponding pronoun *they* depends on where in the discourse *children* appears. For instance,

▶The children had dirty faces. They were eating candy.

versus

▶The children were eating candy. They had dirty faces.

There is no way to consider the syntax of a sentence without considering the larger discourse, for the grammar rules we apply at the sentence level are, to some degree, dependent upon the other sentences surrounding it.

Notice that even what we consider "a sentence" depends on what rules of syntax we have chosen to use. For instance, the above can also be conveyed by the following:

▶Eating candy, the children got dirty faces.
▶The dirty faces resulted from the children's eating candy.

Here, not only have different rules of syntax been applied, but also different words meaning the same things in this context have been used in each paraphrase. There is always more than one way to say anything in any language.

The essence of language lies in the fact that elements must be combined to create messages. Such combining is what makes languages capable of expressing so many meanings. Also, because every part of every utterance does not have to have a specific meaning in human languages, then humans are free to change the meanings of words and phrases, and to make up new ones. Thus, language changes as society changes. Moreover, what people actually say and what they mean may be quite different. "There is no spaghetti sauce" may mean "Go out and buy some spaghetti sauce" or "I can't make supper" or, even "You idiot. You forgot the spaghetti sauce again." As we shall see, much of what we call politeness depends on such disjunction between meaning and the actual words used.

SYNTAX AND GRAMMAR

The term **syntax** was used to refer to the rules for combining words into sentences. The more commonly used term for putting words together into sentences is **grammar**. Unfortunately, as commonly used, grammar is an evaluative term, so that people think of good or bad grammar. Syntax is a neutral term, therefore preferable in a study of social behavior. When discussing different social groups, it is often necessary to speak of differences in rules between their dialects. This is of great importance, both in understanding members of groups other than our own and in teaching.

If a syntax rule is not part of a dialect, we say it is **ungrammatical** for that dialect. The usual word ungrammatical will be used in this book, but with a meaning somewhat different from the one that the reader may be used to. Here it will always mean, 'the speakers of a given dialect do not use a particular form or word order.'

This never implies that using or not using a form or word-order is good or bad. For instance, "I am wanting to know that" is ungrammatical for many Americans, but it is often heard from the British. In dialects of English spoken by urban educated Americans today, "He don't" is ungrammatical, but it is grammatical for most people who have little formal education. Ironically, "He don't" used to be grammatical for all English speakers, educated or not. This shows how arbitrary judgments are about what is proper in language.

Often, ungrammatical constructions are readily understandable. Our judgment of whether or not a construction is grammatical is not determined on the basis of comprehensibility alone. The rules of grammar in human languages constitute a system in themselves and do not have a one-to-one correspondence with meaning. One result of this is that we can understand little children and foreign speakers who do not have all the rules of grammar of our language down pat. We can also understand speakers of other dialects who use rules of grammar somewhat different from our own. Poets often make poetry by deliberately changing some grammar rules for artistic purposes. The human ability for poetry rests on our ability to deal with grammars not exactly like our everyday ones.

Another exceedingly important result of our being able to understand those whose grammar differs from our own is that members of different social groups within the same community can understand one another's speech despite dialect differences between them. Therefore, dialect can be an important marker of social divisions within a community without affecting communication.

Above all is the curious fact that using new or different grammar rules does not cause language to decay. Meaning can still be preserved. Only in the speech of victims of severe mental pathologies, such as those occurring from brain damage, is meaning usually lost. In such instances, few or no words may be recognizable or syntax may be so faulty that it is impossible to figure out the relationship of words to each other.

The grammatical mistakes that most people call "bad grammar" really are social markers. They do not necessarily reflect poor intelligence or faulty knowledge on the part of the speakers. As much as one might deplore "ain't got none" or "him and me went," they are regular productions in some dialects of English.

The fact that two dialects or two languages have different rules does not make one inherently better than another. One may be socially preferred, but that is another matter. Today, for instance, using certain kinds of double negatives is considered incorrect in English. Certainly, no one has any trouble understanding that "I didn't do nothin'" means "I didn't do anything." No one ever takes it to mean, 'I did something' just because, in mathematics, two negatives make a positive. In fact, double negatives are still used by the prissiest of English speakers in sentences like "I was not unhappy." Many languages habitually use double negatives. Italian, for instance, allows *Non ho fatto niente*, and French allows *Je n'ai rien fait*, both of which mean literally 'I haven't done[5] nothing.'

To show how arbitrary the double negative rule is even in English, we can point to older stages of English. Shakespeare used double negatives frequently, especially for emphasis, as in "No sonne were he never so olde of years might not marry" (Abbott 1870, p. 295). Today, the same emphatic use of double and even triple negatives is heard in English considered nonstandard, as in "Ain't no cat can't get into no [pigeon] coop" (Labov 1972 p. 130). The rule forbidding double negatives is arbitrary. Languages work perfectly well with or without double negation. In English today, however, certain double negatives are socially wrong in certain circumstances. That is, although there is nothing inherently wrong with double negatives, there can be something socially wrong with some of them, but not necessarily all, at this time in history.

CHAPTER 1

THE ARBITRARY NATURE OF LANGUAGE

The reader should always bear in mind the difference between the inherent worth of particular kinds of speech as opposed to their social worth. The two are not the same. The particular grammar rules of a language at a particular moment in history are frequently arbitrary. By *arbitrary,* we mean that they don't have to be the way they are, and different languages and dialects have different but equally good rules for such matters. This is in contrast to those features which all languages have in common, such as nouns and verbs. It has been taken as a given that the things all languages have in common are reflections of the human mind and are, therefore, not arbitrary (Chomsky 1972).

Languages are also arbitrary in the sounds they use and in their word choice as well. Just because the English say "tree" for what the French and Germans call *arbre* and *Baum,* respectively, we can't draw any conclusions about their respective national characters. The words themselves and the sounds making them up are arbitrary choices, explicable only in terms of the history of each language. One word does as well as another to designate trees so long as listeners understand what is meant.

Linguists have not been able to find any primitive languages, even among the so-called primitive peoples. All languages spoken in the world as far back as we have any record are equally complex and can potentially do pretty much the same things. For example, every language has some way of indicating whether someone did the action or received it, as a sentence like "The boy bit the dog." English does it by word order. Russian does it by endings on each noun. Swahili does it by prefixes on each noun. Each way is as logical and intelligent as the other. The difference between languages and dialects is not what they can do, but how they do it (Gleason 1961, p. 232).

In their vocabulary and discourse rules, languages may differ in accordance with the values of their societies. Indeed, that is what this book is about. However, no language is fixed at any point. Language is not static. Any language can change in any way its speakers want it to, or need it to, and it can change as soon as speakers wish it to.

Every language has built into its very structure the mechanisms of change. Moreover, all normal speakers of all languages have the ability to:

▶Make up new words.
▶Use old words in new ways.
▶Compose sentences they have never heard before.
▶Combine sentences into wholly new discourses.

Speakers, in short, can say new things in their old language. The corollary is that speakers of a language can understand:

- ▶New words used in a context, often without the speaker's having to define them.
- ▶Old words used in new ways.
- ▶New sentences.
- ▶New discourses.

Noam Chomsky (1959, 1965, 1972) calls the twin abilities of saying and understanding new things the creative aspect of language. He believes there is no way to understand the human mind without understanding its ability to handle creativity in language use. This book will show that there is no way to understand human society without considering this creativity. At the very least, it means that neither individuals nor their societies are wholly bound by the past.

LANGUAGE AND THOUGHT

The very fact that language can be made to take on new meanings shows that language and thought are not necessarily one and the same. So far as we know today there is no one-to-one correspondence between language and thought.

Any thought can be expressed in many ways. That is, all languages allow paraphrase. For instance, if one wishes to inform someone that Jack and Ellen got married after a long courtship, one can express that in at least the following ways:

- ▶Jack and Ellen got married after a long courtship.
- ▶Jack is finally married to Ellen.
- ▶Jack and Ellen are finally married.
- ▶Jack and Ellen finally tied the knot.
- ▶At long last, Jack got married to Ellen.

Any native speaker of English could easily find yet other ways to indicate Jack and Ellen's state of matrimony. Note that the paraphrases are on different levels of the language. Some utilize different **lexical items**. That is, different words or different phrases are used to express the same idea. Notice that individual words may be paraphrased by phrases, as in the alternation between *married* and *tied the knot*, and *finally* and *at long last*. Other paraphrases work by changing **word order**. This last determines whether or not a preposition has to be used, so "Jack and Ellen" may be paraphrased by "Jack...to Ellen."

Furthermore, language also allows ambiguity, so that a word or a sentence can have more than one meaning. Story can mean either 'narrative' or 'level of a building[6].' *Visiting relatives can be boring* can mean either 'relatives who visit can be boring,' or 'it can be boring to visit relatives.' Words and sentences can change meaning according to their contexts.

Not only are utterances potentially ambiguous, but the same words or sentences may be perceived as having very different intentions or forces in different contexts. For instance, "It's cold in here" on the surface means 'The temperature in this place is lacking in warmth.' However, given the right context, such as a hot summer's day in an air-conditioned room, it could mean 'Boy, that air conditioner works well.' Under somewhat different social conditions, it could also mean 'I can see I'm not wanted here.'

The same sentence could also have the force of a command. If the person speaking has a right to command the person addressed, either because of social status or just because the person addressed is closer to the switch, then "it's cold in here" could be interpreted as 'turn the air conditioner off.' If the air conditioner had been reported to be malfunctioning, then the meaning could be construed as, 'this thing is working just fine.'

So important is context to meaning and force of language that to quote someone out of context can constitute an actual lie. The enraged protests of politicians and other often quoted and misquoted newsworthy folks show us how easy it is to twist someone's meaning just by omitting sufficient context.

Later chapters will demonstrate that the context that determines meaning includes among other things:

▶The social status of speakers.
▶The speech event and the social conventions governing it.
▶The social-cultural and physical environment.
▶Previous discourse between the speakers or those known to them.
▶The perceived intent of the speaker.

Meaning, in other words, has a social base. Words do not just mean. They mean in social interaction in a particular society.

FIRST LANGUAGE ACQUISITION

Acquiring language is very much a socially determined phenomenon. No child can learn an oral language without hearing one spoken. If a baby is exposed to more than one language, it will select for learning only those which it perceives have some social function, so in many immigrant homes in the United States children never learned the language of their grandparents—or barely learned that of their parents—although they heard it all the time, unless the family insisted that English not be used within the home or for certain social functions.

One very important consequence of the fact that language is always changing is that it cannot be learned solely by mimicking. The very fact that the same utterance may mean very different things in different contexts shows that people use active decoding strategies in order to understand. They have to match the sentence to the context in order to get the meaning.

Recent studies of how children learn to use language strongly suggest that no one teaches them how to understand. Even little toddlers extract meaning from what they hear by matching it to the context. Toddlers seem to expect that adults will use such a strategy (Baron 1977). The toddler who says, "Mommy sock" will use it to mean 'This is Mommy's sock', 'Mommy put on my sock,' or even, 'I'm putting Mommy's sock on my doll' (Bloom 1970). One wonders how one could explain to fifteen month-olds that they can utter the same words in the same order to give different meanings in different contexts. Again and again while examining the speech of young children, one finds that they are doing such things with words and sentences, things that no one could have taught them.

A simple, apparently trivial example demonstrates this assertion: toddlers habitually make errors in the past tense of irregular verbs, such as saying "comed" for *come*, "goed" for *went*, and "breaked" for *broke*. Interestingly, babies first use *went, came,* and other correct forms of irregular verbs as their parents do (Ervin 1964). However, as soon as they perceive that there is a regular past tense ending *-ed,* as in *played* and *cooked,* they apply it to all verbs to indicate 'past time.' More recently, Bowerman (1985, p. 88) shows that on all levels of language, initially, the child uses many words or other forms separately to give different meanings. Then he or she comes to recognize that several of these can be put together into one class. This is the point at which overregularizing occurs.

Furthermore, even babies growing up in educated homes prove very resistant to correction, continuing in these errors for years, despite the fact that the verbs involved are among the most common in the language, and they constantly hear the correct forms from their parents, on television, and in the streets. Paradoxically, this shows how intelligent children are, not how stupid. For a baby to figure out a form like "goed" when all he or she has probably ever heard is "went" means that the baby is actively figuring out how the language is working. The baby has somehow categorized words into at least nouns and verbs, of course, without calling them that (Berko 1958; Menyuk 1971). The toddler acts as if he or she has categorized words into different parts of speech, some of which take tense endings and some of which do not. Not surprisingly, at the same stage, toddlers are using plural endings on nouns and, again, generalizing them to all nouns, making mistakes like "foots" and "mouses".

What makes the baby's performance all the more amazing is that many languages of the world, such as Chinese, do not use tense markers on verbs or plurals on nouns. Rather, they use words meaning 'before,' 'in the future,' 'next month,' and the like, if it is necessary to note the time. Similarly, if the amount of something talked about is relevant, then a quantifying word is used with the noun without added plural endings. This means that babies cannot be born expecting grammatical markers of any particular kind, as they have to be able to learn whatever language they will be exposed to in infancy.

Babies must be born knowing how to go about learning language, or else they would not be able to figure out the grammatical rules as they apparently do. English-speaking babies notice that there are tense and plural markers. Russian babies have an even more complicated task in learning word endings, for Russian has six different endings on nouns to indicate how they are being used in particular sentences, whether as the subject or the object or in some other function. Furthermore, there are three different genders in Russian: masculine, feminine, and neuter, and each uses a different set of endings. Still, before the age of two, Russian babies have begun to experiment with endings. Typically they are already using at least one to indicate direct objects. Like English-speaking babies the Russian babies start out by generalizing one ending for a function. Just as the English speaker starts out putting -ed on a verb like go, the Russian baby puts the feminine direct object ending -u on all nouns, even masculine or neuter ones. Similar phenomena have been reported for babies who have to learn Turkish, Finnish, or Serbo-Croatian, all languages that use many endings (Slobin 1979).

Babies who are exposed to languages that do not make use of endings, such as Chinese, have to make different kinds of analyses. For instance, Chinese makes use of an intricate set of noun classifiers, each of which is used with a different set of nouns, such as is marginally seen in English in expressions like "a gaggle of geese" or "a pride of lions."

Although the specifics of the task vary from language to language, apparently the task itself is the same for all babies everywhere. They must figure out for themselves how the language around them works. Babies exposed to more than one language have to do this for each, often concurrently. We do not know how conscious babies are of what they are doing, only that their utterances show the result of analyzing language.

Why don't babies just mimic their parents' language? That would seem more efficient than the active analyses just discussed. As mentioned earlier, in order to use language creatively, which is the essence of language use, children cannot just mimic. If that were all they did to learn language, then children would be able to say only what they had already heard. Instead, they have to learn the unspoken rules that will enable them to express new thoughts or describe new situations so that others can understand them. From the start, human beings are not limited to the utterances they have heard.[7] This, of course, argues that there is free will as Noam Chomsky has so often pointed out (Chomsky 1965, 1972).

There may also be a social reason for active analysis in the language learning process. When they are grown up, children do not necessarily talk like their parents. They talk according to the social conditions facing them, not those facing their parents. Parental speech provides a springboard for children, not a template. From the start, human beings learn language for themselves so that they can adapt it to whatever situations they find themselves in.

Another reason babies do not just imitate may be that sheer imitation is not a very efficient way to learn. For instance, the irregular verbs in English today are chaotic. They no longer form regular classes (although once they did). There is no rule to tell which should be irregular, or if they are irregular, in what way. For example, there is an alternation of *i*, *a*, and *u* in a few irregular verbs, as in *sing, sang, sung, ring, rang, rung*. However, there are verbs that rhyme with these in the present tense, such as *bring, sting, cling*, and *think*, that do not follow the same pattern, although they, too, are irregular. Even if there is some discernible pattern in a few of the irregular verbs, there is no single applicable rule that excludes some verbs and includes others. One can only memorize which verbs change and how. Some of the most common irregular verbs, such as *eat* and *go* have no analogues at all; that is, no other verbs change in the past tense as they do.

In terms of communicative efficiency, saying "eated" and "goed" works as well as "ate" and "went." By applying the -*ed* on all verbs and ignoring the exceptions, babies lose nothing in communicability, and free themselves for other learning. When they learn more grammar and basic vocabulary, they can go back and sort out irregular forms.

The actual adult form of many of these verbs varies according to social and regional dialects. Often, the use of one rather than another marks the speaker as a member of a particular group. Saying "knew" instead of "knowed" or "brought" instead of "brang" gives an essentially social message about a person's identity. Such changes in form do not affect the actual meaning of the verb. Therefore, the fine points, so to speak, of verb forms can be deferred until an age when social identity is more important than it is to a toddler.

Another learning strategy that many young children employ is practice drills, repeating a word over and over, altering the context each time. For example, here are two such drills:

Stoly	Turn of de water
Stoly here	I turn de water
Want a stoly	I turn de water
Dave, stoly	I turn [th]is water
Story, story	I turn off de water
Story's de hat	Here Mommy now
Story's de big hat	de bottle
Story's a hat	(Weir 1962)

Readers who have studied a foreign language may note the similarity of these to oral practice drills. Yet, nobody teaches children to create such drills. They do it on their own. They even select the items they choose to practice, here the difference between /l/ and /r/, and /d/ and /ð /[8]. Weir claimed that this is evidence that children are somehow born knowing how to go about learning language.

Kuczaj (1983, p. 12) points out that crib speech may be the first time children use speech that is not tied to the here and now. This is a defining difference between human language and animal communication systems. He also notes that children practise because they are in control of the situation. Children usually play at what they are learning at the time. Given the enormous task of learning a language, it is not surprising that young children practice talk constantly, while playing with toys, or by simply talking to themselves, often in imaginary situations that they have set up for themselves. One could say that the predilection for engaging in such activities is also proof that children have their own inborn strategies for learning.

Even when a young child can be made to imitate, his or her free productions are not necessarily affected. For instance,

Child: Want other one spoon, Daddy.
Father: You mean, you want the other spoon?
Child: Yes, I want other one spoon, please, Daddy.
Father: Can you say "the other spoon"?
Child: Other...one...spoon
Father: Say...other
Child: Other
Father: Spoon
Child: Spoon
Father: Other...spoon
Child: Other...spoon. Now give me other one spoon?
(Fromkin and Rodman 1983, p. 333)

This toddler is not being stubborn or naughty. He shows every sign of trying to cooperate. Although the task clearly makes no sense to him, he dutifully repeats his father's words. The repetition does not make him see his error, however. He has made up a rule, one that works for him, and for the time being at least, he sticks to it. This is the same sort of behavior as continuing to say "goed" in the face of everyone else's "went." It has its analog in the child who has been drilled in school for years in the use of standard English, but never learns it.

It is not only words and sentence patterns that children do not imitate well. They may fail at simply repeating a sound, even one that they can use under some circumstances. In the following example, the little boy, then thirty-three months old did regularly pronounce /p/ in *party* and *piggy*. However, he had misanalyzed the word *pool* as being *cool*.

Mother: Say "pool."
Child: Cool.
Mother: No, say "pool."
Child: Cool.
Mother: No, listen, "puh-ool."
Child: [watching intently, with great effort]: Cuh-ool.
Mother: No! "Puh-puh-ool."
Child: Oh! Puh-cool.

Even when they are corrected, clearly children have difficulty in locating the source of their errors. They don't seem to know what they are being corrected for. Data like those above caused researchers in the sixties to think that children don't learn to speak by imitating their caregivers,[9] that language unfolds naturally as children, on their own, listen to the speech around them and make up their own rules for producing that language. This view was reinforced by the above data which showed that children cannot and do not merely imitate what they hear around them.

Before then, it was assumed that people spoke as they did because of what they heard around them. Thus, it was thought that variation such as regional accents was caused by the density of communication networks (Bloomfield 1933, p. 328). In a somewhat different context, this idea has been recently revived, but not as a matter of behavioral stimulation. Behavioral psychologists such as Skinner believed that children learn to speak the way they do because they receive positive reinforcement from their parents for speaking correctly. However, if children can't pinpoint their errors so that they can correct them, how could they know what part of the speech code they are being rewarded for? Their speech typically is a combination of correct and incorrect forms (from an adult point of view). The ramifications of one's beliefs about language learning are great for child rearing practices and programs for children with pathologies, such as the deaf, the autistic, and the aphasic. Finding out how children actually do learn language is far from a trivial pursuit.

Landau and Gleitman (1985) and Gleitman (1986) discuss the reasons for believing that children are born with biological equipment that tells them how to go about learning a language. Landau and Gleitman cite reasons such as:

▶ 90 percent of the time, children hear contractions like "we'll" for *we will,* but early in the learning period they use the uncontracted form (p. 7).

▶ Deaf children who are isolated in a hearing family make up their own sign language and follow the same developmental steps at the same ages as hearing children. For instance, the hearing-impaired child makes up signs composed of one gesture at the same age as hearing children use single words (pp. 16-17).

▶ Children create a full language from a Pidgin[10] language on their own when there is no one language for them to learn (pp. 17–18) (Bickerton 1981)

▶ Despite the fact that blind children cannot see any of the stimuli that seeing children do, the blind learn language at the same rate and in the same ways as seeing children. On their own, they reinterpret words like *see* and *look* and relational words like *on* and *in* (pp. 19–22).

▶ Down's syndrome children go through the same stages of learning to speak as healthy children. The Down's children just start later and stop earlier, accounting for their diminished speech capacities (pp. 22–23).

▶ Children raised in bilingual homes learn two or more languages at the same time and at the same rates as children learning only one, and they keep the different languages separate. They could not do this merely by imitating both languages (pp. 24–25).

Thus, the child is a born grammarian. According to this view, there is little caregivers can do to teach children to speak. Noam Chomsky, on the basis of taped recordings of academicians at scholarly meetings, claimed that speech input to children is faulty and fragmented, but miraculously, children are able to construct the grammars of any language to which they are exposed. Of course, the language at an academic meeting is loaded with slips of the tongue, hesitations, and false starts because people are thinking out loud and trying to encode new and difficult thought. This is not the usual input to young children.

Subsequent research (Snow 1986; Yamamoto 1990; Huttenlocher, Haight, Bryk, Seltzer et al 1992) has modified Chomsky's idea that children construct grammars out of fragmented adult speech. Rather, social interaction is required. For instance, hearing children of deaf parents don't learn to speak by being placed in front of a TV. From the time a baby learns to wave and say "bye-bye", language learning takes place through social interaction. Even neonates carry on "babbling dialogues" with their caregivers. The baby is encouraged to vocalize if the caregiver responds.

Huttenlocher et al (1992) found conclusively that the amount of time that different mothers spoke to their children was related to their vocabulary growth, and that this was a mother-initiated effect. Interestingly, Yamamoto (1990) found that gender did not have a significant effect on language development, although birth order did, but only in comprehension, not production. First-born children developed earlier than did later siblings. This was seen as the result of greater attention paid to first-born children. This finding is consonant with Huttenlocher et al. in that parental input to first-born children is probably much higher than with later children. Simply put, mothers have more time to speak with the first and only than they do with their siblings.

Actually, many researchers have asserted that the one factor which does seem to accelerate language learning in older babies is parental imitation. Typically, this is done by expanding on the child's utterances, as when a child says, "dat car" and the caregiver expands it to "That is a red car." (deVilliers and deVilliers 1978, pp. 203–209; Kuczaj 1982, pp. 48–49; Kuczaj 1983, pp. 159–162).

Others have found that children who imitate the most are those whose parents imitate them by expanding their utterances (Kuczaj 1983). Speech is ultimately social, so we expect that it will best be learned by social contact, especially if the child feels his or her speech is important to the parent or caregiver. The child feels that his or her speech is important to the caregiver when it is expanded this way. This constitutes an early dialogue between caregivers and children.

It occurs to me that there is another reason for expansions' facilitating language learning. Part of being able to learn anything is feeling that one can learn it. The parent who expands on children's utterances is, in effect, not only saying to the child "What you say is important to me," but also, "I think you can learn to speak like me, and I will help you by providing you with models."

Even so, not all cultures encourage children this way, yet the children belonging to these cultures grow up to be linguistically very able. Shirley Brice Heath (1983) describes in detail how African American children in a Piedmont town acquire language. In this community, caregivers do not expand on a baby's utterances, nor do they use baby talk. In fact, they talk about, but not to the baby (p. 75). They are aware of the way white middle-class mothers talk to their babies, however. One grandmother explains that she thinks it's silly the way white folks keep asking their children questions like "What's this? What's that?" She says that a child has to learn by keeping his (her grandson's) eyes open. She asks:

> You think I kin tell Teegie all he gotta know to get along? He just gotta be keen, keep his eyes open, don't he be sorry. Gotta watch hisself by watchin' other folks. Ain't no use me tellin' 'im: 'Learn dis, learn dat. What's dis? What's dat? He just gotta learn, gotta know; he see one thing one place one time, he know how it go, see sump'n like it again, maybe it be de same, maybe it won't. He hafta try it out...Gotta keep yo' eyes open, gotta feel to know (p. 84).

This sounds like basic training for verbal and mental agility, which it is. Heath says that preschoolers, especially boys, are always being presented with situations and then asked, "Now what you gonna do?" In Chapter 6, we will see the outcome of this kind of socialization in the clever rapping and other oral performances of African American males. Girls, in line with their adult roles, are taught to "fuss," directing complaints about someone or about an incident. Being a good "fusser" is considered an important part of the female role, including being a good mother. Girls, therefore, are encouraged to fuss at others (pp. 97–98).

In this community, babies are constantly around adults, playing at their feet as the adults talk. Although the adults don't direct words at them, babies and toddlers hear discourse constantly, and can be observed repeating the ends of adult utterances (p. 86). This is a different kind of learning through social interaction, one very much in line with the idea that children have to learn for themselves as well as one in line with the expected behavior of adults, male and female.

The question naturally arises of the consequences of such different child rearing practices. The schools are predicated on middle-class folkways. Clearly some children enter school with an advantage conferred on them by their upbringing. In England, class differences in how children are socialized have been directly blamed for the poor showing of the working class in school (Bernstein 1971; Martin 1983). Later chapters will discuss the relationship between school success and language socialization in greater detail.

Chapter 1 Notes

1   Note that this does not mean that other creatures don't think. Nor does it mean that other animals aren't able to solve problems, even come up with new solutions. For instance, a dog I had was forbidden to sleep on the sofa. Every day, when I came home from work, she would crawl out from under the sofa as I entered the apartment. She even made a show of stretching and yawning. Of course, she didn't know that I knew she had been sleeping on it until she heard my step. I could feel the spot still warm from her body, as well as observe the telltale shedding. However, her ploy, pretending to have been asleep under the sofa, showed creative thinking in her quest to circumvent my ban. Both ethological and laboratory evidence have shown that animals do think despite their lack of language.

2   This is not the only way [l]'s and [r]'s can be treated in different languages. In some, an [r] is used at the beginning and end of words, and

an [l] in between vowels. In others, [l] is always used before consonants and [r]'s are used everywhere else. Still others, like English, use
[l] and [r] as two separate sounds. Yet others may lack one or the other
sound completely, if not both.

3   In actuality, this entire account of morphemes is woefully simplified.
Not only can it be difficult to determine whether certain repeated elements are morphemes in a language or not, but it is often not even
possible to come up with a blanket definition of what a word is in a
given language. Literate people usually consider a word to be whatever would be bounded by space in print, but as a definition, this
doesn't work, since many languages are not written, and even those
that are do not consistently write individual words with spaces
between them. For instance, for no reason apparent to me, in
American English, *hairdresser* is written with no space between *hair*
and *dresser,* but *hair net* is written with the space.

4   in any of its forms, such as *am, is, are, was, were, been*

5   Or they can mean 'I didn't do nothing.'

6   The British sometimes spell the word for level of a building as *storey*
in order to distinguish it from the first meaning. Interestingly, despite
the very different meanings attached to *story,* both derive from the
same word, *historia.*

7   Nor are they later limited by the things they have read.

8   Weir's data were collected from her son's presleep monologues.
Although many babies and young children do practice speech while
alone in their cribs, it is not certain that all do. However, children also
practice speech while playing with dolls, playing "house" or "school"
with other children, and related activities. Even much of the mindless
chatter of toddlers and young children, going around pointing to
everything and naming it, may well be a kind of self-instructional
practice.

9   The term *caregiver* is used for "child care" rather than *caretaker*
because the latter implies cold, impersonal institutional care rather
than the nurturing, loving care which we hope children are receiving
in the homes, at day-care centers, or at schools. *Caretaker* can also be
used for inanimate structures, whereas *caregiver* is used only for
children.

10 Chapter 8 deals with Pidgins and Creoles. A Pidgin is a partial language that is used between people who must interact with each other,
but neither side is able or willing to learn the other's language. It is a
highly simplified, limited language form.

Exercises

1. Find at least two examples in speech or print of new words or old ones used in new ways. Using *The Random House Dictionary, 2nd ed.* and/or *The Oxford English Dictionary*, verify that these are new.

2. Observe a young child talking. Tape-record or write down exactly what he or she says. Explain what rule(s) you think he or she has formed that lead to error.

3. Try to correct a young child's speech error. Do your results conform to those noted in the book?

4. On the basis of information presented in this chapter about language acquisition, prepare a lesson to teach a language-impaired child how to describe a picture of your choice.

5. Listen for slips of the tongue in adults. Explain them in terms of what you know about the organization of language.

6. Listen to a foreign person speak English and write down every word for which the English word sounds foreign because the wrong allophone was used. (That is, the sound is close to the way an English speaker would pronounce it, but is a little "off.") Try to figure what the rule for that allophone is in English and how it must differ from the foreign language. Alternatively, try to pronounce words in another language to someone who is a native speaker of that language. Have the person tell you which words are being said with an American or English accent. Can you hear the difference?

References

Abbott, E. A. (1870). *A Shakespearian Grammar* [Reprinted 1966]. New York: Dover Publications.

Baron, N. (1977). The acquisition of indirect reference: Functional motivations for continued language learning in children. *Lingua, 42,* 349–364.

Bellugi, U., & Susan Fischer. (1972). A comparison of sign language and spoken language. *Cognition, 1,* 173–200.

Berko, J. (1958). The child's learning of English morphology. *Word, 14,* 150–177.

Bernstein, B. (1971). *Theoretical Studies toward a Sociology of Language.*(Class, Codes, and Control. Vol. 1). London: Routledge & Keegan Paul.

Bickerton, D. (1981). *Roots of Language.* Ann Arbor: Karoma Publishers.

Bloom, L. (1970). *Language Development: Form and Function in Emerging Grammars.* Cambridge, Mass: MIT Press.

Bloomfield, L. (1933). *Language.* New York: Holt, Rinehart, Winston, Inc.

Bowerman, M. (1985). Beyond communicative adequacy: From piecemeal knowledge to an integrated system in the child's acquisition of language. In K. E. Nelson (Ed.), *Children's Language* (Vol. 5). Hillsdale, N.J.: Lawrence Erlbaum Associates.

Chomsky, N. (1959). Review of Skinner's Verbal Behavior. *Language, 35,* 26–58.

Chomsky, N. (1965). *Aspects of the Theory of Syntax.* Cambridge, MA: M.I.T. Press.

Chomsky, N. (1972). *Language and Mind.* New York: Harcourt Brace Jovanovich.

deVilliers, J. G., & deVilliers, P. A. (1978). *Language Acquisition* (pp. 203–209). Cambridge, Mass.: Harvard University Press.

Ervin, S. (1964). Imitation and structural change in children's language. In E. Lenneberg (Ed.), *New Directions in the Study of Language* (pp. 163–189). Cambridge, Mass: MIT Press.

Fromkin, V., & Rodman, R. (1983). *An Introduction to Language.* New York: Holt, Rinehart, and Winston.

Gleason, H. A., Jr. (1961). *An Introduction to Descriptive Linguistics.* New York: Holt, Rinehart, and Winston.

Gleason, H. A., Jr. (1955). *Workbook in Descriptive Linguistics.* New York: Holt, Rinehart, and Winston.

Gleitman, L. (1986). Biological dispositions to learn language. In W. Demopoulos & A. Marras (Eds.), *Language Learning and Concept Acquisition* (pp. 3–28). Norwood, N.J.: Ablex Publishing Corp.

Heath, S. B. (1983). *Ways with Words.* New York: Cambridge University Press.

Huttenlocher, J., Haight, W., Bryk, A., Seltzer, M., et al (1992). Early vocabulary growth: Relation to language input and gender. *Developmental Psychology, 27*(2), 236–248.

Kuczaj, S. A., II. (1983). *Crib Speech and Language Play.* New York: Springer-Verlag.

Kuczaj, S. A. I. (1982). *Language Development.* Syntax and Semantics. Hillsdale, N.J.: Lawrence Erlbaum.

Labov, W. (1972). Negative attraction and negative concord. In *Language in the Inner City* (pp. 130–196). Philadelphia: University of Pennsylvania Press.

Landau, B., & Gleitman, L. (1985). *Language and Experience.* Cambridge, Mass.: Harvard University Press.

Martin, J. R. (1983). The development of register. In *Developmental Issues in Discourse* (J. Fine & R. Freedle, Eds.) (pp. 1–39). Norwood, N.J.: Ablex Publishing Corp.

Menyuk, P. (1971). *The Acquisition and Development of Language.* Englewood Cliffs, N.J.: Prentice-Hall.

Slobin, D. (1979). *Psycholinguistics, 2nd ed.* Oakland, N.J.: Scott-Foresman.

Snow, C. E. (1986). Conversations with children. In *Language Acquisition , 2nd ed.* (P. Fletcher & M. Garman, Eds.). Cambridge: Cambridge University Press.

Weir, R. (1962). *Language in the Crib.* The Hague: Mouton.

Yamamoto, M. (1990, Sep). Birth order, gender differences, and language development in modern Japanese pre-school children. *Psychologia: An International Journal of Psychology in the Orient, 33*(3), 185–190.

Chapter 2
Bilingualism: Individual and Social

M any people speak more than one language. They may have different levels of proficiency in each of their languages, and use them for very different social purposes and in different social situations. The languages that bilinguals speak affect each other in various ways, so much so that there is regular study of what happens when one language comes into contact with another. In educational and legal settings, it is important to know how a bilingual's native language may affect his or her functioning in other languages. It is also important to find out how to teach people foreign languages efficiently. This entails knowing how people go about learning other languages in adulthood. In countries forged from speakers of many languages, it is important to plan which language or languages are going to be used officially in education, the legislatures, and the courts, as those whose languages are not used may be at a serious social and political disadvantage. In some countries, one or more languages are being abandoned. Many have already disappeared. Efforts to maintain or reinstitute such languages are discussed here.

LANGUAGES

In the United States, many assume that every person usually speaks a language, the language of his or her country. However, in much of the world, it is usual for people in the same country to speak two or more languages. Many countries simply do not have just one language. Different ethnic groups or tribes retain their native languages as well as speak others common to the country. That is, most of the countries in the world are bilingual or multilingual. In contrast, the United States is considered a monolingual nation.

Bilingualism is both a societal and an individual concern. In terms of society, we consider what languages are spoken in a country, by whom, for what purposes, and what effect bilingualism has on the economic and social lives of ethnic groups. Additionally, when considering the individual bilingual, we investigate how best to teach languages, what difference age makes, and what kinds of interference a first language can have on learning a second.

BILINGUALISM IN THE U.S.A

Although the United States is usually considered a monolingual nation, it actually never has been. This supposedly monolingual monolith plays host to Spanish, Italian, German, French, Polish, Yiddish, Swedish, Norwegian, Danish, Russian, Greek, Chinese, several Filipino languages, Portuguese, Japanese, Korean, Navajo, and Vietnamese. Grosjean (1982, p. 45) took this list from a 1976 United States government survey. She added American Sign Language to the list for it, too, is not English. That survey did not pick up other languages that were being spoken in this country in 1976, and still are being spoken, such as Ukrainian, Armenian, Finnish, various languages from India and Africa, Native American (NA) languages other than Navajo, and several varieties of Arabic. There are also pockets of speakers who have retained the language(s) of their native Yugoslavia, Hungary, and Czechoslovakia.

Since the 1976 survey, several other Southeast Asian languages have been added to the pot, especially Hmong, Laotian, Mien, and Cambodian. Not only are these languages different from each other, but so are the cultures of the people who speak them. Because their cultures are so different from that of mainstream urban United States, Southeast Asian refugee youth must contend with significant cultural differences and long-term adjustment problems in school (Ascher 1990). Hmong and Mien speakers have the added problem that they do not have a long tradition of writing their languages, so they are basically oral cultures. As we shall see, people who do not come from literate traditions may have greater difficulty in schools than those who do. As a result of the great cultural differences, often Southeast Asians have not assimilated as well as other non-English speaking groups, including Hispanics (Wong-Rieger & Quintana 1987).

Diversity is even greater than the above listings indicate. What is termed *Chinese* may actually be different languages, such as Cantonese and Mandarin (Beijing speech), and even the Miao-Yao languages spoken by recent immigrants from southern China. German includes both the Pennsylvania Dutch of the Amish and the more "mainstream" German found in groups more assimilated into the general culture. Italian refers to both northern and southern dialects, which differ considerably. Portuguese encompasses both Brazilian and mainland Portuguese, as well as Cape Verdean and Azorean. Similarly, French includes Canadian and Louisiana dialects as well as Haitian, and, of course, Continental French.

CHAPTER 2

The Impact of Bilingualism

What is the impact of our society on the speakers of these languages and on the languages themselves? How many will survive alongside English? What kinds of problems might they pose for our educational system? During the great waves of immigration, foreign-speaking children were simply left to their own devices, being expected to learn English on their own. Those who could manage the feat were able eventually to use the schools as a springboard to a better life. Others who could not learn English were happily absorbed by the great wave of industrialism, the steel mills, and factories. Those who couldn't learn English on their own were not necessarily stupid or backward. Often, they didn't have the leisure. They had to work, to bring money into the house to help support their families. Fortunately for those in the cities, night schools were available for those who worked days, and many were able to get a high school education there after they learned some English on their own. In any event, their children were usually English-speaking, many on their way to assimilating into American culture.

Nowadays, we have bilingual education for children who are immigrants, but this is primarily a stopgap until they learn English well enough to be mainstreamed into English-speaking classes. Language retention is not an insignificant issue. When people lose the language of their culture, their family ties can be weakened, and with them often their religious ties as well, and their sense of ethnic identity and community. A shared language strengthens social and familial bonds, just as a shared dialect does. Only the bilingual speaker knows the rush of warmth of suddenly hearing his or her mother tongue in a land where few speak it.

WHEN LANGUAGES MEET

When two languages come into contact, they inevitably affect each other. In the most extreme cases, languages known as Creoles are formed from the languages in contact (see Chapter 9), resulting in a new language which is actually a combination or blending of two or more parent languages. Although most people think of Creole French in Louisiana when they hear of Creoles, actually any two languages can result in a Creole. As will be demonstrated later, many scholars believe that the many varieties of black speech in the United States and the Caribbean emerged from a marriage between various African languages and English, Spanish, or French. This is an example of a societal change. Creoles are developed, learned and spoken by entire segments of a society.

On the individual level, usually, if adult speakers have to learn another language, they try to learn it in its entirety. Typically, this results in a foreign accent and errors in discourse, syntax, and vocabulary (Odlin 1989). These are usually not shared by the speaker's native speaking offspring. There is no clear evidence that such foreign accents have left permanent marks in American English pronunciation, although certainly, words from many immigrant groups have been adopted.

Commonly a second language learned in adulthood is acquired as if through a filter, the filter being the first language. Some speakers retain strong accents, making grammar errors based on their first language, and misusing words in accordance with their first language even if they have spoken the second for more years than they were monolingual. Moreover, they retain the accents even if they have spoken the second language more frequently than the first during those years. Immigrants who came to America in their twenties may still speak with an extremely thick accent when they are in their seventies. Others will learn the second language with no trace of an accent. The amount of formal education the speaker has received does not seem to be a determining factor in whether or not an accent is retained, although the amount of formal instruction specifically in the new language may be, apparently because adults need somewhat simplified input to help them acquire the second language (Krashen 1973, 1983). This is not surprising if one considers the amount of time that a child can devote to extracting vocabulary and grammar rules from the language he or she has to learn. The adult not only has the interference from a native language, but his or her time to learn is limited. Some immigrants never learn the language of their new country at all. Others learn just enough to get by at work. Social and economic factors, such as a desire to integrate into the new society or to achieve success in business or the professions, probably influence the degree of language learning and the ultimate freedom from a foreign accent.

The movie *Stranger Than Paradise* (1984) depicts the Americanization of Hungarian youths who have recently emigrated to America. The tone is set as the movie opens with the male lead, visibly annoyed by a phone call from his aunt, interjecting "Speak English" to whatever she is excitedly telling him, although he himself certainly can speak and understand Hungarian. When people lose the language of their traditions, they may also start to disvalue the traditions themselves. When that happens, the old who are seen as the guardians of tradition become disvalued as well. What happens to immigrant languages is a vital question for any society, even our own. Can we achieve a melting pot without stirring out all the lumps of different cultures and languages? What do we have to know about language learning and language use to make our decisions wisely?

THE CRITICAL AGE CONTROVERSY

Many linguists believe that sometime after the onset of puberty, a person's ability to discriminate new sounds becomes impaired. *New* here is used in the sense 'different from those in any language(s) already learned by the speaker.' Whether this is purely developmental or whether it is at least partially social is not certain. Folk wisdom claims that adults lose their ability to learn new languages without an accent. It may be, however, that adults do not have the same motivation as children do to learn a new language rapidly without an accent (Lambert 1969; Lambert and Gardner 1972). In light of what we know about the reasons why people retain certain accents (see Chapter 9), it is not unreasonable to assume that adults retain foreign accents as a way of signaling that they still identify with their homeland. There is considerable variation in the degree to which second languages are acquired. One famous and important statesman in the 1970s, Henry Kissinger, could not manage accent-free English although he came to the United States at age 15[1], but many immigrants who also arrive here in their teens speak English with no foreign accent at all. This alone shows that age per se is probably not the sole factor in learning to sound like a native in a second language.

Second languages do not appear to be learned by mimicking any more than first languages are. People who have learned two languages in their childhood seem to learn third or even fourth languages more easily than a monolingual adult can learn a second. Even so, most such bilinguals, but not all, still have an accent in the language learned as an adult. Krashen (1983, p. 30) declares that it is important in language learning to be presented with data just a bit more complex than what is already known. In first language learning, this is typically provided by caregivers' expansions of a toddler's utterances. Few adult language learners get this kind of correction. Therefore, he suggests that one of the most important functions of formal instruction for adults is providing just such input. Many adult second language learners never get formal instruction, however.

Foreign accents are caused by actual misperception of sounds (Odlin 1989, p. 113–119). Speakers seem to hear the sounds in a new language through a filter of their own language, converting new sounds to one already in their linguistic repertoire that shares some features. Some inroads into misperception can be made by good teaching, by focusing the learners' attention on certain sounds and how they should be made.

The attitude of the learner may play a role as well. For instance, German speakers seem to hear the English [θ] and [ð] sounds as [s] and [z], respectively. Many Germans who resettled in America during the 1930's and 40's still say "zis sing" for *this thing*. However, younger Germans born since the end of World War II, who live and have always lived in Germany, often pronounce those sounds as native born English speakers do. One supposes that some teachers of English in Germany concentrate on those sounds. Also, many of these younger Germans are extremely proud of their accent-free English. Such a desire to be proficient in a second language may make the difference in breaking through perceptual barriers.

Grammatical interference may also arise from misperception, or perhaps, failure to perceive at all. The kinds of grammatical errors that bilingual speakers make usually can be traced to the grammar of their native language (Weinreich 1968; DiPietro 1971; Burt and Kiparsky 1972; Odlin 1989). Uriel Weinreich pointed this out in his landmark study *Languages in Contact*. For instance, my grandmother always spoke of "washing her hairs," she always put her hand "in the pocket," not "my pocket," and she often complained "I am waiting since four hours." All of these were transfers from her native languages.

Are Second Languages Learned or Acquired?

Krashen (1983, p. 27), quoting Newmark, attributes such grammar errors to ignorance of the rules in the new language, not to interference. Yet people speaking a second language can make persistent errors in grammar, errors based upon their native language, even after being taught the rules in school. One example that comes to mind is the failure of Russians to use the noun determiners *the* and *a* correctly in ordinary conversation. For instance, Mikhail Baryshnikov, on a TV salute to Broadway, told Liza Minelli that they could "go through mirror" (to Wonderland). A Russian-born friend recently told me about the results of an interview, "I will get letter." A former colleague of mine, a Ukrainian-born anthropological linguist, virtually never used these determiners when speaking.[2] However, in her scholarly writing she always used them correctly. Knowing the rules helped her writing, but not her speaking. Similarly, Germans whose English is otherwise impeccable may still say things like, "I would appreciate to keep in touch." Because the rules of infinitives (in English, *to* + verb) and gerunds (in English, verb + *ing*) differ so from one European language to the next, this often is an area of bilingual error. English speakers frequently fail to use the correct subjunctive forms when speaking French, Spanish, or the other European languages[3] despite the fact that they are drilled over and over on them.

It may be true that people make such errors because they are not wholly sure how and under what conditions all of the grammar rules apply. Alternatively, even if they do know, in the heat of encoding ideas in the new language, they fall back on the grammar they have most thoroughly internalized. Probably both factors are at work in grammatical error, or, for that matter, in any kind of bilingual interference.

Krashen (1983, p. 83–87) has long claimed that there is a difference between acquiring a language, as a baby does naturally, and learning it by being taught. In his view, *acquisition* refers to the process of learning a language without consciously dissecting or otherwise examining its rules. He claims that acquisition is what is responsible for our being able to speak our native language. What he terms *language learning*, on the other hand, is what is formally taught and it may not lead to acquisition. That is, one may learn a language without internalizing it. For instance, as noted above, although English speakers can give the rule for using subjunctives in European languages, in actual unplanned conversation, many still cannot use it correctly.

Krashen's distinction is both precious and doubtful to many scholars. Surely, many people who speak English with foreign accents and who regularly make syntactic errors in it are not stopping to dissect rules or thinking of what rules to apply. If they have not acquired and internalized the language, how can they speak it at all? Moreover, a major problem for the foreign speaker is that he or she often doesn't even hear the errors he or she is making. The same, of course, holds true for English speakers who learn a second language. This is the adult parallel to the child's inability to learn by imitating that we saw in Chapter 1. We have little understanding of how children actually figure out the rules of their native tongues, nor can adults usually articulate exactly the steps they go through in creating sentences in any of their languages. Indeed, native speakers cannot even explicate the rules they use in their own tongue! In any event, one need not be a perfect speaker to be understood and to function well both socially and professionally. One need not be able to rattle off rules. In teaching second languages, the focus should be on teaching people to speak well enough for their purposes. (See Chapter 11).

To me, the interference of rules across languages is reminiscent of the baby who persists in saying "goed" or "'nother one spoon." The rules the child has figured out for himself or herself seem to act as interference, much as the rules of an older speaker's first language interfere with learning a second.

Yet another factor may also come into play in such interference. Unless there is some strong reason for so doing, speakers usually do not remember the exact words and phrases used in a conversation. They remember semantic content or actual lexical choices, not syntactic form. The parallel to this phenomenon is that people do not always notice the syntax that another speaker is using to encode an idea. Much of the so-called bilingual interference perhaps proceeds from the same cause. That is, the speaker simply does not always notice the exact form of the syntax used by native speakers, much less all the particulars of where it differs from his or her own first language. This explains why people can live in a country, not their native one, for most of their lives and never get the grammar rules of the newer language down pat. They can get their ideas across well enough without knowing all the fine points, so they don't necessarily notice them. Furthermore, it is an economy not to get hung up on all the details. Some grammatical errors are acceptable when uttered by persons who are patently not native speakers. If speakers were not willing, or not able, to communicate in a new language without native speaker competence, it would hinder them greatly in social interaction. Imagine if one had to stop and analyze every single grammatical form one wanted to use, making sure one wasn't using one from Language A in Language B! Perhaps bilingual interference results more from the need to hurry up and speak the new language than from any loss of ability to learn new grammars after a certain age, just as baby errors may arise from the need to communicate before all the rules can be learned.

Tran (1990) investigated problems in learning English amongst 327 Vietnamese refugees over forty. In general, older speakers had more problems becoming acculturated than did younger, and women had more problems than men, but these factors seemed to be related to cultural attitudes. Historically, in immigrant groups, women, who were more likely to remain in the home and to be the guardians of traditions, did not learn English as rapidly as men. Even men, if they didn't have to interact with English speakers, as occurred with Portuguese speakers in some of the mills in southeastern New England, did not learn English very well. Again, this can be seen as a cultural influence rather than one of inability.

Vocabulary Borrowings

What people do seem to pick up in the new language, however, are American words for things. In fact, immigrant languages have historically become riddled with Anglicisms in America.[4] There are far more words in any language than there are sounds or grammar rules. Learning new words continues throughout a person's lifetime, especially in societies where there are always new objects being invented, new ideas requiring new labels, even new words for old things. For instance, who today speaks of a *piazza* rather than a *porch* or *deck*? Do you drive a *machine* instead of a *car*? If you do, you would be marked as an out–of–date person. Your great-grandparents probably did not speak of *parenting* a child. They *raised* their children, but younger, educated speakers may prefer the word *parenting* which makes the process seem more scientific, especially if they feel that they have *parenting skills.*

Even if two languages both have a word for the same thing, other meanings of that word will not necessarily be the same. In no language does a word have just one meaning. That would be most uneconomical, requiring that speakers have separate words for each and every concept. Also, it would prevent language from being flexible. Only if a word can mean many things is flexibility ensured, so that old words can be used in new ways. Each word has attached to it a constellation of meanings. During former President Carter's visit to Poland, a United States government translator embarrassed the President by mistranslating the verb *desire,* accidentally choosing a completely inappropriate word translatable by one meaning of English *desire.* Unfortunately for the dignity of the United States, it was the Polish word for 'sexual desire, lust.' The Polish have a completely separate word for English *desire* in the sense of 'would like to,' as in "We desire (would like) to be friends." English happens to attach both meanings to that one word, but Polish does not. The fact that the English word *light* refers both to visual sensation and weight may not be—indeed, probably is not—mirrored in another language, so someone learning English not only has to learn what *light* means, but that it means what two separate words do in their native language.

Similarly, Americans are unfamiliar with the older Germanic meaning of *corn,* meaning 'grain.' They think that the Bette Davis movie, *The Corn is Green* refers to American ears of corn, missing the metaphor of the title completely, since corn on the cob when ripe is green on the outside. In some American cities, there are Jewish bakeries that sell corn bread. Americans, even those who are Jewish,[5] often think that such bread is made entirely of corn meal, such as that used in such American dishes as grits or cake-like corn bread, but it is not. It is made from rye, one of the grains called *korn* in Yiddish. In older English, corn also meant 'rye' as well as other grains.

Often general words, words without very specific semantic features are transferred from one language to another. For instance, the Pennsylvania Dutch say, "It gives rain" under the influence of *es gebt rejje.*

Yiddish speakers (or nowadays, their descendants) might say "Give a look" on the model of "gib a kik." If a bilingual's original language has a word that sounds like one in their second language but has a different meaning, frequently that word will change to the meaning of the new language. This has been the fate of the Italian *fattoria,* which in America means 'factory' but in Italy meant 'farm.' Greek *karro,* now 'car' originally meant 'wagon.' American Portuguese *pinchar* now means 'pinch' as well as its original 'jump' (Weinreich 1968).

Transferring words alone from one language to another is not hard. For this reason, English words have crept into virtually all of the immigrant languages. Florida Spanish developed *pelota de fly* for 'fly ball' (Sawyer 1964). American German has *fleysch pie* for 'meat pie.' Italian restaurants now offer *zuppa di clam* rather than *zuppa di vongole,* a dish of clams in tomato sauce. Mexican-American boys can be very *tufo* (tough) as they race cars with tires that are *eslica* 'slick.' A car has a *breca* 'brake,' *bomper* 'bumper,' and *guipa* 'wiper.' To be out of control is *está de control* (Ayer 1969). A great number of such examples could be supplied from every language spoken in the United States and Canada. Even where immigrant languages have survived, often they have become Americanized in vocabulary.

Fortunately or otherwise, because of American cultural ascendancy in certain spheres of life, English words have crept into many other languages. An Italian-speaking colleague tells how years ago Italo-Americans visiting Italy were laughed at because of their sprinklings of English words as they spoke Italian. Now in Italy, one sees signs like "Snacks" or "Bar." In Beijing in 1991, I saw a restaurant sign proclaiming "California Barbecue." Other examples of such borrowing are French *le weekend* and *le drugstore*, and Japanese *basaboru* 'baseball.'

COMMUNICATIVE COMPETENCE

One usually assumes that if one is fluent in a language, then one can speak it. However, one may be very proficient in a language and still not be competent in using it socially. For instance, one still may not know rules of politeness or shades of meaning not listed in vocabulary lists. Such rules are not usually taught in foreign language classes, which concentrate on the rules of grammar appropriate for formal writing styles. Moreover, most such classes typically concern themselves with the grammar of the sentence. However, it is the requirements of the spoken discourse or written texts which ultimately determine the actual forms sentences take in actual communication.

Because of the attention linguists and sociologists have been paying to the analysis of discourse in the past decade, a whole new set of problems have been uncovered, especially those caused by the unwitting connotation a foreign speaker gives by transferring the discourse rules from their native language to a new one. An excellent example is Gumperz's (1982) study of courtroom testimony. He analyzed the errors made by Filipino defendants on trial in American courtrooms. These defendants were bilinguals with a very good command of English.

One, a doctor, was put on trial for perjury in a child abuse case, one in which the child died of burns. The charge was that he lied to the FBI when he said he did not realize that she had been abused.[6] The FBI claimed that he knew that the girl had been deliberately burned by fuel oil and was not just suffering from a severe sunburn as he had told the authorities. They reasoned that he did not want to get involved in a child abuse case, so he let her go with her parents.

Gumperz shows in detail how the doctor's native language caused him to use English verb forms and pronouns incorrectly, leading the FBI to think he was lying. For instance, the doctor said he noticed the child's "sunken eyes" (p. 179). This made the FBI suspect perjury because he had previously said that he had seen no serious symptoms. In English, the participle *sunken* indicates a preexisting condition, whereas the nearest equivalent in the Phillipine languages, Tagalog and Aklan, does not. At another time, the doctor used the present tense rather than the past, again making it appear as if he had lied. This problem, again, derives from a natural bilingual error because his native languages do not have tense forms on the verbs. Finally, those languages do not have gender in pronouns. The same pronoun stands for males, females, and neuters. Consequently, he mixed up the English *he* and *she,* which further gave the impression that he was lying. Gumperz shows that in another case Filipino nurses were charged with murder because they made the same kinds of errors. The insidious thing about such cases is that the speakers are clearly fluent and may not have too much of an accent. Therefore, English speakers don't suspect the subtle miscuing that is occurring because of first language interference. In instances like this, not to understand how greatly languages differ and what kinds of interference can occur leads to gross injustice, as well as apathy, suspicion, and downright distrust. Conventional translation is not enough. It's the small differences that hurt, those wrought by unintentional and subtle cues of presupposing and implying, of little-expected errors that, in a native speaker, would indicate he or she was lying. Notice that none of this means that either English or Filipino languages are capable of saying or implying different things. It is only that one needs somewhat different grammatical or lexical choices in each for different implications.

DIFFERENT LANGUAGE, DIFFERENT MIND?

Does bilingualism change the workings of the mind? Does it make one more intelligent? Able to think better in any way? Claims and counter-claims have abounded about each of these issues. In the nineteenth and early twentieth centuries, during the great waves of immigration to the United States, it seemed very obvious to earlier comers that foreign speakers were at best stupid. In fact, psychologists "proved" it. Early IQ tests, such as the Binet,[7] were administered to new arrivals on Ellis Island. One director of a school for the feeble-minded virtually greeted 30 Jews just off the boat by having them take this test. Since 25 of them flunked, it reinforced the tester's convictions that Europe was dumping its undesirables on American shores. The fact that the immigrants were in no shape to take such a test seemed not to have occurred to the tester.

Even when the test and the conditions under which it was administered were refined, the less English someone spoke, the worse he or she did on it. It seemed not to have occurred to anyone then that the tests depended on one's command of English and/or American cultural conventions. Rather, it was thought that bilingualism was a mental handicap (Hakuta 1986, p. 21). What is especially ironic about such conclusions is that, in those days, foreign language learning was a large part of both a high school and a college education. The ability of researchers to ignore the obvious in their quest for "scientific" proof can be a never-ending source of amazement.

More recently, studies of bilinguals have sought to prove the opposite, that knowing two languages results in cognitive flexibility. One claim, that knowing two languages allows one to think in two separate systems, is another statement of what is known as the Whorfian hypothesis, which is a belief that one's language influences the kinds of thinking one can do. (See Chapter 6, section 2 and Chapter 10 for further discussion.)

There are, however, recent studies indicating that there are benefits of bilingualism. Before summing these up, it is important to understand that there are many different degrees of bilingualism. Perhaps only a few bilinguals are equally proficient in both or all of their languages. As is demonstrated later, even if bilinguals are equally proficient, they may speak each of their languages only in different social situations or even switch languages in one social situation.

Other bilinguals, and perhaps this is most common, know one of their languages far better than the other. That is, one language is **dominant.** Some may sound very fluent, but when excited or trying to talk of difficult matters, their second language falls apart and they have to fall back on the dominant one. Also, as when comparing monolinguals, one must take care not to compare bilinguals from one social class with monolinguals from another. If one does, then the variable is not necessarily bilingualism vs. monolingualism, but social class.

In order to decide if bilingualism confers mental flexibility or any other benefit, one has to test speakers who are equally good in both languages and who are of the same social class and age group. A pioneer in devising studies which take such care is Wallace Lambert along with his associates and his followers. Starting in the early 1960s Lambert has devoted his academic career to showing the benefits, both social and psychological, of bilingualism. Lambert (1977, p. 24) claims that, through the years, it has been demonstrated that bilingual students in Canada are "...more likely than monolinguals to be advanced in their schooling in French schools, to develop a diversified and flexible intelligence..."(p. 24) Lest one think that it is only the French who fare better when they are also taught English, Lambert says that English-Canadian children also do better when their elementary school classes are conducted in French.

Ben-Zeev (1977) confirms Lambert's position by her studies with English-Spanish bilinguals of low socioeconomic class and English-Hebrew bilinguals of the professional class (p. 32). She devised a series of tests requiring analysis and categorizing. The bilingual children did "significantly better" (p. 34) than the monolinguals. Williams (1984, p. 195) says that one factor in retaining Welsh as the medium of instruction in many schools in Wales is "...the very high academic attainment records of the initial bilingual students..." These results agree with the folk wisdom guiding traditional education. It used to be assumed that studying Latin and Greek as well as modern languages was a necessary component to learning analytical skills. Even today, social groups who insist that their children be bilingual, such as Ukrainians now living in New England, credit their children's success in school to their bilingualism.

Kenji Hakuta (pp. 36–41) considers such studies flawed because the investigators did not utilize random sampling. The very fact that Lambert and his cohorts selected bilinguals equally proficient in both languages **(balanced bilinguals)** may have prejudiced their results. Hakuta asks if those children were balanced bilinguals because they were more intelligent at the outset. Furthermore, Hakuta claims the children should have been tested before they started to learn to speak to see if they had individual differences that would affect their language learning.

One study Hakuta discusses did test prelingual babies, then followed them longitudinally. The investigators, Bain and Yu, advertised for parents of newborns who were going to raise their children either as bilinguals or as monolinguals. They then paired each bilingual family to two monolingual families, one for each language. Hakuta feels that this prejudiced their study because "The bilingual subjects, then, were raised by a set of parents who were probably interested in the language heritage of their children and were perhaps considerably different from parents who...raised their children as monolinguals" (p. 38). Hakuta claims to have "dealt a painful bruise" to Bain and Yu with this objection.

The only problem with Hakuta's objection is that, in a case such as this, it is just as easy to object that the bilingual parents were probably no more concerned with their children's language than uptight middle-class, high-achieving monolingual parents, and perhaps bilingual parents were not considerably different from monolingual ones. In the absence of any corroborating proof that bilingual parents of a given socio-economic group raise their children differently from matched monolingual parents, it is not possible to evaluate Bain and Yu or Hakuta. [8]

A CRITICAL PERIOD?

There is no doubt that children can learn any and all languages that surround them if they perceive a need to do so. The corollary to this, which American and Canadian linguistic history can attest to, is that children will not learn any languages that they see no need for. Before examining this claim, let us consider the question of age itself as a factor in second or third, or more languages. Again, folk wisdom has it that children find it much easier than adults to learn a new language, a position for which there is more than ample evidence, both historically and now.

Although few would doubt that children learn new languages more easily than adults, there is still a question of the degree to which this is a result of changes in the brain as opposed to changes in motivation. One position is that children's brains have a special elasticity, so to speak, and this is what enables them to learn many languages, and that in puberty, this elasticity disappears. This position seemed to be bolstered by the case of Genie, a girl found after puberty who had been confined to a dim bedroom virtually since infancy. No one in the family was allowed to speak to her, and she had been obviously punished for making noise, so she had never learned to control her voice. Despite her willingness and enthusiasm for learning, there were limits to the amount of language she could master. Specifically, her grammatical ability quickly topped out. Her syntax remained that of a toddler, although she would string more words together at a time than a toddler at the same stage would. The reason for this was uncovered when they found that the left side of her brain, the one responsible for syntax, seemed to have atrophied (Curtiss 1977). This was seen as evidence that the language center of the brain loses its plasticity after puberty, making it more difficult to learn new languages. Thus, Curtiss and her cohorts, including Krashen, concluded there is a **critical period** in language learning.

While the Genie tragedy is suggestive, it is not adequate proof for this position. One case doth not a generalization make. Although the researchers claim that she was normal until she was isolated, we don't know for sure that she was. Apparently, one reason that her father confined her was because he thought she was retarded and he was protecting her. Since we cannot repeat the Genie "experiment" to see if the results can be replicated, we cannot prove Curtiss's theory.

Hakuta (1986, p.146) offers some different and more compelling evidence from adult language learners themselves. He cites studies showing that the older adults are when they have to learn a language, the more quickly they hit a plateau. For instance, the level of Hebrew achieved by adult males who emigrated to Israel was directly related to their age. Those in their twenties learned more and better than those in their thirties and forties. Hakuta points out that this doesn't argue so much for a critical period as for a gradual decline with increasing age.

He cites two studies of Spanish-English bilinguals in the United States, both of which confirmed that age is important in foreign language learning (p. 147). One of these actually divided children into two age groups, six to ten and eleven to fifteen. A sixteen to twenty-five year-old group was studied as well. The results showed that the younger the group, the better the English. Another study measured how accurately native Spanish speakers could distinguish between certain sounds as native English speakers pronounce them. Again, the younger people were when they came to the States, the more accurately they identified the sounds (pp. 147–48). However, it has also been shown that individual adults may learn a second language as perfectly as a child does (p. 153). It has even been shown that in at least one instance, twelve to fifteen-year-old youngsters were more accurate in their ability to use and understand a second language, Dutch, than younger ones were. It is difficult to reconcile the critical age theory with such a result. As Hakuta demonstrates, however, it is very difficult, but not impossible, to come up with accurate testing that truly taps the skills learned, and many results are based upon the opinions of raters, not on any objective measures. With the advent of such sophisticated devices as spectrographs and speech synthesizers, Hakuta claims that it has become more possible to devise objective measures, however (pp. 149–153).

Scovel (1988, pp. 183–186) concludes that speech, by which he means phonological output of language, is subject to a critical period. That is, if a language is not heard or spoken before puberty, he claims, the speaker will not achieve perfect pronunciation (p. 122). However, "...other aspects of language—vocabulary and syntax, for example, are free from any ultimate learning period." Still Scovel concludes:

> Indeed, from the experimental studies...we see that regardless of how quickly or slowly you acquire a second language, if you pick it up after the age of 10 to 12, you end up easily identified as a nonnative speaker of that language. (Scovel, p. 123)

Another factor that one would expect to be important in second language learning is that of length of residence. One might suppose that the longer a person lived in a country or spoke a given language, the fewer errors he or she would make. This apparently is not necessarily true. Krashen took as proof of his critical age theory the demonstrable fact that length of residence alone can not explain the degree of proficiency in the new language. What he found was that after a few years, adult learners simply stopped improving. He claims that this has been confirmed in other studies. Somewhere between three and a half and five years of exposure to the new language, improvement stops (pp. 146–149). After that, apparently, only formal instruction can make a difference. It may be that after this time, the person speaks well enough for his or her purposes, so that others can understand, so he or she doesn't concentrate on language per se so much.

It does not seem to me that one can claim that children who are balanced bilinguals simply are "...highly gifted and [have]...a flair for language learning." (Macnamara quoted in Hakuta 1986, p. 39). There are simply too many societies ranging from what we consider the most primitive to the most advanced in which everyone speaks more than one language. There are countries that are officially multilingual like Switzerland and Israel. An American visitor to Israel cannot help but be impressed by the high levels of proficiency in English that one hears from everyone, Israeli Jews and Arabs alike, of all social classes from chambermaids to peddlers to physicians and professors. Everyone in those countries is at least bilingual, not just the gifted or the educated.

Because of the welter of tongues in Africa, many tribal groups were and are at least bilingual, and that means everyone in each tribe. It is quite common—or was before Western culture obliterated all others—in "primitive" societies in places like Africa and Polynesia for people to be required to marry out of their language group so that marriage entailed learning a new language.

Grosjean (1982, p. 176–177) reports that Yaqui Indian children acquire their second and third languages at about ages five or six. Yaqui, of course, is their first language. Spanish learned from Mexican Indian children is learned next, and English is the medium of instruction in school. Tanzanians all speak at least three languages: their tribal tongue, Swahili, and English, again, as the medium of instruction in school. Similarly, in the Philippines, everyone is at least trilingual, speaking a home language like Pangasinense or Aklan, Tagalog as the official "trans-Philippine language" and English as the language of instruction in school.[9] Looking at humankind, not just Western technologically advanced nations, we see that people are naturally as bilingual or multilingual as their societies and their geographies require them to be. Again and again scholars have pointed out that it is monolingualism that is unusual, not bilingualism. Americans say they have no aptitude for languages and do poorly in language studies at school, despite the fact that they may be descended from people who spoke two or more languages. People can speak as many languages as their society expects them to. Language learning does not seem to be a matter of individual heredity, as much as it is of cultural attitudes and social necessity.

Certainly, knowing more than one language is a great resource both in social interactions and in intellectual activities. There is no substitution for bilingualism when it comes to reading or hearing works of art such as novels, poetry, and plays or intellectual works like philosophical and psychological treatises. To have to rely on translations for artistic work is to miss the fusion of form and idea of the original. To have to rely on others' for the intellectual content is to take the chance of getting the message garbled to some degree or other. Still there are brilliant monolinguals and dull bilinguals. There are cognitively flexible monolinguals and inflexible bilinguals and vice versa. The verdict is not yet in.

Americans console themselves for being monolingual by saying that wherever one goes, one finds English speakers. That is true. When one commands the most widely spoken language in the world, one will find someone who speaks it just about everywhere. But, ultimately, it is arrogant to expect that of the 5000 or so languages on earth, everyone should speak to us in our own and no other. The fact that we can make everyone speak to us in English shouldn't blind us to the fact that monolingualism is not particularly natural, nor is it economically or politically beneficial. In both trade and diplomacy, Americans too often rely on the ability of foreigners to speak English, not on American ability to speak "their" language.

LANGUAGE AND THOUGHT

The degree to which our languages control our thoughts has been an important philosophical issue for centuries. Wilhelm Von Humboldt in the nineteenth century and, later, Edward Sapir, argued that people who speak different languages perceive the world differently. That is, people are prisoners of their language. All that we have seen about the flexibility and creativity of language use seems to deny such a proposition. Yet such notions, especially as promulgated by Sapir's protege Benjamin Lee Whorf, persist.

Whorf, like his followers, cites two sorts of evidence for his view. The first is the evidence from translation and the second is evidence from **lexical decomposition** (Lenneberg 1953). The translation evidence always involves an argument that someone has to behave in a certain way because his or her language does or does not say something. The famous Whorfian example is that of the man who tossed a cigarette butt into a gas drum marked *empty*. Whorf claimed that English forces the use of the word *empty* even though fumes are still in the drum. He argued that the use of the word *empty* allowed the careless smoker to think of the drum as having nothing in it, thereby disregarding the vapors and behaving as if they were not there. One flaw in such reasoning is that Whorf did not show that an empty drum could still have dangerous vapors. In other words, the mistake could have been caused by sheer ignorance. Even if it were not, English certainly allows one to say that although marked empty of one substance, gas, a drum still can be full of flammable vapors.

Similarly, Edward Stewart (1979) claimed that the A-bomb was dropped on Japan because the Japanese had marked the Japanese equivalent of *ignore* on the United States communique, informing them of what was going to happen if they did not surrender. Stewart argues that the Japanese, in line with their culture, needed time to deliberate and that is what they meant by their *ignore*. Our culture, supposedly being more hasty, puts another meaning on *ignore*. So we dropped the bomb. To me, this is but an example of poor translation. Hasty and fast-acting culture or not, English is perfectly capable of expressing the idea of holding off on a decision. *Put aside, delay decision* or even *ignore until deliberations are completed* all would have conveyed that idea, and this is not a comprehensive list. Ignore means 'do not pay attention.' Whoever chose that word for "delay decision" was not a proficient translator. Again and again, when Whorfians or others insist that something cannot be said in one language, it turns out to be just such a case of translation difficulty. Having been raised in a multilingual environment, I am familiar with people saying, "You can't say X in English (or some other language)," and then proceeding by circumlocution, to tell the hearer exactly what they have just claimed you can't say in that language!

To be sure, there may be no one word in English to correspond to the one word in the other language. What makes translation so difficult is that no two languages cut up the semantic universe in the same way. Meanings and connotations get attached to words differently. English, for instance, uses *eat* for what both people and other animals do. German distinguishes between human beings, who *ess(en)* and other animals who *fress(en)*. It is not that English speakers do not perceive a difference between animal and human eating. They do, as witnessed in the simile *eat like a pig*. English just does not happen to codify that difference as German does, although it makes other distinctions that German does not make. For example, English distinguishes between *tall* and *long,* whereas German uses the same word for both.

Another problem with translation is that words with the same gloss may have very different sociolinguistic connotations. Eugene Nida, a linguist to whom the science of translation owes a considerable debt (Nida 1975; Nida and Reyburn 1981), gives the example from the Gospels of Jesus calling Mary by the Greek word which means 'woman'. In English, this is intensely rude, but researching other Greek writing of the day, Nida discovered that "woman" was a common, highly respectful address form for 'mother.'

Sometimes these differences do reflect cultural attitudes as we shall see in our discussion of gender (Chapter 10). If so, whole sets of words will be implicated. Sometimes these differences are accidental. No language can have a separate word for each and every concept a speaker might wish to convey. If it did, vocabularies would be horrendously long. Also, language would be static with a one-to-one correspondence between word and meaning. Metaphors and other types of figurative language could not exist, as these are the product of the fact that in all natural languages any given word can mean many different things. Because languages are constructed so as to have a great deal of polysemy (multiple meanings on a word), related words often take on different meanings in different languages or even different dialects. As an example, in Great Britain the notion of a hike in pay is attached to *rise,* but in America to *raise.* The time between acts of a play is called an *interval* in Great Britain but *intermission* in America. Both dialects are perfectly logical. It seems to be quite accidental which one became usual in each dialect.

Research has indicated that people are somewhat quicker to name something for which their language has a specific name, but they are not hindered in their perceptions of things for which the language has no name. Paul Kay has done extensive research into the different systems of color-naming in different languages. This is an excellent vehicle for testing the Whorfian hypothesis because no two languages cut up the color spectrum in the same way. Each has primary colors, but the same ones aren't prime in every language. All languages also have hues, which are not primary colors. For instance, English has blue and green as primary colors, and teal and loden as hues. Furthermore, what our language treats as two colors, another language may have as one. English distinguishes between red and orange, for instance, but other languages treat orange as a hue of another color. By using Farnsworth-Munsell color chips (a standardized set of color chips used in psychology testing) and having people categorize or choose colors in various tasks, we can see if the names their languages encode onto color impairs their ability to discriminate between closely related colors and hues.

Kay and Kempton (1984) investigated whether or not Tarahumara Indians in Mexico would perform differently from Americans in discriminating between blue and green. The Tarahumara use one primary term for both colors. In other words, in Tarahumara blue and green are named by the same color word, whereas two separate color words, blue and green, are named in English. Using eight chips of varying shades of blue and green, Kay and Kempton posited that because English has separate primary terms for those colors, they would perceptually "push" apart the colors of two blue-green chips, which were very close in actual hue, but the Tarahumarans would not, perceiving those chips to be more alike. Indeed, this is what happened when they were asked which of the three was most different from the other two. English speakers said the closely matched green-blue and blue-green chips were farther apart in color than did the Tarahumarans. This showed the influence of having separate categories of blue and green. But in a second procedure, one in which subjects could not use naming strategies because all three chips were not in view at the same time, the difference between groups of speakers disappeared. Kay and Kempton concluded that one's language does affect certain perceptions if one is in a situation that allows reference to the language system (e.g., "hmm, this is green and this is blue"), but this is not a perceptual prison and can be overcome. Most of us have had the analogous experience of buying a shirt or tie to go with a piece of clothing at home. When you visualized the nonpresent article, let's say as red, you selected what seemed to be a perfect match, but when you got the purchase home, it didn't match at all. Often, your mental image of red was primary red, and the clothing turned out to be a different hue.

One problem in measuring differences in cognition is the difficulty of finding appropriate tests to measure the skills we want to know about. Some groups, such as the Kpelle in Liberia, have been found to flunk a supposed test of cognitive abilities, but when they are observed in daily activities, they can be seen using those abilities (Scribner 1977). No one knows how to test unerringly for cognitive abilities. Therefore, we cannot claim that people do or do not have abilities on the basis of what we think we know about their language (Cole 1977).

One other serious problem underlies much Whorfian commentary. Its proponents frequently do not seem to be comparing on the same level. For instance, Whorf (1956, p. 241) waxed poetic about the marvelous ability of American Indians to perceive the world as processes, as opposed to the static compartmentalized perceptions of those who speak what he termed Standard Average European (SAE). As an example, he presented the Apache way of saying, "It is a dripping spring."

> Apache erects the statement on *ga*: 'be white…' With the prefix *no-*, the meaning downward motion enters: 'Whiteness moves downward.'…The result corresponds to our 'dripping spring,' but synthetically it is: 'as water, or springs, whiteness moves downward.' How utterly unlike our way of thinking!

In like manner, Whorf showed that the English *it is* would be rendered in Apache by *golgha* 'the place is white, clear, a clearing, a plain.' According to Whorf, English *It is a dripping stream* has the Apache equivalent of 'the place is white, clear; a clearing, a plain, as water or springs, whiteness moves downward.' Whorf concluded that some languages use a means of expression in which terms flow together into plastic synthetic creations rather than being separate as they are in English.

It should be noted that Whorf derived the supposed Apache meaning from only two Apache words, which he broke down into their component semantic features. Had he done the same for the English sentence, he would have come up with an equally flowing, plastic, synthetic creation

(Lenneberg 1953, pp. 159–160). In English, the phrase *it is* is a dummy with no real meaning beyond marking off positions in a sentence and letting you know that the thing being talked about is coming. The *a* means 'one out of many such.' *Dripping* means 'slow, regular, falling of water or other liquid in drops.' *Spring* means 'active, not static; leap into the air; constant arching of water, so that upward leap is followed by downward movement with water frothing and bubbling continuously.' Translating the English as Whorf did the Apache, one could get, then, 'slow, regular, falling of water after actively leaping into the air, constantly arching so that upward leap is followed by downward movement with water frothing and bubbling continuously.' The English as I translate it is, if anything, more flowing than the Apache, at least as Whorf translated it. If one is comparing two languages, one must be careful to compare the same levels of meaning and not, as Whorf did, compare whole words (in English) with semantic features of words (in Apache).

Comparing semantic features at all is risky business. For one thing, what about synonyms, other ways of saying what we would consider to be the same thing? Before one can say a language does or does not express an idea in a certain way, one must consider all possible ways to express that idea. Whorfians typically do not do this.

Another problem with semantic features is that speakers are not bound by them. We have already seen that people can understand things figuratively as well as literally. Also, morphemes and words can lose some of their meaning in certain contexts or come to mean something quite different from their literal meaning. For instance, how often do you breakfast as an actual breaking of a fast? A dogfight takes place in the air between two planes, not on the ground where dogs fight. Did you ever notice the *-th* in words like *health, wealth, stealth, truth, length,* or *width?* Do you perceive these as resulting from a *-th* tacked onto the *heal, weal, steal, true, long* or *wide?* The *-th* once meant 'state of' but most speakers today perceive those with the ending *-th* as being whole words with one morpheme each, not as one composed of two morphemes. An outsider might nonetheless assume that English speakers break *health* down into *heal* + *th* in deriving meaning. Whorf's breakdown of the Apache words may not represent the way the Apaches themselves derived those words when speaking or listening.

A recent provocative collection of essays (Cooper and Spolsky 1991) suggest that a weak form of the Whorfian hypothesis is highly tenable, however. These show that the way people categorize, the visual representations evoked by words in their individual languages, and the differing semantic loads of words in different languages can lead to cognitive pluralism, making speakers of one language more likely to think in certain terms, or more likely not to challenge certain assumptions. It seems to me that the evidence from English sexist vocabulary supports such a view (Chapter 10); however, as well-oiled as some of our thinking is because of our language, it can always be changed. It is possible to change language and to change one's thinking.

BILINGUALISM ACROSS GENERATIONS

During the great waves of immigration to the United States in the nineteenth and early twentieth centuries, most who came learned English. Their children learned it, often with no trace of accent of the native language. Usually immigrants' children born in this country learned their parents' language at home, sometimes not very well. Often older children knew the language better than the younger. The grandchildren, however, frequently did not learn it at all, except for a few words here and there. Some groups, worried about deculturation, instituted after-school instruction or parochial schools in which at least half-days were done in a foreign language. Greeks, Armenians, French, Chinese, Poles, Germans, Ukrainians, Italians, and Jews are among those who have tried, or are trying, such schooling.

This is quite different from public bilingual schooling for children who come to school already speaking a foreign language which might or might not be their only language. The special after-school or weekend schools usually are a salvaging attempt. Most have been for children who do not know their grandparents' language or do not know much of it. These have become popular with the increased interest in searching for roots. There are also foreign language parochial schools that often have both bilingual and monolingual English-speaking pupils; which language predominates depends upon the particular locale of the school. In New England, there used to be many French Catholic parochial schools which had some or all classes in French. Although the schools themselves may still be operating, most have become English-speaking.

Both after-school instruction and day schools run by Jews and Canadian-French New Englanders illustrate especially well the general factors in keeping second languages alive. Rarely was it the goal of Jewish schools to keep Yiddish alive. Their mission was Hebrew, the language of Jewish prayer, of the Bible, and of much Jewish exegesis of the Bible. Yiddish is actually a form of German and is as different from Hebrew as English is. It was spoken only by the Jews of Eastern Europe, not those from the Mediterranean or the Arab countries. [10]

Most of the Jews in America today are of Eastern European origin. Their ancestors brought Eastern European pronunciations of Hebrew to their praying and Bible reading. Many American Hebrew schools ignored these traditions, teaching instead the pronunciation of Hebrew used in Israel. This is based upon the traditions of Jews in the Arab nations. American Jews largely rejected their Eastern European origins, a fact reflected in the dramatic loss of Yiddish within one or two generations, as well as the change in Hebrew pronunciation. Over 1000 years of degrading and humiliating persecution is associated with both Yiddish and Eastern European pronunciation of Hebrew. The Israeli Hebrew is associated with bravery, independence, and victory. Hence, that is the language taught.

A similar tale can be told of Canadian-French as spoken in southern New England.[11] The language spoken there was not considered proper. The ideal was the French spoken by the educated Frenchman on the Continent, not that spoken by the workers in the shoe and textile factories and the lumber mills. There were French churches, with masses in Canadian-French and the parochial schools run by French-speaking nuns. Classes in religion were taught in French, and there was formal study in continental French, albeit taught by Canadian-French speakers. Because Canadian-French stood in relation to continental French the way Yiddish did to High German, those of Canadian French background who wanted to be French scholars went to great lengths to get rid of their native pronunciations. Over the years, as barriers to higher education and jobs were hurdled, fewer and fewer children from Canadian-French homes learned the language at all, and in time, the French parochial schools, although retaining French names like Mount St. Charles, became like any parochial school with their student bodies drawn from many different ethnic groups.[12]

To some degree, then, one reason for the loss of many languages of different groups is that the variety they spoke was associated with poverty, persecution, and even ignorance. So long as the members of such groups could not get ahead, the principle of solidarity reigned, but as soon as opportunity presented itself, some opted for power (Chapter 3, sec. 8). That is, so long as members of a group feel they cannot get ahead, they retain a native language for intimacy, but they may abandon it when they get an opportunity to rise socially and materially. And, when the language was taught in schools, it was the standard dialect, or as standard as the teachers could themselves use, not the ones the immigrants themselves brought with them. Inadvertently, this, too, led to loss of the immigrant language, as the schools taught the dialect of power, stigmatizing the dialect of solidarity. Ultimately, however, the *coup de grace* for the immigrant languages was the opening of doors for their members.

CHAPTER 2

MAINTAINING BILINGUALISM

The larger the community of speakers of a given language, the longer the language is likely to be retained. In earlier decades, in regions with large populations of non-English speakers, business, social, and church matters were often not conducted in English. Foreign language newspapers, societies, and radio shows flourished for speakers of Polish, German, Portuguese, Italian, Swedish, Norwegian, French, Chinese, Hungarian, Serbian, Yiddish, Japanese, Greek, Ukrainian, and assorted other languages. Over time, except for Spanish, there has been a steady erosion of non-English languages in the United States (Fishman 1966).

The Lutheran churches traditionally have held services in Norwegian, Swedish, Danish, and German in this country (Hofman 1968). Gradually, however, their services have been switching to English. Similarly, many of the older Italian, Polish, Portuguese, and French Catholic parishes now say most of the services in English, rather than in the language of the original parishioners. When Catholic masses were conducted in Latin, still the homilies were in immigrant languages in many parishes, although this practise,too, has been largely abandoned.

Foreign language newspaper circulation has been steadily declining for years (Fishman 1966) for most originally non-English groups. In recent years, the older papers that were not written in English at all have declined. They have been replaced by papers that use both English and another language or are printed solely in English. To me, this is another indication that English is winning out at the expense of other languages. Still, with the advent of new foreign-speaking populations, such as the Southeast Asians, new foreign language newspapers are being published in the United States. Whether or not they eventually give way before English remains to be seen.

It has already been noted that foreign languages survive best where there are large enough populations so that daily social activities can be carried on in that language. The corollary to that is that languages survive where their speakers live together in the same neighborhoods or communities. A further corollary is that the languages survive where people are somewhat isolated physically or psychologically from the mainstream.

As each originally foreign group has produced college graduates and other upwardly mobile young, their old neighborhoods have started to disperse, if they haven't already done so. The population of the German neighborhoods of Chicago, for instance, decreased from 161,567 to 99,413 in the ten years from 1960 to 1970. Despite the existence of German shops, churches, radio programs, children's singing groups, soccer teams, choruses, clubs, and Saturday schools to teach German, the language is less and less spoken (Taylor 1976). Many of those who spoke German, like speakers of other languages, joined the rest of the middle class living outside the ethnic neighborhoods. With this often comes weakening of ethnicity and second-language speaking.

This occurs even in tightly knit groups most determined not to lose their identity. For example, many Ukrainians sought refuge from Communism in America after World War II. Hoping to return to their homeland, they made very sure that their children learned to speak Ukrainian with native speaker competency, to cook Ukrainian foods, to dance all the traditional dances, and to do all the traditional crafts, including the intricate art of dying Easter eggs in exquisite patterns. Above all, they tried to instill in their children a love for their ancestral homeland. To Americans, these Ukrainians seem to have done a marvelous job of keeping their language and traditions alive. However, Olenka Hanushevsky, an American-born Ukrainian, informed me that the older generation exclaims, "How American the young are becoming!" Similarly, Hungarian refugees from the Russian invasion in the 1950s who did not become acclimated to their new homes have children who are proficient in English and are becoming increasingly American (Janda 1975). The only Jews in America who have been able to maintain Yiddish are the minority of ultra-Orthodox and Chasidim who live in largely segregated communities. Most other Eastern European Jews have lost Yiddish as a part of their assimilation to American culture. To a large degree, this movement toward monolingual English may be viewed as natural. The young want to be like their peers, and, after all this is their country. It can be and has been argued that abandoning ethnic languages has been a necessary factor in forging a national American identity. However, the experiences of bilingual countries like Canada and multilingual countries like the Philippines attest to the fact that a country can be open to multilingualism and still share an identity through one or more official languages.

Besides the general intolerance of foreign languages in America, youngsters may see little need to learn other languages because, worldwide, English is the language to know. The young elsewhere identify with American youth, liking their music, their clothes, and, ultimately, their lingo. As already mentioned, foreign scholars and other professionals often feel that some proficiency in English is necessary, especially since so many textbooks are published only in English.

Nor is this an American aberration. In general, worldwide, non-European languages have been disappearing at a rapid rate whenever they come into contact with European ones. Trying to salvage at least descriptions of dying or moribund languages has become a grave concern of linguists. Whether it is the languages of Amazon tribes, Native Americans, or those of the smaller tribes of Africa, many languages are disappearing. The reason is not that English and other European languages are in any way inherently superior to the ones disappearing. It is just that the conquerors of those lands spoke English, Spanish, French, Portuguese, or German, and these are the languages used in textbooks, by the governments, on television shows, and certainly are the languages needed for working in the current social and political scenes.

The original languages of some groups have remained dominant for two, three, and four generations. This includes those such as Mexican Americans, whose ancestors spoke those languages on this continent before English became the rule. Despite this tradition, many younger speakers rely on "Spanglish," a medley of English and Spanish, to the despair of their elders who wish to keep American Spanish "pure." That is, English has invaded Spanish even where it is still spoken in the United States.

Spanish and French in the United States

Clearly, then, language retention in the United States is not only a matter of losing immigrant languages. This, of course, has been the case for Native American languages. Southwest Hispanics were here when the Anglos came. Their language and traditions were usurped. Furthermore, they were long shut out of all but menial and low-paying jobs. Both factors for retaining their ethnic language took place: lack of chance to get ahead, hence why bother learning English, and fear of the loss of solidarity if they gave up Spanish. These, of course, are the factors that lead to retention of nonstandard dialects as well.

Donald Lance (1972) offers a neat example of generational differences in speaking Spanish, an example verified by Garcia (1981). The grandmother did not speak English at all, although she appeared to understand it. She was only receptively bilingual. The grandfather, a gardener, spoke English only if the hearer did not know Spanish. The daughter and her husband seemed equally proficient in both Spanish and English, although when speaking Spanish they would throw in a few English words. When speaking English, they did not seem to interject Spanish words. In the presence of an "Anglo," they relied on English. Their children were also bilingual but were inhibited about using Spanish and could not talk into a tape recorder at all in Spanish. Although they admitted they could talk Spanish with a Hispanic person, they found it almost impossible to do with an Anglo. This could indicate that they had been socialized to speak Spanish only with Spanish speakers and to do so with others would be as impossible as arguing with a priest's homily during a mass at St. Patrick's Cathedral. The words just would not come out! One is reminded of schoolchildren who do poorly in testing situations that do not conform to the conditions for verbal performance for their culture.

Janet Sawyer as far back as 1964 found that Southwest Spanish speakers avoided using Spanish terms whenever they could, even terms that Anglos typically use like *corral, lariat, frijoles,* and *chaps.* If they had to utter a Spanish word, even their own names, they would anglicize it. Such behavior is typical of other originally foreign-speaking groups as well. Yiddish speakers anglicized the names of their foods, so in New York City, *kishke,* a kind of sausage, became *stuffed derma* on many a menu. *Kneydlach,* literally 'little dumplings' became *matzoh balls.* People with Yiddish names Americanized them so that *Bayla* became *Bella* and *Tible* became *Toby.* Italian *Roberto, Vincenzo,* and *Allessandro* became *Robert, Vincent,* and *Alex.* Like the Spanish, the Italians have anglicized Italian words borrowed into English including names. In Italy, a *g* before a consonant is pronounced like a *y,* so that last names like *Migliaccio* are pronounced "Milyachio" in Italy, but in America they turn into "Migliachio." Names like *Cedrone* which has an Italian pronunciation of "Chedrone" are anglicized to [sIdron]. Such anglicizing has generally characterized those who eventually gave up the languages of their ancestors.

Until recently, Spanish has been retained for two reasons: the real alienation of a large proportion of Hispanics by their inability to enter the mainstream, and the solidarity provided by maintenance of social networks. The former situation is slowly changing so more Spanish speakers may achieve upward mobility. This does not mean that Spanish is necessarily going to suffer the same fate as so many other languages. There are several reasons for this.

First, the very numbers of Spanish speakers in the United States are a big factor in that language's not dying out. Not only are there the Southwest Spanish speakers in Arizona, Texas, and California, and the Puerto Ricans and Cubans in the East, but there are now Spanish speakers from South America, such as those from Colombia, and others from Central America. Those who move upward still have plenty of relatives and friends who speak Spanish. The need for Spanish bilingual professionals is very great: Spanish-speaking physicians, nurses, lawyers, teachers, and social workers. In these days of international business, both business and financial institutions also need Spanish-English bilinguals. Moreover, Spanish is the second most widely spoken language in the world, with English being the first. None of the earlier immigrant languages were needed for middle- and upper middle-class jobs and professions as Spanish is, nor was any other immigrant language spoken by such numbers of people spread all over the country and all over the world. Except for Native American languages, no other language had as much legitimacy as Spanish has in the Southwest, a legitimacy conferred because the Spanish speakers were there before the English ones. In many states, Spanish is not truly an immigrant language.

Two other factors bode well for Spanish bilingualism. One is the continued Hispanic immigration into this country, and the other is ready contact with families and friends in their countries of origin both by phone and by plane. Earlier languages were retained as long as there was immigration from the old country, but immigration from much of Europe was cut off by 1924 and by the time easy access by phone and plane came, the language was no longer being spoken by descendants.[13]

The Louisiana and French-Canadian speakers also have as much historical justification for their languages as do the English speakers. Still, in the United States, nowadays, those who speak French usually also speak English and, as with other language groups, there has been a falling off of younger bilingual speakers. Even the Native Americans have, by and large, become speakers of English (Leap 1993). The trend is usually toward the language of those who wield the power. For instance, Spanish supplanted the original native languages of the peoples in Mexico, Central and South America, including the ancestors of the Spanish-speaking Americans today.

Still, the non-dominant language does leave its traces in the dominant one in names for food, geographical features, and other common words. Many Spanish words have entered American English, like *mesa, canyon, tostada, frijoles, nada, dinero,* and even *amigo.* This can happen with nonnative languages as well. Despite the near demise of Yiddish, for instance, words like *shlepp* 'to drag', *shmuck* 'a fool' and *spiel* 'a story' or 'salesman's pitch' have been absorbed into English.

Native American Languages

Ironically, the original inhabitants of America, the Native Americans (NAs), commonly called Indians, were never able to claim their languages as American after the Europeans colonized. Many people naively think of NAs as being a monolithic group. Actually, different tribes with very different cultures and languages extended from Maine to Florida, Alaska to California, and all points in between. It is estimated that there were between 500 to 1000 separate languages spoken in America north of Mexico. Arlotto (1972, pp. 57–61) shows twelve large and extensive Indian language families. Each family has or had several separate languages and dialects. A language family is a group of languages that can be shown to have sprung from one common language. For instance, the Algonquin family included several languages spoken throughout central Canada, the Great Lakes, parts of the Southwest, and the Eastern seaboard, with two distant relatives in California. Some examples of these were Narragansett, Cree, Cheyenne, Delaware, and, of course, Algonquin itself (pp. 59–60)[14].

The true extent of this diversity can perhaps best be seen by comparison with one language family. Most of the languages of Europe and some of India descended from one now dead language called Proto-Indo European. English, Russian, German, French, Italian, Spanish, Swedish, Hindi, and Rumanian are all members of this family, for example. Imagine 12 language families among the American Indians! The languages within each could be as different as Sicilian is from Prussian, and the language families themselves could be as different as Gaelic is from Chinese.

Perhaps, one factor contributing to the demise of NA languages was the very fact that there were so many different ones, most spoken by a relatively small number of speakers. There was no one widespread Indian language that could have been used to unite the NAs. This, of course, was a reflection of the fact that the social organization of the NAs was tribal with no larger governmental authority to unite them. Therefore, they were virtually sitting ducks for the technologically superior European colonists who came armed as well with the concept of governmental authority that made it possible for them to mobilize more efficiently than the NAs.

The other factor in the loss of NA languages, and the major one, is the "time-honored" circumstance that the vanquished lose their language. The original language of England was a Celtic one. It disappeared when Germanic tribesmen overstayed their welcome and took over England. Originally, in what is now Italy, there were four Italic languages: Oscan, Umbrian, Faliscan, and Latin. But when the Latin-speaking Romans took over the rest of the peninsula, the language of Rome overcame the others. Then, as the Romans fanned out over Europe, their spoken language[15] fanned out with them, leading eventually to the Romance languages. Romance here does not mean a love story. It simply means 'of Roman origin.'

Needless to say, when Europeans came, saw, and conquered the New World, they were not terribly interested in the NA languages. As conquerers, we wouldn't expect them to care a fig about the language of the conquered. Besides in this instance, the conquered were far more primitive both in social organization and technology than were the conquerors. Consequently, many NA languages disappeared with their tribes.[16] Grosjean (1982, pp. 82–84) reports that according to the 1970 census, there were an estimated 764,000 NAs in the United States, belonging to about 150 distinct cultures. Most of these, however, were English-speaking as only 34 percent reported an NA or Eskimo language as their first language. About 25,000 reported Spanish and 8,000, French. Grosjean claimed then that there are about 300 NA languages still in use, mostly by older speakers, but Leap (1993) estimates that now there are only about 206, including dialects.

Even this figure is misleading. Leap (1993, p. 207) declares that a 1962 survey showed that 49 of these languages had fewer than 10 speakers, all over 50 years of age. It would be safe to assume that these are moribund if not dead by now. Six other languages in 1962 could report more than 10,000 speakers "within all generational groupings in each community" and fluency in the remaining 151 "can fall at any point between those extremes." Similarly, levels of English fluency vary widely, especially amongst the generations (Leap, p. 208). Not surprisingly, younger speakers may be more fluent in English than the oldest members of their tribes. This situation is enhanced by the fact that more than 70 percent of NA children are enrolled in public schools rather than in the older, segregated Bureau of Indian Affairs schools. Of course, television has had its impact as well.

At least part, if not most, of the reason for the rapid disappearance of NA languages can be attributed to early government policy. Compulsory schooling run by the Bureau of Indian Affairs made children board at school, did not allow them to speak their NA tongues, and discouraged their parents from visiting them. Grosjean (1982, p. 84) says that "All ties with the nation or tribe were broken…"

Since 1979, however, the government has funded bilingual education for 14,000 NAs in 14 states. Some of these even attempt to revive languages like Seminole, teaching them as second languages. As with African American parents who complain if Black English (Chapter 8, sec. 11) is encouraged in the classroom, some NA parents want their children schooled in English so that they will not continue to be second-class citizens.

We have already seen that the particular language that a speaker already knows when learning another will influence the second language. This was true of NAs as well, so that Leap (p. 209) reports that NA English varied according to the languages of each tribe, pointing out that "Tribally distinct English codes emerged—each formed off the grammar of the particular Indian language" (p. 209). To some degree, these differences have remained with consequent results for education and for the students' eventual success in Anglo society. For instance, NA students may "interpret material on the printed page in terms quite different from those intended by the writer…" (p. 210). This occurs even when the NA speaker no longer speaks the original tribal language. Studies with speakers of other dialects (Chapter 11) have shown that such problems in dialect differences contribute to failure in Anglo education, thus resulting in lower socioeconomic status for the speakers.

The Aleuts, Eskimos, and NAs in Alaska have maintained their languages well. And about 82 percent of the Crows in Montana speak their language as a mother tongue, but by 1960 only a third of the Cherokee did. That fraction is undoubtedly far smaller now. The Crows feel that teaching their language is a task for the home, perhaps explaining their high success rate. The kinds of salvage work on fast-disappearing languages[17] that we have seen for other groups is being attempted for some endangered NA languages, but the fate of Gaelic (next section) suggests that governments would do well to assess the attitudes of the speakers before setting up programs.

The Fates of Gaelic

On another continent with a situation parallel to the United States, the Irish, despite centuries of brutal treatment by the British, largely abandoned Gaelic as their first language. By 1850, only about 5 percent of the Irish were monolingual Gaelic speakers. Macnamara (1971) claims this is because English is the language one must know in order to get and hold a job. Of course, this doesn't explain why Irish Gaelic has all but died out even in Southern Ireland, which has been independent of British rule for decades now.

Furthermore, Irish has steadily declined even though the Irish government has made a strong effort to save it. When the Irish government took over in 1922, most of its speakers were in the poorest, rural parts of Ireland. To save the language, then, the government poured money into that region, elevating it considerably. They made Irish the national language, gave subsidies to families whose children spoke it, as well as other perks such as house-building grants and scholarships. Teachers were specially trained to teach all subjects in Gaelic (Fennell 1981). The result? Irish has been steadily eroding. Fennell blames the Irish government because all of these programs were administered in Dublin. Ultimately, however, he correctly attributes the failure to the fact that the Irish simply had no will to save their language (p. 39), something that requires a "prophetic individual" to inspire the people (p. 39). If people don't want to speak a language, they won't and, apparently, Irish Gaelic did not have enough reason for being for most of the Irish to retain it. Alternatively, it may be that the Irish perceived Gaelic as the language of the oppressed and so preferred not to speak it. This certainly is one reason for the near-demise of Yiddish amongst Eastern European Jews, and shows how important it is to discover the attitudes of speakers towards a given language if one desires to teach it.

There are fears of a similar fate befalling Welsh Gaelic (Jones 1981; Ambrose and Williams 1981) which, in many respects, has been and still is more robust than Irish despite 800 years of Anglicization. One factor that saved it from the Irish fate, was that evangelical Methodists in the eighteenth century adopted it as their church language, thus tying the national tongue to religion. Still, perhaps as one would expect, it is declining even in areas with many bilinguals, and despite the fact that there is Welsh-language television, and books in Welsh are still being published (p. 48). In some respects, Welsh has actually extended in use in that it is now used for public administration and is utilized more in education, including government schools. Jones says that Welsh-speaking people say they see no need for it. Because of the widening of social networks and the general utility of English, Jones fears the same homogenizing of language use that has occurred in America. Ambrose and Williams paint a less bleak picture, however. They have not only mapped the geographical extent of Welsh speakers, but they have also mapped areas according to the social situations in which Welsh is still spoken. As they say, the fact that Welsh is now a minority language is no cause for alarm. Languages have died out even when their speakers were a majority, and many minority languages have survived. The key is whether or not the language is used for many social purposes or not.

The original language of Scotland, Scots Gaelic, a relative of Irish Gaelic, has been all but dead for centuries, except amongst isolated populations, such as rural fisherfolk in East Sutherland (Dorian 1982, p. 25). The British actually banned its use after they conquered Scotland. The Scots, however, developed their own brand of English. The issue in Scotland now is not to resuscitate the Gaelic, but to keep Scots English alive as a separate dialect of English. Educated Scottish speakers are more and more learning British English. Aitken (1981) feels that without their own dialect of English, the Scotch will completely lose their identity.

There is concern in Europe today that minority languages like Romansch, Basque, Walloon, and Flemish will die out in the general crush towards speaking the major European languages. Therefore, the European community funds committees whose business it is to foster the speaking of minority languages, such as the Bureau for Lesser Used Languages, which is situated in Dublin, and the International Association for the Defense of Menaced Languages in Liege, Belgium.

OFFICIAL LANGUAGES

Despite the extensive bilingualism in the United States, for official purposes, so to speak, it is essentially a monolingual country. Therefore, it is hard to realize how important the issue of language choice is in much of the world. The issues have always been clear for our own foreign speakers. English is the official language of the land for all purposes and if one wishes to enter into mainstream society, one must learn it. This is not entirely a bad thing. A unified country requires that one language be understood and be used by virtually everyone.

We have already seen that a common language forges social bonds. The corollary is that different languages reinforce separation, even hostility. For example, utility bills are now printed in English and Spanish throughout most of the country. In southern New England, they are in Portuguese as well. As harmless as this may seem, it has excited irritation and hostility. While traveling in Florida, one sees bumper stickers with sentiments like "one language, one country." All over the country, English speakers resent laws requiring bilingual education, bilingual notices, bilingual directions, and bilinguals. Americans certainly feel that if immigrants are going to come here, they can jolly well learn English. In California, Arizona, Texas and New Mexico, Anglos conveniently forget that they are the "immigrants." Spanish speakers settled those states first. And, of course, everyone forgets the Native Americans' claims to their language. Clearly, who actually came first is not the issue in the United States or anywhere else.

All modern nations require official languages in fact if not in law. As of this writing, even though a country like the United States has no law proclaiming that English must be its official language, in fact, English operates as one. Laws are written in English. The courts are conducted in English. Classrooms are conducted in English unless they are specifically set up as part of a bilingual program—or, in higher education, as foreign language classes. Other countries that have recognized the legitimacy of more than one language have actually set up official languages by law.

In Canada, the French have an equivalent, actually a prior, claim to official status for their language. They bitterly resented the concept of

English as the official status for everything, wanting French to have equal status in education and law. Accordingly, recent laws have instituted bilingual education so that younger speakers can converse with each other and even read the same books. Now some English speakers resent having to learn French.

Teaching in French legitimizes that language. Children taught French as a medium of education are more likely to feel that it is as "good" as English than they do if French remains only the language of the home and the streets. It must be emphasized that in Canada, bilingualism extends through the university levels. French is equal to English at all ranks of education. Laws are written in both languages as are contracts. Advertisements appear in both, as do signs, road markings, and the like.

Various ethnic groups in the United States want similar bilingual education. When the United States government funds bilingual programs, typically they cover the elementary grades, and most have the aim of turning foreigners into English speakers. Since English has become the language of scholarship throughout the world, it is considered important to teach in English. Many textbooks are written solely in English. Academic conferences, including those in non-English-speaking countries, are often held in English. As students go further up the educational ladder, English becomes more and more important.

There is some question about teaching basic skills in one language when the higher studies based on those skills have to be done in another language. This is a consideration especially in mathematics. It is not known to what degree, if any, learning basic mathematics in one language can hamper a student in complex mathematical formulations in advanced studies.

Paradoxically, it would be advantageous to teach reading to future English users in languages like Italian and Spanish rather than English. Once someone learns to read in one alphabetic system, it is not difficult to transfer those skills to another, especially to one that uses pretty much the same letters. Since both Italian and Spanish spelling have a good fit with the actual pronunciation of both languages, it is relatively easy for their speakers to learn them.

English spelling shows a very poor fit to even the standard forms of the language. Furthermore, it is chaotic: [š] can be spelled <sh> as in *shoot,* <ch> as in *machine,* <shi> as in *fashion,* <ssi> as in *mission,* <su> as in *sure,* <ti> as in *nation,* <ci> as in *crucial.* Besides the superfluity of having one sound represented by so many spellings, the same spellings can indicate different sounds, as <ch> in *child,* <su> in *Susan* (where one <s> is [s] and the other is [z]), <ti> as in *till,* and <ci> as in *city.*

It is far more difficult to learn to read English than it is to read Spanish and Italian. Because of this, the children who learn to read in those languages learn more quickly and are thus able to get a jump start on subject matter. It has been found that if Spanish-speaking children are taught to read first in that language, they accelerate more rapidly than when they have to learn to read in English. Once children have cracked the code, so to speak, it is easy for them to transfer their reading skills to English.

TRANSLATING

Americans assume that bilinguals are able to translate from one of their languages into the other. Given the traditional American-style language teaching, this is not an unlikely assumption. Typically, we assume that what one does in a foreign language classroom, translating English into the target language, and the foreign language back into English, is what bilinguals do. More usually, it seems that the bilingual keeps his or her languages separate, drawing on one or the other as the occasion demands. They may be able to switch very rapidly from one to the other, but it seems as if they draw upon each as a separate system rather than trying to find the equivalents from one to the other.

Actually, bilinguals may find it very difficult to translate from one language to another. Neither words nor grammar of languages show a one-to-one correspondence with each other. One has to use a phrase in one language to translate a word in another and vice versa. Even when one can translate by substituting one word for another, the rest of the grammar of the sentence may have to be very different. And always there is the problem of connotations that occur in one language, but not the other, connotation that the bilingual is very attuned to. Grosjean (1982, p. 256) mentions the case of a French-English bilingual who wrote his dissertation in English but then couldn't translate into French. His wife had to do it for him.

Many foreign language teachers are themselves not native English speakers and regularly make all sorts of errors in English, which nobody ever seems to remark on. It's all right to make errors. Too fine an attention on every single point defeats the purpose of trying to learn another language. All it does is inhibit the would-be speaker, confirming them in their belief that they can't learn another language. Interactive computer programs can be used for correcting many grammatical errors, leaving more class time for encouraging actual conversation.

CHAPTER 2

LANGUAGE PLANNING

Many modern nations have been forged from disparate groups or tribes, all speaking radically different languages, all having a stronger commitment to those languages than to their governments or other peoples in the new nation. Yet official languages are needed both for government and education.

In most instances, a colonial power bequeathed its language: French, Dutch, Spanish, Portuguese, or English. By itself or with other language(s), the colonial language is retained for government and higher education. To be able to read advanced textbooks, students going on to college must know a European language, with English increasingly taking the edge. The colonial languages might seem to be good choices as national languages for the new countries that inherited them. But language is a very personal, very emotional issue. Former colonies often hated their European rulers. European languages, therefore, are anathema to many in the Third World. Even those who see the need for French, Spanish, or English in international affairs or at the university level in education deplore such languages for primary-school children or even for local government. They do not want four-year-olds to have to learn any of them as the sole language of school. Nor do they want business conducted in the colonial language, or broadcasting in it on radio or TV shows. In regions where as many as ten or even 20 languages are spoken, this is no trifling matter.

The problem is compounded by the lack of writing systems for many native languages. Phonetic transcriptions can be devised by linguists, but even if they are, what will become the official orthography of the country? What script will newspapers use? What will be chosen for business communication? All of these problems are further complicated by the intense emotional commitment of people to their own language. After generations of terrible oppression, the blacks in South Africa finally rioted over the issue of what language would be used in the schools of Soweto. Language riots have occurred in other countries as in India after the British withdrew.

Because of the problems caused by multilingualism in new nations, some linguists and sociolinguists have become involved in language planning. Before a language is made official, a careful study is needed to determine the attitudes toward it. Planners must decide what language(s) will be employed in elementary schools. It must be one that will not repulse natives, one that they feel comfortable speaking in social situations, including school and business.

Planners must acknowledge that such decisions have far-reaching social and political effects. If a given language is not used for schooling, business, or government, it is likely to lose prestige socially. Judging by the experiences of the United States, if enough speakers get an opportunity to learn an official language, their children will make less and less of an effort to learn their family's original language(s). This can lead to weakening of both family and social bonds. The old grandmother or grandfather who cannot speak the new language cannot converse readily with the younger generation, thereby losing prestige.

Worse, perhaps, grandparental authority is weakened. If the language becomes outdated, then the traditional wisdom of the old is also considered outmoded. Many an immigrant mother found herself in such a position. And, many an immigrant grandmother in twentieth century America found herself denied traditional grandparenting because her children's children literally could not speak her language. If she could speak theirs, it was with an accent, perhaps one lampooned in jokes or in the movies.

Choosing official languages must take such potential problems into account. What is the role of the elderly in a culture and what language(s) are these roles encoded onto? How can these language(s) be preserved as worthy means of communication even if another must be made official for other reasons? Such questions and their solutions must be a part of any language planning.

When an official language (or languages) are chosen, those to whom it is not native can be encouraged to speak it, but not give up their home language. For, ultimately, that does have repercussions both on the extended family and the feelings of self-worth on the individual. One way that schools can help is to set up mock situations in which the different languages would be switched into and out of according to the drama being enacted. Studies like history, sociology, and psychology lend themselves to such role playing techniques. Such activities can also be used to spur discussion. In other words, bilingual schools could teach and encourage code-switching as part of their regular curriculum.

Language planners, in their selection of one language over the other, must also be very aware of political consequences. Natives who already speak the language selected have an advantage over those who do not. In terms of carving out sinecures and of getting advantageous connections, this edge can last for generations. The fact that one language is chosen also makes its speakers seem more important than those of languages not chosen. If Western experience is any guide, usually the language not chosen is doomed unless its speakers are isolated. The reverse may also become true, as those who do not speak the official languages are likely to become isolated. Remedies for these eventualities must be part of the original planning. When we think of Hispanics and NAs in the United States itself, we must remember that this country still needs language planning.

There is no way to consider language use without considering its impact on the very fabric of society and government. There is no way to consider any human group without considering how it uses language. There is no way to investigate and learn language fully without considering its social uses, nor to consider any society without considering how they employ language.

ESPERANTO

One way to overcome these problems would be to use a language which has no political or social connotations. Devotees of Esperanto think that is the answer (Quick 1989; Carvalho 1990; Fettes 1991; Welger 1992). Esperanto is an artificial language created in 1887 by L. L. Zamenhof. Noting that natural languages were all capable of ambiguity and variable interpretations, he decided to develop a completely neutral, unambiguous language in which a word or sentence would always mean just one thing. The advantage to Esperanto, besides its precision, would be that ostensibly it would offend nobody's nationalistic feelings. Unlike English or French or any other candidate for an international language, Esperanto would not be associated with any one political or cultural group.

However, Zamenhof was writing during the heyday of colonialism, and formed his language out of European, specifically Latinate, features. Thus, it is hardly neutral to the mass of Chinese, Thai, Japanese, Native American, Austronesian, and other non-European languages, which, it must be noted, comprise most of the languages of the world. Esperanto is as Eurocentric as English or French. Moreover, any language in use, if it is a full, flexible language, allows speakers to use old words and constructions in new ways. Ambiguity is a by-product of flexibility. Communication would be severely hindered if people had to think up a brand-new word each time they wanted to convey a new shade of an idea, then had to explain what the word was and what its meaning was for all time. Rather, language is structured so that one can use an old word in a new way in such a fashion that another speaker can instantly fathom the new intended meaning. Nobody has ever found any way to stop living languages from changing, so how would we stop Esperanto from gaining new meanings? And why would we want to? If we did, it would then be isomorphic, with a one-to-one correspondence between message and meaning. This, of course, is the defining characteristic of nonhuman communication systems vis-à-vis human language.

Moreover, people learn the languages they want, and one thing that makes them want to learn certain languages is that they admire the culture of those who speak it. We know of no way to force people to speak a language not identified with a culture. Certainly, if Esperanto were adopted as an international language, then the spread of English as the international language would be checked. However, English is already spoken all over the world, more widely than any other language has ever been. People have already learned it. They have shown that they want to learn it. What are we to do? Tell Africans and Japanese and Chinese and the French and Spanish and Germans and Dutch and Russians and Yugoslavians and Aleuts to forget English and try to learn a new made-up Eurocentric language just because it is not identified with any one culture? One could say that English is no longer identified with any one country. It is so widespread. I have had academics from Germany, for instance, proudly tell me that they have held scholarly meetings in Germany in which all papers were delivered in English and the proceedings were published in English. This is purely voluntary on the part of the Germans. It is difficult to see another way for an international language to take hold.

Chapter 2 Notes

1   My father and his sisters immigrated to America when they were twelve, fourteen, and fifteen, respectively, and all three gained complete native speaker competency in English with no accent or evidence of interference from their original languages.

2   Speakers of declined languages like Russian are accustomed to endings on words that show what part of speech they are and how they are being used in a sentence. In languages like English, both word order and noun determiners like possessives, articles, and auxiliaries give the same information. Typically, then, declined languages do not use articles before nouns and may rely more on verb endings than auxiliaries with verbs. As a language changes from declined to nondeclined, determiners develop. One can often tell if a speaker's native language is declined because, if it is, he or she will make many errors in using determiners.

3   Americans are typically told that English no longer has subjunctives other than the "If I were..." variety used to indicate an impossible

situation, as in "If I were 6 feet tall, I'd become a Rockette." Since I am 4'11", this is a statement contrary to fact. However, there is another subjunctive used daily, but largely unnoticed in English grammar books, to wit:

1. I prefer that you **be** here.
2. I insist that he **come** immediately.
3. He suggested that she **leave** by the first boat.
4. They preferred that Patriarca **flunk** the lie detector test.

The use of *be* with no auxiliary is subjunctive, as is the lack of agreement on third person singular verbs. Since this is the only agreement marker left in English, it is the only one usable for marking a subjunctive. As in other European languages, however, the subjunctive occurs following a verb of indirect speech or when stating a proposition that is not necessarily going to happen. Just because someone prefers, suggests, or insists something doesn't mean it will necessarily happen.

English also expresses subjunctives by use of the infinitive, as in

▶I asked him **to come**. (equivalent to: I asked that he **come**)

and use of

▶*would, should, might, may, could.*

4   This is now happening all over the world because of the influence of American popular culture.

5   They are monolingual speakers of English.

6   Sunburns and other burns may not appear fully until hours after exposure, and severe sunburn can look like any other severe burns.

7   This was originally created in French and was translated into English in 1910. Later, it was improved, becoming the Stanford-Binet, long used to assess the IQ's of American schoolchildren .

8   The clearest example in modern scholarship to this kind of objection is the classic behaviorist's claim that if we knew all of the stimuli that impinged on every individual from before birth to time of discussion, we would see that every response of that individual was caused by some stimulus. To this I can only respond that it is just as likely that we would see that every response wasn't caused by stimuli.

9   Ayessa DeLeon, a native Filipino who speaks Panasinense, Tagalog, English, and Spanish, tells me that there is no concept in the Philippinesof having a special flair for languages. Everybody just expects to learn more than one. Although English is not formally introduced until about the third grade, children learn English words for common objects before they go to school. Also, they regularly hear English and Tagalog along with their native language. This is not a

matter of social class. The servants also speak Tagalog and English along with their native tongue.

10 Spanish and Portuguese Jews spoke Ladino, based upon an early form of these Romance languages. As with Yiddish, this was a language born of isolation and persecution. This is another reflection of what we saw in dialects: people who are not allowed to assimilate, develop or retain their own forms of speech.

11 It may well be true of the French throughout New England. My direct experience, however, has been with the southern New England populations.

12 This is decidedly not true of Canada. There, educated varieties of Canadian French are considered as proper as educated varieties of American and Canadian English.

13 It is still the case that most Jews of Eastern European origin can not go back to the Ukraine or the Polish hinterlands, and even if they could their families' have long been obliterated.

14 The distribution of these languages shows the migrations of the earliest speakers of Algonquian. As separate groups settled elsewhere, their language changed over time, eventually splitting off from the parent group. This is how all the languages belonging to a parent language are formed. We can learn a good deal about the prehistory of a language by determining which languages are related. This was one of the earliest tasks of linguistics.

15 This was not, as popularly believed, Latin, but a later spoken version of the Roman language. One proof we have that this was different from Latin is that certain words for common things occur in all of the Romance languages, but not in Latin. For instance, in Latin the word for *mouth* was *os~oris,* but in all of the Romance languages, the word is related to a word for *mouth* that derives from *bucca,* which originally meant 'cheek.' What had to have happened is that the Romans transferred the meaning of *bucca* from 'cheek' to mouth. Then, over time, as Roman started to break up into separate languages, the word for mouth was derived from *bucca,* such as French *bouche.*

16 Sometimes an interested European wrote down lists of words with or without grammatical descriptions, and missionaries and anthropologists did get some languages well described in this century and the latter part of the last.

17 Disappearing in the United States, that is, when we are considering European and Orientals. Their languages are alive and well in their countries of origin.

Exercises

1. If you come from a bilingual or multilingual home, try to observe code-switching in your family or amongst your friends. Chart the topics of conversation which seem to cause the code-switching. What emotional message, if any, does each language seem to signal? Do more formal situations elicit one form of language rather than another?

2. Do a computer search, such as a Dialog search, or look in published abstracts, such as *Language and Linguistics Abstracts* or those for sociology and anthropology. Create a bibliography of recent works on retention or loss of Native American languages. Check the same sources for studies of Southeast Asian languages in the United States and create a parallel bibliography. Do the research efforts in each area seem equivalent? (This exercise is probably best undertaken by two or three students working together. Perhaps a jointly authored term paper could result. This exercise could also form the basis of a paper on the likely survival of Native American languages, or a report on the extent of loss of those languages.)

3. Check a historical dictionary such as the *Oxford English Dictionary* or the *Random House, 2nd ed.* as to the origin of words used in science, religion, music, native American animals (such as the raccoon, possum, and squirrel) or any other sphere of interest you wish. Does the set of words you chose show heavy borrowing from another language or languages? By checking an encyclopedia or other source, try to formulate a hypothesis to explain the borrowings from the language. Remember that no language ever has to borrow a word from another language. There is always some way to create a new word in one's own language. Consider the reasons that people are likely to borrow in your response.

4. Poll your English-speaking peers as to their attitudes toward foreign languages. How many languages does each speak? What languages would he or she be willing to learn? Why would they or would they not want to learn any other language? How do they feel about the foreign language classes they have already taken. Alternatively, poll immigrants or other bilingual peers, creating a questionnaire that would uncover their attitudes to English and their other language.

5. Look up five words in a bilingual dictionary (such as Spanish/English or German\English). Note what English words are used to translate the non-English word. Then look up each of those English words in an English dictionary. How different is the translation of the English word from its non-English equivalent? Does the English word contain more meanings or

different meanings than its equivalent in the other language? Alternatively, look up the English word in a thesaurus and see how different its equivalents are to the foreign word.

6. Look up newpaper and magazine articles written in the past two or three years about resistance to bilingualism in the United States. This has taken the form of organizations—or individuals—devoted to making English the official language of the United States or of severely limiting such conveniences as bilingual signs in public places or bilingual notices on telephone bills. What are the arguments given for 'English only' sentiments? In light of what you have learned in this chapter about bilingualism, prepare a short report on the wisdom of such attitudes towards bilingualism.

7. Pretend that a position becomes available to head up a new bilingual program for speakers of a language or group of languages of your choice. Apply for the position, explaining why a study of sociolinguistics and bilingualism is vital to setting up an effective program. Consider especially issues in individual bilingualism, such as problems of languages in contact, attitudes toward native and target languages, and the social situations in which bilinguals are likely to use each language.

References

Aitken, A. J. (1981). The good old Scots tongue: Does Scots have an identity. In *Minority Languages Today* (E. Haugen, D. McClure, & D. Thomson, Eds.). (pp.72-90). Edinburgh: University of Edinburgh Press.

Ambrose, J. E., & Williams, C. H. (1981). On the spatial definition of "minority" scale as influence on the geolinguistic analysis of Welsh. In *Minority Languages Today* (E. Haugen, D. McClure, & D. Thomson, Eds.) (pp. 53–71). Edinburgh: University of Edinburgh Press.

Arlotto, A. (1972). *Introduction to Historical Linguistics*. Boston: Houghton-Mifflin.

Ascher, C. (1990). Southeast Asian adolescents: Identity and adjustment. *Equity and Choice,* 6 (2), 46–49.

Ayer, G. (1969). Language and attitudes of Spanish-speaking youth of the Southwestern United States. In *Applications of Linguistics* (G. E. Perren & J. M. Trim, Eds.) (pp. 115–120). New York: Cambridge University Press.

Ben-Zeev, S. (1977). Mechanisms by which chilhood bilingualism affects understanding of language and cognitive structures. In *Bilingualism: Psychological, Social, and Educational Implications* (P. A. Hornby, Ed.) pp. 29–55). New York: Academic Press.

Burt, M., & Kiparsky, C. (1972). *The Gooficon: A Repair Manual for English*. Rowley, Mass: Newbury House Publishers.

Carvalho, L. (1990). Esperanto—the international neutral language. *CTJ Journal*, 22, 47–50.

Cole, M. (1977). An ethnographic psychology of cognition. In *Thinking: Readings in Cognitive Science* (P. N. Johnson-Laird & P. C. Wason, Eds.) (pp. 468–482). New York: Cambridge University Press.

Cooper, R. A., & Spolsky, B. (Eds). (1991). *The Influence of Language on Culture and Thought: Essays in Honor of Joshua A. Fishman's Sixty-Fifth Birthday*. New York: Mouton de Gruyter.

Curtiss, S. (1977). *Genie: A Psycholinguistic Study of a Modern Day "Wild Child"*. New York: Academic Press.

DiPietro, R. (1971). *Language Structures in Contrast*. Rowley, Mass: Newbury House Publishers.

Dorian, N. C. (1982). Defining the speech community to include its working margins. In *Sociolinguistic Variation in Speech Communities*. (S. Romaine, Ed.) (pp. 25–33). London: Edward Arnold.

Fennell, D. (1981). Can a shrinking linguistic minority be saved? Lessons from the Irish experience. In *Minority Languages Today* (E. Haugen, D. McCLure, & D. Thomson, Eds.) (pp. 33–39). Edinburgh: University of Edinburgh Press.

Fettes, M. (1991). *Europe's Babylon: Towards a Single European Language?* Esperanto Documents 41A. Rotterdam: Universal Esperanto Association.

Fishman, J. (1966). *Language Loyalty in the United States*. The Hague: Mouton.

Garcia, M. (1981). Spanish-English bilingualism in the Southwest. In *The Writing Needs of Linguistically Different Students*. (B. Cronnell, Ed.) Los Alamitos, CA: SWRL Educational Research and Development.

Grosjean, J. (1982). *Life With Two Languages*. Cambridge, Mass: Harvard University Press.

Gumperz, J. (1982). Fact and inference in courtroom testimony. In *Language and Social Identity* (J. Gumperz, Ed.) (pp. 163–195). New York: Cambridge University Press.

Hakuta, K. (1986). *The Mirror of Language*. New York: Basic Books.

Hofman, J. E. (1968). The language transitions in some Lutheran denominations. In *Readings in the Sociology of Language*. (J. Fishman Ed.). The Hague: Mouton.

Janda, I. H. (1975). English Hungarian and Hungarian English interference in Chicago. In *Second LACUS Forum*. (P. Reich Ed.) Columbia S.Carolina: Hornbeam Press.

Jones, B. L. (1981). Welsh:Linguistic conservation and shifting bilingualism. In *Minority Languages Today* (E. Haugen, D. McLure, & D. Thomson Eds.) (pp. 40–51). Edinburgh: University of Edinburgh Press.

Kay, P., & Kempton, E. (1984). What is the Sapir-Whorf hypothesis? *American Anthropologist*, 86, 65–79.

Krashen, S. (1973). Two studies in adult second language learning. [Paper Delivered Linguistic Society of America, 48th Annual Meeting]. San Diego.

Krashen, S. (1983). *Principles and Practice in Second Language Acquisition*. New York: Pergamon Press.

Lambert, W. (1977). The effects of bilingualism on the individual: Cognitive and sociocultural consequences. In *Bilingualism: Psychological, Social, and Educational Implications* (P. A. Hornby, Ed.) (pp. 15–27). New York: Academic Press.

Lambert, W. (1969). Psychological aspects of motivation in language learning. In A. Dil (Ed.), *Language, Psychology, and Culture: Essays by Wallace Lambert*. Stanford, Calif.: Stanford University Press.

Lambert, W., & Gardner, R. (1972). *Attitudes and Motivation in Second Language Learning*. Rowley, Mass.: Newbury House Publishers.

Lance, D. (1972). The codes of the Spanish-English bilingual. In B. Spolsky (Ed.), *The Language Education of Minority Children* (pp. 25–36). Rowley, Mass.: Newbury House Publishers.

Leap, W. L. (1993) American Indian English and its implications for bilingual education. In *Linguistics for Teachers*. (L.M. Cleary & M.D. Linn, Eds.) (pp. 207–219). New York: McGraw-Hill.

Lenneberg, E. (1953). Cognition in ethnolinguists. In P. Adams (Ed.), *Language in Thinking*. Baltimore: Penguin.

Macnamara, J. (1971). Successes and failures in the movement for the restoration of Irish. In *Can Language be Planned?* (J. Rubin & B. Jernudd, Eds.) (pp. 65–94). Hawaii: University of Hawaii Press.

Nida, E. (1975). *Language Structure and Translation: Essays by Eugene Nida* (selected by A. S. Dil). Stanford, California. Stanford University Press.

Nida, E., & Reyburn, W. E. (1981). *Meaning Across Cultures*. Maryknoll, N.Y.: Orbis Books.

Odlin, T. (1989). *Language Transfer: Cross-linguistic Influence in Language Learning.* Cambridge Applied Linguistics. New York: Cambridge University Press.

Quick, V. (1989). Does anyone here speak Esperanto? *Gifted Child Today,* 12(3), 15–16.

Sawyer, J. (1964). Social aspects of bilingualism in San Antonio, Texas. In *Readings in American Dialectology* (H. B. Allen & G. N. Underwood, Eds.) (pp. 375–381). New York: Appleton-Century-Croft.

Scovel, T. (1988). *A Time to Speak: A Psycholinguistic Inquiry into the Critical Period for Human Speech.* Issues in second language research. Cambridge, Mass.: Newbury House.

Scribner, S. (1977). Modes of thinking and ways of speaking: Culture and logic reconsidered. In *Thinking: Readings in Cognitive Science* (P. N. Johnson-Laird & P. C. Wason, Eds.) (pp. 483–500). New York: Cambridge University Press.

Stewart, E. (1979). Talking culture: Language in the function of communication [Paper Presented at the First Delaware Symposium on Language Studies]. Newark, DE.

Taylor, D. Linguistic change and linguistic challenge: Preserving a native language in a foreign environment: German in Bethlehem, Pennsylvania in the mid-1700's and Chicago, Illinois in the mid-1900's. In R. DiPietro & E. Blansett (Eds.), *Third LACUS Forum.* Columbia, S. C.: Hornbeam Press.

Tran, T. V. (1990). Language acculturation among older Vietnamese refugee adults. *Gerontologist,* 30(1), 94–99.

Weinreich, U. (1968). *Languages in Contact.* The Hague: Mouton.

Welger, H. (1992). A brief introduction into the legal constitution of the international language. *Grundlagenstudien aus Kybernetik und Geisteswissenschaft,* 33(1), 32–40.

Whorf, B. L. (1956). *Language, Thought, and Reality.* Cambridge, Mass.: MIT Press.

Williams, C. H. (1984). More than tongues can tell: Ethnic separatism. In *Linguistic Minorities, Policies, and Pluralism* (J. Edwards Ed.) (pp. 179–219). New York: Academic Press.

Wong-Rieger, D. &. Quintana, D. (1987). Comparative acculturation of southeast Asian and Hispanic immigrants and sojourners. *Journal of Cross-cultural Psychology,* 18(3), 345–362.

Chapter 3
Style of Speech

S peech, like dress, varies with the situation. Styles used only in certain locales and occasions are called registers. Voice quality is learned, not completely inborn. Different aspects of voice have been shown to correlate with the way one's personality is perceived. Style forms a communication system apart from linguistic messages given in words and sentences. In fact, these messages are not supposed to be conveyed by the linguistic code itself. Style controls social interaction subliminally. Messages of power and solidarity between interactants is an important function of style. Each society has its own rules of politeness. It is not certain that one society is more polite than another. What is true is that politeness may be encoded on different parts of the language.

STYLE AS COMMUNICATION

Style refers to the selection of linguistic forms to convey social or artistic effects. In recent years, the term *style* has also been used to indicate different modes of communicative strategy associated with ethnicity (see Chapter 9). In this chapter, we consider style as alternate forms to convey mood or other social or artistic messages. In these guises, style often acts as a set of instructions. The messages it conveys are not normally conveyed in words. Indeed, the idiom "didn't get the message" refers to listeners' not picking up on style, even though they understood the actual words. Interactants mutually apply style both to guide and manipulate others. In any conversation, we often rely upon style to get others to conform to our wishes without coming right out and saying what we want. Curiously, such manipulation—or guidance, depending on how you look at it—like other backgrounded matters in social uses of language, facilitates the smooth progress of ordinary daily interaction.

Style forms a communication system in its own right, one that determines how a social interaction will proceed. Or if it will proceed at all. If it is to continue, style tells how, whether formally or informally. Style may also tell listeners how to take what is being said: seriously, ironically, humorously, angrily, lovingly, or dubiously. Style is also intimately bound up with our presentation of self, the image we convey to others.

Often when the meaning of the style of an utterance contradicts the meaning of the words and grammar used, the style is believed (Mehrabian & Ferris 1967; Mehrabian & Wiener 1967, Bugental, Kaswan, & Love 1970.) Since style tells us how to interpret a message, this is not surprising. For example if "Greg is nice" is said sarcastically, the style instructs 'take these words to mean the opposite of what they actually say.' Thus, "Greg is nice" means 'Greg is not nice.' Similarly, a timid "I'm not afraid" still conveys 'I am afraid.' And, an imperious "I do hope we will be friends, Miss Tippett" is not likely to yield close confidences. Style forms a communication system that works along with language itself, yet is apart from it. Many stylistic messages are countered only with other stylistic messages. Style uses all the resources of language: tone of voice, different pronunciations, even the choice between synonymous words and grammar. The number of possible variations of style is far more limited, however, than the possible choices of words and their combinations in sentences.

Style overlaps with ritualistic uses of language, as in greetings and forms of address. Each language or dialect usually has several of these, each marked for a different style. Considering the function of style as the controller of the interaction, this is hardly surprising. Greetings and address start interactions. One expects heavy style-marking on them because they set the tone for what is to follow.

Registers

Also, a style may be associated with a particular social occasion. Then it is called **register** or **functional variety** of speech. One uses one register at a funeral and another in the receiving line at a wedding. Sometimes, an occasion calls for switching into a second dialect for bidialectal speakers, or even into another language for bilingual speakers. Both dialect and language switches are associated with occasion or even mood. We cannot make neat categories for style, dialect, and language. There is a continuum from style to register to dialect to language. This may disconcert readers who wish that everything can be divided into nice tidy labels and definitions. The fuzzy borders between language categories are what ultimately make language flexible. To put it another way, human beings can handle variation. The thing to remember is that the elements of speech that get varied are the same in style, dialect, and language. Styles differ from one another in the same features as dialects and languages do. Since dialect and language differences will occupy the rest of this book, only style will be discussed here.

Choosing Linguistic Alternants

John Gumperz (1971) pointed out that one's choice of linguistic **alternants** "reflects the positions actors [parties in an interaction] assume relative to each other." By linguistic alternants, he meant sets of words and/or phrases that share meaning but differ in that one or more members of the set carries a social connotation. This connotation gives information about the speaker's social status and about how he or she wishes to be treated.

In an earlier piece, Gumperz (1964) gives the example of *dine* versus *eat*. Both denote consumption of food, but *dine* connotes more formal surroundings calling for formal manners. It also implies certain kinds of food: *coq au vin* as opposed to fried chicken. Choice of the verb *dine* also carries implications about those who are doing it. Gumperz (1964, p. 139) says "Not everyone can 'dine'. Certainly not two laborers during a dinner break no matter how well prepared the food...and how good their table manners."[1]

One way to verify Gumperz' insight is to notice the difference in **co-occurrence restrictions**. These are restrictions on what words can go together. For instance, in English, both people and animals can be killed, but only people can be murdered or assassinated. The latter two verbs imply the victim was a human being.[2] Similar restrictions determine which style goes with certain words. Words that differ in the degree of formality do not usually **co-occur** (to use the linguistic terminology), nor do words that give conflicting information about social status. Note, for example:

1. Let's dine on fried chicken.
2. Hey, baby, wanna dine tonight?
3. Me and Bob are dinin' out.
4. Wouldja dine with me tonight?
5. Would you dine with me tonight?
6. Mrs. Whitmore wishes you to dine with her.

The first four sentences are humorous. The joke for each lies in the violation of co-occurrence restrictions. Except for *hors d'oeuvres*, food eaten with the fingers is not an appropriate object of *dine*. "Hey, baby," implies that the speaker is a young male trying to put forth a macho image. Since, in our society, being macho is not associated with refinement, such speech forms clash with the formal *dine*. In 3, the grammatical variant "me and Bob" is a marker of nonstandard speech, thus clashing with the formality of *dine*. Additionally, the pronunciation 'dinin'' is humorous because the -in' replacement for -ing is reserved for informal speech. Similarly, *wouldja* is a more casual pronunciation than "would you." The last two sentences are not humorous because they are entirely formal, hence appropriate for *dine,* although they too could be used facetiously by, say, a person adopting a formal tone for comic effect.

Speakers give a great deal of information about themselves just by the words, grammar, and pronunciation they choose both unconsciously and consciously. This information reveals to the hearer such things as the speaker's social or educational background and regional affiliation. The style markers of a particular social group or region may be deliberately used for other purposes. For instance, the man who approaches a woman with "Hey baby. I like yo' gear" may not be an inner city youth. Middle and upper class whites and African Americans have adopted such speech. Although his own usual dialect does not normally greet with "Hey, baby..." nor use *gear* to mean 'clothes,' he still may choose that terminology as a way of asserting his masculinity. His "hey, baby" lets the woman know that he does not want their encounter to be formal. It is an invitation to intimacy. Of course, she may not be in accord. If she is not, she responds in a style appropriate both to her status and the degree of intimacy she prefers, as in the following:

> ▶"I'm busy tonight, thank you."
> ▶"Were you talking to me, sir?"

She does not need to comment overtly on his style. Rather, by her responding with a formal style, she instructs him to keep his distance. Her style alone says, "Back off, Jack," although her words do not. The message is also conveyed by her intonation, inflection, and precise pronunciation. For instance, the second of the above responses uttered with a rising inflection might be interpreted as a coquettish response. In fact, it would be downright odd if she said something explicit like "I do not want you to be so familiar to me. I do not consider myself a sexually available woman, nor do I wish to be intimate with you." Such messages are usually given by style. Actual words are used only on the rare occasions that the offending party is too obtuse to "get the message." It must be emphasized that the social message conveyed by style is not coded directly onto actual words that mean what the intended social message is.

GREETINGS

Greetings are an excellent example of style as communication. Have you ever answered someone's "Hi! How are you?" with a brisk "Lousy" or its equivalent, only to get a cheerful response of "That's good." as the greeter traveled on. Conversely, have you ever answered "Fine" in a glum voice, only to have the greeter stop and ask, "Oh, what's the matter?" In both cases, clearly, the words were ignored, but the style was not. (Chaika 1973.)

How something is said takes precedence over what is said. Indeed, in greetings and some other social routines, it is inappropriate to state one's real feelings in words, unless the response indicates happiness and/or satisfaction and the responder genuinely has those feelings. If he or she is not happy or satisfied, he or she still must use words that indicate good feelings. Note the criticism if one describes someone as being 'the kind of person who, if you ask him how he is, tells you.' That is, she or he is a socially inept individual. The implication is that this person tells others that she or he doesn't feel good, and why.

Ritual greetings are supposed to convey information about someone's well being, but not in words. Nor are words usual for the messages of status and intimacy today in our culture. There seem to be three reasons for this: **phatic communication**, **control of interactions**, and **protection of the ego**, what is commonly called **face** (Goffman 1955; Brown and Levinson 1978, pp. 70–83).

The rules for greeting and other social routines are unspoken, but they are rules nevertheless. It is not surprising that in activities as complex as much conversation is, sometimes speakers unwittingly—or wittingly—break the rules. When this happens, co-conversationalists typically do not overtly comment on the infraction.[3] There are several kinds of repairs, each appropriate to particular facets of social interaction. For this reason, we shall discuss the ways repairs are carried out as we examine the unspoken rules of conversation: the style, kinesics, and discourse routines that have to be adhered to. In each instance, the offended party attempts to right the situation without overtly commenting on the other's infractions, so that, for instance, style is repaired by one's manipulating style. We will be coming across the concept of repairing as a regulator of interactions throughout this book, but the repair differs from an overt correction in that the former always gives the offender a chance to make her/his correction without losing face; that is, without being embarrassed.

Greetings have two functions. One is to initiate interaction; the other, which will concern us first, is what cultural anthropologist Bronislaw

Malinowski (1923) called phatic communication, speech not to convey thoughts, but to create "ties of union...by mere exchange of words." Phatic communication is speech for the sake of social contact, speech used much the way we pat dogs on the head as a way of letting them know we care.

Greeting, even if in passing, is essential to let members of society know that they count, and that "everything is all right." Most often, this is to indicate that there are no hard feelings or anger on the part of the greeter, although, in the event of a cold greeting, it may indicate that there are still hard feelings. If an acquaintance fails to say "Hi" when we know that he or she has seen us, we feel hurt. Such a trivial omission, yet we give it a name, a *snub*. We are obliged to greet even when we cannot or do not want to get into a conversation. For this reason, perhaps, the person greeted is supposed just to acknowledge the greeting phatically, not launch into a recital of "What's 'happenin'" or even the ills of the day. The response "Fine" can properly end the greeting sequence. Whether or not the person is truly fine is immaterial. Phatic communication has been completed with its utterance. If the greeter wants to know more, such as why "fine" was uttered glumly, he or she can stop and ask for more information. At this juncture, it is proper to go into details. Greeting, then, fulfills two functions: first, it is a requirement of phatic communication, and second, (if desired on the part of the greeter) it opens further interaction.

It is amazing how much we can be controlled by the style of a greeting, especially if it is appropriate to the person who uses it. The person with higher rank, if there is one, has the privilege of controlling interaction. This is done simply by choosing the style. Then the lower-ranking person is constrained to follow suit.

One's superior may maintain authority merely by consistently choosing formal greetings. The underling who must always respond to "How are you today, Mr./Mrs./Ms.... ?" with "Fine, thank you" is kept at a distance. Each time the greeting is given, the social distance is reinforced. Casual chitchat and easy confidence are almost impossible with someone who consistently greets and addresses one formally. Most important, it is difficult, even impossible, to challenge aloof, formal authority. The words metaphorically stick in one's throat. Most of us have had the experience of being at a loss to "speak up" to a teacher, employer, parent, member of the clergy, or any other dominant person. In earlier, more formal and more authoritarian times, it was perhaps a more familiar experience than it is today in our egalitarian culture.

ADDRESS FORMS

In the United States today, the person we cannot address by a first name is not a peer. In other words, we are expected to address peers by their first names. However, this was not always so. In earlier, more formal times here, it was common even for longtime friends to address each other by titles like Miss or Mr. This is very noticeable in nineteenth and early twentieth century novels, as well as in plays, older movies, and newer movies seeking to recreate older times.

Today in America, it is possible for someone to force deference by maintaining the formality of [Title + Last Name]. Such a person can be most difficult to confront. Perhaps this is why respect always takes the form of formality. Respect implies social distance, and social distance defines formality. Being casual implies social intimacy or equality. One need not obey one's equals nor show them any particular respect beyond the bounds of normal politeness and mutual consideration.

Even if we understand how style controls us, we cannot break its barriers. My immediate superior, a courtly gentleman who outranked me both in position and age, for ten years greeted me, "How do you do, Dr. Chaika?" Thus, he affirmed his own higher status and announced that he wished to maintain distance. Because he unfailingly greeted me that way, I, of course, was forced into a wholly uncharacteristic "How do you do, Dr. X." Even at parties, I found it impossible to say, "Hi, P...How's it goin'?" The round of greetings typically was, "Hey, Rich! Hi, Jane! How do you do, Dr. X?" The first time he saw me after announcing his retirement, Dr. X greeted me with, "Hello, Elaine" finally establishing us as equals.

Not all superiors wish to maintain distance, or at least not so overtly as using formal titles plus last names. Nowadays, especially, it is not at all unusual for bosses to first-name their employees, and to request first names back. The late Robert DiPietro (personal communication) pointed out to me that such first-naming is "... at least on the surface, a state which is intended to avoid confrontation." In other words, first-naming allows a pretense of equality even though one outranks the other; thus allowing the subordinate to save face. As we shall see, saving face is frequently the force behind choosing one linguistic alternant over another. This does not mean that the subordinate has no choice at all. Strangely enough, although they cannot bridge social distance by initiating first-naming, inferiors can maintain it by refusing to first-name superiors. Sometimes such refusal is virtually involuntary, as when a person simply cannot bring himself or herself to call an elder or a boss by a first name.

CHAPTER 3

STYLE AND INTERACTION

Style is so integral a part of social functioning that interaction cannot go ahead if one party to it does not speak with the right style for the occasion. Whether or not style is right depends partially on the social identity of the speaker. If a style is perceived as correct for a given speaker, then the respondent has to obey that style or, at least, normally does. Style also has to fit the social situation: A funeral does not allow for the same range of styles as a backyard barbecue.

Repairing Style

Correct use of style is a delicate matter. If the wrong style seems to have been used by one party in a dialogue, **repairs** often will be attempted by the other. These repairs take the form of the respondent's manipulating his or her own style in an effort to get the first speaker to change style. This happens typically when one person speaks too intimately to another. A response in a superformal style is a clue to the first speaker that distance is to be maintained. Style is elevated often far above what is normal in an effort to make someone switch to more formal speech. Saying, "Were you talking to me, sir?" in response to someone's overly casual style is a common example as is a salesclerk's, "May I help you, sir?" to a too-forward customer. These illustrate both the way that style itself is the message and the way we try to control others through style.

It certainly does not seem surprising that we slap someone down for being too intimate. What is surprising is that being too polite seems just as bad socially. Politeness, as much as rudeness, calls for stylistic repairs or even anger. Garfinkel (1967) had his students act too politely at home. The results were disastrous. Mothers cried. Fathers became furious. Since politeness indicates formality, therefore social distance, the parents' reactions were perhaps to be expected. One's family interprets intimacy as a sign of affection and belonging. The converse must seem like rejection. Then, too, since the privilege of initiating a style belongs to the socially superior, and since those in authority have the right to maintain distance by maintaining formality, the students were acting wholly inappropriately to their parents; that is, the students' style usurped their parents' authority.

In a near replication of Garfinkel's work, I instructed my students to act too formally to their friends. Their results illustrate the social functioning of style even between peers. (Names changed to protect identities.)

In the dormitory:

7. *Trish*: Would it be possible for you to wait for me after class?
   Ann: Yes, of course it's possible. Why are you talking so proper?

In a car on a date:

8. *Pat*: Jacques, could you tell me how far we are from our destination?
   Jacques: (sarcastically) Yes, Patricia. We are about 50 miles from our destination. Are you satisfied?

9. In the cafeteria:
   Robert: Hi, Dave!
   Dave: Hello, Robert. How are you?
   Robert: Not bad. You take a test or somethin'?
   Dave: Why, no. Of course not. Why do you ask?

[Robert looks strangely[5] at Dave, and leaves without replying.]

10. *Tom*: Is this seat taken?
    Al: Why, no. Won't you join us?
    Tom: [looking puzzled] How was logic today?
    Al: Very instructive.
    Tom: Oh, was it? What did he talk about?
    Al: He talked about fallacies and associated topics.
    Tom: [laughs, looks puzzled, mimics Al, and hits him].
    Would you care to come over for tea?

11. *Ernie*: Hello. How are you?
    Andy: Tired.
    Ernie: And why is that?
    Andy: [suspiciously] Because I haven't gotten any sleep this week.
    Ernie: Oh, that is too bad. I feel sorry for you.
    Andy: [antagonistically] Why are you smirking when you say that?
    Because you're a louse!

[The experimenter and an observer both claim that Ernie was not smirking and his tone was not sarcastic.]

In 7, Ann responded to both the linguistic and the stylistic message. She answered the question, then attempted to find out why the style was wrong. Notice, athough, that when Ann answered the question, she matched Trish's formal style (Giles, Taylor, and Bourhis 1973)."Yes, of course it's possible" is not a usual college girl's response to her roommate. "Yeah, sure" is more likely.

We see style matching as well in 8. The respondent uses the formal variant of his girlfriend's name: Patricia. Even the "yes" is a formal answer. He continues in a superformal style, to the point of actually mimicking Pat's words. His sarcastic tone throughout indicates that this is more than mere style matching. Normally, it is very rude to mimic someone whom you perceive as not having spoken correctly. It would be unthinkable to do that to a foreigner or someone with a speech impediment, for instance. If someone uses the wrong style with you, however, apparently the social conventions can be dismissed.

We see another social convention dismissed in 9. Usually, it is the height of rudeness to leave a conversation without saying "good-bye" or one of its equivalents. It is doubly rude simply not to answer a question. Robert, like the respondents in the preceding examples, immediately perceives the inappropriate formality. His repair takes the form of asking why they are "talking so proper." His "You take a test or somethin'?" is another way of saying that.

We see a slightly different tactic in 10. Here, Tom uses humor to repair the too-formal style. He mentions "coming over for tea," which in American culture usually indicates a formal afternoon gathering, one as inappropriate for buddies as is Al's style.

Unfortunately, Andy in 11 had another typical reaction. He got angry, assuming that Ernie either was making fun of him by speaking too formally, or thought so little of him (Andy) that he was not to be given an opportunity to make amends if he had done something to offend Ernie.

Unless one considers style as a communication system in its own right, the responses in 9, 10, and 11 could seem bizarre. In 9 and 10, the responses have no relevance to anything that has been said in actual words. Clearly in 9, Robert means 'Is something wrong?' He wonders whether something unsettling happened to his friend to cause him to seem remote or cold. Tom's bogus invitation to tea in 10 is a way of saying 'Come off it.' Andy's anger results from his frustration because Ernie is not playing by the rules of the game: Use correct style for the occasion.

Naturally, the receiver of too formal a style, especially if normally intimate (as is a buddy, family member, roommate, or lover) wants to know what is wrong. If the first speaker does not use an appropriate style in responding that nothing is wrong, then the other party, far from being reassured that the world is all right, is getting cues indicating that it is not. Properly, if someone has offended one, and that is why he or she is being too formal, then the offender has a social right to find out what is wrong and try to make amends. It shows little regard for the offender if he or she is not given this courtesy. Until and unless the hearer can localize the source of the inappropriate behavior, he or she cannot behave normally. This, in itself, bars interaction; hence the anger and the termination of conversations.

Why do people respond to style with style? Why don't they just say, "Your style is inappropriate." The most overt comments on style are of the variety "Why are you talkin' so proper? You take a test or somethin'?" These are attempts at repair, at finding out why the style is off so that the hearer can deal with the situation, but as with style, the message is often not overt.

It has already been demonstrated that style gives messages about the social status and mood of the speaker. It would be very odd to say, "I am a middle-class educated female from Rhode Island. Today I am feeling tired and irritable, and I do not wish intimate conversation with you, although I consider you my peer and acknowledge your existence." Yet, a greeting, in both the form chosen and the tone of voice of its delivery, conveys that meaning. Also, the style selected during the entire conversation either reinforces or contradicts that information. Using style carried along with a greeting and conversational message is more efficient than having to encode that information at the outset or continually during a conversation.

Having such information given via style has another advantage. It allows status and mood to be known, without ever bringing them to the fore. It saves face. The lower-status person does not have his or her social inferiority rubbed in, so to speak. Constant assaults to the ego are spared by placing messages of rank in the background, by having style carry them.[6]

Then, too, people can behave in accordance with style without any arguments about it. If stylistic messages were overtly encoded, they could as overtly be commented on. The person who said, "I am of higher status than you. Treat me with respect."—or even, "I am your equal," would be inviting comment. Wrangling about status, intimacy, and mood is kept to a minimum if they are signaled only by style. By keeping such information backgrounded, it can be acted on virtually automatically.

Style, then, serves social interaction three ways: It saves time and egos, as well as cuts down on friction. Finally, if the style is perceived as wrong, as we have seen, style rather than overt comment is used to effect change. This can be viewed as an extension of using style to control social interaction.

THE ELEMENTS OF STYLE

Just as the language itself can be broken down into elements that combine in various ways, so can style. There are three important differences, however. Whereas the elements of language proper can be combined and recombined into an infinite number of sentences, the system of style appears to be finite. Whereas language can be used to say anything, style is confined to messages about social status, moods, and desired degree of intimacy between speakers. Whereas language must be broken down into elements if it is to be understood, style is virtually **isomorphic** with the message. That is, in contrast to language itself, there is a one-to-one correspondence between the message given by style and its meaning.

Style is akin to the signal system of animals. It is not as inherently ambiguous as language itself. Any word or sound in the linguistic system proper can be used to mean many different things, and their meanings can change in new situations. Since style is processed separately from the meaning of words and grammar, it is not surprising that its messages are unambiguous. To have two sets of messages coming at once and to have both potentially ambiguous would multiply the complexity of the task of understanding. Style is an instruction to hearers superimposed upon the content of the communication. The less ambiguous the instruction, the more likely it will be understood.

The messages given by style depend heavily on features like tempo, pitch, loudness, intonation, and timbre. This last refers to voice character or quality—whether it is resonant, harsh, thin, nasal, breathy, creaky, mellow, musical, twangy, or the like (Abercrombie 1967).

Voice

The **voice quality** we use is not entirely the one we are born with. To be more accurate, each person is born with a possible range of voices, one of which we adopt as the base or normal voice. Most of us could talk either on a lower or a higher pitch than we do, and we can vary our timbre, making it more or less resonant, twangy, mellow, or harsh, for instance. Sometimes we do change our voices, making them sexier or kinder or sweeter. When we mimic others, we may change our voices so radically that we do not even sound like us anymore.

The linguist Edward Sapir noted in 1927, "On the basis of his voice, one might decide many things about a man...that he is sentimental...sympathetic...cruel...[or] kindhearted." Experimenters like Allport and Cantril (1934), Kramer (1963) and Laver (1968) have found that people judge personality and even physical appearance on the basis of voice alone. For instance, we associate a deep, loud, resonant voice with a tall, stocky man, although a skinny wimp is able to have such a voice. Many radio announcers lost their jobs when television arrived because their appearance didn't match their voices.

To some degree, the voice quality we adopt is that of our social group or dialect (Wells 1982, p. 91–93). The reedy California valley girl, the African American man's deep resonance, and Midwesterner's twang are all examples. This does not mean that all members of a group adopt the same voice, but rather, that certain voices are associated with different groups. Individuals who fit those categories may choose not to sound that way, however. They may adopt a voice quite different from that of the group to which they belong. Alternatively, they may switch into and out of particular voices at different times.

Switching from one voice to another is part of the larger phenomenon of being bidialectal. It can also show change in topic. Blue-collar males of Italian ethnic background in southern New England may speak in a raspy, harsh, loud voice when talking about fights or other street concerns, but adopt a smooth, mellow one for recounting personal memories of a less hostile nature. Voice switching can yield voices so different that students evaluating speakers on tape consistently fail to recognize two segments as belonging to the same speaker. Furthermore, they consistently rate the supposedly different speakers in very different ways, according to the voice used.

The same voice quality can give different messages to different cultural groups. What is a normally loud, friendly, and warm voice in one culture can be judged as pushy and crude in another. Similarly, what is submissive in one can indicate great inner strength in another. Each culture has its own norms for pitch and loudness, as well as ranges of pitch for signaling masculinity or femininity, dominance and subordination, politeness and rudeness. But within those ranges, how deep or high the voice, and what other qualities occur, such as raspiness, breathiness, resonance, or reediness may give clues as to personality and mood. People project images with their voices.

Just as a particular voice quality is associated with a particular style, such as being tough or formal or intimate, so may a voice quality be associated with a particular dialect or language. One melds into the other.

Style is relatively minor variation in usage. Dialect indicates rather more difference, and language, the most. It is virtually impossible to pinpoint exactly when a style switch graduates into a dialect change. A working rule is that dialect signals regional variety of speech, or one associated with a social group, either social class or ethnic group, whereas style signals only a change in mood or intimacy.

People from the same social groups seem to assign the same meaning to intonation, tempo, and voice quality. How could it be otherwise, if such factors are to be useful in communication? However, different languages and different dialects use the features of style somewhat differently, leading to cross-cultural misunderstanding. Moreover, the same elements that go into stylistic variation may be part of dialectal variation. That is, it seems as if some languages or dialects are spoken at higher or lower pitches, slower or faster rates, or with more or less of a twang in their voices.

Pitch

Like voice, **pitch,** how high or low the voice is, is also somewhat culturally bound. Although, as with voice, pitch is partially inborn and is also a physiological correlate of age, different cultures habitually keep the voice at different pitches. Moreover, as with voice, changes in pitch can be correlated with different emotions or styles. These also yield different messages in different cultures. Whereas some cultures indicate threats by lowering pitch, others do so by raising it. This can cause grave cross-cultural miscommunication in public settings in which people of different cultures come in contact with each other, such as sporting events or public schools.

Many Americans feel that there are specifically black voices that have racial characteristics, but this is not so. Part of the stereotype of black males in America is that they have deep, resonant, loud voices. However, Nigerian black male Yoruba speakers of my acquaintance have high, thin voices as compared to the American stereotype. Labov (1964) showed that many black voices cannot be identified as such on the basis of recordings.

There are definite ranges of pitch which members of a culture will consider masculine, feminine, aged, babyish, and so on. Within these ranges, how deep or high the voice is gives definite personality cues. Surprisingly, Scherer (1973) found that, for American and German males, high pitch within the masculine range correlated with men's self-evaluations of their own personality as being sociable, dominant, and aggressive. Also, their peers judged them to be dominant and aggressive. Scherer explains (p. 154) that the fact of competent and dominant speakers having higher pitch than submissive speakers does not really violate expectations because these voice don't necessarily sound high-pitched so long as they don't get into the feminine range. Scherer explains that high pitch is evocative of "habitually elevated level of arousal" (p. 157). Since arousal leads to muscle tension, competence and dominance may be reflected in heightened muscle tone. Depressed mental patients on the other hand are characterized by low pitched voices.

Tempo

The actual tempo of speech is confounded by one's familiarity with it. Students learning a foreign language often find that it seems spoken too rapidly at first, but the more proficient they become at it, the slower the speech occurs. Within a language, typically, speakers feel as if some dialects are spoken more slowly than others. For instance, the normal tempo of some dialects of the American South seems slow to Northerners. Consequently, they may label Southerners as lazy or stupid. In turn, Southerners may find Northerners brusque and impatient.

Interestingly, people differ in their judgments of tempo. Although New Englanders may judge urban Midwestern speech as being rapid, there are Midwesterners who find New England speech fast. Many adults find that Rap songs are chanted so rapidly that they have difficulty decoding the words, but younger listeners, familiar with the idiom of Rap, report no such difficulty. The less familiar a dialect or language, the more rapid it may sound. This may be caused partially by the miscuing that results from slight differences in using allophones in different dialects, or even from differences in points of articulation for the same phonemes. As we shall see, there are also cross-cultural differences in such matters as how long a pause one requires before one can jump into a conversation. This can cause those who wait longer to feel that the other party keeps cutting them off.

Loudness

Loudness also differs according to social, ethnic, or language groups. This can lead to serious misunderstanding. In England, the voices of American tourists seem to boom out in country pubs. Apparently, many American dialects are spoken more loudly than British ones. The stereotype of Americans as brash and rude may derive from such differences. Closer to home, a second-generation American who has strong ethnic ties to the Italian American community once approvingly told me about a diet lecturer, "I knew she was one of my kind. She talked so loud." The friendly, happy unself-conscious talk of Americans of Italian background, especially those who still identify with their ethnic group, often seems to be somewhat louder than, for instance, speech of descendants of the English settlers. Jews of Eastern European origin, especially those with strong ethnic identities, also seem to speak louder. It must be emphasized, however, that many people of Italian or Jewish background have adopted softer voices than are usually associated with those ethnic groups.

As with tempo, however, the loudness perceived by listeners of another culture may not be actual loudness at all. Many factors may lead to a judgment of loudness when, in fact, a speaker is not talking especially loudly. If the rules of conversation of one group of speakers do not usually allow one person to break into another's speech, dialogue with a member of a group that does allow such interruptions may be uncomfortable. The member of the former group may feel that the interrupter is speaking too loudly. The same perception can occur if someone breaks into speech after a shorter pause than another person's rules for conversation allow. Speaking loudly is a way of impinging on conversational space. Therefore, if someone breaks into someone else's speech in violation of that person's conversational practices, the behavior is perceived as speaking loudly.

Whether differences in loudness are real or imagined, misunderstandings result if people feel someone speaks too loudly or too softly. People accustomed to soft voices may misinterpret louder voices as being overbearing or vulgar. However, people accustomed to louder voices often judge softer-voiced speakers as cold, distant, unfeeling, unfriendly, or mousy. Currently it seems as if adolescents adopt louder voices than their elders. The elders find them rude and loud, and they in turn find their elders cold and stiff. Such judgments are easily gathered by playing tapes of people speaking with different degrees of loudness and asking subjects to rate them on a questionnaire.

MARKED AND UNMARKED VALUES IN STYLE

There does seem to be one difference between stylistic variation and that of dialect. For each feature such as tempo, pitch, loudness, timbre, or intonation there seems to be a base that indicates that everything is fine. The base is not a fixed point or line, but a range within which no special message seems to be given. In linguistic terms, we would say that staying within the base is an **unmarked** situation. Moving out of that range indicates that something is wrong or out of the ordinary. Hence, it is a **marked** situation.

Each dialect or language seems to be spoken at a characteristic rate. Speeding up indicates excitement. Slowing down may indicate exhaustion, boredom, or uncertainty. Raising the normal pitch may indicate a number of emotions: anger, fear, surprise, or excitement. Lowering it can be a sign of happy excitement or even rage. If loudness and slow tempo are combined, it can be a signal that the speaker's patience is wearing thin. One's normal voice can be made more honeyed when an attempt is being made to ingratiate oneself with another. That one wants unquestioning obedience may be evinced by making one's voice harsh and raspy. One's normal intonation (rise and fall of the voice) changes to show surprise, sarcasm, or exasperation. In combination, especially, these features allow the full range of human emotion to be expressed. Remember, however, that different languages may use them differently to signal somewhat different messages.

Using a Moog synthesizer, Klaus Scherer (1973) created tone sequences by varying tempo, pitch, loudness, and intonation. He found that judges could assign meanings to each sequence, such as pleasantness, activity, potency, interest, sadness, fear, happiness, disgust, anger, surprise, elation, or boredom. There was good interjudge reliability in the task. That means that a significant number of people had the same opinion about each sequence.

In general, Scherer found that moderate pitch variation in intonation indicates generally unpleasant emotions, such as sadness, disgust, and boredom. Extreme pitch variation produces ratings of pleasant, active, and potent emotions, such as happiness, interest, and surprise. Fast tempo is more active and potent than slow, with the former indicating interest, fear, surprise, or anger, and the latter indicating boredom, sadness, or disgust. Both fear and anger can be indicated in diametrically opposed ways, either by low, slow sounds with moderate intonation or high, fast sounds with extreme intonation. The difference seems to be that of potency with the lower, slower, flatter variation indicating cool anger or fear without activity. The faster, higher, more extreme tone sequences indicate hot anger and a more potent, excited fear.

Indexical Meaning

Within a culture, people assign what Laver (1968) calls **indexical** meaning to voice quality, intonation, pitch, and other features of style. Laver means that these features serve as indexes, or markers, indicating social status, age, and personality characteristics. This is hardly surprising. It would be of little use to signal that I am angry if others in my culture do not understand my cues for anger. Laver notes,

> Listeners, if they are from the same culture, tend to reach the same indexical conclusions from the same evidence, but the conclusions themselves may on occasion bear no reliable relation to the real characteristics of the speaker.

In other words, we judge voice quality according to our stereotypes of the people who, we believe, use a particular voice or style. The American stereotyping of black male voices mentioned above is a case in point. This is not so contradictory as it sounds, for members of a group do assign the same messages to certain styles, but someone need not use those styles even if he or she belongs to a group which is stereotyped as using it. Similarly, one need not indicate anger or impatience if one does not desire to. Hence, the absence of a style or even the presence of one, e.g., friendliness and warmth, may not correlate with actual feelings.

A person can adopt a particular style to project a false image. Laver mentions that a harsh voice "...is correlated with more aggressive, dominant, authoritative characteristics" so it is likely to be adopted by, say, drill sergeants. Scherer (1979, p. 158–159) suggests that resonant, metallic voices seem to indicate emotional stability, extroversion and dominance. He quotes Laver's doctoral research as support, saying that passive, submissive people could be assumed to have rather lax voices, but disciplined and controlled speakers would have tenser ones. A breathy voice projects an image "more self-effacing, submissive, meek." That description aptly describes the sex kitten voice, such as the late Marilyn Monroe's.

Scherer also notes that breathy voices may be indicative of introversion, neurotic tendency, and anxiety. In a study of jurors, German speakers with such voices were judged by their peers as dominant and neurotic, but not sociable. In this light, it is interesting to consider Henton and Bladon (1985). They show that breathy phonation occurs consistently in females speaking two accents of British English, despite the fact that such breathiness actually creates preceptual problems for the hearer (p. 225). It is not a feature of male speech. Noting that breathiness is associated with "sexiness," they suggest that "...if a woman can manage to sound as though she is sexually aroused, she may be regarded as more desirable ..." and that such a voice may be seen as "... a part of courtship display ritual" (p. 126).

In America, high pitch in females correlates positively with judgments of femininity and socialization, but negatively with capacity for achieving status, sociability, social presence, and self-acceptance. In other words, women who use high-pitched voices are felt to be well socialized into being women, but they are not felt to have much capacity to achieve high status, aren't self-confident, and aren't sociable. This probably says more about stereotypes of what constitutes femininity in our culture. Assertive, self-confident women do not fit the cultural ideal of the passive, non-assertive woman. In any event, women who prefer to break out of the latter mold would probably enhance their chances by developing a low pitched voice.

Scherer (1979) rightly deplores the copious writings purporting to designate specific voice qualities with personality types. Far too few of these have ascended above the plane of anecdote. He accuses "the happy consistency of findings and interpretations... which one sometimes finds in American[7] textbooks or review chapters... " These, he notes, are not due to lack of research. He himself, admirably, uses excellent field methods, including acoustic analyses, expert ratings, and systematic codings. He relates these to standardized personality measures (p. 151).

Voiceprinting

In recent years, American courts have allowed identification by voiceprinting. It is popularly believed that people's voices are as individual as their fingerprints. James Milroy (1984, pp. 52–53) criticizes such a belief. First, "voiceprints" are only printouts of spectographic data. It has long been possible to record pronunciations to get a visual "picture," just as we can get one of brainwaves or heartbeats. The problem is that these visual prints only substitute for aural ones. That is, the phonetician has to interpret what he or she hears or what he or she sees, and, at the point of present knowledge, even the best phoneticians are likely to be wrong sometimes. A second reason for approaching voiceprinting with caution is that "no one can define a finite population from which the data-sample to be analyzed is drawn; therefore, there is no way of knowing how many individuals have similar vocal characteristics" (p. 52).

Testing for Cultural Differences in Style

How can we ascertain what attributes members of a society ascribe to features of style? There are two kinds of tests used extensively to measure reactions to dialects that are equally useful for testing features of style:

matched guise and subjective reaction testing. The first of these entails recording the same person speaking in different styles or dialects, and then measuring reactions to each version of his or her voice. The reason that the same person is used is to ensure that reaction is to the feature tested, not some accidental feature of voice quality between two speakers. Besides asking listeners to evaluate the matched guise voices, one can use other measures, such as giving directions over a loudspeaker and seeing how many people comply. In a subjective reaction test, people are asked to evaluate speakers who speak as they do, that is, use certain target features. It has been found that the features that people most disvalue in themselves, they also disvalue in others, even when they are unaware, as they usually are, of how they are really speaking.

Knowing how members of social groups actually evaluate stylistic features can be very important in the training of teachers and social workers who need to realize that they may unconsciously evaluate pupils and clients unfavorably just because of their pitch, loudness, tempo, timbre, and intonation. One of the complaints that people make when they have to deal with members of other cultures is "You never know what they are thinking." Actually, one never knows what anyone is thinking, but one automatically responds to cues of style.[8] If those cues differ from the ones we have internalized, then we do not quite know how to react. Perhaps this explains the preference of some people to "be with their own kind."

LEXICAL AND SYNTACTIC ALTERNANTS

The features of style so far delineated are nonlinguistic. These, along with the kinesics discussed in the next chapter, are the **paralinguistic** component of language. They do not involve the system of sounds, words, and grammar that make up language proper. Some other aspects of style do, however. These are **phonetic variants**, different ways of pronouncing the same things, **lexical variants**, different words for the same thing, and **syntactic variants**, different grammatical constructions for the same meaning. For instance, it is normal and usual in American English to convert a word final /t/ into [č] if the next word starts with a [y] as in [donča]. These variants are stylistic when choice of one or the other does not change the content of the message, but does signal a different social or emotional message, or belongs to a different register.

The technical term for this process is **palatalization**. That this is in the realm of style, not language proper, is shown in two ways. First, one variant is normal and usual, and a departure from it signals that the circumstances are not ordinary. Second, the words are perceived as remaining the same, whichever pronunciation is adopted. In contrast, *tin* and *chin,* are perceived as being different because of the differences between /t/ and /č/. The meanings and possible contexts of usage are changed because of the presence of one or the other sound. There is no such difference between "won't you" and "wonča," despite the fact that the same sounds are alternating. We perceive the change from /t/ to /č/ as linguistic in *tin* vs. *chin*, but as stylistic in "won't you" and "wonča". For instance, if one says to a peer or inferior "Won't you come afterwards?" with a clearly articulated /t/ and /y/, this indicates a formal party, or anger or upset on the part of the speaker. In the encounters described above, a prime signal of superformality was the lack of palatalization, and it caused strain between speakers. If one, instead, asks "Wonča come afterwards?" it connotes that everything is all right. Relations are normal.

Words, more technically termed lexical items, may also show stylistic variation. In 7–10 above, we saw several lexical variants: "destination," "very instructive," "associated topics," even phrases like "would it be possible...?" and "And why is that?" The choice of one word or phrase rather than another gives a stylistic message although the linguistic meaning remains the same. In all of these instances, the message given by style indicates that the speaker outranks the hearer and wishes formality, hence distance.

Lexical variants can also give quite the opposite stylistic message. For example, choosing "I'm outa here" over "let's go" shows one's identity with youth and establishes an informal, casual mood. Referring to a man as a "dude" shows one's hipness. Saying "dichotomy" instead of "split," "division," or even "two sides to the question" shows that one is educated. The person who speaks of "shooting the breeze" instead of "chatting" is referring to a very casual conversation, and is more likely to be a male than one who "chats".

Laver and Trudgill (1979, p. 26) feel that lexical markers are the least interesting and the hardest and least profitable to study. They feel that linguistic analysis has little to offer in this area, that they occur infrequently, and are "liable to conscious repression." Given the strong role of lexical markers in jargons and slang, however, they are not uninteresting sociolinguistically. For instance, semantic features indicating sexuality and weakness abound in American terms for females, and these are usually used wholly unconsciously even by women. Even after these biases have been uncovered, such gender marking in the English lexicon is alive and well. (See Chapter 10).

Syntactic variants involve the choice of one rather than another grammatical construction for the purpose of giving a different social message.

Saying "Have I not?" instead of "Haven't I?" is one example. Although the use of double negatives and *ain't* are often differences between educated and uneducated dialects, in actual fact, many educated speakers will on occasion use such forms stylistically. At casual parties, rock concerts, and sports events, educated middle-class speakers can be heard saying such things as "Ain't no way that's gonna happen," and "He never brings no beer." Use of such forms heightens camaraderie and the general informality of the occasion. Occasionally, these forms are also heard as being extra emphatic. There are actually very few syntactic markers for style in American English, and many of those that do occur are important mostly for formal writing, not speech.

Linguistic meaning can only be extracted from speech by an active decoding process during which the hearer has to figure out what sounds have been used, which meanings should be extracted from the words used, how to fit the meaning of the words into the syntax used, and which way to interpret a syntactic construction if it is ambiguous. In contrast to these complex decoding strategies, to decode style the hearer must only determine which variant was used. There is little, if any, segmenting out of features and fitting them to the context. This is true even in those instances in which style is carried by phonological, lexical, or syntactic variants. All the hearer has to do is note which variant has been used in order to get the stylistic message.

Language itself is open-ended. There is no limit on the number of different utterances a person can make. Although there are limits on the possible meanings of a given sentence or word, both can change meaning to some degree in different contexts. Style, on the other hand, is virtually a closed system. There are a limited number of pitches, tempos, timbres, and intonation contours available. There are bounds on softness and loudness. There are relatively few sounds involved in phonetic variation, and only a few syntactic constructions for stylistic manipulation, compared to the language as a whole, that is.

Perhaps the most open-ended feature of style is the lexical variation which bears the brunt of adapting rapidly to new situations. Even so, the number of lexical items available for purely stylistic choices is very limited in contrast to those in one's entire vocabulary. Furthermore, far from the changeability of meaning that characterizes language, the elements of style are quite fixed, with the element given and the message it gives being virtually one and the same. This makes it possible for style to function as it does, as a set of instructions telling the speaker how to take whatever is being said. A hearer need only note the markers of style as he or she decodes the sentence proper.

POWER AND SOLIDARITY

Brown and Gilman (1960) in a pioneering work defined social relationships in terms of **power** and **solidarity**. Both of these are matters of degree and they work together to produce various combinations of distance and intimacy. A person in power, for instance, may elect to use some markers of solidarity with her or his employees to maintain friendly relations. Forms which indicate power establish who has authority and how much that authority is. Forms which indicate solidarity establish the degree of intimacy in the relationship. These concepts have been very useful in analyzing social variation in uses of style and body motion **(kinesics)**; however, it should be remembered that there are many social limitations on who can signal power or lack of it, and who can signal solidarity, and how much of it, and that these often are beyond the choices of the individual speaker. Since power and solidarity are the two major variables in interactions, it is not surprising to find them well-marked in most languages, especially at the outset of interactions, such as introductions, greetings, and summonses.

Interactions typically have a formal beginning. This is an indication that the hearer is supposed to start decoding a linguistic message. At large gatherings or in public places, we hear talking all around us, but it is only a jumble of sound. Then suddenly amid the babble, a name or a key word penetrates our consciousness and we find ourselves hearing what one voice out of the many is saying. People usually tune out conversation not relevant to them, even when conditions are fine for hearing. One of the reasons that Robert Altman's films like the original *M.A.S.H., McCabe and Mrs. Miller,* and *Nashville* are so confusing to some people at first viewing is that, in an attempt to simulate actual social situations, he has several people talking at once, often carrying on several conversations. In many scenes for the first few seconds, viewers are given no clue as to which conversation to focus on. In actual social situations, we typically zero in on one and ignore the rest.

One sure way for a conversation to become relevant is for someone to give a summons or greeting. This summons grabs one's attention. This need not include names. A simple "uh" or "excuse me" can function as a summons. A summons is the verbal equivalent to catching someone's eye. No conversation is likely to proceed without one or the other.

It is not surprising that style is especially heavily marked at the outset of conversations. A summons may take many forms—*uh, excuse me, waiter, Joe, Dr. Dreidel*—and may or may not be combined with an address form. Lexical variation is prominent at the outset of conversations, although the other features of style certainly are also used. These may also be modified by varying timbre, loudness, and the like, but the prime marking usually is by the form itself. This seems to be a reflection of the importance of this initial style-marking. Perhaps word variation is more perceptible, especially in the flurry of greeting, than general tone of voice.

A summons typically is followed by a conversation (or other action), whereas greetings may or may not be. Whereas the function of greeting is phatic, that of summons is not; it has a purpose. Catching someone's eye may be followed only by a greeting with no other conversation, but the fact of summoning implies more is to come. If address forms precede a greeting, they may function as a summons. A few greetings may also function as summons, notably the shorter, more informal ones, such as *hi!* or *hey!* Pitch and intonation distinguish between the summons *hi* and *hey* and the greeting version.

Address is often part of greeting. When it is, it must match the greeting in style. Together they can signal the same messages of power and solidarity. Greetings also occur once at the outset of an interaction, but no conversation necessarily ensues. Address differs from summons and greeting in two ways. First, summons and greeting are used only at the outset of a conversation and are not repeated, whereas address may be repeated throughout the interaction. Second, we have seen that summons is used to get someone to attend to the summoner, and greeting may be used phatically. Address, however, is used almost solely for power and solidarity. Between two people, then, it remains constant throughout a relationship unless that relationship changes. An example is an older person's saying, "Oh, call me Marge" when previously she was called "Mrs. Doohickey." She is signaling that she wishes more solidarity in the relationship. My superior's eventual "Hello, Elaine" when he retired was a clear shift away from power.

If a stranger is summoned, polite forms, those that signal that social distance is to be kept, are used. An example is the common, "Excuse me, sir. Could you please tell me the time?" If a person approaches a stranger and asks, "What time is it?" without at least an "uh" or "excuse me" to act as summons, the person spoken to usually ignores the question. If the asker persists, the stranger may turn, saying, "Were you talking to me?" or its equivalent. This occurs even if the two involved are the only two present, as at a bus stop or waiting for an elevator. "Were you talking to me?" is not a request for information. It is really a repair meaning 'you are not using the correct form for this conversation.' This is generally invoked for any inappropriate approach, as when males come on too strong to females. A *sir* attached to the question has the added effect of 'keep your distance.'

The use of formal distancing style to strangers is an indication that, although a request must be made, there is no intention of intruding on the person's privacy. The request is not to be construed as a bid for friendship. If, being bored or whatever, one of the parties does wish to continue a conversation, polite forms are still used until it is evident that both wish to talk further. If the person approached does not want to converse, he or she need only answer briefly and turn away. Notice that this option is open only after the original summons and request are answered.

People feel compelled to answer a summons. If someone does not, we assume that something is wrong. Moreover, despite the fact that it is a stranger ignoring a summons, the one who gives it feels hurt and even angry, as if receiving a slight. Indeed, one has, considering the social rules that decree that people are supposed to answer appropriate summonses for appropriate purposes. In our society, queries to strangers about time or location are proper if preceded by a summons using polite forms. Their obligatory nature can be seen by the declaration "I wouldn't give her or him the time of day." Since we are obliged to give that to anyone who asks for it, provided that they have used the correct summons, the declaration is tantamount to saying "She or he is beneath my notice as a human being."

If a casual, informal style, normal between two persons who are acquainted, is used with a stranger, the recipient is under no obligation to answer. "Hi there. Know the time?" is fresh and rude. If a male says that to a female and she answers, he may well assume that she is willing to give more than the time. If a female uses a casual, informal style to summon a male, he is more likely to assume that it is a sexual invitation. Even if a same-sex stranger asks it, formal interactions with strangers protect our privacy. It ensures that we need not spend time with a stranger. At the same time, it ensures that strangers can get necessary information such as time or directions. This is another example of how crucial style is to social interaction. It also illustrates the rigid conventions that govern even trivial interactions, as well as the social reasons for those conventions.

Speakers of European languages, excepting of course English, have another resource of address open to them—two forms of the second person pronoun. For instance, French has *tu* and *vous,* and German has *du* and *Sie.* This variation can be, and is, used to control social interactions by indicating the degree of power and solidarity (Brown and Gilman 1960) between the parties. As we shall see in later chapters, many other facets of communication also signal messages of power and solidarity.

On the model of French, Brown and Gilman called the singular of the second person pronoun the T form and the plural the V form. However, when they speak of T forms, they include the German *du* and, indeed, all singular 'you's' and the term V form includes German *Sie* or *Ihr* as well as all plural 'you's'. English, too, once had this variation, the old *thou* versus *you,* but the distinction all but disappeared after Shakespeare's time, and is seen today virtually only in the *thou* of prayers.[9]

If a **dyad,** two interacting parties, exchange mutual T (the singular), they are signalling intimacy, that is, solidarity. However, if one member of the dyad gives the singular and the other has to use the plural V back, then power is being signalled by the one who gives T and gets V.

It is quite usual in many societies to find the same address forms being used both to keep inferiors in their place and as a sign of intimacy. Those who have studied European languages may recall that the intimate form of *you* is also the one used to inferiors. In French, for instance, one says "I love you" using the *tu* form as in *"je t'aime."* The late Robert DiPietro told me that today, young French people *tutoyer* (use *tu* to him or her) each other as a sign of acceptance as an equal, but, in earlier, less casual times to *tutoyer* someone who was not an intimate could be an insult. The parallel use in English of using *thou/thee* for intimacy was pretty much gone by Shakespeare's day, and, by the later plays, we find the familiar *thou/thee* co-occurring with insults and the *you* for more ordinary speech.

Formality implies distance. Both intimacy and insulting imply little social distance. Hence, the same form can be used to insult and to show endearment. The insult occurs when the intimate form is used inappropriately to someone of higher rank who has not been given permission to use it.

Because of the social upheavals of two World Wars and the urbanization of society, many of the old rules for using T and V forms have changed. For instance, in World War I, officers in France used *tu* when speaking to subordinates. It also used to be correct to *tutoyer,* as the French call using *tu,* waiters, but nowadays with less social stratification, *vous* is used in both situations.

Throughout Europe there has been a steady erosion of T forms to indicate that the person addressed is inferior. There has, however, been an increase in its use to indicate equality. Bates and Benigni (1975) investigated such changes in Italy. They administered a questionnaire orally to 117 adults between the ages of fifteen and sixty-five, so that they would get both pre- and post-WWII adults. The oral format was used so that those with poor reading skills would not be at a disadvantage. The participants, who came from different social classes, were asked to imagine 23 different social situations, including those in which there would be conflict, such as speaking to the seven-year-old son of the President. They were allowed to tell the interviewer what forms they would use, and also were allowed to comment on their choices.

Italian not only has the T and V forms, *tu* and *voi,* but also *lei,* a formal marker meaning roughly 'her ladyship'. They quote a university student who says that everyone uses *tu,* unless the person to whom they are speaking refuses to respond with *tu.* Then, the student said, they use *lei.*[10] He claimed that nobody uses *voi.* By nobody, he apparently meant 'nobody amongst university students'.

The working-class youth did use *voi* to older members of their family, a practice largely abandoned by the students. Moreover, the workers still used *lei* to shopkeepers and other such contacts. In other words, the working class was much more likely to preserve the older forms of respect than the middle and upper classes. The young of the latter groups were the most likely to use *tu* to everyone, implying a comradeship with everyone. They used *lei* to shopkeepers. Interestingly, on Italian television and in the comics, the working classes are portrayed as always using *tu* inappropriately, of not knowing the niceties of address,[11] when, in fact, they do. This shows the danger of assuming things in sociolinguistics.

If we consider the shifts in American address forms in the past 20 years or so, we see a parallel situation. If a society wishes to even out social class differences, there are two ways it can move. One, the "solution" adopted by English speakers in the seventeenth century, is to use the polite form to everyone. Originally, in England, as on the Continent, the *thou* was used to inferiors as well as to intimates. By adopting the *you* for everyone, the pretense was that everyone was upper class. This is essentially what happened in France when officers began to give *vous* to the lower-ranking troops.

The opposite can also occur with the same motive: the intimate form can be chosen for all, thus also leveling out social differences. This is what the Italian university students claim. Fairclough (1989, p. 72) avers that the reason that overt marking of power relations is soft-pedaled in Europe and America today is that "power-holders have been forced into less direct ways of exercising and reproducing their power..." because the formerly powerless and disregarded people have protested, gone on strikes, and actively rebelled.

Address forms seem quite uniform throughout the United States, although some regional variations exist, notably the southern *Miss* + [first name] to an older woman, as in *Miss Lillian,* even if she is married. Why married women should be "demoted" (if it is a demotion) to *Miss* under these circumstances is quite mysterious. This allows the solidarity of first-naming to be combined with the social distance of a title. [Title + last name] generally indicates social distance. That address is given both to one's superiors and to relative strangers. What constitutes superiority in this country is, in itself, quite a complex business. For instance, age is one clear determinant of use of the form [title + last name]. An older person usually commands *Mr., Mrs.,* or *Miss,* especially from younger people. What happens, however, when a younger person is the boss of an older one? Sometimes age wins out, so that the boss calls his or her employee by [title + last name]. Sometimes it does not and the employee is first-named.

There is no such ambivalence for medical doctors in the United States. They are almost always and everywhere called *Dr.* Even if a physician is younger than the patient, *Dr.* is the usual address. Occasionally, one hears someone consistently refer to his or her physician by first name as in "I told Mitchell just before I was put under..." Since it is, indeed, a privileged patient who first-names his or her physician, one cannot help feeling, in many instances, that this is a way of affirming special status.

There are two reasons for the consistency in addressing medical doctors. Their position is virtually exalted. Despite backbiting at the profession in recent years, medicine is still a highly respected endeavor. The second reason for always calling a doctor *Dr.,* may be for control. Doctors have to be, or feel they have to be, obeyed. Those whom we first-name are our peers. We do not usually obey them. It is difficult to argue with those who are always above us, always at a distance, by virtue of address forms. The address form governs us.

Interestingly, the address *Dr.* can be used alone without a last name, and still be respectful. This is not so true of *Mr., Mrs.,* or *Miss.* If those titles are used without last names, they become impersonal, as in

▶Hey, Miss, your lights are on.
▶Hey, Mister, you dropped your wallet.

or even rude, as in

▶Where do you think you're going, Mister?

But the title *Dr.* retains its respectability with or without a last name. Oddly enough, doctors who do not have M.D.'s are properly addressed only by [Dr. + last name]. The exalted *Dr.* by itself is denied them.

Whenever he goes out of his office, one Ph.D. of my acquaintance tapes a sign on his door that says, "The Doctor is not in." The humor lies in the fact that *Dr.* without a last name refers to a medical doctor, not a Ph.D.

Other titles that can or must be used without last names are *Father, Sister, Rabbi, Reverend, Your Eminence,* and *Your Honor.* These denote either the religious or judges who, by definition in our society are morally better and certainly above the rest of us. The most respectful terms, *Your Eminence* and *Your Honor,* cannot be used with last names at all. It is as if their position takes precedence over their individuality. In monarchies, *Your Honor* or *Your Highness* is used this way. In line with our own country's political base, our leader is called "Mr. President," a title that combines the everyman's *Mr.* with the respected *President,* and like titles of the Your Honor or Your Highness category, is not used with a last name.

The form of address in itself is a powerful controller. Susan Ervin-Tripp (1972) recounts a sad example. Dr. Alvin Poussaint, a well-known African American psychiatrist and author, was riding in his native Mississippi in 1967. A white policeman stopped him.

What's your name, boy? [the policeman asked]
Dr. Poussaint. I'm a physician.
What's your first name, boy?
Alvin.

In a *New York Times* article, Dr. Poussaint[12] admits, "As my heart palpitated, I muttered in profound humiliation..." Ervin-Tripp explains that the source of Dr. Poussaint's extreme emotion was that he was forced to insult himself publicly and that this was done through widely recognized American rules of address. We have already seen that medical doctors are accorded exceptional respect in American rules for address. The policeman's refusal to use Dr. Poussaint's correct and deserved title was tantamount to stating that no black is worthy of adult status or earned respect, even one who has a medical degree. The officer's use of address form alone conveyed that message without his having to put it in actual words.

Ervin-Tripp calls *boy* "a social selector for race." That is not entirely true. To call a male of any race "boy" in American society indicates that he is a servant—not a personal servant who has an identity, but an anonymous servant to anyone. Note, for instance, the terms *busboy, bellboy,* or *messenger boy.* All of these are called "boy" regardless of age or color. Dogs are also called "boy," faithful servants that they are. The word *boy* refers to a faceless person who is there to carry out a function, but whom one otherwise barely notices. By extension, *boy* can be used as a wholly impersonal form of address to any male inferior, as in "Hey, boy! Get off my car." I heard this spoken to a white teenager in front of a theater.

Special nicknames are often used among close friends or members of teams. Certain kinds of nicknames are signs of intimacy, those like "Bubba" or "O.J." or "Sliv," nicknames that can't be predicted and are idiosyncratic to a certain person in a group. On athletic teams, where special bonds have to be forged between players, nicknaming is common. One is reminded of the German and French mountain climbers who, after they reach a certain height, start to use the intimate *du* and *tu* respectively, but, on their way down, revert to the usual *Sie* or *vous*.

In contrast, many names have recognized nicknames that are used as a matter of course, with the given name virtually never being used. If it is, something is unusual, typically anger, exasperation, or humor. It is the rare *William* who hasn't turned into *Bill* or *Willy*. *Robert* usually becomes *Bob(by)*. *Charles* almost always becomes *Charlie* or *Chuck*. Of course, *James* is doomed to *Jim(my)*, and *Daniel* to *Dan(ny)*. This also occurs with female names like *Patricia* who used to be *Pat*, but, for many younger females now is *Trish*. *Katherines* by any spelling become *Kathy*, more rarely *Kate* or *Kitty*. This does not seem to be a matter of solidarity, but of common usage. People with certain names are always called by the recognized short forms of those names. To be sure, an occasional recipient of such a name insists on the full form, and, even more occasionally, manages to get it.

Some common first names are actually old nicknames. *Wendy* comes from *Gwendolyn*, *Stacy* from *Eustacia*, *Nancy* started life as *Hannah*, and *Sally* as *Sarah*, *Beth* as *Elizabeth*. Also, it is certainly not unusual for a girl to be given for her full name what is still recognizable as a nickname or even two, such as *Peggy Sue*, *Cathy Jo*, or *Liz Anne*. It seems to me that this is more prevalent in our society in names for women than for men. I have met a handful of men christened with nicknames like *Sam* or *Benny*, but, in my personal experience, it is more common for women to be given nicknames as full names than it is for men. Since the usage of nicknames implies that the one so called is to be treated as an intimate and not as one in power, it would be pertinent to investigate whether or not this practise is more prevalent for women than for men.

One curious disparity in American naming practises is that names for men can cross the line and become names for women, but the reverse does not happen. For instance, the names *Shirley, Joyce, Brook, Marion, Ashley, Whitney* and *Dorian* were all originally names for men. Once the names become used for females, however, they pretty much cease being used for men. One might say that the names then become stigmatized for men. This, too, suggests that females don't have quite the positions of males in our society, even now.

The function of address forms in creating solidarity has resulted in more ready first naming than was common even 50 years ago. This probably results from the increased mobility of our population. In the old days, when people lived in the same neighborhoods for most of their lives, as did their neighbors, the progression from formal to casual, if it occurred at all, often did so slowly. After all, casual address goes with friendship. If neighbors are likely to be stuck with each other for life, they have to be careful to whom they extend the privileges of friendship. Also, in the days when people were occupied with large families, unto distant cousins, and work weeks were far longer than today, many did not have time for a large circle of friends. In modern transient neighborhoods, however, if people waited a long time to become friendly, many would never make friends at all. With the breakdown of the extended family, that would leave many mighty lonely. Easy first-naming seems to me to be a response to the need to replace the family with other networks of relationships. It is apparently furthered by the circumstance that the ways of youth are the reference point for much of society. Tradition, with its respect for old ways, formality, and titles, belongs to the aged, and they no longer set the pace for society.

In sum, then, the forms of address in a given society reveal a great deal about social stratification and attitudes. The intricacies of address forms in some cultures indicate how much more important social rank is than in others. For instance, it is well-known that the Japanese have an extensive system of **honorifics**, address forms attached as suffixes to names. For instance, in normal conversation, most adults would append -*san* to another's name (Coulmas 1992). That is ordinary politeness. -*sama* is even more polite, and indicates a somewhat higher status. Japanese exchange students in my classes have told me that -*dono* is the most polite. Traditionally, only men are accorded -*dono*. At really formal occasions like weddings and funerals, people use -*shi* to a man and *hujin* for a married woman. -*jo* is used to an unmarried woman. Boys either do not use honorifics with each other, or use the casual -*kun,* but girls, supposedly being more polite, use either the ubiquitous -*san* or -*chan,* the latter being a term of endearment often used to little children.

The fact that women are not accorded the highest titles makes one suspect that women are inferior to men in Japan. Examining terms for married women confirms this suspicion. Although men do call their wives by their first names with no suffix, they also use the term *omae* 'you', a pronoun for a person with lower status than the speaker, and *kimi* 'you', a pronoun for an intimate, equal, or inferior. Men do not address their wives by the pronoun to indicate a superior to the speaker (Lee 1976). A man may also call his wife by *okaasa* 'mother' or *okaacha* 'mommy.' If a man has to address another man's wife, he may refer to her as *okusan*. *Oku* means 'the inner part' and the *-san* is the honorific suffix. Women traditionally belong in the inner part of the house. A woman who works outside of the house will get the *-san* attached to her surname, which, as in Western cultures, is the husband's. She may also be addressed as *anata,* the politer form of 'you.'

Two other forms deserve mention, both now usually in the written language only: *tuma* and *gusai*. The former means 'a vegetable used as a garnish with raw fish' or 'the side plank supporting a roof,' and the latter means 'stupid wife' (Lee 1976, p. 995). *Tuma,* then, means 'something of secondary importance.' Lee says that *gusai* is "rather archaic" but older men use it in letter writing. It's not so much that he really thinks she is stupid. Rather "he intends to honor the person to whom the letter is addressed by lowering the status of his wife and therefore himself (p. 995)." Most telling is that there isn't even a form equivalent to 'stupid husband'.

We can look at these data and pretend horror at such sexism, but as we shall see, English does much the same thing, only we don't do it so heavily on address forms. It's done in other spheres of language. Our address system is not totally blameless. We still identify women as being sexually available or not by indicating *Miss* versus *Mrs.* I teach at a Catholic college with both priests and nuns on the faculty. Whereas priests are always Father + *Last name* (even if they have a Ph.D.), the nuns with Ph.D.'s are frequently Sister + *First name*. At a meeting or party, one says "How are you, Father Kenny? How are you, Sister Leslie?" First names are more intimate than last. This is equivalent to using *tu* or *omae* to women and *vous* and *dono* to men.

UNIVERSAL POLITENESS

Yet, even the most apparently polite of cultures may allow some behaviors which others find quite rude. For instance, when two Japanese exchange students in my class gave a talk on Japanese honorifics, mitigators, and dishonorifics, the female startled the class by saying in a rough, strong voice, one which sounded like scorn to our American ears, "You Americans are so rude. You come right out and say things!" We Americans all felt immediately that she had insulted us. Afterward, I asked her if it was considered in line to say such things to people. She said, brusquely (or so it sounded to us Americans), "Yes!" I told her that it is very rude in America to tell someone bluntly that he or she is rude. Only during an argument would such a thing be said. Both Japanese students were shocked. It never occurred to them that there are ways in which Americans are polite and ways that the Japanese are rude according to our standards.

The Japanese often feel that Americans are rude because they do not use **dishonorifics**, suffixes that indicate that what one has is not very good (Lakoff 1972) . In English translations, these dishonorifics are usually equated with a word like *humble,* as in "Have some of my humble apple pie" or "Please enter my humble home." Such translations render the Japanese ridiculous.

Actually, what the Japanese do is put a suffix after the word. This suffix means, roughly,[13] 'Eh! It's not so hot,' backgrounding it more than the English translation of 'humble' suggests. Lakoff (1972) points out that, actually, we have our own version of dishonorifics in English, but we don't put them on the noun. Our version of saying "my humble home" is "Please excuse the mess." Typically this is said as one enters a spotlessly neat abode, and it serves the same social purpose as the Japanese suffix.

As for humble cakes, we allow our system of modal auxiliaries[14] to take on this semantic load. Thus, Lakoff says, if we are offering someone cake that we ourselves have baked, we would normally say "You **must** have some of this cake." In other circumstances, must is used if we are commanding someone to do something distasteful, such as "You **must** clean the toilet!" Therefore, by saying that someone **must** have the cake, one is pretending that a person has to be forced into eating the cake, even though we think the cake is actually delicious. The polite fiction, then, is parallel to the Japanese dishonorific. Presumably, the Japanese speaker would not think of offering someone cake which is actually 'humble.'

Notice that it would actually be somewhat rude to use *should* in this context, as it would be too close to bragging about one's baking prowess, although I can use *should* when offering cake I neither baked nor selected, as in "You **should** have some of this cake. My mother baked it." The rudest of all to an adult is the one most accurate in terms of semantics, "You **may** have some of this cake." This is rude because it implies the speaker is socially superior to the one being offered the cake. This may be true, but our society, like the Japanese, usually adheres to the social fiction that all parties to the interaction are equal.

CHAPTER 3

The Japanese may perceive that Americans "just come right out bluntly and say things," but that they, the Japanese, mitigate verbs by using prefixes that, in effect, mean 'I humbly say that I heard you perhaps say, O honorable one that...' Again, there are American analogues to such softening of assertions, as when one says, "I thought you said..." "Gee, it seemed to me, and I may be wrong, that you said..." or "Maybe I didn't hear you correctly, but I interpreted what you said to mean..."

English speakers also soften assertions by casting them in the future or past tenses. For instance, *will* functions as a politeness marker in:

▶That will be five dollars.
▶And this will be Mrs. Jones.

Typically, this last is said upon meeting someone one knows with a companion, and one presumes the companion is a spouse one knows of. Taking the assertion away from the present tense, makes it not so direct. Compare, for instance:

▶And this is Mrs. Jones.

Similarly, the past tense in English is often used to indicate a situation which is imaginary. Compare

▶The unicorn **was** at the pond.
▶The unicorn **is** at the pond.

or to indicate that someone is no longer alive:

▶My uncle **had** blue eyes

indicates that my uncle is dead, whereas

▶My uncle **has** blue eyes

indicates that he is still alive.

Because both the future and the past indicate nonreal or nonexistent situations, they combine to produce polite forms. The auxiliary verbs used to indicated politeness typically have a sense of futurity combined with a past tense. *Would,* for instance, a combination of [*will* + past tense], gives the polite:

▶ *Would* you *hold* this for me.
▶ *Would* you *stand* over here, please.

Similarly, *could* (a combination of *can* + past tense) and *might (may* + past tense):

▶ *Could* you please *lend* me a hand right now?
▶ Do you think you *might be* able to lend me five dollars?

The frequent use of questions rather than statements in politeness routines also mitigates the requests or comments. Americans don't have a specific set of formal honorifics and mitigators as Asians do, but we indicate that someone is of honored status by such verb usage. That is, by using verb tense and questions to soften statements and requests, we are, in effect, saying to the other person, "I am humbler than you. You are superior to me. I am showing deference to you." The social effect is the same as that of honorifics and mitigators, helping to avoid confrontation and saving face. The same social effects may be achieved by manipulating different language features in different languages.

Not surprisingly, some Asian speakers do not recognize the way we achieve politeness in English. They simply see the lack of overt honorifics and mitigators, not realizing that English uses syntactic means to achieve these effects. Consequently, when they request or criticize, they sound to Americans as if they are being brusque. My editor at Heinle and Heinle, David Lee, recounted two incidents involving very polite and friendly Taiwanese coworkers, people with whom he has had very cordial relationships. Mr. Lee was taken aback by a fax from his Taiwanese colleague which states simply, "Include market surveys in all subsequent reports, please." This was the first time such a request was asked for, but it sounded to him almost like a rebuke. As an American, he would have requested by saying something like, "I meant to tell you at our last meeting that it has been decided to include market surveys with all reports, so from now on, could you please include market surveys? Thank you." The Taiwanese colleague seemed to think that the inclusion of please alone was sufficiently polite even though no market surveys had ever been requested before. To an American, however, such a brusque, direct request can be made only if several earlier, polite requests have been tendered.

Mr. Lee had an even more unsettling correspondence from Taiwan. He had written an article about the company at the request of the Taiwan affiliate, who did reply with a simple thank you. However, the affiliate also sent Mr. Lee a note saying,

I'm sorry can't be adopted. Please have H&H to rewrite. Please try to be interesting, knowledgeable, intelligent, and not too commercial.

Mr. Lee said that he was sure the affiliate didn't intend to have a message conveyed that he, Mr. Lee, was stupid, much less do so not by "telling him to his face," but complaining to a colleague. The effect, of course, was doubly insulting. One doesn't complain about a person behind his or her back in American culture. This is a shocking breach of American etiquette, but, apparently in Taiwan, it is most polite not to tell the offender to his or her face directly. I asked Mr. Lee how an American would express dissatisfaction with an article. He offered as a typical rejection: "This isn't quite what we wanted to say. How about something that talks more to the teachers?" Americans always try to give a piece of direct advice about what to do. Moreover, note the indirectness of the American response, the hedging with *quite*, as if the article were almost all right, and the almost casual question "How about...?" There is no actual criticism in the American response, whereas the Chinese response, saying "try to be" (a command) and then using words like *intelligent*, clearly implies that the article was none of these things: neither intelligent nor knowledgeable, nor interesting, and, finally, it was too commercial. Notice also that the Chinese complaint did use overt politeness markers like "I'm sorry" and "please" whereas the American one did not. The Chinese rely on overt politeness markers, but the Americans rely on mitigating through understatement and questioning.

If we are willing to look at the language system as a whole, we can often find equivalencies in politeness and face-saving rituals; that is, we must never expect the same measures of politeness to occur in the same places across languages. Still it is difficult to say that all languages do exactly the same things in politeness (Werkhofer 1992). That is, although many languages do allow the pretense that what the giver has to offer is inferior, this is not to say that all cultures ascribe to this fiction and, certainly, all cultures do not codify a pretense that the speaker is of humbler status—or of an equal status—than the person addressed. Two examples from western culture immediately present themselves, both tragic. The first is the treatment of Jews in Europe where, repeatedly, in many countries for long periods of time, it was permissible to insult Jews to their faces, speak to them scornfully, and even attack them physically without impugnment. In eastern Europe, for instance, it was common for Jews to hear contemptuous *zhid* from their Christian neighbors. The Nazis merely intensified what had been a *de facto* situation. The second is the American treatment of people of color who also were routinely insulted to their faces, ordered about, even physically attacked, and generally rudely treated. Certainly, in highly stratified societies with noble ranks, often the upper classes make no attempt to save the faces of the poorer or to mitigate the lack of equality. Ideologically, the doctrine of equality amongst men has led to politeness routines that are geared to save face even amongst those of lower rank.

Negative and Positive Face

Coulmas (1992) recounts the true story of a Japanese man who killed a stranger who dared to use the suffix -*kun* to him. Yet, in our culture, the equivalent of -*kun*, first-naming, is quite common amongst strangers. To us, the solidarity marker would be a way of showing respect for someone else's worth, but to the Japanese, it is disrespectful. Apparently, this is because of different ways of maintaining face in each culture.

Wood and Kroger (1991) show that a useful concept in distingushing between cultures is that of **positive** and **negative** face. Positive face is achieved by "positive rites of approach, exaltation, and affirmation" (Wood and Kroger 1991, p. 146). They claim that positive face "requires the achievement of closeness and common identity (p. 147), such as using first names or address forms like "brother" or "darling." Negative face distances, overtly shows deference, and acknowledges "the lack of common status"(p. 146). Saying "Your Majesty" or attaching a -*dono* or even just using [Title + Last Name] are all ways of maintaining negative face. Some societies seem to rely more on positive face rituals to protect their faces, and others rely on negative ones for the same purpose. In either event, egos are spared. Hurt feelings are minimized, but the means of achieving these common ends differ. Japanese society operates more on negative face. Americans rely on positive face. Many European societies have been going from a situation in which negative face was more usual (hence the strict rules of T and V forms of address) to the American situation of positive face (hence the increased adoption of the T form to everyone.)

Chapter 3 Notes

1   Since he wrote this so long ago, he may have changed his mind about it. In any event, I'm not sure this applies. A laborer, dressed in a good suit, and eating at a "fancy" restaurant would, to me, still be dining. Nowadays that scenario certainly occurs.

2   Figurative language is excepted. For instance, when organizations like Greenpeace speak of the murder of the baby seals, they do so to imply that baby seals feel the same pain as humans.

3   Unless the rule-breaker is a child or is in a classroom situation.

4   *Dreamchild,* a 1985 movie about the Alice for whom Lewis Carroll wrote *Alice in Wonderland,* depicts the brashness of American reporters who failed to use the titles an English lady expected. Much of the tension of the movie is centered on the business of address forms.

5   The student who reported this used the term *strange.* Although he didn't elucidate, as a native-speaking American, I could picture the look and even reproduce it. This is a normal circumstance with metaphorical or idiomatic speech, as discussed in George Lakoff's (1987) *Women, Fire, and Dangerous Things.* For instance, he gives the example of how all get the same picture from "She held him at arm's length, & prototype stuff."

6   As we shall see, however, not all members of society may be equally spared indignities to face, nor have all societies necessarily considered this a high premium.

7   He is not American.

8   One also reacts to kinesic cues. (see Chapter 4)

9   Shakespeare and other writers of and before his time thus had a resource open to them which is denied to us. Shakespeare, for instance, played with the usage of *thou* and *you* to indicate extreme anger, humor, and sarcasm. A character, such as one of the Henry's, would use *you* until he got angry. Then he would slip into *thou.* Often such switching is the strongest linguistic evidence of emotion.

10   Professor Rodney Delasanta, a native speaker of a northern Italian dialect, and a frequent visitor to Italy tells me that the university students he has known while teaching in Italy always use *lei* to him. In fact, he says, *lei* is prevalent everywhere, from and to shopkeepers, within families, between friends.

11   This is like the portrayals of the mythical American cabbies who call everyone "Mac".

12   This is the same Dr. Alvin Poussaint who has taught at Harvard University for years, and is the psychologist who advised the Cosby Show.

13   Robin Lakoff is not responsible for this translation. It's my own.

14   These are the verb auxiliaries: *shall, should, may, might, must, can, could, will,* and *would.*

Exercises

1. How many registers do you think you usually command? Give examples of each along with a description of the circumstances that evoke each. What are the components of each register?

2. Observe the difference in address forms that you give and receive in two different social situations (work, school, home, church, party, etc.) Do not work from memory. From these forms can you make any judgments about the social structure of the community you observed?

3. If you were writing an etiquette book, what rules for address forms, offering, asking, inviting, accepting, greeting, register and style would you include for work, school, parties, sporting events, funerals, weddings, formal dances, or graduation ceremonies? Try to think of some rules which were not covered in this chapter.

4. Compare your politeness rules to that of another culture. For instance, if you are a native English speaker what do you do in your speech to compensate for the lack of distinction between formal and informal *you*? Or what do you do to compensate for the lack of honorifics or dishonorifics in English?

5. Try to violate co-occurence restrictions in greetings and address with people you know well. How do they respond? Do they attempt repairs, and, if so, how? Can you formulate any general principles of repair?

6. Describe the voice(s) of a character or characters on a television show or commercial and try to explain how this voice presents the person's personality. Alternatively, discuss why such a voice was adopted in this circumstance.

7. Observe the same person speaking in two very different situations, such as at a funeral and at dinner. What changes in style do you notice alternatively; notice whether someone's style changes as topics of conversation change. Does a person speak of a death in the same way as a party, for instance? What are some of the signals which signal 'this is unpleasant/serious/funny, etc.?'

8. Note all the instances of positive and negative face rituals in contrasting interactions. For instance, what differences do you find between same-sex peers and an older high status person with a younger, lower status person (such as a professor and a student)? Do your observations substantiate the idea that Americans rely on positive face rituals? If you use interactions between people of another culture, analyze whether or not they use positive or negative face rituals and when.

References

Abercrombie, D. (1967). *Elements of General Phonetics.* Chicago:Aldine.

Allport, G. W. & Cantril, H. (1934, reprinted 1972). Judging personality from voice. In *Communication in Face to Face Interaction* (J. Laver & S. Hutcheson, Eds.) (pp. 155-171). Baltimore: Penguin.

Bates, E., & Benigni, L. (1975). Rules of address in Italy: A sociological survey. *Language in Society. 4,* 271-288.

Brown, P., & Levinson, S. (1978). Universals in language usage: Politeness phenomena. In *Questions and Politeness* (E. Goody Ed.), (pp. 56-289). New York: Cambridge University Press.

Brown, R., & Gilman, A. (1960). The pronouns of power and solidarity. In *Style in Language.* (T. Sebeok Ed.), (pp. 253-276). New York: Cambridge University Press.

Bugental, D. E., Kaswan, J. W., & Love, L. R. (1970). Perception of contradictory meanings conveyed by verbal and nonverbal channels. *Journal of Personality and Social Psychology, 16,* 647-655.

Chaika, E. (1973). Hi! How are you? Paper delivered at the Linguistic Society of America 48th Annual meeting. San Diego, Calif. (ERIC Documents).

Coulmas, F. (1992). Linguistic etiquette in Japanese society. In *Politeness in Language: Studies in its History, Theory, and Practice.* (R. J. Watts, I. Sachiko, & K. Ehlich, Eds.), (pp. 299-323). New York: Mouton de Gruyter.

Ekman, O., & Frisen, W. (1976). Measuring facial movement. In *Nonverbal Interaction , 2nd ed.* (S. Weitz, Ed.) (pp. 64-76). New York: Oxford University Press.

Ervin-Tripp, S. (1972). On sociolinguistic rules: Alternation and co-occurrence. In *Directions in Sociolinguistics* (J. Gumperz & D. Hymes, Eds.), (pp. 213-250). New York: Holt, Rinehart, and Winston.

Fairclough, N. (1989). *Language and Power.* New York: Longman.

Garfinkel, H. (1967). *Studies in Ethnomethodology.* Englewood Cliffs, N.J.: Prentice-Hall.

Giles, H., Taylor, D., & Bourhis. R. (1973). Towards a theory of interpersonal accommodations through language: Some Canadian data. *Language in Society, 2,* 177-223.

Goffman, E. (1955). On face work. *Psychiatry,* 18, 213-231.

Gumperz, J. (1964). Linguistic and social interaction in two communities. *American Anthropologist, 66,* 137-153.

Gumperz, J. (1971). Social meaning in linguistic structures. In *Language in Social Groups: Essays by John Gumperz.* (A. Dil, Ed.) (pp. 247-310). Stanford, Calif.: Stanford University.

Gumperz, J. (1971). Social meanings in linguistic structures. In *Language in Social Groups: Essays by John Gumperz* (A. Dil Ed.) (pp. 247-310). Stanford, Calif.: Stanford University.

Henton, C. G., & Bladon, R. A. W. (1985). Breathiness in normal female speech: Inefficiency versus desirability. *Language and Communication, 5,* 221-227.

Kramer, E. (1963). Judgment of personal characteristics and emotions from non-verbal properties of speech. *Psychological Bulletin, 60,* 408-420.

Labov, W. (1964). Stages in the acquisition of standard English. In *Readings in American Dialectology* (H. B. Allen & B. N. Underwood, Eds.), (pp. 491-493). New York: Appleton-Century-Crofts.

Lakoff, G. (1987). *Women, Fire, and Dangerous Things: What Categories Reveal About the Mind.* Chicago: University of Chicago Press.

Lakoff, R. (1972). Language in context. *Language, 48,* 907-927.

Laver, J. (1968). Voice quality and indexical information. *British Journal of Disorders of Communication, 3,* 43-54.

Laver, J., & Trudgill, P. (1979). Phonetic and linguistic markers in speech. In *Social Markers in Speech.* (K.R. Scherer & H. Giles, Eds.), (1-32). New York: Cambridge University Press.

Lee, M. Y. (1976). *Journal of Women in Culture and Society, 1,* 991-999.

Malinowski, B. (1923). Phatic communication. In *The Meaning of Meaning (Supplement to)* C. K. Ogden, & I. A. Richards. London: Routledge and Kegan-Paul.

Mehrabian, A. &. Ferris, S. (1967). Inference of attitudes from nonverbal communication in two channels. *Journal of Consulting Psychology, 31,* 248-252.

Mehrabian, A. & Wiener, M. (1967). Decoding of inconsistent communications. *Journal of Personality and Social Psychology, 6,* 109-114.

Milroy, J. (1984). Sociolinguistic methodology and the identification of speakers' voices in legal proceedings. In *Applied Sociolinguistics* (P. Trudgill Ed.), (pp. 51-71). New York: Academic Press.

Sapir, E. (1927). Speech as a personality trait. *American Journal of Sociology, 32,* 892-905.

Scherer, K. (1973). Acoustic concomitants of emotional dimensions: Judging affect from synthesized tone sequences. In *Nonverbal Communication , 2nd ed.* (S. Weitz Ed.), (pp. 249-253). New York: Oxford University.

Scherer, K. (1979). Personality markers in speech. In *Social Markers in Speech* (K. Scherer & H. Giles, Eds.), (pp. 147-209). New York: Cambridge University Press.

Wells, J. C. (1982). *Accents of English, 1-3.* New York: Cambridge University Press.

Werkhofer, K. T. (1992). Traditional and modern views: The social constitution and the power of politeness. In *Politeness in Language: Studies in its history, theory and practice* (R. J. Watts, S. Ide, & K. Ehlich, Eds.) (pp. 156-199). New York: Mouton de Gruyter.

Wood, L. S., & Kroger, R. O. (1991). Politeness and forms of address. *Language and Social Psychology, 10,* 145-168.

Chapter 4

Kinesics: The Silent Language

Kinesics is the study of body motion. Under it, we subsume also all matters of interaction which are not carried out by actual words, including such matters as the amount of talking which may be done, regardless of the content of that speech. Although humans share a basic repertoire of kinesics (body motions, eye contact, facial expressions, gazing, postures, touching, and proxemics), each social group may have somewhat different rules for using them. There may be national, tribal, ethnic, or gender differences in all aspects of kinesics. Since these matters are important for regulating interactions and for showing interest, politeness, submission, approval, or disapproval, people who do not share the same repertoire of kinesics may misunderstand each other. This causes cross-cultural difficulties and becomes crucial when one group of people is in a position to dominate another whose kinesics are substantially different. Special attention is paid in this chapter to the valid ways of researching these behaviors.

BODY LANGUAGE

Communication is not achieved by voice alone. It comprises posture, gesture, facial expression, gaze, even how we space ourselves relative to others. As with the vocal cues such as pitch and timbre that give purely social and emotional information, body movement is difficult to describe and analyze because we respond to it subconsciously. In fact, it is extremely difficult to talk without using body motion and facial expression (Hall 1959; Kendon 1983). Frequently if we are miscued or feel something is wrong, we simply feel uncomfortable without quite knowing why. As with style, this can be a basis for discomfort when interacting with people from cultures different from our own. It may also cause us, in all innocence, to ascribe the wrong characteristics to those whose "silent language," to use Hall's and Critchley's (1975) term, differs from our own.

Kinesics is the technical term for all aspects of this silent language. Along with those elements of style that we have already discussed it forms the **paralinguistic** system that operates with the linguistic system proper.

Like language itself, kinesics seems to be both inborn and culturally determined. There seem to be certain facial expressions, gestures, and body motions that generally mean the same things in all cultures. There are other kinesic messages that have specific meanings to particular cultures. Even if they are seen in more than one culture, it may be that they are evinced at different times in different cultures.

Charles Darwin (1965) felt that human expressive movements are the vestige of biologically useful movements that later became innately linked to emotional experience. A pushing away movement of the hand accompanying a negative response, for example, may be viewed as the vestige of actually pushing away a danger.

Darwin and, later, ethologists like Konrad Lorenz, Jane Goodall, and Dian Fossey noted the similarities of expression between man and other animals. One example is the brief raising of the eyebrows to indicate recognition. This has been observed in wolves and apes as well as man. In many human cultures, this has been extended in its meaning to indicate sexual desire or invitation. Old movie buffs will recall that both male and female movie stars in the 1920s had the entire area from eyebrow to eyelid painted to emphasize looks of sexual invitation. Groucho Marx's exaggerated eyebrow lifts were a parody of this sexual message. With or without paint, raising of the eyebrows is used for flirting in many cultures. The Polynesians carry it one step further, using an eyebrow lift alone to mean 'yes' (Eibl-Eiblesfeldt 1972.) Universally eyebrow liftings mean 'yes' to social contact, sexual or not.

Raised eyebrows signal to another that she or he is being looked at. In our own culture, the idiom "looking at him/her/them with raised eyebrows" means that the looker disapproves of a particular behavior. *Raised eyebrows* in this instance refers to staring as the idiom implies that the eyebrows remain lifted for more than the split second necessary to signal recognition or invitation. Like so many other idioms this one reflects our virtually subconscious knowledge of what is going on in ordinary interactions.

Goffman (1963, p. 86) says that normally we give "civil inattention." We don't usually stare at strangers. He notes that one of the trials of the handicapped is that people do stare at them just as they stare at animals in the zoo. Staring is often done to those with whom we do not speak.

Although raised eyebrows universally signal that someone is being looked at, still the degree of raising, the duration of raising, and whether it is with or without eye widening may all be manipulated to give different messages within cultures and cross-culturally.

When comparing American college students to the Fore tribesmen in New Guinea who had virtually no contacts with Westerners, Ekman and Frisen (1976) found that there is great similarity in signaling specific emotions by facial expression. Each group looked at pictures of the other one and was asked if the faces were happy, sad, disgusted, surprised or fearful. The instructions to the Fore were couched in small narratives, like, "His or her friends have come and he or she is happy." They found that both the Fore and the Americans made similar judgments. Because people could identify emotions on the faces of people from other cultures, Ekman and Frisen concluded that specific facial expressions are associated with particular emotions for all human beings.

Eibl-Eiblesfeldt (1972) offers even more conclusive evidence for the same position. He noted that three children who were both deaf and blind and had no hands still smiled, sulked, laughed, and showed surprise and anger with expressions like those of children who can see. He also observed blind children with hands, but critics were quick to point out that such children could have learned normal facial expressions by touching faces making different expressions.

Keating, Mazur, Segall, Cysneiros, Divale, Kilbride, Komin, Leahy, Thurman, and Wirsing (1981) specifically compared facial gestures[1] indicating dominance cross-culturally and across species. They noted that nonhuman primates such as Old World monkeys and apes signal dominance and submission by their degree of eyebrow raising, with lowered brows being dominant.

When I read Keating et al., it occurred to me that, as so often in the social and behavioral sciences, everyday idiomatic usage indicates a recognition of social cues and rules, in this instance of the lowered brow. We have words in English which refer specifically to the message of the lowered brow seen in us and the other primates: *glowering, glaring,* and *browbeaten.* Note that the first two describe the dominance expression of lowering the brows and sending the emotion of justified authoritarian anger. The third refers to a submissive person, one who is metaphorically, of course, beaten by the brows of a dominant person.

Keating et al. note that all primates use such expressions because they signal social status and help regulate relationships by "forecasting the probable nature of impending interaction" (p. 615). Although humans also have language to help this along, still the facial gestures do the same work. As with features of style carried paralinguistically with speech, signaling dominance via kinesics helps avoid confrontation and battling over power. However, Keating et al. found that human facial expression of dominance is homologous with that of other primates. Before we can accept such a parallel, we have to see if all cultures signal dominance this way. If they do not, then, despite the similarities between English and nonhuman primate dominance displays, we can't say with assurance that we have a true connection.

These researchers showed pictures of smiling and nonsmiling people with or without lowered brows to a wide variety of cultural groups: Zambians, Brazilians, Kenyans, Germans, Canary Islanders, Thais, Texans, and New Yorkers. What they found was that Westerners, including Americans, did associate lowered brows as an indication of dominance, but other groups did not or did so weakly. They found "neither observers' gender nor familiarity with models' ethnic facial characteristics had any important influence on dominance attributions (p. 624).

Similarly, they investigated whether there was a correlation between smiling or not smiling and dominance. This seemed mostly culturally determined. Texans and Canary Island workers did not find that nonsmilers were dominant, but New Yorkers and Canary Island students did. Why the Canary Island students and workers have different judgments about smiling and dominance is not clear. As it happens, in many societies different social groups may interpret the same cues differently, a phenomenon we will see in the United States in subsequent chapters. Keating et al. do suggest that a dominant person can manipulate another by smiling when giving commands (p. 624) and that smiling can indicate social dominance.

In short, although some humans do signal dominance the way other primates do, human facial gestures are culturally influenced as well. Apparently, the other primates' expressions can also be modified by their experience as well (p. 625).

Smiles

Although the basic human repertoire for facial expression may be the same, there is plenty of evidence showing that each culture modifies that repertoire. Smiles provide us with a good example. All human beings smile, but there are many kinds of smiles. Each culture smiles in somewhat different ways for somewhat different purposes. Even within a culture, there are many smiles. In the United States, for instance, there are friendly smiles, sly smiles, skeptical smiles, derisive, threatening, and sick smiles. And there are also grins. Some cultures demand a wide smile, teeth showing, upon greeting. Others find this too forward, greeting people with close-mouthed or only narrowly open-lipped smiles. Others greet each other deadpan. Some smile when scolded or asking a favor. Others do not.

The situations that call for smiles and call for each type of smile seem to be culturally determined. In a multicultural society, this can cause misunderstanding. Persons who do not smile enough for one group are pegged as cold and unfeeling. Frequent smilers, or those whose smiles are broader than other groups, strike nonsmilers as being phony or stupid. One of the most often quoted examples of cultural misunderstanding because of differences in smiling habits is that of Japanese-American children. As a sign of respect to their elders, these children smile when they are being scolded. Their Anglo teachers construe this as rudeness. LaBarre (1947) mentions the Japanese custom of smiling even at the death of a loved one. This is not because of any hard-heartedness. Rather, the bereaved smiles so as not to inflict his or her sorrow upon others.

A particularly gruesome instance of cross-cultural misunderstanding because of smiling as a sign of respect was portrayed in the movie *Platoon*. This involved a Vietnamese peasant who was brutally beaten to death because, in his attempts to be ingratiating, he kept smiling at American soldiers, one of whom interpreted this to mean the man was laughing at them.

Birdwhistell (1970) found that there were differences in frequency of smiling in different regions of the United States, even neighboring ones. For instance, people from Memphis and Nashville, Tennessee, smiled more than Northerners, but people in the Appalachian areas of the South smiled much less. Keating et al. (1981) said that Texans and New Yorkers should have agreed on their correlations between dominance and smiles, but they do not (p. 264). When we look at data such as Birdwhistell's, however, we see that such variation in meaning should be expected. It must be noted that Americans, at least, think that people who don't smile as much as they do are cold. Hence, Southerners complain that Yankees are cold. As the next section shows, such feelings don't stop at a country's borders.

Babad, Alexander, and Babad (1983) show that smiling is clearly inborn, but how much smiling someone does, and the intensity with which it is done seems to be cultural. Specifically, they show that children by the age of three show clear differentiation in returning the smile of a stranger. Israeli children and adults smile far less than Americans do. Harter in Babad et al. (p. 83) comments that the Israeli children do not smile as much as American children because of the constant threat of war in Israel. However, Babad et al. (p. 91) point out that it is Israeli Jewish children who don't smile very much. Israeli Arab children smile a great deal, and they are in the same danger as the Jewish children. Moreover, American Jewish children smile at strangers a great deal, as much as any other American child in the region in which they are being raised. Clearly, the correlation is between culture and smiling. What is the prime cause of such cultural differences? This, at least in such behaviors as smiling, we don't know.

What we do know, however, is that there is considerable misunderstanding between peoples with such differences. Americans feel that Israeli Jews are rude and hostile because they don't smile "enough," and Israeli Jews feel that Americans are insincere because they smile so much. These Israelis don't see themselves as rude and hostile, however. They see themselves as natural and sincere (p. 6).

Smiling often figures into ratings of competence. Israeli elementary school teachers rated nonsmiling children as more competent socially than those who smiled a great deal. American teachers thought smilers were more socially competent, since, in America, smiling is the social norm.

In general, a cultural group which smiles less than another, seems to feel that smilers are either insincere or not too bright. Although America is a smiling culture, compared to the Israeli, as noted above, there are clear regional differences in smiling. Note, for instance in the United States, the unflattering image of salespeople with superwide, toothy smiles often depicted in commercials.

Culture-Specific Gestures

Studies of kinesics and culture usually confine themselves to culture-specific gestures; that is, they are concerned with the way a given message is expressed in the kinesics of a given culture. Many, if not all, human groups often express 'yes' and 'no' kinesically, although not necessarily with the nodding and head-shaking that we associate with positive and negative. Examining the signs for 'yes' and 'no' is a study in how varied kinesics can be in different cultures, even though there are some widespread similarities. For instance, we have already seen that eyebrow raising is universally a 'yes' to social interaction. The Dyaks of Borneo raise their eyebrows to mean 'yes' and contract them, thus frowning, to mean 'no.' Actually, so do Americans under certain circumstances, as when surreptitiously trying to 'throw' a message to someone. The contracting eyebrows is often accompanied by a slight shaking of the head to mean 'no. This head shake is very common among both humans and other animals. Darwin related it to a baby's refusal to nurse when it is full. Eibl-Eiblesfeldt found it in deaf-blind children. He feels it stems from the way animals and birds shake themselves to be rid of water or the like.

Still, there are many culture-specific ways to say 'no'. The Abysinnians jerk their heads to the right shoulder, in a sort of modified head shake. They indicate 'yes' by throwing the head back and raising the eyebrows. This is a neat combination of a culture-specific motion with the apparently universal eyebrow lifting motion. Just how different cultures can be may be seen in the Maori 'yes' and the Sicilian 'no'. The two cultures use the identical motion, but for the opposite meaning they raise their chins, tilting the head back (LaBarre 1947).

Even a transparent gesture such as pointing with the finger to indicate location is not universal. The Kiowa Indians point with their lips. Sherzer (1973) found that the Cuna Indians of San Blas, Panama, use lip pointing to indicate direction, to acknowledge a joke, especially one mocking one party to the interaction, or as a greeting between people who have a joking relation. Interestingly, Americans, although pointing with fingers, not lips, can use a pointing gesture in the same ways that the Cuna do.

Efron (1972) attempted to relate differences between kinesic systems to cultural facts. He studied Jews and Italians in New York City in the 1920s at the end of the great waves of immigration. He found that Eastern European Jews (henceforth EEJs) who had been persecuted for centuries had confined gestures with elbows close to their sides. They walked with a shuffle and stood hunched with rounded shoulders. Their entire appearance was apologetic, timid, and depressed.

Italians moved the whole arm widely, expansively. Efron felt that the Italians' feelings of personal freedom are expressed in their arm movements, as the Jewish feelings of repression and inhibition are expressed in theirs. Studying first-generation Americans as well as immigrants, Efron found that persons who retained ethnic loyalty retained their group's gestures, but the assimilated adopted more American gestures. The accuracy of Efron's analysis is confirmed both by current-day Israeli and American Jews. Members of both groups maintain confident postures and gestures. Gender and social class may still result in different kinesic displays, as may regional loyalties. The general loss of specifically Italian or Jewish kinesics mirrors the loss of specifically Italian and Jewish ethnic dialects in northern cities, a loss evident by the 1960s (see Chapter 9)

PROXEMICS

In order to carry on an ordinary conversation, people have to learn the correct patterns for their society. This includes learning how near or far to stand from those with whom they are conversing. Normal distance between speakers varies from culture to culture and between subcultures of the same society (Hall 1959).

Typically, Americans stand with more distance between them when they are speaking than do Latin Americans and Middle Easterners. Scheflen and Ashcraft (quoted in Milroy 1980, p. 90–91) claim that Cuban men stand only 18 inches apart when talking in quiet and uncrowded places, but African Americans (by which I suppose they mean males) stand more than 36 inches apart even in fairly intimate conversations.

One of my students, Paul Goebelbacker, decided to investigate how consistently students at our college maintained distance while standing in line. He chose this situation because every day there are lines formed in the cafeteria, and at the ATM machine in the student center, so he could easily observe it on successive days and even photograph it. Fortunately, there are 30-centimeter tiles on the floor, so he could measure distance between students maintained from the photos. What he found was that students spontaneously, but consistently placed themselves at a distance of 45 centimeters from each other. The lines are very orderly, even in this casual setting, and the equality of space between members is very striking. One would almost think the students measured. Paul concluded that a line is a social structure and people unconsciously follow the rules for its formation as part of their socialization. His argument is bolstered by the fact that frequently one person would come up to another in line to talk to her or him, but they never got in between that person and the next one in line. Rather, they stood just outside the line, positioning themselves at right angles to the one they were talking to, so that the 45 centimeter distance was maintained and the line was not disrupted, but the conversation could still go on.

This lining up seems to be a self-regulatory behavior, and one which helps maintain an orderly society. These students stayed far enough from each other so that their bodies did not touch at all. This is not at all surprising amongst middle- and upper-middle class students from the Northeast. Theirs is not a "touchy-feely" culture, and even when engaging in casual conversation on campus, one notes distance being maintained amongst speakers.

If someone stands too far away in an interaction for a given culture, it is virtually impossible for others in the culture to continue a conversation with that person. In fact, one good way to signal the end of a conversation is to walk backward slowly even while maintaining eye contact. As one crosses the invisible line, the boundary of conventional distance, the speaker will suddenly stop even in midsentence, saying the equivalent of "Oh—see ya!"

Cross-culturally, since the distance considered normal varies, those who are used to less distance will keep moving closer if they are conversing with one used to a greater gap. The latter will keep stepping backwards, and so it goes. Once, entangled in just such an uncomfortable conversation, I realized that I was dancing around my office with my co-conversationalist in hot pursuit. What made it even more uncomfortable was that I am less than five feet tall and he is over six feet. To minimize the distance between us, as he was explaining his problem, he also kept leaning toward me. There seemed no way he could talk over my normal distance, and no way I could listen if he tried to lessen that distance.

The extreme discomfort caused by someone's moving in too close was well illustrated when one of my students did so experimentally. She placed her tray adjacent to that of a casual acquaintance in the cafeteria. Returning from getting some drinks, she found her tray had been pushed across the table. She pushed it back and sat next to the hapless acquaintance. The victim sat fiddling with her napkin, not contributing much to the conversation. When the experimenter moved even closer, the subject moved away, and finally asked, "What's your problem?"

Repeating this procedure in a student lounge, the experimenter kept moving in too close to a boy eating a grinder.[2] He abruptly picked himself up, leaving about three fourths of it. Before his hasty departure, he signaled discomfort by looking tense, speaking abnormally little, and nervously jabbing at the ice in his glass. A third subject, approached while sitting in a library carrel, finally laid her head down and said, "I really can't help you anymore. I'm so tired from studying." Perhaps the most original repair tactic was displayed by a girl chewing bubblegum. When the experimenter started walking out of class far too closely by her side, the gum chewer proceeded to blow a huge bubble. This forced the experimenter to move aside before the bubble burst in her face. As with style, it is rare for violations of proximity to be commented on overtly. Rather, people try other adjustments to force a proper distance to be maintained.

The delicacy with which we must obey the unwritten rules of distance in conversation should underscore for the reader how intricate our socialization into a society really is.

The amount of space one takes also gives clear messages about dominance. It is well known that dominant mammals take up more space than those who are nondominant; that is, the dominant ones demand that more space be left around them than for inferiors. Thus the image of inferiors huddling together with a space between them and their leader. Examining the behaviors of American males and females gives us some disquieting confirmation of this.

American males tend to fill up the spaces around them. They stand with their legs wider apart than females do, although this may be changing. In social situations, men spread their arms out over backs of chairs, assume asymmetric leg positions with one leg up on a chair and the other on the floor or another chair or stool, legs as far apart as the human body allows. Men lean their torsos way back while their legs are stretched forward. It often seems that the males at a social gathering expand in every possible direction.

Women, on the other hand, sit with their knees together or legs crossed tightly, arms close to their sides, or hugging their knees close to their chests. My student Elizabeth Brown, who did a term paper on elevator behavior, carefully noted the different behaviors of men and women. Women took up less space than men, crossing their arms and even legs, often also keeping their heads down, another way to minimize space. If they carried a briefcase or bag, they held it close to their legs or chest, thereby setting up a physical barrier between themselves and others. Men are more likely to spread their legs apart, keeping their arms at their sides. Some put their hands in their pockets with their elbows out to the sides, another way of maximizing their space. Whereas women could best be described as being huddled, men leaned against the walls with legs stretched forward.

Men walk with a wide-legged stance, a ten to fifteen degree angle, but many women walk, literally, with legs not only close together, but even with one leg crossing in front of the other. Men often appear far more relaxed both when standing and sitting than women do. Only when women become old are they likely to sit with legs wide apart. In old age, many gender markings become less overt.

Other studies have shown that behaviors evinced toward inferiors are regularly evinced toward women but not men. For instance, both men and women stand closer to women than to men. Invading another's space is permissible for the dominant party, so this is a sign of nondominance in women. Both men and women touch women more in conversation than they touch men, another sign of feminine lack of dominance.

EYE CONTACT

Very rarely can interaction begin until eye contact is made in our culture. When a person is summoned by another, it is not sufficient to answer verbally. One must turn his or her head toward the summoner. Then the interaction can begin. In many, but not all situations, once eye contact is made one is compelled to respond. This is why waitresses as they rush about will not look at patrons. By looking away, they are not compelled to take any more orders. Once they allow eye contact, they might feel that they have to stop and listen even at another waitress's table.

Anger is frequently signaled by refusal to make eye contact. Such refusal means 'no' to social interaction. We have all known the discomfort of waiting for elevators with strangers. Where to put one's eyes? If we inadvertently make eye contact with strangers, either we look away quickly, embarrassed, or we are compelled to engage in chitchat. That is how strong a signal eye contact is for beginning social interaction. Elizabeth Brown, in her study of elevator behavior, previously mentioned, rode up and down in a commercial building for two hours. She found that everybody walked in the elevator without making eye contact and proceeded to look straight forward at the door or the floor indicator. Nobody risked eye contact.

During a conversation, eye contact is never steady. Steady gaze is staring. In most if not all cultures, staring is impolite. Perhaps this is because, even in other species, in creatures as lowly as chickens and turkeys (Sommer 1965), staring is both threatening and cowing. If dominant birds, for instance, stare at lower-ranking ones, the latter look away submissively. Staring in human beings can also be a sign of dominance and may be taken to mean haughtiness. Only a dominant person can "stare another down." Many a teacher knows how often a class can be quelled simply by staring. And many a mother controls her children in public just by staring at them across a room. Staring also implies that the one stared at is outside the pale of society. One deserves staring if one's behavior is out of normal bounds or if one is some sort of freak to society. That is another reason that staring is rude. It implies that the one stared at deserves it, and only outcasts are believed to deserve it.

During conversation, regular fluctuations of eye contact are followed by looking away. The length of time eye contact is held and the number of times it is made during a conversation depends partly on the topic of conversation. Within cultures, there may be differences in eye gaze between the sexes, different age groups, and those whose status differs on other parameters.

Culture determines both the frequency and length of eye contact. This can cause severe cross-cultural discomfort. Those who are used to little eye contact feel that those who habitually engage in more are staring. This is a common complaint about Anglos by members of some tribes of Native Americans. Conversely those who are used to more eye contact, the Anglos, feel that those who give less, the Native Americans, are not paying attention, are passive, or sneaky.

As with features of style, deviation from the conversational norm connotes a special message. For example, in American culture, sexual attraction is signaled by two people looking into each other's eyes. Thus, flirting can be initiated by prolonging eye contact.

Women look at one another more while they are speaking, while they are being spoken to, and while they exchange simultaneous glances. Whatever the sex of the other partner in the dyad, women look at him or her more than men do. There are two possible reasons for this. One is that women are more willing to establish and maintain eye contact because they are more inclined toward social relations (Grumet 1983, p. 117). Another is that women are more sensitive to visual cues (Eakins and Eakins 1978, p. 50).

However, another explanation is more likely. It seems that, frequently, the subordinate person in an interaction looks at the superior more than the superior looks at the subordinate. Looking to the superior is a way of getting approval, of gauging the effect they're having on the one whom they wish to please. In conversations, listeners look more at speakers than speakers look at listeners. One is reminded of the stereotypical blushing bride who keeps looking adoringly at her husband to see his reactions to her words.

This is not to say that gazing is always an indication of inferiority or of willingness to have social interaction. Kleinke (1986, p. 80) shows that "Gaze influences evaluations of liking and attraction, attentiveness, competence, social skills and mental health, credibility, and dominance." Kleinke notes that studies have shown that Americans say that people like each other if they gaze into each other's eyes.

One disquieting discovery is that people gaze more at interviewers when they are intentionally giving false information (p. 82). Yet, Americans rate people as being truthful if they look directly at someone. The shy person who can't bring herself or himself to look into another's eyes, or one whose culture forbids such gazing, is likely to be rated as being shifty and dishonest.

Having people rate participants in movies of job interviews indicates that the interviewee who gazed at the interviewer 80 percent of the time was rated more favorably, but more tense, than those who gazed less (p. 80). Gaze seems to indicate intensity of feelings, but the feelings can be either good or bad (p. 81). As we have seen, prolonged gazing, what is considered staring, can be threatening or an indication of dominance, as well as an indication of interest and liking. Within a culture, the particular meaning given to the gaze depends on mutual social rankings, situation, posture, facial expression, voice quality, and, of course, what is being discussed.

There is a body of research which says that people are likely to increase their gaze when they are trying to be persuasive (p. 82), as well as when they want to be friends. In fact, gazing seems to be the thing to do to get others to comply with one's requests. People have been shown to be more willing to accept leaflets, to donate money to charity, and to change money for experimenters who gazed at them. Similarly, drivers were more likely to pick up hitchhikers who gazed at them. People were more likely to pick up coins or leaflets that were dropped by someone who gazed at them (p. 83). Professors who make a good deal of eye contact with students not only get rated highly, but their students perform better than those under the tutelage of professors who gaze less (p. 84). We must remember, however, that the amount of gazing and what it means varies from culture to culture. Those students who come from cultures in which direct gazing is avoided might feel threatened by teachers who gaze at them. In turn, the teachers might construe the student who refuses to gaze back as being uninterested, bored, or even sneaky. It is imperative that teachers and others who deal with the public understand the differences in kinesics.

Gaze also helps regulate social interaction. Typically, in many but not all American social groups, listeners look more at speakers than vice versa. When the speaker does look at the listener, it can be a cue that the speaker is willing to give up the floor (p. 81). However, looking can mean other things, such as disapproval, approval, anger, or flirting. Other factors, including the appearance of the gazer, will also influence the message of the eyes. It has been shown, for instance, that an unkempt person staring at pedestrians at a stoplight will make them hurry across the street. Kleinke (p. 82) says that the function of gaze in regulating interactions will be understood better when we better understand such effects as motive and context. Clearly, the amount of gazing and the conditions under which it is carried out are supremely important in how one is evaluated and how one evaluates. How we get treated and how we treat others is tied up in gazing.

Head position and eye gaze serve both to regulate interaction and to underscore the purpose of actual words. The interpreting posture and direct eye contact in psychiatric interviews alone give the message 'These words explain what you just said.' In teaching or punishing situations, the direct eye gaze at the recipient says in effect 'pay attention. I'm the dominant party in this interaction.' Most of us at some time or another in our childhood have had an adult reprimand 'look at me when I talk to you' as the start of a complaint about our actions.

Like style, eye gaze and head position must be correct for interaction to continue smoothly. We are all familiar with the discomfort caused by the person who persists in looking down or away as we attempt to talk with her or him. As parents know, young children have to be taught to look at someone who is talking to them or to whom they are talking. Two-year-olds for instance, often look down at their toys while talking to parents or when they are spoken to.

In an Anglo group, those addressed behave differently from others in the group. This does not seem to be so among the Warm Springs Native Americans. Speakers do not align their bodies toward anyone in particular. Non-Indian observers get the feeling that speakers are talking in general to the entire group because no one in particular aligns herself or himself with the speaker. In the interactions between other Americans, aligning motions are prime determinants in who will take the next turn. In classrooms, for instance, often the student who aligns her or his body motions to the teacher is the one who gets called on. Such alignment is taken as a sign of interest. One can see where Anglo teachers might misinterpret NA or other children whose kinesics do not align themselves to show their interest. This doesn't mean that they don't have other subtle ways of indicating interest. It is just that the teacher may not recognize another culture's way of doing so.

TOUCHING

Cultures also vary in the degree of touching that they do during normal social interaction. When we think of touching, frequently we think of sexual advances, such as pinching bottoms or making "a pass." This does not mean that we don't ever touch or are never touched. We greet each other with a handshake. Heslin and Alper (1983, p. 51) say that the handshake "neutralizes status." Handshaking "...is used to signal that the persons involved are starting off on status levels that manifest each other's personhood." So long as it can't be construed as a sexual advance or sign of superiority, touching can be bonding (p. 54).

Although little has been written about it, touching in the course of professional activity is allowed and even sought out by the middle class. Many people are routinely touched by hairdressers, manicurists, masseuses, estheticians,[3] tailors, and of course, doctors and nurses.

Typically, we barely notice certain kinds of touching: the unintentional and unavoidable, as when one is jammed together in a full bus or standing in a long line to get tickets for a rock concert. Bumping, momentary contact, is also often permissible, as when trying to navigate an airplane aisle while carrying a suitcase. The "sting" of such touching is lessened by the one bumping repeating, "Excuse me, Excuse me" while making her or his way. Other kinds of touching can set off an argument. If one male pokes the other on the shoulder as they argue, that can be construed as inciting blows.

Very little research has been done on these impersonal or threatening kinds of touching, but there is evidence, even for middle-class Americans, that some touching by strangers and acquaintances can have a positive effect. For instance, people have been shown to comply with requests more frequently, perform favors more readily, are more likely to sign a petition, fill out a questionnaire, and even return money found in a phone booth when they are touched lightly (Heslin and Alper 1983, p. 68).

As can be inferred from the data on proxemics, most Americans are not "touchy-feely" people, although there may be some ethnic variation. Brady and Eckhardt (1975) studied African American girls in the schoolyard in the South. They found that for these girls, the welfare of the group is more important than individual success. Everything is done in terms of the group, both to get its support and to give it. Although there is competition, it always involves the group. It is not for personal gain. Understandably, then, a major component of play is hand-clapping. The girls clap in time together, sing the same ritualized tunes in unison, and form circles when playing, thus invoking strong bonding and solidarity.

All of these behaviors indicate strong bonding and solidarity. Clapping, of course, is touching, and touching can be bonding. Singing together is also bonding, which is why in many countries there are national anthems which citizens sing together, and, of course, it is why hymns and responses are sung by the congregations in churches and synagogues. And, the circle itself is universally a symbol of solidarity. Hence, camp-fires, powwows, square dancing (which is actually circular), and folk dancing take place in circles.

So important is the concept of the circle to these girls that even when they are sitting around just talking, they form a rough circle. At the same time, they touch each other, even if it is a foot stuck out to touch someone else's foot. In most of the circle games, they hold each other's hands, a further display of solidarity.[4]

Brady and Eckhardt show that these girls don't lose all individuality. One at a time, they go to the center of the circle and there they can dance and sing as they wish. As Brady puts it, "Surrounded by the support of her friends, which is echoed in every clapped beat, [she] is free to act out whatever she wishes." Moreover, what the girl does in the center, the others will imitate, showing that they accept her both as a performer and as a member of the group.[5]

One thing that strikes many observers is the degree to which these girls look out for each other. They constantly literally look at each other, too, reinforcing solidarity with eye contact. They also teach each other, and make sure none of them is in trouble. They have very few of the competitive games that middle-class girls indulge in, games in which one person emerges as the winner. Given the degree to which the usual classroom in America is organized on competitive principles, one sees that these girls could be at a great disadvantage in school. Yet, schools could just as easily be organized on cooperative principles.

Although middle-class Britons and Irish, like many Americans, do little touching, (Milroy 1980, p. 91), the working-class in Belfast,[6] differ. Milroy (p. 91) describes a common occurrence especially among women there. Women who are not especially intimate sit "squeezed" together with arms linked. Sometimes a hand was placed on her arm or around her shoulder. As they conversed, they slapped, squeezed, and nudged to reinforce what they were saying. Note that in America, a "squeeze" is someone with whom you have a romantic relationship. We don't normally squeeze anyone else. Note that the American usage couldn't be used in working-class Belfast, as, there, squeezing is not sexual.

Men, too, evince both closer proximity and touching in daily interacting. A speaker places a hand on a listener's shoulder, standing within a foot of each other, at right angles, with his mouth only inches from the listener's ear. Eye contact is avoided. Milroy observed two men who had never met previously adopt this pose for over an hour in a crowded dance hall. The speaker was talking about the fact that he was illiterate, a fact which he wished to keep secret.

Milroy says, and I agree, that, in Belfast such proximity and touching, is not intimate, but it is done to achieve solidarity. The male-to-male conversational stance also signals that the conversation is private and shouldn't be interrupted. Also note that neither the female nor male stances foster eye contact, although there is touching.

Eye contact frequently interacts with touch. Both give strong messages about intimacy, solidarity, and power. For instance, it has been long known that couples who make a great deal of eye contact are perceived as liking each other more than couples who make less eye contact (Abbey and Melby 1986, p. 285). They also found that both males and females perceived females, but not males, in terms of their sexuality when viewing photographs of males and females in different poses involving touch, gaze, and proximity. The woman who touches a man, and/or gazes into his eyes, is very likely to be interpreted as having sexual interests (pp. 284, 296). In Chapter 10 we will see that this is part and parcel of a larger tendency to define women in terms of their sexuality.

In many cultures, if not all, touching between adults can indicate sexuality; however, the conditions under which it does vary greatly. For instance, in the United States men do not walk around holding each others' hands, unless one is blind or otherwise infirm and the other appears to be helping him get around. Otherwise, this is seen as a strong indication of homosexuality. This is true of female pairs as well. Yet, in some countries, such as Egypt or at least some of Latin America, same-sex handholding or arms around the waist or shoulder indicates solidarity only. In those cultures, typically, one wouldn't touch a decent woman in public, although in the United States, hand-holding across sexes is considered harmless enough.[7] Similarly, the American locker room habit of one man playfully slapping another on his behind is misconstrued by those of other cultures as being homosexual, although, in the United States, this only indicates camaraderie.

Recall that, in Belfast, neither males nor females make eye contact, although they certainly make physical contact. Perhaps having both kinds of contact at the same time is simply too powerful and indicates too much solidarity or even sexuality or both. Eye contact, so long as it isn't construed as staring, indicates willingness to interact. When combined with touching, it can be a potent force. As such, the combination can be threatening especially when given to strangers. For instance, Goldman and Fordyce (1983) had a confederate approach a passerby and ask people to participate in a survey. Just before the last question was to be asked, the confederate touched some of the passersby softly on the shoulder. Others weren't touched. The touching was combined with eye contact for some, but not others, and some eye contact was made without any touching. Variation in voice was also combined with the touching and eye contact, so that some heard a "warm and expressive" voice, and others a flat monotonous one. After the last question was asked, the confederate "accidentally" dropped the sheaf of questionnaires. The dependent variable was whether or not the passerby helped to pick them up.

Every possible combination of touch, eye contact, and voice was used. The most help was obtained if the confederate did one or the other, but not both. That is, the confederate made no eye contact, but did touch, or he or she made frequent eye contact but didn't touch. Making both eye contact and touch, or no eye contact and no touching got the confederate less help.

One of my students, Susan Pinkerman, replicated this study. She confirmed their results, except that she found a gender difference: Males helped females far more than the reverse under all combinations of touch and gaze. Apparently, both together are perceived as an invasion or even a threat of undesired intimacy. Pinkerman saw this nonhelping behavior as an attempt at repairing the situation, a way of keeping the experimenter at bay. A little friendliness goes a long way.

I suspect that using two such signs of intimacy to strangers is very threatening; however, using one or the other makes the encounter just personal enough so that the respondent feels cooperative.[8] If the person asking another to respond neither touches nor gazes, the respondent gets no bonding whatsoever, no feeling except that of being a cipher. Ciphers don't fill out forms or do favors. Also, Fordyce and Goldman found that significantly more help was also forthcoming when requests were made in a warm, expressive tone rather than in a flat one.[9] Again, the feeling that someone cares is conveyed by expressive tones, whereas flatness conveys a lack of interest.

The degrees of solidarity that we see in both the African American southern girls and the Belfast working class are, as noted, not usual in more competitive groups in Western cultures, especially amongst the upwardly mobile middle and upper middle class. In fact, one requirement for such upward mobility is the willingness to become more competitive and to lessen behaviors intended primarily to achieve solidarity. Milroy cites the cases of bright working-class children in Belfast who reject scholarships because they do not want to have to leave their neighborhoods. It seems to me that the major reason for this is that people raised in neighborhoods in which solidarity is constantly affirmed find middle class culture frightening with its apparent coldness. Moreover, those who are used to having the support of the group in their endeavors find it difficult to stand alone, so to speak, and constantly have to compete against others. Mere money and elevated social position aren't always enough reward to those used to being part of a close and caring group that reinforces its strength by constant touching, looking, talking, visiting, and general caring.

Actually, there seems little reason beyond custom for the "every person for himself or herself" ethic in business or the professions. Rather than requiring those who are raised with solidarity to learn the ways of power, perhaps those who are raised with power should learn how to achieve solidarity in education and industry. That is, instead of blithely assuming that, in order to get ahead, one must learn competitiveness, perhaps the upper middle-class in Europe and America can learn achievement through solidarity. Typically, the assumption is that those who wish to raise their socioeconomic status must become like those who have higher status, but it is just as reasonable to change educational practises so that co-operative and caring group behaviors lead to higher socioeconomic goals.

AMOUNT OF TALKING

People often seem to judge each other on the basis of social behavior rather than on acuity. It is not always what people say that cause others to evaluate them in a certain way, but how they say it, and even how much they say. Bales (1955) found that people in small group interactions who speak more than average and give more than the average rate of suggestions and opinions will be judged as "having the best ideas." This is true regardless of the worth of the ideas expressed. In getting others to think that one is bright, one's ideas themselves are not as important as their frequency. Furthermore, the member ranked the highest by a group addresses considerably more remarks to the group as a whole than to individuals. Lower-ranking members address individuals more than the group.

Riecken (1958) went one step further than Bales. Riecken provided both high-ranking and low-ranking members of groups with a solution to a human relations problem that the groups were considering. Using 32 four-man groups, he verified Bales' finding that those who talk the most are ranked the highest. He also found that those who are ranked highest by the group got their ideas accepted. Lower-ranking members who advanced the same ideas did not get them adopted. Moreover, Riecken found that the high-ranking members influenced others because of their ability to win support by talking the right way and using the right techniques of kinesics and eye contact. Neither measured IQ nor fluency in speaking seemed to be important factors in determining who could persuade.

This is to be expected in cultures which value the printed page over the oral word, but we should not assume that this is true for all cultures. Fluency may count strongly in cultures which don't value book-learning, those known as oral cultures, and is frequently the most important factor in becoming a leader in those cultures. In such cultures, oral displays of verbosity can be brilliant. (see Chapter 6).

BODY MOTION IN CONCERT

It can be seen that even the simplest of conversations requires a good deal of learned behavior, all fine-tuned. Whether or not one may speak at all depends on the situation and whether one's culture allows speech in it. Not only does the content of the message have to be appropriate for the context, but the speaker has to encode her or his meaning with words and grammar that hearers can understand. Even that is not enough. The style used must be appropriate for the occasion. Then, too, the speaker must stand just the right distance away, making the right amount of eye contact, holding it just the right length of time, tuned to the requirements of turn-taking as well as topic of conversation. Heads must move to signal points as well as to signal turn-taking. Gestures must correlate with meaning and, again, with turn-taking.

This is part of a larger phenomenon of the way interactants organize their postures, patterns of looking, proxemic configuration, nods, and gestures in "cooperative, reciprocal, rhythmically coordinated ways (Chick, 1990, p. 227). In a successful interaction between members of the same culture, conversational behavior is synchronized "like ballroom dancing partners of long standing...moving in smooth harmony," whereas interactions between persons from different cultures may be "marked by a series of uncomfortable, asynchronous movements" (Erickson, quoted by Chick, p. 227). As we shall see, maintaining synchrony is part of doing a conversation successfully, including giving appropriate turn-taking cues (Pelose 1987, pp. 186–204). Typically, we are so unaware of these behaviors that when we can't get in synch with another, we find the interaction stressful, thinking that person is uncooperative, aggressive, or otherwise difficult. Different cultures maintain different rhythms in their conversations, use more or less subtle body motions, and so on, making intercultural interaction difficult and leading to negative cultural stereotypes (Chick, p. 228).

Although so far as we know, all cultures have such restrictions on speaking and how it may be done, the exact rules for interaction vary from society to society.

Whether or not participants in an interaction are aware of the fine adjustments they are making while talking, still they have to be made. As Harumi Befu (1975) has shown, this can occur even when participants cannot see each other, as in Japanese bowing. Both the depth and the timing of each bow vary with the status and degree of intimacy of participants. Furthermore, the bows have to be synchronized with the other party's. Once a bow has begun, however, one cannot see the other. "Bowing occurs in a flash of a second, before you have time to think. And both parties must know precisely when to start bowing, how deep, how long to stay in a bowed position, and when to bring their heads back up" (Goody 1978). With the changes in Japanese society in the past decades, bowing behaviors seem to be being modified especially amongst younger Japanese in the workplace.

American cultures do not include such bowing, and in fact, during and after World War II, Japanese bowing was frequently ridiculed or held up as an example of Japanese slyness and deception. Of course, the Japanese evaluated American failure to bow very negatively, thinking that Americans were rude and aggressive. These are typical reactions of people to those from different cultures. Actually, every culture has its ways of moving, looking, standing, and "talking with their hands." We find our own so natural, we usually don't even notice them consciously.

Violations of Expectations

It has generally been assumed that all facets of gaze, kinesics, and proxemics must be exact for interactions to take place successfully. If someone violates expectancies, it prompts changes in others' behavior and evaluations. For instance, as seen above with proxemics, the offended person tries to repair the situation by putting up barriers or walking backward. However, Burgoon (1983) claims that there are situations in which it is beneficial to violate **expectancies**, her term for 'expectations'. In studies of small group interaction, it has been found that high status members get better evaluations by not following the group's consensus when given a task demanding creativity (p. 77). However, low-status people who conform to group norms are more attractive to others.

Burgoon found that one important variable in how people are rated is how physically attractive[10] they are. For instance, attractive people are more likely to be rated as sociable, composed, and extroverted. When distance norms are violated by someone coming in too close, the attractive people are rated as sociable. Furthermore, attractive people stand farther away than our social norms dictate. They communicate an unspoken message of high status.

Burgoon also finds that if someone speaks unexpectedly temperately in an intense situation, they will be judged more favorably and they will foster greater changes in attitude. It seems to me that this is not really acting against social expectancies. It is to be expected that the one who keeps coolest shall prevail, since we associate overt anger and emotional stress with unclear thinking. The assumption is "hotheads" are incapable of thinking straight or planning wisely.

Moreover, it must be stressed that the violations of expectations that Burgoon cites are quite different from what has been shown in previous sections. She does not show, for instance, that the Japanese can interact successfully without bowing. Nor does she show that an American woman—or man—can interact successfully by hiding her—or his—mouth behind a hand while he or she is trying to talk. In fact, her violations do not seem to be violations at all. They are variations in gaze and proxemics, variations which convey definite messages of authority when done by those who are perceived as having the right to do them. I would even quarrel with her lumping together creativity and unexpected response. She does this by giving as an instance of unexpected response the creativity of a high ranking member in a small group. Presumably, if a group is getting together to solve a problem, it is hoped that at least one person will have some new and unusual ideas. The true violation of expectation in such a situation would be for no original ideas to come forth, or for one member suddenly to haul out a whip and start beating others into submission, or for one to suddenly pelt the others with rotten eggs.

Regulating Conversation through Kinesics

Like gaze, body motion is implicated in regulating conversations. Again, like style, this backgrounds messages of control, submission, and cooperation. Since conversations are regulated differently from culture to culture, often outsiders do not catch the cues. Members of the Warm Springs tribe in Oregon, for example, use much less body motion, shifting of body and moving of head, than most other Americans to indicate the course of an utterance (Philips 1976). Instead, these Native Americans rely on movement of the eyes and eyebrows: widening, lifting, and narrowing. They themselves refer to the eyes most when describing emotions. For instance, "they were snapping eyes" means 'they were very angry.' Lips are not moved much in this culture. Arm and hand movements are also more confined than for most Anglo groups. They make much less eye contact and complain that Anglos stare too much even when Anglo observers verify that the Anglos were just glancing. One person's glance is another's stare.

For most other American groups, however, kinesics plays a large part in controlling turns. There are speaker-distinctive movements such as head bobbing in rhythm with speech and gesturing to punctuate speech. By stopping such movements, a person signals that she or he is giving up the floor. In general, in our culture listeners look at speakers more than speakers look at listeners. When a speaker gets ready to let another take over, she or he will look at that person. Before long utterances, speakers look away until nearing the end. Looking away prevents the listener from breaking in (Clarke and Argyle, 1982). Looking at the other person invites that person to speak. If someone actually stops talking in most Anglo groups, someone else rushes in to fill the silence.

Susan Philips, who sat in on meetings at the reservation, says that Warm Springs interactions seem vague and unstructured to outsiders, so much so that they get the feeling that nothing is being responded to at all. At the reservation, if an issue is raised or an accusation made, the next speakers do not necessarily even mention it. If someone does bother to comment, she or he may do so almost as an afterthought.

Philips gives the example of a woman who complained, "[a tribal member] goes to Washington too often." After eight others spoke, the apparent accused got up, read a 15 minute report, then entered into a discussion of the report. During this discussion, the accused said, "I can account for all of my trips to Washington." During the entire meeting, Philips notes, no one spoke directly to anyone, and no one ever asked for any response to the statement. Nobody interrupted, and there were no visible kinesic clues that someone was no longer listening or wanted to talk as there are in Anglo conversations. Philips feels that the Native Americans control when they speak. They are not "forced" into it as Anglos are by having to respond to another's statement. Also since nobody interrupts, the Indians control the length of their own turns.

Actually, Anglos also exercise control over when they speak and for how long. They just do it differently. The Native Americans' control over their turns is not necessarily greater than that of other Americans. If someone is not free to interrupt or to give kinesic signals that he or she wishes to speak then that, in itself, is a very great restriction. One is not controlling when and for how long one may speak if one has no way to make the other person give up the floor.

In any event, it is not an issue of one culture's being superior to another, but of understanding how each culture signals such matters. Anglos might misinterpret tribal members as being unresponsive and vague, but, in turn, tribal members might misinterpret Anglos as being too intense and impatient, just because of differences in eye contact and kinesics.

PROBLEMS IN RESEARCH IN PARALINGUISTICS

We can close this chapter with some observations by Knapp (1983) on some problems in all aspects of studying kinesics, gaze, and proxemics. He points out that most studies of paralinguistic communication are based upon studies of people who are not intimate and haven't had a relationship with each other. Furthermore, he points out, that the way that we judge the same actions varies when done by those we are intimate with as opposed to those we are not. For instance, if we see an interviewer lean forward in a video, we would judge that he or she shows rapport, but that doesn't mean that you'd rate your spouse or sibling as showing the same if he or she does the same thing. Furthermore, Knapp points out that researchers are concerned with visible behavior but in ongoing relationships it's often the nonvisible behaviors which are important. One certainly doesn't have to inquire phatically after the health of intimates or preface remarks to them with address forms. The timing and location of behaviors is often the most important. He gives the example of someone holding out a hand to someone with whom one has just had a vicious fight. This is more important and has a greater meaning than the number of times the same pair has been observed holding hands (p. 184). Most of our knowledge of paralinguistics has been gleaned from nonintimate encounters, and this makes it all woefully incomplete.

Knapp also points out that nonverbal behaviors often mean more than one thing. For instance, silence can be used both for intimacy and remoteness. Squeezing a child's shoulder can mean 'pay attention', (do what you were told), and/or 'I am capable of really hurting you' (p. 188). He has also found that one must consider interaction of behaviors. For instance, although it has long been accepted that invasion of someone's space leads to that person stepping back, he has found that, in an argument, the person who "has made a strong stand" is not vulnerable to those who invade space (p. 189). Again, we see a common idiom accurately encoding what is going on socially.

Finally, Knapp sees as another serious problem in paralinguistic research the problem of training a confederate to behave in a "neutral" or even deviant manner as in participant observations. He points out that the "neutrality" actually may give a message of lack of interest. Similarly, if one is instructed to gaze 100 percent of the time in an experimental situation, or to gaze 50 percent, these gazing behaviors are so abnormal, that it simply isn't safe to generalize to the population at large (p. 190).

We must recall that Knapp is concerned with the paralinguistics of ongoing relations, what happens when relationships become more or less intimate. This doesn't invalidate research with those who have transient or distant relations. Papers like Knapp's are invaluable in their ability to prod us, to ask questions we haven't thought of asking, and to make us look carefully and with clear eyes at the research we read about.

Chapter 4 Notes

1   Strictly speaking, of course, only hands make gestures. Faces make movements, but since these perform the same function as gestures, many writers on kinesics speak of facial gestures.

2   Known in various places in the United States as a *hero, hoagie, submarine, poor boy, wedgie,* or *torpedo.*

3   These give facials and apply cosmetic makeup.

4   An even more solid display of solidarity in play is seen in scenes of apparently usual play amongst children of the Bushmen in the Kalahari Desert in the movie *The Gods Must be Crazy.* Here children are shown dancing in a circle, each on one leg, and the other leg lifted and entwined in the leg of the child behind him or her. The entire group hops around thus intertwined as if it is one creature.

5   Again, this is generally human behavior. A close parallel occurs in Ukrainian folk dancing in which women dance in a circle, and men go into the center to show off their acrobatic ability. Women are cooperative and men competitive.

6   Although she specifically studied those in Belfast, one would not be surprised to find the same proxemics in rural Ulster as well as Eire proper, at least amongst the working class and its rural counterparts.

7   Except amongst Orthodox Jews who refrain from handholding or touching a member of the opposite sex except for one's spouse, and then only in private.

8   Goldman and Fordyce made no such interpretation and aren't responsible for this one.

9   Pinkerman did not attempt voice quality as a variable.

10 Many studies of nonverbal behavior use as one variable the dimension of physical attraction. Interestingly, however, this is never really defined. One assumes that the researchers assume that certain metrics of attractiveness are uniform within a society, an assumption which I suspect should be investigated.

Exercises

1. Watch a video of at least one blind entertainer (or observe a blind person of your acquaintance). Describe his or her facial expressions, gaze, head movements and hand movements. To what degree do these seem to differ from those of seeing persons? To what degree are they the same? From this, what conclusions do you draw about the relation of nature and nurture in kinesics?

2. Observe people interacting in public places, such as the library or cafeteria. Compare a dyad or a group that seems to be very much involved with each other as opposed to one in which the members are not. What behaviors distinguish between the two groups. How accurate is the idiom "in synch with" in describing the involved versus the uninvolved groups? Alternatively, you may analyze a television commercial or other video.

3. Observe a group at a party or other gathering. Is there a difference in the amount of space around different members? That is, do some members take up more space than others? If so, what is the gender, social class, and/or ethnicity of those who do? What conclusions can you draw about power and/or solidarity from these observations?

4. Observe eye contact in your home or social group. What seems to be the "normal" amount of eye contact in an interaction? What topics or situations seem to call for longer eye contact? Alternatively, try to compare the eye contact behavior of two different groups (ethnic, gender, social class) and determine what differences there are, if any, between them.

5. Keep a log of all the touching you do and all those who touch you at school, work, or home for part of a day. How much touching actually goes on, under what conditions, and for what reasons? What kinds of

touching evoke excuses and what seems to be unnoticed? Exclude sexual touching from your observations.

6. Watch a group of children at play. In what way(s) do they signal solidarity and/or competitiveness? Alternatively, watch a team sport on television and describe the kinesics of members of the team to each other as opposed to nonmembers.
7. Try to analyze a few minutes of a movie or other video source, correlating facial expressions and kinesics to the verbal message. How much of the message is being given in words alone? How much in kinesics alone? How much by interaction of both? Alternatively, observe people interacting and estimate how much of their messages are being overtly stated and how much is given in kinesics.

References

Abbey, A., & Melby, C. (1986). The effects of nonverbal cues on gender differences in perceptions of sexual intent. *Sex Roles, 15,* 283-298.

Babad, Y. E., Alexander, I. E., & Babad, E. Y. (1983). *Returning the Smile of the Stranger: Developmental Patterns and Socialization Factors.* (Vol. 48, pp. 3–93). Monographs of the Society for Research in Child Development.

Bales, R. F. (1955, March). How people interact in conferences. *Scientific American,* pp. 3–7.

Befu, H. (1975, April 28). Konnichiwa, an essay read at The Japan Society luncheon, San Francisco. In E. N. Goody (Ed.), *Questions and Politeness* (1978). (p. 9). New York: Cambridge University Press.

Birdwhistell, R. L. (1970). *Kinesics and Context.* Philadelphia: University of Pennsylvania Press.

Brady, M., & Eckhardt, R. (1975). *Black Girls at Play: Folkloric Perspectives on Child Development.* Austin, TX: Southwest Educational Development Corporation.

Burgoon, J. (1983). Nonverbal violations of expectations. In *Nonverbal Interaction.* (J. M. Wiemann & R. P. Harrison, Eds.) (pp. 77–111). Beverly Hills: Sage Publications.

Chick, J. K. (1990). Reflections on language, interaction, and context: Micro and macro issues. In D. Carbaugh (Ed.), *The Interactional Accomplishment of Discrimination in South Africa.* (pp. 225–252). Hillsdale, N.J.: Lawrence Erlbaum.

Clarke, D., & Argyle, M. (1982). Conversation sequences. In C. Fraser & K. R. Scherer (Eds.), *Advances in the Social Psychology of Language*. New York: Cambridge University Press.

Critchley, M. (1975). *Silent Language*. London: Butterworths.

Darwin, C. (1965). *The Expression of Emotions in Man and Animals*. Chicago: University of Chicago Press.

Eakins, B. W., & Eakins, R. G. (1978). *Sex Differences in Human Communication*. Boston: Houghton-Mifflin.

Efron, D. (1972). *Gesture, Race, and Culture*. The Hague: Mouton.

Eibl-Eiblesfeldt. (1972). Similarities and differences between cultures in expressive movements. In *Nonverbal Communication, 2nd ed.* (Weitz, S. Ed.) (pp. 37–48). New York: Oxford University Press.

Ekman, O., & Frisen, W. (1976). Measuring facial movement. In *Nonverbal Interaction, 2nd ed.* (S. Weitz, Ed.) (pp. 64–76). New York: Oxford University Press.

Goffman, E. (1963). *Behavior in Public Places*. New York: The Free Press.

Goldman, M., & Fordyce, J. (1983). Prosocial behavior as affected by eye contact, touch, and voice expression. *The Journal of Social Psychology, 121*, 125–129.

Goody, E. N. (1978). *Questions and Politeness*. New York: Cambridge University Press.

Grumet, G. W. (1983). Eye contact: The core of interpersonal relatedness. *Psychiatry, 46*, 172–179.

Hall, E. (1959). *The Silent Language*. Doubleday.

Heslin, R., & Alper, T. (1983). Touch: A bonding gesture. In *Nonverbal Interaction* (J. M. Wiemann & R. F. Harrison, Eds.). Beverly Hills: Sage Publications.

Keating, C., Mazur, A., Segall, M., Cysneiros, P., Divale, W., Kilbride, J., Komin, S., Leahy, P., Thurman, B., & Wirsing, R. (1981). Culture and the perception of social dominance from facial expression. *Journal of Personality and Social Psychology, 40*, 615–626.

Kendon, A. (1983). Gesture and speech: How they interact. In J. M. Weimann, & R. P. Harrison (Eds). *Nonverbal Interaction*. Beverly Hills: Sage Publications.

Kleinke, C. L. (1986). Gaze and eye contact: A research review. *Psychological Bulletin, 100*, 78–111.

Knapp, M. (1983). Dyadic relationship development. In *Nonverbal Interaction* (J. M. Wiemann & R. P. Harrison, Eds.) (pp. 179–207). Beverly Hills: Sage Publications.

LaBarre, W. (1947). The cultural basis of emotions and gestures. *Journal of Personality, 16*, 49–68.

Milroy, L. (1980). *Language and Social Networks*. Baltimore: University Park Press.

Pelose, G. C. (1987). The functions of behavioral synchrony and speech rhythm in conversation. In *Multichannel Communication Codes*. (S. Sigman, Ed). Research on Language and Social Interaction. (vol. 20.) Canada: Boreal Scholarly Publishers.

Philips, S. U. (1976). Some sources of cultural variability in the regulation of talk. *Language in Society, 5*, 81–95.

Riecken, H. (1958). The effect of talkativeness on ability to influence group solutions of problems. In *The Psychosociology of Language*. (S. Muscovici Ed.) (pp. 308–321). Chicago: Markham Publishing Co.

Sherzer, J. (1973). Nonverbal and verbal deixis: The pointed lip gesture among the San Blas Cuna. *Language in Society, 2*, 117–132.

Sommer, R. (1965). Further studies of small-group ecology. *Sociometry, 28*, 337–343.

Chapter 5

Pragmatics

Much speech is a way of effecting actions, a way of doing things with words. In the law, many crimes consist merely of such speech acts, as do contracts, wills, and other legal instruments. Cultures have different rules for when people can speak and when they must be silent, including rules for interrupting. We use shared discourse routines for much interaction. Utterance pairs must be responded to in certain ways, and if they are not, repairs are attempted. Simply knowing the language is not sufficient because true meaning often lies not in the actual words uttered but in a complex of social knowledge.

DOING THINGS WITH WORDS

People usually think of speech as a way of stating propositions and conveying information, and they think that this is done by selecting the exact words and grammar that add up to what they are trying to convey. So persistent is this "commonsensical" idea that for generations, linguists were primarily concerned with trying to elucidate the rules of grammar and the meanings of words in order to explain language.

It remained for philosophers to point out the obvious. Much of what we say means things quite different from the words and grammar used. Furthermore, much of what we say is not concerned with conveying ideas, even those utterances which are not part of phatic communication. Austin (1962) stressed the functions of speech as a way of "doing things with words." For instance, one may use the same proposition to do quite different things. Searle (1969, p. 23) says one may use it "...to 'describe', 'assert', 'warn', 'remark', 'comment', 'command', 'order', 'request', 'criticize', 'apologize', 'censure', 'approve', 'welcome', 'promise', object', 'demand', and 'argue'. These are all examples of **illocutionary** force. The illocutionary force, expressed implicitly or explicitly, tells how the proposition is to be taken. For instance, if I say, "I'm eating with Berthold tonight.", I might mean this as a warning to Berthold's girlfriend that I intend to steal him from her. Or, I could mean it as a description of my current social life. I could phrase it as, "May I eat with Berthold tonight?" if Berthold is a student who needs permission to go out. Again, I could mean it as an apology to someone who has asked me to dinner.

Sometimes it is clear from the context what the illocutionary force is. For instance, one could say, "I'll clean up that mess before you come back." This is clearly a promise even without prefacing it with, "I promise..."

Verbs like *bet, promise, guarantee, order,* and *request* are known as **performatives**, and these explicitly state the illocutionary force of one's utterance. Frequently, one can determine that a verb is performative by putting hereby before them, as in "I *hereby* request that you leave this property." In contrast, note the absurdity of "I hereby detest chocolate soda." That is because one's detestation of chocolate soda is a conveying of information, and not doing something with words like betting, promising, guaranteeing, and the like.[1] If one's utterance actually makes another person do something, such as carry out a command or take defensive action, then the speech is a **perlocutionary act**.

Speech Acts and the Law

The reality of speech acts has long been recognized in law. The Bill of Rights protects freedom of speech so long as the speech is about personal opinion or statement of fact, but it does not protect all speech acts. That is why crying, "Fire!" in a crowded building is a crime. Despite the fact that it is clearly speech, it is also primarily an act, as it is intended to make people flee the building. It is not someone's opinion, or shouldn't be since it has the perlocutionary effect of panicking people, potentially causing a great deal of harm. The fact of crying out "Fire" is tantamount to commanding everybody to get out as fast as possible.

Similarly, conspiring to bribe a jury or to commit another crime is illegal even though both are done in speech, because they have the effect of inducing illegal actions. Other crimes which are essentially speech acts are perjury, libel, and slander. Wills, contracts, and appointment of an agent on one's behalf are also speech acts. Wills give something to someone. Contracts are reciprocal acts of offering and accepting (Tiersma 1993, p. 133). Appointment of an agent permits that person to buy or sell for you, to act, in other words.

Speech Acts and Social Interactions

Speech act theory has prompted sociologists, anthropologists and educators to investigate the ways people use language to manage social interactions. Threatening, complimenting, commanding, even questioning can all be manipulative, as we shall see. Another person's behavior may be affected quite differently from what one might expect from the actual words used. "See the belt?" may be sufficient to restrain a child from wrongdoing. The words themselves are an action to which the child imputes the intention of a threat of a spanking. Moreover, it has prompted linguists to consider how meaning is achieved regardless of what words are actually used (Chaika 1990). As we shall see, this has impacted on the study of literature, legal documents, psychotherapy, and a myriad of other human activities.

SPEECH ACTS AND DISCOURSE ROUTINES

Because speech acts operate by what amounts to pragmatic principles, the study of speech acts in daily interaction is called *pragmatics* to distinguish it, for instance, from rules of syntax and lexical choice, such as the rule for making a passive sentence or using a word denoting time with the verb *lapsed*. Speech acts carry heavy social implications. Moreover, the responses to them are typically conventional, so that we speak of **discourse routines**, such as questions and answers.

Much of our everyday talk consists of discourse routines and cultures vary considerably in the modes of routines they prefer. The degree to which one requests or orders directly, the occasions on which one compliments and one's response, how one invites others to do something, all of these are done by socially recognized discourse routines, which are speech acts. Asking questions causes others to answer; therefore, questions are speech acts. So are apologies and excuses. All of these are embedded in our daily conversation. Since cultures vary in how they carry out discourse routines, learning them is an important task if one is to become socialized. Unfortunately, foreign language classes often focus on correct grammar and vocabulary building. They teach us how to speak directly, how to say what we mean. However, much interaction has to be effected by not speaking directly, by not saying what one means. One also has to learn to make the proper responses in one's culture in discourse routines. This can also cause cross-cultural difficulties. The social facts of responsibility and saving face determine how discourse will be routinized in a culture. That is, whether or not one can issue a command to another is determined according to whether one has the obligation or the right to do so. How one phrases a request or a criticism may be determined by the desire not to insult another, but to make them lose face.

FRAMES

Many scholars have shown that the way we make sense of the myriad impressions that assail us daily is to use **frames**, also known as **scripts**, **schemata**, and **structures of expectation**. (Tannen 1979b; Gumperz 1982, p.21–2). We use these to decide what is important, what inferences we can and should be getting from an interaction, why someone is speaking the way he or she is, and what our reaction should be. If we did not use such interpretive frames, we would have to treat every conversation separately, examining it word by word. This would hinder communication drastically. Nothing would ever get done. We would never be able to make sense of things.

Goffman (1974) speaks of frames somewhat differently, as self-presentation. Generally, Goffman portrays people as giving performances as they go about their daily business. He is very insightful but rarely mucks about with hard data. As Corsaro (1985 p. 178) complains, "Goffman makes major assumptions about what people do in discourse without ever studying discourse," a practice also criticized by Stubbs (1983, p. 91). This doesn't mean you should ignore Goffman. His works are seminal and should—and do—inspire research. Since subsequent chapters will show how people use language to project an identity, in this one we will consider only frames as expectations.

Ironically, one obstacle in using frames to interpret is that they are based upon an individual's personal experiences. Another is that cultures differ in their frames. Tannen (1979a) illustrates how we can figure out such differences by analyzing what people say. She specifically analyzes how Greek and American women narrate what they have just seen in a short film and how their frames can be deduced from what they say. The film showed a pear picker in a tree, who had left his fruit in a basket under the tree. A boy came along, and stole the pears. Then, he fell from his bike and dropped the pears. Other children riding by helped him pick up the pears, so he gave each one. When the picker came down from the tree, he discovered his empty basket. Then he saw the children eating the pears (Chafe 1980).

Americans revealed more expectations about what a film should be than Greeks did. For instance, several commented that the film had no dialogue, showing that they expected it (p. 151). Tannen explains that negative statements are the most frequently used clear indications that an expectation is not being met (p. 148). Americans also thought that the task was a test of memory. This was revealed in comments like "How picky do you want?" and "That's all I remember." "You should have caught me... ten minutes ago when I remembered..." Greeks, on the other hand, expected the film to have a message (pp. 155, 160) which they revealed by their judgmental comments. For instance, one woman commented on the pear picker, "He lived that which he did, he liked it." Of the children she said, "...this was something that showed how children love each other" (p. 156).

Other kinds of expectations are similarly revealed. Both Greeks and Americans commented on the fact that the picker didn't see the boy. Clearly, they expected that the worker should have seen the boy. This is very evident in "...But he's [the boy] very brazen. I mean...they're only three feet apart." Tannen points out that the words *brazen* and *only* both show that the speaker would normally expect to see the boy (p. 161).

Speech Events and Genres

A **speech event** is the situation calling forth particular ways of speaking (Gordon and Lakoff 1975). **Genre** refers to the form of speaking. Usually, it has a label, such as *joke, narrative, promise, riddle, prayer*, even *greeting* or *farewell*.

Members of a speech community recognize genres as having beginnings, middles, and ends; they also recognize it as being patterned. "Did you hear the one about...", for instance, is a recognized opener for the genre *joke* in our society. "Once upon a time..." is a recognized opener for the genre *child's story*, and "And they lived happily ever after" is the *stock ending*. The end of a *joke* is a *punch line,* often a pun, an unusual or unexpected response to a situation or utterance, or a stupid response by one of the characters in the joke. Typically, the stupid response to a situation is one that reveals that the character is lacking in some basic social knowledge. For instance, an old Beetle Bailey cartoon shows Sarge saying to Zero, "The wastebasket is full." Zero responds, "Even I can see that." The joke lies in the fact that Zero took Sarge's words literally rather than interpreting them as a command, which was their actual social force.

Sometimes, but not always, the genre is the entire speech event. Church services are speech events, for instance. *Sermons* are a genre belonging to church, but sermons do not cover the entire speech event. Prayers, responsive readings, hymn singing, and announcements also constitute the speech events of church services.

The way that participants carry out the demands of a genre is their **performance**. In some communities this is more important than others. Also, performance is more important in some speech events than others. A professor's performance is usually far more important than that of students in her or his classroom.[2] Perhaps *important* is not quite the right word. It might be more accurate to say that the professor's importance will be judged more overtly than a student's and will be judged according to different criteria. These are the criteria judged in public performance, such as clarity of diction, voice quality, logic of lecture, and coherence. Correct performance in less formal speech events is just as important, but judgments may be limited to how appropriate the speech was to the situation. Everyday discourse routines are as much performances as are preaching, joke-telling, and lecturing.

Intention

In all interaction the parties assume that each person is speaking with a purpose. Hearers get meaning partially by what they think the speaker's purpose is. Esther Goody (1978) says that people impute intentions to others' words. In fact, she notes, they "...positively seek out intentions in what others say and do." What people assume is another's intention colors the meaning they get from messages. How often has someone suspiciously said to a perfectly innocent comment of yours, "Now what did you mean by that?" The question is not asking for literal meaning but for your intention in saying what you did.

One important determinant for interpretation of intention is the **presequence**. Presequences are recognized opening sentences which signal that a particular kind of speech act will follow, such as commands, demands or threats. For example, the child who hears an adult's, "Who spilled this milk?" may rightly perceive the question as the precursor to a command, "Wipe it up!" So important is intention to verbal interaction that deBeaugrande and Dressler (1981, p. 112) say that the only way utterances can be used to communicate is if the speaker intends them to be communicated, and the hearer accepts them as intended.

Often intentions are not perceived correctly, causing misunderstandings as harmless as hearing an honest question as a command or as serious as hearing an innocent comment as an insult.[3] To illustrate, consider a man who, in front of his slightly plump wife, looks admiringly at a model. "Wow! What a body on that one." The wife immediately bridles or dissolves in tears, depending on her personal style. She assumes that his comment is a way of complaining about her fat.

If a speaker gives false information, then his or her intent will largely determine whether or not it is a lie, an error, or fantasy. If the speaker gives false information, but believes that it is true and is intending to inform, then he or she is simply mistaken. If the speaker gives false information, but knows that it is false and is intending to make the hearer believe it is true, then he or she is lying. If he or she gives false information and knows it and is representing it as not true, then he or she is creating fantasy. The difference between an error, a lie, and a fantasy, then, is not only a matter of actual truth, but of the speaker's belief and intent.

CONVERSATION

We are not mere creatures of conditioning when it comes to language. Noam Chomsky's most potent insight, perhaps, was that we can say things we never heard before as well as understand what we have not previously heard. Language, then, makes us free as individuals but chains us socially. Fairclough (1989, p. 24) points out that **discourse**, any connected body of speech or writing, such as conversation, is social interaction. He claims that "people internalize what is socially produced and made available to them" and that what they internalize gives "the forces which shape societies a vitally important foothold in the individual psyche, though...the effectiveness of this foothold depends on it being...below the level of consciousness." Discourse, then, involves social conditions, and thus helps maintain the social order (Fairclough 1989, p. 25). In other words, our unconscious compliance with social rules of discourse helps keep us and others in their place.

In contrast to Chomsky's dictum, when we consider discourse rules we find that the social rules of language often force us to respond in certain ways. We are far from free in forming sentences in actual social situations. Frequently, we are at least constrained, if not forced, to limit sentences to conform to a topic previously introduced by another (Duranti and Ochs 1979), although there are socially acceptable ways to change it. The topic need not be overtly stated, and seldom is. And, there are times when we must respond whether we want to or not and, even, to respond in very limited ways (e.g., Sacks 1964–1972, 1970; Schenkein 1978).

Grice (1975, pp. 45–47) claimed that there are certain maxims which guide conversation. He calls these the **maxims** of **quantity**, **quality**,

relation, and **manner**.[4] By *quantity,* he means that one should say no more nor no less than is required for current purposes. By *quality,* he means one should say only what one has evidence for, and what you believe is true. By *relation,* he means that everything one says should be relevant to the interaction. And, by *manner,* he means that one should try not to be obscure or ambiguous, or say anything more than necessary, and that one should be orderly. These maxims can be **flouted**, that is, not obeyed. When they are, they typically entail or imply another meaning. Thus meaning is effected both by adherence to the maxims and by their being flouted.

For instance, Grice says that the person who is overinformative may mislead hearers into thinking that there is a reason for the excess of information. One possible reason that something is mentioned when it could be presumed to be known is to put someone down, to say in effect, the speaker thinks you're so stupid that he or she has to tell you the obvious. Unless, of course, the information could be construed to be newly important. Years ago, when I brought my computer in for repair, the technician, a male, patronizingly said, "You know you have to put in a diskette." (This was before hard drives.) Since this was so basic to operating a computer, it was as if the technician assumed that I didn't know how to operate my own computer. I naturally took this as an insult.

Gordon and Lakoff (1975, p. 92) give a wonderful example of the violation of quantity. If you were to go up to a married friend and say, "Your wife (or husband) is faithful," the friend would probably do a double-take and even get angry. If you tell someone something that he (or she) either knows or takes for granted, that person would figure that you were actually casting doubt on his (or her) spouse's fidelity. Otherwise, why say it at all? Part of the reason that it means this is also that there is a violation of the maxim of relation. Why would you say such a thing? What relation does it have to the interaction?

Of course, if there had been an earlier interaction in which the spouse's fidelity had been an issue, the married friend would be glad to hear the news. The maxim of relation would not have been violated, as the utterance would be related to the prior one. Nor would the maxim of quantity have been violated. Notice that there is a meaning **entailed** by "Your wife is faithful," a meaning not directly attributable to the actual words used. In a very real sense, words in an interaction usually mean a great deal more than they say. We "get at" that surplus of meaning by our assumptions

Intentionally or not, people frequently violate the maxim of quality. That is, they misinform unintentionally or misinform intentionally (that is, lie) or both. The lie consists as much in the hearer's assumption that the speaker is telling the truth as it does in the actual words of the speaker. Similarly, the unintentional misinformation is effected because of the hearer's assumption that the speaker knows what he or she is talking about.

All people at some time are obscure when they are trying to explain or recount something, thus violating the maxims of relation and manner. Fortunately, the hearer can initiate repairs so the speaker can sharpen his or her manner. People who wander off the topic or who say things with no apparent relation to the context can also be asked for repairs, unless, of course, they are insane or under the influence of drugs or alchohol. Indeed, one of the criteria for insanity is that the speaker not only violates the maxim of relation, but also can not repair what was said. For instance, one schizophrenic in an interview said,

> I have distemper just like cats do, 'cause that's what we all are, felines. Siamese cat balls. They stand out. I had a cat, a manx still around somewhere. You'll know him when you see him. His name is GI Joe. He's black and white. I had a little goldfish, too, like a clown. Happy Hallowe'en down.

Mentioning too much, even if it is related to the topic and can be construed as being new information to the hearer, can be as distracting as actual departures from the topic itself. People assume that anything known to all parties in a given conversation will not be overtly stated unless there is some special reason for so doing. Searle (1975) says that mentioning extraneous matters leads listeners down false trails as they try to figure out how those matters fit the topic at hand. It seems to me that this is why our courts of law have such strong rules against introducing irrelevant matters. To do so clouds the issues for the judge and jury.

Applying these maxims, which are actually presuppositions about discourse, is one factor in our being able to make sentences cohere so that they are perceived as being a discourse. Since the term maxims has long been in use in discourse analysis, I use it here, but, actually, they are **strategies** based upon presuppositions about conversations and text which we use to interpret.

Although Grice is not wrong, more detailed analyses of conversation by linguists have shown that adherence to the maxims is not quite so cut and dried. Indeed, in order to do conversation skillfully, sometimes more needs to be said than is strictly necessary for conveying information. This, as we shall see, however, does not take the form of overinforming in a business encounter, such as dealing with repair technicians. Moreover, the entire concept of a topic around which all statements revolve belongs more to writing than to speech.

It has become increasingly clear that people do a conversation together as a social action. Both hearers and speakers are involved, and their roles rotate in the course of a conversation. If one person speaks and the others just listen, then one is hearing a lecture or a sermon, either of which primarily inform. In contrast, while conversation may inform, it just as importantly serves as a bonding activity, a way of maintaining social relations with others. Examining actual conversations, one sees that the maxims are often not so much flouted, as that they are irrelevant, and that society cannot be understood without understanding conversations, just as a sentence cannot be understood without considering the entire discourse in which it is embedded. Linguists, therefore, have become very interested in **discourse analysis**, both written and spoken.

Strictly speaking, the term *discourse* refers to any stretch of language above the level of the sentence which, in some sense, coheres as a unit. The term *text* usually refers to written language rather than spoken, although some use the term discourse for writing as well.[5] People who come from cultures which have writing systems typically think of language as being what is on the written page, and are frequently amazed to discover that ordinary speech is as important an object of study as texts are. Indeed, it can be argued that analyzing ordinary speech is more important for understanding a society than analyzing texts is. As Stubbs (1983) says,

> Conversation is basic: the commonest use of language, a pervasive phenomenon of everyday life that deserves systematic study... If only because of its massive occurrence, spontaneous unrehearsed conversation must provide some kind of baseline or norm for the description of language in general. (p. 10)

Clearly, there is no way of understanding any society unless one understands its conversation. There are cultures which have no writing, but none which have no conversation. Besides conversation, there are more formal uses of spoken language, such as lectures and eulogies, which are quite different in form and purpose from conversation.

Topic

One consequence of assuming that texts are no different from conversation has been the insistence that all sentences must be governed by a topic (Van Dijk 1977). The earlier models of conversation assumed that everything had to be subordinated to topic, whatever is being talked about. Once a topic is introduced, it must be adhered to unless some formal indication of change is being made. Paradoxically, in American English, this often is "Not to change the subject, but..." which always changes the subject. "By the way..." also indicates that the topic is about to be changed to something which has been mentioned before. It may also be used when one wishes to mention something that is not so nice or something likely to bother the hearer. Among the other changes of topic signals are, "Ooooh, I meant to tell you" or "That reminds me..." or "Speaking of Harry..." It is also possible for a speaker to announce a topic, as when one prefaces a remark with phrases like, "About last night..." and "You'll never believe this one..."

These are valid ways of changing a topic. The very fact that we have so many devices to do this indicates the importance of keeping to a topic in some situations at least. In any conversation, however, one's response or utterance must relate in some way to what has already been said, or is about to be, but frequently one can't show that the utterance adheres to an overriding topic which governs the entire conversation.

In a casual conversation, the interactors are typically limited only by the speakers' ingenuity in presenting statements so that hearers can deduce the "point." Erickson (1984, p. 126) speaks of **topic associating** in a conversation. As people talk, giving anecdotes, listeners use a strategy of figuring out what the semantic connections between the anecdotes are. It is the listeners as much as the speakers who create the topic. Erickson speaks of **rhapsody**, a stitching together of a conversation (p. 97) between speaker and hearer. Thus, often a friendly conversation starts out on one subject and ends on quite another without anybody overtly announcing change of topic. Still, it will be a coherent, sensible conversation because the adjacent parts of it go together in a relevant way.

When conversation is going well, when the speakers are all "in synch" with each other, it can be set to a metronome (Erickson and Schultz 1982). Movements, whether micromovements like head nodding, or larger ones like legcrossing, are synchronized with utterances. Tannen (1989, p. 18) likens joining a conversation to joining a line of dancers. One must first be able to share its rhythm. Erickson and Shultz found that people being counseled were able to derive more usable information from interviews when they and counselors were able to establish such a rhythm.

Maxim of Quantity and Conversation

The maxim of quantity is constantly being violated in conversation. For one thing, repetition which does not further a storyline or add new information is, nevertheless, a very important part of successful conversation. Tannen (1989) shows that repetition serves many conversational purposes. It is a way of showing that one is still participating even if he or she has nothing new to add. It is a way of showing support for the views of a co-conversationalist, or of agreeing. It is a way of showing that one understands what the other is saying. It is also a way of showing appreciation of what the other has said. It is also a way of emphasizing a point, and a way of establishing a rhythm. For instance, in telling about a fight:

And I says to him, you're bleeding, you're bleeding. Jack, you're bleeding.

At the dinner table:

Bobby: I've stopped drinking.
Susanne: He's stopped drinking.

Mother: Use your napkin, Johnny.
Father: Use your napkin, Johnny.

Or, upon leave-taking:

Mother: You'd better button up. It's cold out.
Aunt: Yes, it's very cold out.

Similarly, when one repeats the punch-line of a joke while laughing, one is letting the joke-teller know that one thinks he or she is very funny. Orators like Dr. Martin Luther King and Jesse Jackson make great use of repetition to keep their speeches memorable and rhythmic.

Another way in which the maxim of quantity is violated, and has to be violated, is that in conversation, a good speaker will pepper his or her talk with details not strictly necessary to convey the information, or will supply anecdotes by way of illustration. Parables, in which the stories illustrate one main idea, are an extreme example of the latter. Tannen shows that use of details and anecdotes is a way of involving others in the conversation. They help the other(s) to visualize events being spoken of, so that they feel as if they have actually participated. For example, in telling a friend how my husband always buys more than he is supposed to, I recount a time when I asked him to bring me home some candy:

> Well, he stuck his hand in his pocket and out came jujubes and fruit drops. Then he went to another pocket and produced crunch bars and chocolate covered cherries, light and dark. He handed me a bag too. I opened it. Baby Ruths™ and sour balls, caramels. So I screamed, "Why did you get so much?" He answered, "I wasn't sure what you were in the mood for."

Interestingly, the friend then repeated, laughing, "He didn't know what you were in the mood for," showing that she appreciated the story. The reporting of actual dialogue even though it is not strictly necessary for the message adds to the immediacy of the scene; hence, adds to the hearer's involvement. It helped that I can imitate my husband's facial expressions, shoulder shrugging, and intonation when repeating his words. Had I merely said, "He brought me too much." the friend couldn't have visualized the scene, wouldn't have seen the latent humor in the situation. It occurs to me that by recounting this story in such detail, I conveyed to the friend a great deal about my husband's character and behavior, which wouldn't have been conveyed had I strictly adhered to the maxim of quantity.

It is not that the maxims do not guide much of our speech and writing, but that they don't explain a good deal of our ordinary conversation. What is needed, perhaps, is a strict taxonomy of when the maxims apply and when and how they should be ignored. Notice that the examples given of violation of the maxim of quantity are not just any old violations. They still have to do with the topic, and they are demonstrably ways of enhancing what is said.

THE ETHNOGRAPHY OF COMMUNICATION

Studying the dynamics of communication within or between social groups is the ethnography of communication (Hymes 1972). The ways that one studies and records such fluid phenomena as ordinary speaking is **ethnomethodology**. Garfinkel (1972, p. 309) says he uses that term to refer to "various policies, methods, results, risks, and lunacies" to localize what parts of behaviors are important to study as well as to investigate the reasons for the "...organized artful practices of everyday life." The work of the ethnographers has shown us that the seemingly random behavior of ordinary daily activity is actually highly structured, often as much so as texts are. It has also been discovered that the rules for carrying out conversation and other speaking activities vary not only from country to country, but within a country both regionally and ethnically.

In order for social interaction to proceed smoothly, all societies employ some kind of speech exchange system. Some cultures allow the person speaking to continue until he or she wishes to give it up. Others regulate turn-taking more overtly. The early research on turn-taking gave us a picture of a smooth transition between conversationalists with little or no interruption of the speaker. At some point in the speaker's turn, he or she was signalled by a downward intonation curve that it was the other person's turn. If one participant overlapped his or her words with the speaker's, it was considered an interruption. After a suitable pause to ensure that the speaker really was giving up the floor, the other person would speak. As it happens, length of pause varies cross-culturally, causing problems. For instance, Southern friends and colleagues have complained about how difficult it is to interject their words in conversations with Northerners (like me), because just as the pause was long enough for them to take the floor, the Northerner figured that the other didn't want to say anything and took the floor back. Thereupon, the Southerner feels as if the co-conversationalist is not giving him or her a chance to speak, and is being very rude. Even within a region this can happen with people from different ethnic groups.

The person who interrupts another's turn is felt to be invading the space of the other. In fact, Tannen (1984, p.78) cites an article about a psychologist who considers "fast talkers," and those who don't allow a pause between turns to be "conversational menaces" who "crowd" others, thereby leading to lack of communication.

But what of the invaders? Do they perceive themselves to be rude? Are they being rude? Tannen (1979b, 1984) in her study of spontaneous conversation between friends at a Thanksgiving dinner shows that, to the contrary, for members of certain cultures, overlapping is a sign of bonding (1984, pp. 83–87), of showing rapport (1979b, p. 8; 1984, p. 56), even of helping the other speaker (1984, pp. 118–119). Tannen says that overlappers are members of **high involvement** (HI) cultures (as opposed to those who don't overlap, members of **low involvement** [LI] cultures.)

Rapport and bonding are shown by clearly extraneous questions and comments as the other talks. Tannen gives as an example, **cooperative prompting** (1984, p. 118), in which a listener keeps asking things like "What'd she say?" "Did it really?" "What did you say?" This is done although it is very clear that the speaker is going to tell all with or without prompts. The prompting is a way of showing enthusiasm, interest, and encouragement for the other's narrative. Obviously, when she says "Did it really?" for instance, she was not maligning his veracity. There is variation in how this is done in different HI cultures, as when ethnic blacks murmur, "Tha's right," "Talk dat talk!" "Right on brother!" and other such encouragements. This is done in church in response to a preacher's words, at banquets when the formal speech is given, as well as to each other in intimate conversations. These responses are frequently accompanied by overt head nodding. To those used to such encouragement when speaking, it is extremely unnerving to face people who remain silent when another is speaking.

Perhaps the most important thing to remember in dealing with those from other cultures is the list of common misperceptions that HI and LI members of society have of each other. We have already seen that LI conversationalists may consider HI ones to be rude and pushy. In turn, the HI speakers may feel that the LI ones are cold and wishy-washy. The Scollons (1981, p. 36) present lists of misunderstandings between Athabaskans, who are LI, and non-Native Americans, who are not. The Americans are "confused" (their term) because the Athabaskans don't speak, keep silent, never say anything about themselves, talk in a flat tone of voice, are slow to take a turn in talking, talk only to close acquaintances, avoid direct questions, and other LI traits. The Athabaskans, in their turn are confused by English speakers who talk too much, always talk first, talk to strangers, brag about themselves, always interrupt, don't give others a chance to talk, always get excited when they talk, only talk about what they are interested in, and so on. These are virtually classic LI versus HI conflicts arising from the differences in speaking styles.

Bonding through the act of conversing seems to be widespread if not universal, especially if the parties are able to agree. Adrienne Lehrer (1983) reported that her subjects in a wine tasting experiment expressed good feelings when they were able to negotiate an agreement about what words to describe wine they had just tasted. Many of the words, like oaky, were not usual words for beverages. Since she did her study somewhat in advance of the evidence about high and low involvement cultures, we don't know which kind of culture her subjects came from or if it would have made a difference in that task, but informally I have noticed that when people can reach agreement in a discussion, they feel warm towards each other. Conversely, it's very difficult to love those with whom we disagree.

In the thick of talking, speakers often can't think of an event or a place, or the right word or wording. They make slips of the tongue and false starts. In some HI cultures, co-conversationalists feel free to break in on the speaker and help him or her by supplying the right word or fact (1979, pp. 9–11). Tannen points out that not only is this expected, it is virtually required. Such overlapping gives a message of, "I understand you so well that I know what you are going to say." In HI cultures "...overlap not only does not impede but in fact enhances communication" (1984, p. 79). Overlapping is a sign of interest, enthusiasm, and encouragement. Tannen sums it up saying that, in such cultures

> ...it is not the business of listeners to make sure that others have "room" to talk. It is their business to show interest and enthusiasm. Finding room to talk is up to speakers. Indeed, it is incumbent upon speakers, if they are observing this system, to find things to say and places to say them. A person who gives up after a single try is perceived by overlap-favoring speakers as being uncooperative, withholding, even sulking. (Tannen 1979, p. 13)

Tannen's observations were specifically on Jews from New York City of Eastern European background and may not be true of Jews from other backgrounds or locations. Also, it may be that Eastern Europeans in general, or New Yorkers in general would fit Tannen's description of members of HI cultures. She did not explore these possibilities. Certainly Jewish New Yorkers are not the only people who overlap other's words in conversations. Several of my students have attempted to replicate Tannen's investigation at family dinners. So far, it appears from these studies that people who identify ethnically with being Italian, African American, or Irish seem, generally, to be HI. This doesn't mean that all members of any group are equally talkative or verbally aggressive or equally quiet and passive. There are always variations in individual personalities, but those from HI culture, for instance, are not likely to be offended by someone's butting in as much as an LI person is.

Another thing that must be borne in mind is that there is probably no sharp dividing line between HI and LI cultures. For instance, Native Americans in the West are clearly LI. But virtually all other groups in America, including LI groups like descendants of French Canadians in New England and the original English settlers, would probably be more HI than the Native Americans, but still far less HI than Russians. The studies of HI and LI behaviors are relatively new. But, these classifications do fit with the voluminous ethnographic literature. It is doubtful, however, that the bundles of behavior patterns that have been labeled HI and LI will be shown to be all or nothing. We should think, instead, of a cline, with a gradient of HI to LI characteristics, with different cultures and individuals fitting relative to each other on the gradient.

Those who come from LI cultures were probably shuddering as they read about those who interrupt, overlap, and leave no pauses. The normal conversational behaviors of high involvement cultures is exceedingly rude in the eyes of others. An anecdote illustrates: My, friend, B, from a high involvement culture, married a man from a low involvement one. When B's mother-in-law regaled her with the doings of illustrious ancestors, B would, of course, constantly ask little questions and make little remarks, whereupon her mother-in-law would stop and glare at her for her rudeness. As it happens, B is an exceptionally quiet, polite, and soft-spoken person. The impression she gave of rudeness rested solely on the fact that her way of being polite did not jibe with that of her husband's family.

Note that someone who is considered *pushy,* metaphorically, crowds others. The feeling that certain ethnic groups are pushy seems related to their normal practices of overlapping and interrupting. Social scientists again and again have shown that, often, the way we perceive people is not always the way they actually have behaved. For instance, the common belief that women talk more than men has been disproven. Men talk more than women, and even interrupt women more than women do to men (Chapter 10). Tannen counted the amount of time and the number of turns taken by each of the guests at the Thanksgiving dinner. Afterwards when she interviewed the participants in the Thanksgiving dinner, everyone was surprised that David (HI) had actually spoken less frequently than had Chad (LI) (1984, p. 132). Everyone had come away with the impression that Chad had talked very little. One thing that caused this misperception seemed to be that David made a far greater percentage of ironical or humorous remarks than Chad, who made virtually none. In fact, the three HI speakers in the group were most likely to indulge in humor which seems to be part of their normal style, especially irony and self-mocking, such as exaggerating their own ethnic speech styles (pp. 133–136). This implies that the "use of humor makes one's presence felt..." (1984, p. 132).

Tannen (pp. 54–58) shows also that HI conversationalists talk about themselves a great deal and do this as an invitation for the others to do the same. LI speakers often view this with distaste. Not only are they unlikely to reciprocate with tidbits of their own lives, but one has to drag things out of them by questioning. In turn, HI speakers may find LI ones secretive and cold.

Finally, the persistence of HI speakers (pp. 87–94) bears mentioning. Not only do they overlap when they wish a change of topic or a chance to question or comment. This persistence takes the form of talking while others are, and the persister usually persists until he or she gets the floor.

DIRECT AND INDIRECT STATEMENT

We all are willing to say some things directly, and others we have to indicate indirectly. Still, as perhaps might be expected, it seems that frequently, HI speakers prefer more bald on-record statements. By this, I mean bald statements, statements that are on the record, as opposed to off-the-record implications. LI speakers may prefer subtlety, whereas HI speakers prefer to "lay it on the line." Again, it is Tannen (1981, 1982, 1984) who provides succinct examples:

1. *Wife*: John's having a party. Wanna go?
   Husband: OK.
   Wife: (later) Are you sure you want to go?
   Husband: OK, let's not go. I'm tired anyway.

2. *Husband*: Let's go visit my boss tonight.
   Wife: Why?
   Husband: All right. We don't have to go.

Tannen asked both Greek and American informants to interpret 1. More Greeks than Americans felt that the husband's "OK" meant that he really didn't want to go, but he thought she wanted to go, so he would go along with it. They thought this because of the brevity of his first response. In contrast, the Americans thought that the very brevity of "OK" is what showed he really did want to go. The Greeks wanted a greater display of enthusiasm to indicate genuine willingness, and the Americans felt that intimates say what they really mean. Moreover, the husband, when later asked to comment, said that since she mentioned the party in the first place, to him that meant she wanted to go, but by asking the second time, it meant she had changed her mind. He was trying to be solicitous and caring, so he made up an excuse for not going. The real problem is that the wife expected to give and understand outright statements, not subtle cues, but the husband was responding, he thought, to subtle cues.

In 2, the husband reported that when she countered with "Why?" He assumed she didn't want to go and this was her way of saying so. On her part, the "Why?" was a genuine request for information. The wife felt that her husband was very erratic because he was "Always changing his mind."

CHAPTER 5

Both thought the other mercurial. The husband in both sequences was Greek, and the wife an American of HI culture. Miscommunication resulted from the use of directly opposing strategies. Such are the shoals of communicating in a marriage between people of such different communication styles.

SPEECH OCCASIONS

The occasion itself is crucial in determining who will speak and even if anyone will. There are times when it is all right to speak and times when it is not. These are frequently bound with place. For instance, in a Northern European or American middle-class neighborhood, if a group of adults congregate in the streets, everyone would assume that something bad has happened, such as someone's house catching fire. In other neighborhoods, however, it is usual to see groups talking and laughing on the street. In some cultures, it would be fitting only for men to do this; in others, both men and women would. In African American neighborhoods of some Northern cities, men congregate on the street corners or in front of a business establishment. Women sit on front porches or "stoops" of residences. What middle-class people do once they cross the thresholds of their home, other groups will do in public. Milroy says that working-class men in Belfast congregate in the streets to talk and they will have very personal discussions in quite public places.

There are great differences in speech practices in places of worship. For instance, in a great cathedral if a worshiper disagrees—or even agrees—with the homily, she or he does not stand up and comment to the preacher and certainly doesn't encourage by shouting out "Ain't it so, brother" or "Hallelujah!". But in an English chapel or an American Pentecostal church service, parishioners do just that, but they would never criticize. Their calling out is considered evidence of strong religious feeling, of really feeling the spirit, just as silence is evidence of deep religious feeling in Cathedral masses.

In an Orthodox Jewish congregation, each individual is free to chant the prayers at his or her own speed regardless of where the rabbi and cantor are. This is a reflection of the fact that, in Judaism, the rabbi has no special powers and members of the congregation can and do participate in every aspect of the service. The congregation is not in a subservient position, and every man in it has a thorough enough religious background, including knowledge of Biblical Hebrew, to officiate at services. In Reformed Jewish services, however, in which the congregations are frequently less versed in Hebrew, such fluidity would be unthinkable. There is no individual calling out frequently not even of "Amen" or "Hallelujah." The congregation speaks out and sings only at prescribed times.

SILENCE

In order to carry on a successful interaction, one must know the rules of silence, as well as the ones for speech. Silence can say as much as speech. Accompanied by the correct kinesics and amongst those of the same culture, it says "We're friends," "I'm hostile to you," "This is a reverent occasion," "I disagree with you," or, even, "Shut up!"

It would be hard to find any communicative behavior that causes more intergroup misinterpretation than the rules of silence. For many Americans and Europeans, silence when with another indicates hostility or social malpractice. The ideal is to fill silences up, and this is not done by the awkward or the angry, but, even in Northern Europe there is variability in silence practices. Milroy (1980, pp. 87–89), quoting Coulthard, tells of a Danish couple who were so exhausted and angered by an American guest's constant chatter that they had to retreat to the privacy of their room. Of course, the American was just trying to be polite. Milroy herself suffered from a disjunction between her rules of having to fill up the silences and those of the Belfast working-class Catholic Irish she was investigating. You may recall from Chapter 4 that Irish female guests would sit with their elbows entwined and bodies otherwise touching, and when they did talk, they gave little slaps and pokes to each other. What was even worse is that they didn't often speak. They sat close together, arms entwined, and silent. Guests frequently entered the home and sat down, sometimes for hours not saying anything. In contrast to most American and Northern European groups, stepping over someone else's threshold clearly was not a signal for chit-chat. Milroy (p. 89) suggests that this is similar to what has been reported of Eskimos who would visit a researcher every day for an hour to make sure he was all right. It has occurred to me that one reason that such rules of silence are prevalent in working-class Belfast and the Eskimos is that if groups are closely knit, with everyone pretty much knowing each other and visiting is done frequently and homes are always open to visitors, and frequent visiting is an important mark of solidarity, talking is both superfluous and beside the point. It would be too exhausting otherwise. Requiring talk as a show of solidarity seems more necessary in a society in which people visit far less and, typically, only by invitation. Milroy (p. 89) says that "A fairly familiar (but not necessarily intimate) visitor…in Belfast may sit in total silence without the host feeling the slightest obligation to say anything at all." In such a culture, people in the family usually go on with their business, even when visitors drop in. This makes perfectly good sense. If people stop by frequently, how would anyone get their work done if a host had to be one in the American middle-class sense.

Another sphere in which there is great misunderstanding is behavior in houses of worship. Maltz (1985) explains that, among Pentecostals, speaking out in church is both a way of showing their commitment and of demonstrating their joy. He says "The expression of joy is not merely permitted, but openly encouraged" (p. 126), especially since Pentecostals believe that calling out "Amen," "Hallelujah," and other such expressions of support shows that one has received the Holy Spirit. "Speaking in tongues," that is, producing streams of sounds not identifiable as a language, is another such expression also associated with the Pentecostals. Although Americans often identify such a display as being a feature of certain American Protestant churches, this is prevalent in Scotland and England as well. It has to do with Pentecostalism, not ethnicity.

To show how variable practices for the same ends can be, the Quakers, in order to let the Light of Christ enter into them are silent at worship, with individuals speaking out only when they are sure that they have received a message from the Light (Maltz, p. 123 quoting Bauman).

For traditional Jews, noise other than that from the pulpit is fine as it indicates that congregants are praying the entire service usually by chanting, sometimes for hours on end, in a one-on-one communication with God. A cantor, choir, lay-leader and/or rabbi will also be praying, speaking, or singing from the pulpit. They are singing or saying prayers for the congregation. Even if the members of the congregation just say, "Amen," it is considered that they have each sung the prayer themselves so that both individual and group prayer can go on at the same time. Similarly, sporadically through a service, one will hear a voice singing a short refrain, or joining in on the last few words being sung by the cantor or choir. Heath (1983, p. 209) chronicles the same kind of "support" in an African American church when a layperson is praying in her own words. "On one occasion...a member of the congregation broke in with a supporting bar of melody..."

If each person is capable of chanting the entire service and is free to move along at his or her own pace, then noise other than that from the pulpit is all right, providing of course that the noise is associated with praying. Since many Orthodox Jewish services are very long, children may be running around, some adults may get up to leave for a few moments, or someone might pause to greet a latecomer. It is even all right to make occasional soft comments to someone. All of this is taken to be evidence of being "at home" with God. Less Orthodox Jews are more likely just to follow in the prayer book and, like non-Pentecostal Christians, to do responsive readings and sing hymns together as directed by the pulpit, not going at their own speed.

Although little of the "controlled chaos" of Orthodox services survives amongst the less traditional, one thing does: When they are sitting and waiting for a service to begin, Jews are likely to be chatting with their friends and families. When they are invited to Catholic or mainstream Protestant weddings or other church services, the Jews enrage the Christians because they sit and talk, not knowing that this is not done in churches.

The thing to remember, however, is that these highly diverse and conflicting practices are all intended to enhance communication with God, and those who practice them feel that they are evincing true piety.

RITUAL NATURE OF CONVERSATION

The ritual nature of conversation as well as the role of social convention in determining meaning is easily seen in rules for the telephone (Schegloff 1968). Telephones have been common in American homes only for the past 50 years or so. Yet very definite rules surround their usage. Exactly how such rules arise and become widespread through society is not precisely known; they just do. Usually, when a social need arises, language forms evolve to meet the need.

The first rule of telephone conversation in the United States is that the answerer speaks first. It does not have to be so. The rule could as easily be that the caller speaks first. That makes perfectly good sense, as it means that the one who calls is identified at once. Of course the American way makes equally good sense, as it ensures that the receiver is at someone's ear before the caller starts to speak. There are often several equally logical possibilities in conversation rituals, but any one group may adopt just one of the possible alternatives. In other words, if we come across ways different from our own, we should not assume that "theirs" are better or worse than "ours".

In any event, in the United States the convention is that the answerer speaks first. If the call could conceivably be for the answerer because she or he is answering the phone at her or his home, the usual first utterance is "Hello." In places of business or in a doctor's or lawyer's office, wherever secretaries or operators answer the phone, "Hello" is not proper. Rather, the name of the business or office is given, as in "E.B. Marshall Co." or "Dr. Sloan's office," or "George J. West Junior High." Giving the name in itself means, 'this is a business, institution, or professional's office'. At one time it was appropriate for servants in a household or even friends who happened to answer a phone while visiting to answer "X's residence," unless the call might conceivably be for the answerer. Increasingly, however, it seems to me that people answer "Hello" to a residential phone in someone else's home or just let the phone ring.

Godard (1977) recounts the confusion on both her part and on the part of American callers because her native French routine requires that callers verify that the number called is the one reached. Violation of discourse routines, like violations of style, hinders social interaction at least a little even when the violations otherwise fit the situation.

As simple as the telephone rules seem to be, and they surely constitute one of the simpler social routines, there are still many other rules to follow for a "good" result. After the answerer says "Hello," (or its variants), the caller asks "Is X there?" unless the caller recognizes the answerer's voice. In that instance, the caller must greet the answerer before asking for the party she or he wishes to speak with. Some do not bother to greet the answerer first. Whether or not hurt feelings result seems to depend on the length of acquaintanceship and degree of intimacy. Students in my class report that their parents feel snubbed if a frequent caller does not say the equivalent of "Hi, Mrs. Jones. Is Darryl there?" Sometimes callers wish to acknowledge the existence of the answerer (phatic communication) but do not wish to be involved in a lengthy conversation, so they say, "Hi, Mrs. Jones. It's Mary. I'm sorry, but I'm in a hurry. Is Darryl there?" On the surface, "I'm sorry, but I'm in a hurry" seems to have no relevance to phone greetings. It makes perfect sense, however, if one takes phatic communication into account, as well as telephone routines. The apology acknowledges that the caller recognizes acquaintance with the answerer and, therefore, the social appropriateness of conversing with her or him.

In terms of social rules, perhaps what is most interesting is that the person who answers the phone feels compelled to go get the one the caller wants. This compulsion may be so great, that answerers find themselves running all over the house, shouting out the window if necessary to get the one called.

One ex-student of mine, John Reilly, reported an amusing anecdote illustrating the strength of this obligation. He called a friend to go bowling and the friend's sister answered the phone. She informed John that her brother was cutting logs but that she would go fetch him. John, knowing that the woodpile was 100 yards away, assured her it was not necessary. All she had to do was to relay the message. Three times she insisted on going. Three times John told her not to. Finally, she said, confusedly,

"Don't you want to talk to him?" John repeated that she could extend his invitation without calling the friend to the phone. Suddenly, she just left the phone without responding to John's last remarks and fetched her brother.

As extreme as this may sound, it is actually no more so than the response of a person in the tub when the phone rings, and she or he leaps out of the tub to answer it[6] and, still dripping wet with only a towel for protection, proceeds to run to another part of the house to summon the person for whom the caller asked. It is the rare person who can say, "Yes, X is here, but I don't see him. Call back later." Indeed, there are those who would consider such a response quite rude. It is as if the person who answers has tacitly consented to go get whomever is called, regardless of inconvenience, unless the called one is not at home. The sense of obligation, of having to respond in a certain way, is at the core of all verbal social routines.

Actually, if the one called on the phone is not at home or does not live there anymore, or never lived there at all, the semantically appropriate response to "Is X there?" should be "No." In fact, however, "No" is appropriate only if X does live there, but is not now at home. For example, if X once lived there, but does not now, an appropriate answer is:

1. X doesn't live here any more.
2. X has moved.
3. X lives at ___ now.

Although a plain *no* carries the correct meaning, it cannot be used if X no longer lives there, but once did. If X has never lived there, one may answer:

4. There is no X here.
5. What number are you calling?
6. You must have the wrong number.

Again *no* would seem to be a fitting response, but it cannot be used to "Is X there?" Notice that 4 semantically fits for a meaning of 'X no longer lives here' but it never would be used for that meaning by someone socialized into American society.

In discourse routines, frequently an apparently suitable response cannot be used in certain social situations or the response will have a greater or different meaning than the words used. For instance, one apparently proper response to:

7. Where are the tomatoes? (in a store)

is:

8. I don't know.

Most people would find such an honest answer rude, even odd. More likely is:

9. I'm sorry, but I don't work here.
10. I'm sorry, I'll ask the manager.
11. I don't work here, but the tomatoes are in the next aisle.

If one is not an employee, then she/he explains as in 9 why no answer is forthcoming. If the one asked is an employee, then 10 is appropriate. As with the telephone, the answerer feels obligated, as evinced by prefacing each remark with "I'm sorry." This apology makes no sense if we consider the question alone. It makes perfectly good sense, however, when we realize that the response is to the **precondition** that there is an assumption that an employee knows where items are. Notice that there is no reason at all to say "I don't work here" in 11, except that the respondent is correcting the asker's assumption that she or he works there. That is, again, the response is understandable only if we realize that people respond to the social assumptions behind questions and other remarks as well as to the actual words given.

Preconditions for asking questions in our society are:

I.   The questioner has the right or duty to ask the question.
II. The one asked has the responsibility or obligation to know the answer. (Labov and Fanshel 1977)

Preconditions for speech acts are as much a part of their meaning as actual words are. The giveaway in 11 is the *but*. It makes no sense at all unless it is seen as a response to precondition II. When *but* joins two sentences it often means 'although' so that 11 means 'although I don't work here, I happen to know that the tomatoes are in the next aisle.' That is, 'although I am not responsible for knowing since I don't work here, I will tell you anyhow.'

The phenomenon of responsibility as in telephone routines and answering questions is part of a larger responsibility that adheres to the discourse routines that Harvey Sacks called **utterance pairs**.[7] These are conversational sequences in which one utterance elicits another of a specific kind. For instance,:

- ▶greeting—greeting
- ▶question—answer
- ▶complaint—excuse, apology, or denial
- ▶request/command—acceptance or rejection
- ▶compliment—acknowledgment
- ▶farewell—farewell

Whomever is given the first part of an utterance pair is responsible for giving the second half. The opener of such a sequence, in our society, commands the person addressed to give one of the socially appropriate responses. As with the telephone, these responses often have a meaning different from, less than, or greater than the sum of the words used. The only time that we are freed from the obligation to carry out the socially prescribed roles in conversation is when the other party is incapable of acting with a purpose, as when drunk, stoned, or insane (Frake 1964). Perhaps one of the reasons that we get so angry when someone does not act or speak appropriately for the situation is that we cannot figure out his or her intentions. Without knowing those, we do not know how to act ourselves when dealing with the person.

Furthermore, the first half of the pair does not necessarily have to sound like what it really is. That is, a question does not have to be in question form nor a command in a command form. All that is necessary for a statement to be construed as a question or command is for the social situation to be right for questioning or commanding. The very fact that a speech event is appropriate for a question or a command may cause an utterance to be perceived as such even if it is not in question or command form. As with proper style, situation includes roles and relative status of participants in a conversation. Situation, roles and social status are an inextricable part of meaning, often as much as, if not more so, than the actual form the utterance takes in terms of words used and sentence construction.

Utterance pairs are not necessarily universal, at least not in demanding a rapid response. For instance, for mainstream American society if a question is asked, it must receive an answer even if that answer is "I don't know." The Warm Springs Indian does not have to answer right away. One may be asked a question but may not receive an answer for hours or even days. Similarly, in much American culture, if one receives an oral invitation, one must give some sort of answer right away. If a Warm Springs Indian gets one, she or he need not respond at all (Philips 1976).

CHAPTER 5

Goody (1978) points out that questions, being incomplete, are powerful in forcing responses in our culture. We have already seen that certain preconditions exist for questioning and that an answer may be to a precondition rather than to the question itself. In the following discussion, it is always assumed that the preconditions for questioning are fulfilled. We will then be able to gain some insights into how people understand and even manipulate others on the basis of social rules.

There are two kinds of overt questions, *yes-no* questions and *wh-* ones. The first as the name implies, requires an answer of *yes* or *no*. In essence, if the *yes-no* question forms are used, one is forced to answer "yes," "no," or "I don't know." There is no way not to answer except to pretend not to hear. If that occurs, the asker usually repeats the question, perhaps more loudly, or even precedes the repetition with a tap on the would-be answerer's shoulder (or the verbal equivalent). Alternatively, the asker could precede the repeated question with a summons like, "Hey Bill, I asked..." It is because members of our society all recognize that they must answer a question and they must respond "yes" or "no" to a *yes-no* question that the following question is a recognized joke:

▶Have you stopped beating your wife?/husband?

Since you must know what you do to your spouse, "I don't know." cannot be answered. Only a "yes" or "no" will do. Either answer condemns. Either way, you admit to spouse beating.

Yes-no questions can also be asked by ending a statement with a **tag**:

▶You're going, *aren't you?*
▶It's five dollars, *right?*

If the preconditions for questioning are present, as Labov and Fanshel (1977) point out, a plain declarative statement can be construed as a *yes-no* question as in

▶Q: You live on 114th Street.
▶A: No, I live on 115th.

The *wh-* questions demand an answer that substitutes for the question word. An "I don't know" can also be given. The *wh-* words are *what, when, why, who, where,* and *how* appearing at the start of a question. These words are, in essence, blanks to be filled in. *What* has to be answered with the name of a thing or event; *when* with a time; *why,* a

178

reason; *who,* a person; and *how,* a manner or way something was done. There is actually yet another *wh-* question, "Huh?" which asks 'would you repeat the entire sentence you just said?' That is, the "huh" asks that a whole utterance be filled in, not just a word or phrase.[8]

The answer to any question can be deferred by asking another which creates **insertion sequences** (Schegloff 1971) as in:

▶A: Wanna come to a party?
▶B: Can I bring a friend?
▶A: Male or female?
▶B: Female.
▶A: Sure.
▶B: O.K.

Note that these questions are answered in reverse order, but all are answered. Occasionally insertion sequences can lead conversationalists "off the track". When this happens participants may feel a compulsion to get a question answered even if they have forgotten what it was. Hence, comments like

▶Oh, as I was saying...
▶Oh, I forget what we were talking about.

Note that **oh** serves as an indicator that the speaker is not responding to the last statement but to a prior one. Such seemingly innocuous syllables frequently serve as markers in conversation.

The actual meaning of any utterance depends partially on the social context in which it occurs (Brown and Yule 1983, pp. 27–58). Rommetveit (1971) gives a classic example of this. He tells a story about a man running for political office who is scheduled to give a talk in a school auditorium. When he arrives, he sees that there are not enough chairs. He calls his wife at home. Then he goes to see the janitor. To each, the candidate says, "There aren't enough chairs." To his wife this means 'Wow! Am I popular!' To the janitor it means 'Go get some more chairs.' The full meaning evoked by the statement "There aren't enough chairs" is largely a product of the context in which it is said, including the relative social statuses, privileges, and duties of the speaker and hearer. Society places obligations upon us in discourse, and the real meaning of an utterance cannot be derived independently from social context.

CHAPTER 5

MANIPULATING BY THE RULES

It is easy to manipulate people subtly by plugging them into the presuppositions and preconditions behind statements (Elgin 1980; Labov and Fanshel 1977). We have already seen that the use of *even* entails the proposition that everyone is doing something except the one being addressed. There is a further unspoken proposition that if everyone else is doing something then so should the addressee. Hence, "Even Oscar is going" means 'Oscar usually doesn't go, but he is now. That means everyone is going, and so should you.' Readers may recognize in this rather common ploy, the childhood, "Everyone else has one" or "Everyone else goes to sleep at ten."

Elgin (1980) also discusses the manipulations of the "if you really love me" variety. These are actually subtle accusations. What they mean is 'you should love me but you don't. The guilt you feel for not loving me can be easily erased, though, by doing whatever I want.'

Another manipulation is the "even **you** should be able to do that" type. Here we have *even* again, the word that tells someone that she or he is alone in whatever failing is being mentioned. Its use with *should* is especially clever because it implies that the hearer is stupid or some sort of gross misfit, but it backgrounds that message so that it is not likely to be discussed. Rather, the hearer is made to feel stupid and wrong, so that she/he will be likely to capitulate to the speaker's demands in an effort to prove that if all others can do it, so can the hearer.

A variant to this is "even a child (baby/idiot/moron/...) can do it." This is a gross insult, as it says that those with little intelligence can do it, so if you can't you are stupid. Using *even* in this way may uncover social attitudes, for the person(s) who are the butt, so to speak, of the *even* are inferior in the activity under discussion. For instance, it is possible to find contexts for "Even a woman can do it" as in "Even a woman can handle this truck." This implies that women usually cannot drive trucks. The contrasting phrase, "Even a man can do it," as in "Even a man can boil eggs" seems to be used mostly for trivial matters, matters typically relegated to women. The "Even a woman..." putdown always refers to more masculine, hence important and powerful activities, showing that sex-stereotyping is alive and well even after decades of feminism.

One can achieve manipulation and insult by preceding a comment with "Don't tell me you're going to..." or "Don't tell me that you believe..." Notice that these are questions in the form of a command. They are actually a way of asking:

Are you really going to ___?
Do you really believe ___?

Both of these also mean 'Your action or belief is stupid.' A likely response to either of these is:

Well, I thought I would, but now I'm not so sure.

But responses like:

Of course I am. Aren't you?
Of course I do. Don't you?

while rarer, could be humorous simply because they violate the presuppositions behind the *don't tell me's*. In any event, such rejoinders certainly would deflate the manipulator and make her or him seem to be the stupid one. Moreover, they are a way of informing the *"Don't tell me..."* speaker that you are not going to be manipulated.

The really clever ploy of the "Don't tell me..." variety is that the hearer, H, is instantly made to feel foolish because of the presuppositions. However, since the speaker, S, has not overtly accused the hearer of stupidity, argument is difficult. H is not even allowed the luxury of anger at the insult because it has not been overtly stated. It is contained only in the presupposition. H might become immediately defensive but still feel quite stupid because of the implied insult. Not only does S usually get H to capitulate, but also S establishes that H is the stupider of the two. As a manipulatory device, this is a "double whammy," (unless, of course, H stands her or his ground and delivers the unusual retort.)

Labov and Fanshel (1977) show that some people manipulate in even more subtle ways by utilizing common understanding of social and discourse rules. Using patient-therapist sessions, which they received permission to tape, Labov and Fanshel describe the struggle of a woman named Rhoda for independence from a domineering mother. The mother finally leaves Rhoda at home and goes to visit Rhoda's sister Phyllis. Rhoda cannot cope, but neither can she ask her mother to come home because that would be an admission that the mother is right in not giving Rhoda more freedom. Rather Labov and Fanshel say that Rhoda employs an indirect request both to mitigate her asking her mother for help and to disguise her challenge to the power relationship between them. Rhoda calls her mother on the phone and asks

CHAPTER 5

►When do you plan to come home?

Since this is not a direct request for help, Rhoda's mother forces an admission by not answering Rhoda's question. Instead she creates an insertion sequence:

►Oh, why?

This means 'Why are you asking me when I plan to come home?' In order to answer, Rhoda must admit that she cannot be independent, that the mother has been right all along. Furthermore, as a daughter, Rhoda, unconsciously abiding by the questioning rules in our society, is forced to answer her mother's question. Her mother has the right to question by virtue of her status and Rhoda has the duty to answer for the same reason. So Rhoda responds

►Things are getting just a little too much…it's getting too hard.

To which the mother replies:

►Why don't you ask Phyllis [when I'll be home]?

Since it is really up to the mother when she will come home, and also, since she has a prior obligation to her own household, Labov and Fanshel say that it is clear that Rhoda has been outmaneuvered. The mother has forced Rhoda into admitting that she is not capable and she has, in effect, also refused Rhoda's request for help.

It seems to me that this mother has also conveyed very cleverly to Rhoda that Phyllis is the preferred daughter and has said it so covertly that the topic can't be openly discussed. Clearly it is the mother's right and duty to come home as she wishes. By palming that decision off on Phyllis, she is actually saying to Rhoda, "No matter what your claim on me is, Phyllis comes first." That is, for Phyllis's sake, she will suppress her rights as a mother and allow Phyllis to make the decision. Notice that all of this works only because at some level both Rhoda and her mother know the rights and obligations of questioners and answerers.

All indirect requests do not arise from hostile situations although most are used when individual desires conflict with other social rules or values. Classic examples, spoken with an expectant lift to the voice, are

▶Oh, chocolates.
▶What are those, cigars?
(Sacks, 1964–1972).

Assuming that the above are spoken by adults who have long known what *chocolate* and *cigar* denote, these observations are perceived as requests. This is shown by the usual responses to either:

▶Would you like one?
▶I'm sorry, but they aren't mine.

or

▶I have to save them for X.

Toddlers just learning to speak do practice by going about pointing at objects and naming them. Once that stage is past, people do not name items in the immediate environment unless there is an intent, a reason for singling out the item. All properly socialized Americans know that one should never directly ask for food in another's household or for any possibly expensive goods like cigars. That would be begging. Therefore, one names the items in another's home or hands so that the naming is construed as an indirect request. There is rarely another reason for an adult to name a common object or food out of the blue; that is, in the absence of a previous question or utterance which could elicit the name of the object. The responses to "Oh, chocolates" and "What are those, cigars?" make sense only if the hearer construes those as really meaning 'I want you to offer me some of those chocolates/cigars.'

Commands and Questions

Requests for food are not the only discourse routines arising from conflicts between general social rules and the will of the individual. Commands share virtually the same preconditions as questions:

▶The speaker who commands has the right and/or duty to command.
▶The recipient of the command has the responsibility and/or obligation to carry out the command.

The problem is that, even more than with questioning, the one who has the right to command is usually clearly of higher status than the one who must obey. The United States supposedly is an egalitarian society, but having the right or duty to command implies that some are superior to others. This runs counter to our stated ideals. Therefore, in most actual situations in American speech, commands are disguised as questions. The substitution of forms is possible because both speech acts share the same preconditions. Moreover, phrasing commands as questions maintains the fiction that the one commanded has the right to refuse even when she or he does not. Consider:

▶Would you mind closing the door?

Even though this is uttered as a *yes-no* question, merely to answer "No" without the accompanying action or "Yes" without an accompanying excuse would either be bizarre or a joke. In the movie *The Return of the Pink Panther*, the late Peter Sellers asks a passerby if he knows where the Palace Hotel is. The passerby responds, "Yes," but keeps on going. The joke is that "Do you know where X is?" is not really a *yes-no* question, but a polite command meaning 'tell me where X is.'

Direct commanding is allowed and usual in certain circumstances. For instance, parents normally command young children directly, as in:

▶Pick those toys up right away.

Intimates such as spouses or roommates often casually command each other about trivial matters such as:

▶Pick some bread up on the way home.

Often these are softened by *please, will ya, honey*, or the like.

Direct commanding in command form occurs in the military from those of superior rank to those of inferior. During actual battle it is necessary for combatants to obey their officers without question, unthinkingly, and unshesitatingly. Direct commands yield this kind of obedience so long as those commanded recognize the social rightness of the command or the need. It is no surprise that direct commands are regularly heard in emergency situations, as during fire fighting or surgery:

▶Get the hose! Put up the ladders.
▶Get me some bandages! Suture that wound!

In situations that allow direct commands, the full command form need not always be invoked. Just enough has to be said so that the underling knows what to do, as in:

▶Time for lunch! (meaning 'come in for lunch').
▶Scalpel! Sutures! Dressings!

Note that such commands are contextually bound. They are interpretable as commands only if the participants are actually in a commanding situation. Similarly, Susan Ervin-Tripp's (1972) comment that:

▶It's cold in here.

can be interpreted as a command only in a specific commanding context. The speaker must somehow have the right to ask another to close a window if that is the cause of the cold, or to ask another to lend his or her coat. In this situation, the fact that one person is closer to an open window may be sufficient reason for him or her to be responsible for closing it. The duty or obligation to carry out a command need not proceed only from status, but may proceed from the physical circumstances in which the command has been uttered. That is why in the right circumstances, ordinary statements or questions may be construed as commands, as in:

Tom: Any more coffee?
Ann: I'll make some right away.
Tom: No, I wanted to know if I had to buy some.

If it is possible to do something about whatever is mentioned, an utterance may be construed as a command. It was possible for Ann to make some more coffee, and she must have been responsible for making it at least part of the time. Hence, Tom's question was misinterpreted as a command to make some. The same possibility of misinterpretation can occur in questions like:

▶Can you swim?

Said by a poolside, it may be interpreted as a command, "Jump in!" but away from a body of water, it will be heard merely as a request for information.

Although questions are often used as polite substitutes for commands, the question-command can sometimes be especially imperious:

▶Would you mind being quiet?

Similarly, an *if* clause by itself yields an especially haughty command:

▶If you would wait, please...

I suspect that both of these carry special force because the high formality signalled by *would you mind* and *if you would... please* contrast so sharply with the banality of keeping quiet and waiting, that the effect of sarcasm is achieved.

Compliments

Compliments are another utterance pair type that can create conflict. There is a great deal of cross-cultural variation in the amount of complimenting that is done, on what one may be complimented, and if complimenting should be done at all. Basso (1989) shows how the Apaches ridicule the amount of complimenting by "the whiteman." The overabundance of complimenting is actually embarrassing to them. Sometimes, even in the Anglo culture, people feel that a compliment is an implied judgment that the complimenter had no business to make. For instance, when I heard a supervisor of student teachers complain in high dudgeon, "What a colossal nerve!" because one of the students had dared to say after observing the supervisor's class, "That was wonderful!" There is a feeling in such a case that the supervisor is of course wonderful. What else would the student expect? In contrast, in situations, or between people, where a great deal of complimenting is expected, the person who doesn't compliment may be found too demanding or cold.

Knapp et al. (1984, p. 13) report that two thirds of 245 people who were observed while being complimented reported later that they felt "uncomfortable, defensive, or cynical" about the praise and, to me most telling, have problems responding appropriately. I strongly suspect that this is because of general social convention and the rule that the first part of an utterance pair must evoke a response. Compliments call for an acknowledgment. The acknowledgment can properly be acceptance of the compliment, as by saying, "Thank you." The problem is that to accept the compliment is very close to bragging and bragging is frowned upon in middle-class America. Hence, one typical response to a compliment is a disclaimer like:

▶This old rag?
▶I got it on sale.
▶It was a Christmas present.

An exception is special occasions when compliments are expected, as when everyone is decked out to go to a prom or a wedding. Then, not only are compliments easily received with "Thank you," but not to compliment can cause offense or disappointment.

Except for such situations, complimenting can lead to social embarrassment. If one persists in complimenting another, the other person often becomes hostile, even though nice things are being said. At the very least, the recipient of excessive praise becomes uncomfortable and tries to change the subject. Often she or he becomes suspicious and angry or tries to avoid the person who is heaping praise. The suspicion is either that the complimenter is being patronized or is trying to get something or "butter the person up." The overenthusiastic complimenter is in danger of sounding smarmy, especially if she or he is lower in status than the object of praise (p. 25). I suspect that anger results from the social precariousness of being complimented. As with style, when a person is put at a social disadvantage so that she or he does not know how to respond, anger may result. Too much praise is tantamount to being continually asked to tread the line between gracious acceptance and boasting. Most people prefer to ignore anyone who puts them in that situation. Probably equally as important, one gets suspicious of the motives of those who "butter us up" with too many compliments.

Still, Knapp et al. (p. 27) claim that most people who give compliments and who receive them say that the compliments are deserved. So, although compliments may be perceived as being false, they are not always perceived that way. Of course, who doesn't want to believe that others admire them, and few would admit they are themselves insincere.

Requesting and Apologizing

The speech acts of requesting and apologizing vary greatly across cultures, both in what must be apologized for, what may be requested, and how either is to be carried out.

Requesting varies according to whether or not the speaker chooses a more or less direct request in a given situation, such as requesting a ride from someone (House 1989, p. 111). Some apologize first, explain why they need the ride, and then make a request, as in:

▶Excuse me, I'm Bob Miller. I live on the same street you do. I wanted to ask you if you may possibly take me along in your car because I missed my bus and the next bus goes in one hour.

This was elicited from an American. Note the degree of apology and indirectness: *Excuse me, I wanted to ask you if you may possibly...*followed by the request for a ride. In contrast, a British speaker simply said,

▶Look, if you are going my way, could you possibly give me a lift? I've missed the bus and there isn't another for an hour.

The British man also uses politeness markers like *could you possibly*, but doesn't embed it in a string of *if you may possibly*. Note that the British request starts with a simple and direct, "Look, if you are going my way..." whereas the American both excuses himself, gives his name, explains his relationship, and then says, "I wanted to ask you..."

House (1989, p. 107) establishes that such differences depend on the degree to which the requester has a right to ask, the hearer has a social obligation to comply, and the request is associated with social or communicative difficulty. For instance, if the person asked would lose face by complying or violate the hearer's privacy, then the requester would have to hedge the request in increasingly more convoluted politeness phrases. Apparently, the American feels that asking for a ride is more of an imposition than the English person does. If the same request were made to a spouse, the American might simply say "Hey, I need a ride. I missed the bus." One must be less direct with strangers, as they don't have the same obligations to do one's bidding.

Blum-Kulka and House (1989) show that, in many instances, the tendency toward a particular speech act pattern may be similar, although there are always differences. Whereas we might suspect that one culture is more polite than another, it is equally true that cultural attitudes and facts are important determinants in how a request or apology will be conveyed. For instance, Israeli Hebrew speakers and Germans show close agreement on avoiding overt apology words like "I am so sorry" for insulting a worker, but they vary in apology strategies in other instances. In general, however, it was found that there weren't significant differences in the kinds of strategies used in different situations eliciting apologies. This may be because the four groups studied, Israelis, Germans, Australian English, and Canadian French, are all basically, Euro-centered Western industrialized cultures who share similar values.

Presequences

An interesting class of discourse rules is what Harvey Sacks called **presequences** (lecture, November 2, 1967), particularly **preinvitations**. Typically, someone wishing to issue an oral invitation first asks something like:

▶What are you doing Saturday night?

If the response includes words like *only* or *just* as in

▶I'm just washing my hair.

or:

▶I'm only studying,

the inviter can then issue an invitation for Saturday night. If, however, the response is

▶I'm washing my hair.

or:

▶I'm studying.

the potential inviter knows not to issue the invitation. Following such responses, the inviter typically signals a change in conversation by saying, "Uh..." and then speaks of something other than Saturday night. Issuing of preinvitations is an ego-saver like the use of style to signal social class. Having been spared overt refusal, the inviter is able to save face (Goffman 1955). Additionally, Blum-Kulka and House (1989 p. 130) suggest that pre-requests check the feasibility of compliance, thereby overcoming grounds for refusal.

Collapsing Sequences

Sometimes utterance pairs are collapsed (Sacks, November 2, 1967) as in the following exchange at an ice-cream counter.

A: What's chocolate filbert?
B: We don't have any.

B's response is to what B knows is likely to come next. If B had explained what chocolate filbert is, then A very likely would have asked for some. By explaining what it is, B would be tacitly saying that she or he had some to sell. In a selling situation in our society, explaining what goods or foods are is always an admission that they are available. Imagine your reaction, for instance, if you asked a waitperson what some food was like and she or he went into detail telling you about it. Then, if you said, "Sounds good. I'll have that," and the response was, "We don't have any" you would think you were being made a fool of.

Another common collapsing sequence is typified by the exchange:

Q: Do you smoke?
A. I left them in my other jacket.

Such collapsing sequences speed up social interaction by forestalling necessary explanations. They are used for other purposes as well, as when a newcomer joins a discussion in progress.

▶Hi, John. We were just talking about nursery schools.

This either warns John not to join the group or, if he is interested in nursery schools, gives him orientation so that he can understand what is going on.

Although, in utterance pairs, the first half strongly controls what is coming next. The larger conversation beyond these is not so strongly constrained as to form. The syntax of the language can be drawn upon to encode new ideas, not just the syntax of greetings or questions. In questions, for instance, the first sentence or so is predetermined by the question just asked, but the speaker becomes even freer as soon as an answer is given that fills in the *wh-* word or supplies the *yes, no,* or *I don't know.* The constraints upon topic, however, remain very strong.

REPAIRS REVISITED

As we have already seen, if a person uses the wrong style for an occasion, the other party(ies) to the interaction try to repair the error. Schegloff, Jefferson, and Sacks (1977) collected interesting samples of self-correction in discourse: people repairing their own errors. Sometimes this takes the form of obvious correction to a slip of the tongue, as in

▶What're you so *ha*—er—unhappy about?

Sometimes speakers make a repair when they have made no overt error, as in

▶Sure enough ten minutes later the bell r—the doorbell rang.

Because such repairs do not show a one-to-one correspondence with actual spoken errors, Schegloff et al. preferred the term *repair* over *correction*. In both of the following, for instance, neither repair is preceded by an error that actually occurred in speech.

Schegloff et al. found an orderly pattern in speech repairs. They did not occur just anywhere in an utterance. They occur immediately after the error as in the previous two, or at the end of the sentence where another person would normally take the floor as in the following:

▶...all of the doors'n things were taped up—I mean y'know they
put up y'know that kinda paper stuff, the brown paper.

or right after the other person speaks:

Hannah: And he's going to make his own paintings.
Bea: Mm hm.
Hannah: And—or I mean his own frames.

If the speaker does not repair an obvious error, the hearer will. Usually this is done by asking a question that will lead the speaker to repair his or her own error. Some examples:

A: It wasn't snowing all day.
B: It wasn't?
A. Oh, I mean it was.

A: Yeah, he's got a lot of smarts.
B: Huh?
A: He hasn't got a lot of smarts.

A: Hey, the first time they stopped me from selling cigarettes
was this morning.
B: From selling cigarettes?
A: From buying cigarettes.

Often the hearer will say, "you mean..." as in

A: We went Saturday afternoon.
B: You mean Sunday.
A: Yeah, uhnn we saw Max...

In most of the repairs by hearers, it seems that the hearer knows all along what the intended word was. Still, it is rare, although not impossible, for the hearer only to supply the word without at least putting it in a question. It seems to me that this is a face-saver for the person who made the error. The hearer often offers the correction or the question leading to correction tentatively, as if she or he is not sure. That way, the speaker is not humiliated as she or he might be if the hearer in positive tones asserted that an error was made. I also suspect that another reason that hearers offer corrections tentatively may be that in doing so, the hearer is in the position of telling someone else what must be going on in her or his mind, a right we accord only to psychiatrists.

Schegloff et al. (1977, p. 38) state that "the organization of repair is the self-righting mechanisms for the organization of language use in social interaction." In other words, it maintains normal social interaction. We have already seen this in attempted repair of inappropriate style. Fairclough (1989) suggests that this is also a way of maintaining the status quo in society.

The importance of the self-righting mechanism is shown in the following almost bizarre interactions. These involve repairs in greetings and farewells collected as part of a participant observation by a student, Sheila Kennedy. While on guard duty at the door of her dormitory, she deliberately confounded greetings and farewells, with fascinating results.

Sheila: Hi. [pause] Good night.
Stranger: Hello, take it easy.

Note that the stranger also gave both a greeting and a farewell, even matching the pause that Sheila used between them. This is highly reminiscent of the exchanges in which subjects so frequently matched the experimenter's style even when they questioned it or objected to it. Another exchange was:

Friend: Bye, Sheila.
Sheila: Hello.
Friend:Why did you say "hello"? I said "goodbye". [pause] Hi.

Even though the friend questioned the inappropriateness of Sheila's response, she still felt constrained to answer the greeting with a greeting.

> *Friend*: Hi!
> *Sheila*: So long.
> [both speak at same time, so Sheila starts again.]
> *Sheila*: Hi!.
> *Friend*: Bye. [laughs] Wait a minute. Let's try that again. Hi!
> *Sheila*: Hello.
> *Friend*: Bye.
> *Sheila*: So long.
> *Friend*: That's better.

What is interesting here is the lengths the subjects went to in order that the appropriate pairs were given. Note that she had to get both greeting and farewell matched up before she would leave.

The degree to which we are bound by the social rules of discourse is well illustrated by the phenomenon of repair. The very fact that people go to so much trouble to repair others' responses seems to me to be highly significant. It shows the importance of discourse routines to social interaction and that one cannot be divorced from the other. Even when people know what the other must mean, they want the discourse righted. And, even when it makes no difference in a fleeting social contact interactors demand that the right forms be chosen. This establishes the importance of maintaining social routines in the overall maintenance of social order, and that such maintenance is not merely a matter of overt laws and policing, but of our internalized assent to modes of conversation. This is another example of Fairclough's (1989) thesis that ordinary speech activities have as part of their purpose the maintaining of the status quo in society.

JARGONS

The sensitivity with which language mirrors society is highlighted in jargons. **Jargons** are varieties of language created for specific functions by the people who engage in them regularly. They are like minidialects, but used only for the activity for which they were created. Jargons are not only sensitive to the requirements of the activity but to the personal and social needs of the speakers. Jargons arise so rapidly and are so fitted to specific events that they give us insights into both the mechanisms and causes of language change by ordinary conversational practices.

A student of mine, Timothy Rembijas, an experienced league bowler, took down a conversation between a nonbowler, F, and another member of the league, S, during a match. S used jargon words like *cranking, turkey, bellying, gyro*, as well as common words used with special meaning, such as *buried, inside, outside*, and *carry*. In this lingo, *cranking* means 'throwing ball with much velocity and curve'; *turkey* means 'three strikes in a row;' *bellying* is 'too much curve,' *gyro* is a kind of bowling ball; *buried* is a way of saying 'perfect'; *inside,* 'left side of approach;' *outside* 'right side of approach;' and *carry* is 'get strikes or knock down pins consistently.' F pretended that he understood S by comments like "Yeah, I thought so too," but his kinesics told the story.

Dell Hymes (1974) mentions two ways in which speech function can be mismatched to the participants in the speech event: The intent is understood, but not the actual words; or, the words are understood but not the intent.[9] The one-sided commentary just quoted is a beautiful instance of the first. Given the nature of jargons, the situation is not unusual. One function of jargons is to exclude lay persons or novices, those who do not belong. It is well-known that speakers adjust to listeners' needs (Giles, Taylor, and Bourhis 1973) defining words when they notice confusion, slowing down speech to foreigners or speaking more loudly. Despite F's overt kinesic signaling that he was bewildered, S barreled on, piling jargon word on jargon word.

S behaves like those who display their brilliance by spouting jargon, cowing lesser beings who do not know it. Doctors and lawyers are often accused of such behavior, but the practise is not confined to them. Displays like S's underscore that those who do not understand are outsiders. In other words, jargons are one way to play one-upmanship. Rembijas explains that in order to be regarded as an expert bowler, one must not only bowl well but be able to use the language. The bowler who cannot, even if she or he gets high scores, will be regarded by bowling peers as being simply lucky. Jargon is a clear case of language being used for social identification.

Jargon also serves the purpose of bonding. Whenever people use special words to let others know that they share interests or background, this bonding is achieved. Claiming something in common, especially language use, is a request for at least some degree of intimacy. "We are friends and others aren't invited to share our special bond." We have seen that style may be used the same way. In both jargon and style, the choice of word itself, not its actual meaning, gives the social message. If jargon is used for bonding, it is a request for less social distance between parties. Also, as in style selection, using features that heighten differences between speakers is a way of forcing distance. Thus, the jargon word lessens distance between those who know it and heightens difference between the person uttering it and those who do not know it.

Sometimes close friends will create their own jargon. Bridget Hurley and Maureen Sullivan, my students, made me promise that I wouldn't use theirs until they graduated because they didn't want friends not in their immediate circle to understand it. They devised this to comment on male-female relationships in close contact. Their jargon centered on words for kissing. They give as a typical conversation:

(topic is previous night's dating)

M: What time did you get in this morning?
S: Early enough to reap the crops.
R: How was the harvest?
S: Better than last season's crops, but not as good as consistent corn that other people get.
      (group laughter)

What this meant was that S found her date's kissing to be better than the last boy she kissed, but not as good as one would expect from a steady relationship with real involvement between a couple. In this jargon, *corn* means 'kiss'; *reaped the crop* means 'a casual date'[10], *last season's crop* is 'male previously kissed'; and *consistent corn* is 'involvement in a relationship'. There are other words in this jargon, all related to corn, such as *kernel's worth of corn* 'a kiss on the cheek', *imported corn* 'males visiting females', *potential corn* 'looking towards the prospect for involvement'; and *bad crop*, 'male expecting too much'.

Only words associated with the activity eliciting the jargon are used for excluding and identifying those who belong. All of the jargon words for bowling describe different aspects of the game. If the markers for a jargon center on the activity that calls for it, they will normally appear early on in an encounter. Thus, they are effective as signals for identification.

Another motivation of word creation in jargons is communicative efficiency. If something has to be mentioned often, it is more economical to have a single word to refer to it than a lengthy phrase. It is more efficient to say "carry" than "get strikes or knock down pins consistently," especially in the heat of a bowling contest, when rapid encoding of the events is important.

CB jargon, so prevalent a few years back,[11] was developed for quite different reasons: to prevent boredom and to keep drivers informed of police monitoring of speed. Because of the noisy road conditions under which it operated, CB actually developed new syntactic forms so that its messages could be more readily interpreted. This gives us insight into how grammars of a language can change, and how rapidly if need be. (Chaika 1980, 1982). There was (and is) a great deal of noise on CB channels, both static and road noise. Since it was necessary to locate where the police were, new markings developed on expressions showing location. In mainstream English, most locative phrases do not take demonstratives and articles, such as *the, this,* or *that,* but in CB talk these were used:

	CB English	Mainstream English
1.	this 95	95
	That exit 23	exit 23
	That Maine town	Maine

Similarly, names for people also took on demonstratives, as in the handles (on air names for people):

2.	The one outlaw	Outlaw
	The Jungle Jim	Jungle Jim

By violating the usual grammar rules of English and putting *the, this,* and *that* where they do not usually appear, two things are achieved. The ones who really belong use the new grammar rule, thus being identified as real CBers. The innovative use of demonstratives warns listeners to be alert, that a location is about to be named. This helps counteract the noisy conditions of the road. The reasons for the same kind of marking on names are that it is difficult to know to whom one is speaking as, typically, several conversations are going on at once, making a generally noisy environment even more confusing.

Oddly, CBers never use their own names. Instead, they give themselves **handles**. Why, then, do they want to mark these names? After all, one would assume, they want to keep their identities secret. DiPietro (1977) says that these are handles that only open outward, and that they are "devoid of any allusion to [the CBer's] own social status." As an instance, he comments that Henry Ford II preferred his handle to be "Beer Belly" rather than "Hank the Deuce" or "Chairman." Therein, I believe, lies the answer. The kinds of handles they choose indicate that they wish to project an image. They prefer pseudonyms like "Outlaw," "Rocky Racoon," and "Jungle Jim." Typically, handles seem to refer to stereotypical lower-class images, fighting prowess ("Rocky"), and animal imagery. We see these last two combined in "Rocky Racoon." Racoons are animals noted for their thievery. The animal imagery also conjures up back-to-nature images with its overtones of sexuality and toughness unrestrained by civilization. "Jungle Jim" was a seminary student and is now a priest. "Outlaw" was a happily married college graduate. Thus, through their handles, CBers can hide their true identity and vent their most taboo fantasies. But what fun would it be if nobody knew whose voice and handle it was? Even in fantasy, people usually want to be somehow identifiable.

Chapter 5 Notes

1   However, one could say "I detest chocolate soda" in response to someone's offer of one, so that the person will not actually place a chocolate soda in front of you. Notice, however, that saying this does not prevent someone from trying to force the soda on you, anyway. Conveying one's dislikes does not necessarily do or prevent anything, whereas a bet or a promise is doing something even if it is ignored. That is, the bet has still been made, as has the promise.

2   The exception would be those classes in which students have been assigned special speaking tasks, such as oral reports.

3   The adjective *innocent* refers to the fact that we so associate intention with speech that we must distinguish between comments meant with the intent to insult and those which have no such intent. When such matters get encoded as part of the speech activity, we know how ingrained it is in our everyday use of language.

4   Gordon and Lakoff's term "conversational postulates" refers to essentially the same phenomena, although their term does convey the idea that we are operating on these assumptions.

5   See Stubbs 1983, pp. 9-11, for a full discussion of the different implications of using these terms.

6   Not to answer at all is very difficult. The ring itself is akin to a summons which cannot easily be ignored, if at all.

7   These are also called **adjacency pairs**. Some authors use the terms interchangeably. Because it is possible to have utterance pairs without their being adjacent, this text uses the former term.

8   This can also be used to indicate disbelief. The meaning of the *huh* used that way is "Say it again. I couldn't have heard you correctly."

9   This commonly occurs with psychiatric patients. Since Freud, psychoanalysis has the function of providing an intent because therapists could not understand why patients talk that way by using everyday decoding strategies (Chaika 1977, 1990).

10 At Providence College, the word for this is *scoop,* as in "I scooped a great guy last night." It also seems to imply 'going home with someone one has met at a party or mixer.'

11 Throughout here I use the present tense even though most of the craze for CB is over. However, there still remain some CBers. And, the reasons for the CB jargon taking the form it did are still current.

Exercises

1. Record a short, but not intimate, conversation in a setting of your choice and count all of the repetitions in it. Did they enhance the conversation or make it boring; what seemed to be the purpose of the repetitions? Warn the speakers that their words are being recorded.

2. Poll friends of different religions about when it is all right to talk in church and when it is not and under what conditions one calls out responses. How much variability do you find? Try to explain the varying practices in accordance with religious beliefs.

3. Observe two or more people in conversation. What evidence do you see for synchrony between them?

4. Using evidence from dinner-table conversation, explain whether your family belongs to a high or low involvement culture. Alternatively, determine the kinds of culture friends belong to by observing their behavior during a meal or a visit.

5. Give the first part of utterance pairs to friends or family and record the responses. Do your results conform to those presented in this chapter? Can you find a type of pair not mentioned here?

6. Collect several instances of repair and explain how they work. Do these verify the regulatory nature of repair and/or the ways that repair helps maintain the status quo?

7. Try to tell the same story in two different frames. What is the effect of the frame on how the story is perceived? Alternatively, collect an example of misinterpretation because the hearer misperceived the speaker's intent.

8. Collect examples of speech acts as opposed to communicative speech amongst your friends or family. How can you distinguish between the two?

9. Do you participate in a jargon? If so, describe it and show how it fulfills its purpose.

References

Austin, J. L. (1962). *How to do Things with Words* (2nd ed.). (J. O. Urmson & M. Sbisá, Eds.) . Cambridge, MA: Harvard University Press.

Basso, K. H. (1989). *Portraits of "The Whiteman": Linguistic Play and Cultural Symbols among the Western Apache.* Cambridge, England: Cambridge University Press.

Blum-Kulka, S., & House, J. (1989). Cross-cultural and situational behavior in requesting behavior. In *Cross-cultural Pragmatics: Requests and Apologies* (S. Blum-Kulka, J. House, & G. Kasper, Eds.) (pp. 123–154). Advances in Discourse Processes. Norwood, NJ: Ablex Publishing Corporation.

Brown, G., & Yule, G. (1983). *Discourse Analysis.* Cambridge Textbooks in Linguistics. New York: Cambridge University Press.

Brown, P., & Levinson, S. (1978). Universals in language usage: Politeness phenomena. In *Questions and Politeness* (E. Goody, Ed.) (pp. 56–289). New York: Cambridge University Press.

Chafe, W. (Ed.). (1980). *The Pear Stories* (Vol. III). Advances in Discourse Processes. Norwood, N.J.: Ablex Publishing Co.

Chaika, E. (1977). A linguist looks at "schizophrenic" language. *Brain and Language, 1,* 257–276.

Chaika, E. (1980). Jargons and language change. *Anthropological Linguistics, 22,* 77–96.

Chaika, E. (1982). *Language the Social Mirror, 1st ed.* Rowley, Mass: Newbury House.

Chaika, E. (1990). *Understanding Psychotic Speech: Beyond Freud and Chomsky.* Springfield, Ill.: Charles C. Thomas.

Corsaro, W. (1985). Sociological approaches to discourse analysis. In *Handbook of Discourse Analysis.* (T. A. Van Dijk, Ed.) (pp. 167–192). New York: Academic Press.

Critchley, M. (1975). *Silent Language.* London: Butterworths.

deBeaugrande, R., & Dressler, W. U. (1981). *Introduction to Text Linguistics.* New York: Longman.

Dillard, J. (1973). *Black English: Its History and Usage in the United States.* New York: Random House.

DiPietro, R. (1977). Got your ears on? *Interfaces, 7,* 1–3.

Duranti, A. & Ochs. E. (1979). Left dislocation in Italian conversation. In *Discourse and Syntax.* (T. Givon, Ed.) (377–417). New York: Academic Press.

Elgin, S. H. (1980). *The Gentle Art of Verbal Self Defense.* Englewood Cliffs, N.J.: Prentice-Hall, Inc.

Erickson, F. (1984). Rhetoric, anecdote, and rhapsody: Coherence strategies in a conversation among Black American adolescents. In *Coherence in Spoken and Written Discourse.* (D. Tannen, Ed.), (pp. 81–154). Norwood, N.J.: Ablex Publishing Corp.

Erickson, F., & Shultz, J. (1982). *The Counselor as Gatekeeper: Social Interaction in Interviews.* New York: Academic Press.

Ervin-Tripp, S. (1972). On sociolinguistic rules: Alternation and co-occurrence. In *Directions in Sociolinguistics.* (J. Gumperz and D. Hymes, Eds.) (pp. 213–250). New York: Holt, Rinehart, & Winston.

Fairclough, N. (1989). *Language and Power.* New York: Longman.

Frake, C. O. (1964). How to ask for a drink in Subanum. *American Anthropologist, 66,* 127–132.

Garfinkel, H. (1972) Remarks on ethnomethodology. In *Directions in Sociolinguistics: the Ethnography of Communication.* (D. Hymes and J. Gumperz, Eds.) (pp. 301–324). New York: Holt, Rinehart, and Winston.

Giles, H., Taylor, D., & Bourhis. R. (1973). Towards a theory of interpersonal accommodations through language: Some Canadian data. *Language in Society, 2,* 177–223.

Godard, D. (1977). Same setting, different norms: Phone call beginnings in France and the United States. *Language in Society, 6,* 209–220.

Goffman, E. (1955). On face work. *Psychiatry, 18,* 213–231.

Goffman, E. (1974). *Frame Analysis: An Essay on the Organization of Experience.* Cambridge, Mass: Harvard University Press.

Goody, E. N. (1978). *Questions and Politeness.* New York: Cambridge University Press.

Gordon, D.; & Lakoff, G. (1975). Conversational postulates. In *Speech Acts.* Syntax and Semantics. (Vol. 3, pp. 83–106). (P. Cole & J. L. Morgan, Eds.) New York: Academic Press.

Grice, H. P. (1975). Logic and conversation. In *Speech Acts.* Syntax and Semantics. (P. Cole & J. L. Morgan, Eds.) (Vol. 3, pp. 41–48). New York: Academic Press.

Gumperz, J. (1982). *Discourse Strategies.* New York: Cambridge University Press.

Heath, S. (1983). *Ways with Words*. New York: Cambridge University Press.

House, J. (1989). Politeness in English and German: The functions of *please* and *bitte*. In *Cross-Cultural Pragmatics: Requests and Apologies*. (S. Blum-Kulka, J. House, & G. Kasper, Eds.) (pp. 96–122). Norwood, NJ: Ablex Publishing Corporation.

Hymes, D. (1972). Models of the interaction of language and social life. In *Directions in Sociolinguistics: The Ethnography of Communication* (J. A. Gumperz, & D. Hymes, Eds) (pp. 35–71). New York: Holt, Rinehart, and Winston.

Hymes, D. (1974). Ways of speaking. In *Explorations in the Ethnography of Speaking*. (R. Bauman & J. Sherzer, Eds.) (pp. 433–451). New York: Cambridge University Press.

Knapp, M., Hopper, R., & Bell, R. A. (1984). Compliments: A descriptive taxonomy. *Journal of Communication*, pp. 12–31.

Labov, W., & Fanshel, D. (1977). *Therapeutic Discourse*. New York: Academic Press.

Lehrer, A. (1983). *The Semantics of Wine Tasting*. Bloomington: Indiana University Press.

Maltz, D. (1985). The significance of noise in Pentecostal worship. In *Perspectives on Silence* (D. Tannen, & M. Saville-Troike, Eds.) (pp. 113–127). Norwood, N.J.: Ablex Publishing Corporation.

Milroy, L. (1980). *Language and Social Networks*. Baltimore: University Park Press.

Philips, S. U. (1976). Some sources of cultural variability in the regulation of talk. *Language in Society*, *5*, 81–95.

Rommetveit, R. (1971). Words, contexts, and verbal message transmission. In *Social Contexts of Messages* (E. A. Carswell & R. Rommetveit, Eds.) (pp. 13–26). New York: Academic Press.

Sacks, H. (1964–72). *Lecture notes*. Mimeo.

Sacks, H. (1970). *Discourse analysis*. Mimeo.

Schegloff, E. A. (1968). Sequencing in conversational openings. *American Anthropologist, 70*, 1075–1095.

Schegloff, E. A., Jefferson, G., & Sacks, H. (1977). The preference for self-correction in the organization of repair in conversation. *Language, 53*, 361–382.

Schenkein, J. (Ed.). (1978). *Studies in the Organization of Conversation*. New York: Academic Press.

Scollon, R., & Scollon, S. B. K. (1981). *Narrative Literacy and Face in Interethnic Communication*. Norwood, N.J.: Ablex.

Searle, J. R. (1969). *Speech Acts: an Essay in the Philosophy of Language.* New Rochelle: Cambridge University Press.

Searle, J. (1975). Indirect speech acts. In *Speech Acts.* Syntax and Semantics. (Vol. 3). (P. Cole & J. Morgan, Eds.). New York: Academic Press.

Stubbs, M. (1983). *Discourse Analysis: The Sociolinguistic Analysis of Natural Language.* Chicago: University of Chicago.

Tannen, D. (1979a). What's in a frame? Surface evidence for underlying expectations. In *New Directions in Discourse Processing.* (R. Freedle, Ed.) (pp. 137–196). Norwood, N.J.: Ablex Publishing.

Tannen, D. (1979b.) When is an overlap not an interruption: one component of conversational style? Paper presented at the first Delaware Symposium on Language Studies. Newark, Delaware. October 18, 1979.

Tannen, D. (1981). Indirection in discourse: Ethnicity as conversational style. *Discourse Processes, 4,* 221–238.

Tannen, D. (1982). The oral/literate continuum in discourse. In *Spoken and Written Language: Exploring Orality and Literacy.* (D. Tannen, Ed.) (pp. 1–16). Norwood, N.J.: Ablex Publishing.

Tannen, D.(1984). *Conversational Style: Analyzing Talk Among Friends.* Norwood, N.J.: Ablex Publishing Corporation.

Tannen, D. (1989). *Talking voices: Repetition, Dialogue, and Imagery in Conversational Discourse.* Studies in Interactional Sociolinguistics 6. New York: Cambridge University Press.

Taylor, D. (1976). Linguistic change and linguistic challenge: Preserving a native language in a foreign environment: German in Bethlehem, Pennsylvania in the mid-1700's and Chicago, Illinois in the mid-1900's. In *Third LACUS Forum.* (R. DiPietro & E. Blansett, Eds.). Columbia, S.C.: Hornbeam Press.

Tiersma, P. (1993). Linguistic issues in the law. *Language, 69,* 113–137.

VanDijk, T. (1977). *Text and Context.* New York: Longman.

Chapter 6

Orality and Literacy

A ll societies grade members on verbal skills, either oral or written. Literate societies prefer displays of book learning, although there is a continuum from oral to literate activities even in literate societies. It has been difficult to prove that being literate creates new mental skills, although oral cultures seem to stress thematic thinking more than literate ones do. Uneducated people may display very sharp logic and often show greater knowledge of vocabulary and history than the educated would assume they have. People use verbal displays as a way to boost their egos and to relieve tensions safely in a community. The topics of verbal displays reveal social attitudes and underscore social conditions under which participants live.

VERBAL SKILL

Almost every social group grants high status to members with good verbal skills, but different social groups value different skills. In middle-class American culture, the skills most respected are those associated with formal schooling: reading books designated as texts and reproducing part or all of their contents on paper. This is known as "passing tests." A good deal of adult rank depends upon the skill with which this was done in childhood and how long into adulthood test passing was carried on. Cultures which value this are **literate**. But there are more kinds of verbal activity than book learning. So much do we forget this fact that when we come into contact with people to whom book learning is not important, we assume that they are nonverbal. They, too, have their tests, but these are spoken. Such cultures are considered to be **oral**.

Nonliterates and those to whom written skill is not important engage in oral dueling of all sorts. Ong (1982, pp. 43–44) takes this to mean that oral cultures are **agonistic**, that is that much of their speech is combative and strains for effect. He feels this is an inevitable characteristic of oral societies, and he certainly implies that this is a limitation. Here, I will develop the thesis that people lacking formal education and formal high status use such oral displays as a way of gaining status. Wit, repartee, and drollness are all admired by the formally educated, but for them, a person's ultimate status is not determined by oral performance but by bookish or business skills, both of which demand their own kind of competitiveness, and both of which are relatively recent arenas.

Literacy

For most of human existence, language and the knowledge based upon it resided only in the human brain. Writing systems, even primitive ones, have been in existence for only about 5000 years. See Gelb, 1963, for chronology of writing. Those of us raised in a largely literate world assume that writing is language. Indeed, it is difficult for us to think of language as being anything but what is written. For instance, most of us think of ourselves as pronouncing letters, not sounds. We even justify our pronunciation on the basis of letters in the spelled version of a word. Midwesterners visiting Eastern New England, complain that the natives don't pronounce /r/'s resulting in *heart* and *hot* being homonyms. They base this judgment on the standard spelling. Of course, the Midwesterners don't realize that they may not distinguish between certain "letters" themselves, as when they make homonyms of *walk* and *wok*. In other words, for the literate or for those familiar with literacy, true language is thought to be writing. For those with no writing systems, and that includes most of the human beings who ever lived, and most of the time that Homo Sapiens has lived, language is what is in the mind.

In the modern world, a world in which increasingly everyone must be able to handle reading and writing, literacy has become not only an educational concern, but a political one as well. Those who are illiterate are severely handicapped. And, if these illiterates disproportionately belong to certain ethnic and racial groups, many suspect deliberate neglect of those groups. Since we can certainly find that those are the people who have historically been shortchanged by those in power, it is easy to blame their lack of success on the government and schools. In all fairness to politicians and teachers, however, we should remember that literacy is not inborn in humans the way spoken language is. Children don't have to be taught to speak, but they do have to be taught to read and write. Although children denied language through normal channels will create a language on their own, they will not create an **orthography** writing system in the absence of written input.

Indeed, we could make quite a case for saying literacy is unnatural, an accident of human history. We find many middle-class people from very literary environments who have difficulty learning to read. Some, severe dyslexics, may even be pathologically so. Thus, it is not only the economically disadvantaged who have such problems, although the burden may be heavier on them than on dyslexics from other groups.[1] It has only been comparatively recently that we have begun to learn the dynamics of culture on successful literacy.

ORAL AND LITERATE CULTURES

In the 1960s it was assumed that all we had to do to create a literate society was read to little kids, to have books lying around the house, and have adults be seen reading. For those children who didn't come from such homes, we assumed that Head Start programs and the like would be adequate substitutes, as would remedial reading classes. In those halcyon days, we thought money spent on "programs" was the answer.

Then came the first disquieting observation: There are literate and oral cultures, and, some think, these produce children with different kinds of minds, different ways of interacting with the world. This was not to say that those from oral cultures were stupid or deficient in any way. In fact, the entire *oeuvre* of scholars like Labov and Abrahams showed that those from oral cultures are as intelligent and logical as those from literate ones. What is different is what they are intelligent about.

Ong (1982, pp. 44–45) thinks that oral cultures foster "a celebration of physical behavior" and that they are far more violent than literate cultures are, an arguable premise at best. Professor Robert DiPietro has rightly pointed out to me that American culture hardly bears out such a conclusion, and, he added that he was not convinced that the illiterates in literate societies are necessarily more violent than others. I concur.

In general, Ong's explanations of the differences between oral and literate cultures depend on *post hoc* analyses, not from a consideration of the functions of oral language in nonliterate cultures. For instance, he says that the reason for oral descriptions of violence is that gore is "less revulsive" when spoken than when read. Actually, gore might well be more revulsive when described orally, complete with intonation and verbal sound effects. The printed word is not so immediately graphic. Whenever we try to construe the meaning of any social act, we must first consider its function in society, and then see how it fits its purpose.

Scholars have long known that nonliterates are often capable of prodigious feats of memory, feats we literates are frequently incapable of. Poetry seems to have as its origin the need for remembering in the absence of writing. If one encodes thoughts in rhyming words, so long as one retrieves one member of the pair, the other is likely to come. If one encodes using a strong repeated beat and/or latches the words to a tune or chant, then one need only recall the beat or the tune to start remembering. If one encodes thoughts in highly unusual language, metaphor, simile, and metonymy, one is more likely to recall the image. Keyser (1976) observed that most poems say quite ordinary things, but do so in extraordinary language. Poetry once served the function of record-keeping: genealogies to inspire great deeds, information on weaponry, food finding and/or growing, and even records of attacks and defeats so that warriors could be whipped into enough frenzy to fight victoriously. This is the stuff of *The Iliad, Beowulf,* and even parts of the Bible.[2] Ong (pp. 38-39) sees the necessity for such devices as leading to redundancy in thought. In contrast, he finds literate thinking sparse and analytic as a consequence that one need not fill up one's mind with what can be looked up in a book.

The Oral and the Literate Mind

Because they perceive regular differences between oral and literate cultures, some scholars theorize that there are differences between oral and literate minds. With much justice, Ong (1982), for instance, declares that literacy restructures consciousness (pp. 78–108). Because writing transfers speech to the visual plane, Ong maintains that the literate are capable of more abstraction and distancing. Thinking becomes less bound to a specific or personal context. He points out that the Sumerians developed a code of law almost as soon as they developed writing, a feat not feasible in the absence of writing. Even our concept of time, our habit of dating from specific years, is a matter of literacy (p. 98). Our seeing history as the accumulation of points in time is a literate habit (p. 98). And, I am certain, so are the kinds of categorizing which are dependent on outlining, diagramming and other visual displays of language. One would expect that the kinds of accumulated fact learning typified in game shows like *Jeopardy* and board games like *Scrabble*—or in "objective" tests—are not found in oral cultures. Bits of information not related to themes is not a concern of such cultures.

The Scollons (1981) maintain that oral cultures rely on thematic abstraction both for memory and for making sense out of the world. They show that the Athabaskans abstract themes from what they observe and hear (pp. 159–162). Knowledge is organized around central themes. Consequently, narratives are important in socializing children. The Scollons claim that in this culture, "Human variability is organized around typifications and the typifications further are taken as norms for behavior" (p. 159). Those from literate societies have to be taught to abstract themes from what they read. They have to learn such abstraction in formal lessons in school, but those from oral ones learn to do this on their own as a vital part of their socialization.

Scribner and Cole (1981) investigated literacy among the Vai in West Africa. The Vai are exposed not to one, but to three kinds of literacy: English, via formal schooling; Arabic, taught by the local Imam who teaches children to chant the *Qur'an* each morning at daybreak (p. 30); and Vai script which had been developed by the Vai themselves in the nineteenth century. Scribner and Cole tested both literate and nonliterate Vai with a battery of tests designed specifically to see if does have an effect on the mind. They came up negative on almost all counts:

> On no task—logic, abstraction, memory, communication—did we find all nonliterates performing at lower levels than all literates...We can and do claim that literacy promotes skills ... but we cannot and do not claim that literacy is a necessary and sufficient condition for any skills we assessed. (p. 251)

Any advantage literacy conferred was highly specific, being related to given tasks associated with that script. Literacy didn't even make individuals more objective about parsing sentences grammatically (p. 157). Nor did literacy lead to superior communication skills (p. 212). Each kind of literacy was virtually exclusive of the others (p. 107). This last suggests to me that there is no generalized literacy effect. Being literate in Vai script confers no educational or vocational advantage. Nor does it "...open doors to vicarious experience, new bodies of knowledge, or thinking about major life problems" (p.238).

Scribner and Cole's conclusions directly contradict those like Ong who assume that literacy restructures the mind. More recently, Scinto (1986) has objected to their conclusions on two grounds. First, Scribner and Cole based their conclusions on a separation of literacy and schooling practices themselves. Scinto (p. 94) points out that the use of a written language norm and the process of schooling are interfunctional. One is learned in the context of the other, and both together determine how literacy will be used. Moreover, Scinto (p. 96) points out that literacy is marked by **decontextualization**. That is, one learns to handle language apart from the physical context one finds oneself in. This is a sharp difference from most oral communication which depends on the social and physical context of utterance for its meaning and force. This decontextualization involves learning different means of expression from those used in oral production, and this learning is effected in school and by literacy together. Scinto (p. 96) avers:

Schooled discourse values knowledge insofar as it is objective and depersonalized, that is, knowledge or rules of inquiry into things which are divorced from immediate perceptual experience...Schooling as an institution honors rational and logical knowledge that in its most extreme form is what we have come to call science.

This does not mean that nonliterates are not as capable of thought or reasoning as literates. Indeed, we shall present much evidence that it is entirely possible to be logical in an oral culture.

The Oral/Literacy Continuum

Moreover, there is no sharp break between oral and literate language. Rather, there is a continuum. There are oral productions which are very "literary" in character. These range from papers given at scholarly meetings, to sermons, to political speeches, to inaugurals, eulogies, and valedictorian speeches. These are more literary than oral because they use the grammatical devices of writing: a great many subordinate clauses, long sentences, words usually only seen in print, and a tightly organized structure, complete with topic sentences and formal summations. Then, too, there is writing which is oral in structure: humorous pieces, novels like *Catcher in the Rye* and *Finnegan's Wake*, and informal notes or lists. Tannen (1982) shows that telling someone to "get to the point" is an extension of requirements of writing (p. 3). It also seems that much of what has been deemed oral vs. literate may really be a matter of focus (Scollon, R. and S. Scollon 1984). If the focus is on the social interaction itself, oral strategies are more likely. If it is on content, then literate ones are. Moreover, all oral cultures are not alike, nor are all literate ones. Tannen demonstrates this in her comparisons of Greek and American narratives. The Greeks use what Ong and others have regarded as "oral" strategies, such as insisting on a moral in a movie. (Tannen 1980.)

Interaction, Depersonalized Knowledge and Literacy Skills

It may be, however, that those from cultures which focus on interaction rather than depersonalized knowledge have difficulty making a transition to what schools teach. Gumperz, Kaltman, and O'Connor (1984) show that an ethnic Black college student transferred his oral narratives to his written themes with little use of literary techniques. Similarly, in the same volume, Michaels and Collins show that the African American children they studied used an **associating** style (p. 224) in Show and Tell rather than a **topic-centered** one as did the white children in the class. Apparently, the African American children they studied were not from middle-class homes. It is unfortunate that these authors—and so many other researchers—use African American non-middle-class children for their examples as they then confound issues of race, ethnicity and social class. Middle-class African American children from literate homes behave like white children from the same kinds of homes.

The associating style of these African American children is characterized by using seemingly unrelated anecdotes to tell their story, using prosody instead of actual words to show connections (p. 234). Of course, prosody is denied to writers, but it is "normal" in speech. One thing a literate person has to do is to learn to use actual words and grammatical forms to do what one does with voice in speech.

At first blush, it appeared that these children were flitting from topic to topic (p. 224), but careful analysis showed that there was an implicit theme of the story which one had to deduce. White children in the class subordinated all of their sentences to an overtly announced topic and used actual words as connectors (pp. 236-238)

Shirley Brice Heath (1983) in a monumental study of African American and white rural families in the Piedmont of the Carolinas, investigated both the ways that children learned how to use language in their social group, and how they used literacy. Like Scribner and Cole, she found no sharp division between oral and literate traditions. The two function together as "part of the total pattern of communication..." For both groups, as for the Vai, the residents turn from spoken to written uses of language...as the occasion demands..." (p. 230). One surprise in this study is that African American children actually begin to read before entering school (pp. 192–194). Despite this, they do poorly once in school. The reason they fail is that their socialization with regard to language use differs so drastically from what schools require. At home, they are allowed to break into adult conversations (p. 167); they are not socialized to answer factual questions directly, nor to be still when others are talking. Also, they don't come from a culture in which activities occur at a special time or place. Even their church services are open-ended, ending when they end, so to speak. Also, in their communities, reading is done aloud as a performance, not silently. Even so in school, the African American children seek out books, reading them through again and again (p. 295).

White rural children are socialized to answer factual questions and to be silent until called upon. Although they do well at the outset, they, too, fail as time goes on. It is their socialization as well that causes this. At home, great store is set on their learning facts and accepting what they are told. Life is explained in proverbs and other pat sayings. Creativity is often considered lying. In their narrative performances, these children show no evaluation of what they have related, no indication of emotional involvement, and no causal links between events (p. 304). Although they seem to start out more in tune with the schools, they fall behind once creativity and problem solving become more highly valued by teachers.

Logical Argumentation in an Oral Culture

Labov, Cohen, Robins, and Lewis (1968) give a very good example of logical argumentation in a speaker of a nonstandard dialect, one from a clearly oral culture. At the time of their investigation, the Harlem street gangs were heavily involved in the Muslim religion. The same boys who were virtually illiterate in regular schools were studying history, science, and reading in the Muslim schools. They often took oral tests, which was called "being put on the square" or displaying "heavy knowledge": although that terminololgy may not have been used in other Black communities. The ability to win arguments by quickness, facts, and logic is at a premium.

Labov et al often took gang members on trips. Since one tenet of the Muslim religion is vegetarianism, this posed a problem in providing lunches. Once, unthinkingly, Labov and his team prepared tomato sandwiches with mayonnaise. Since mayonnaise has eggs in it, several boys objected, saying, in effect, eggs are from chickens, chickens are meat, so eggs are meat. To this, one boy, Quahab, responded, using the dramatic intonation of Black preaching style. This includes a chanting, as well as an elongating of the final word of a sentence, often the one crucial to the argument. The hairsplitting arguments are worthy of theologians, even those who write their thoughts for others to read.

> No, bro', we din't eat no meat. You might as well say we drunk
> it because it was in a liquid fo-orm. (Labov et al, 1968, p. 143)

In other words, the injunction is against eating meat, not drinking it. Eggs are liquid. One drinks liquid, so it's all right to consume eggs. To hammer home his point, Quahab continued,

1. Dig it, it ain't even in existence yet, dig that. It ain't even in existence yet. If didn't come to be a chicken yet. You can detect it with a physical eye, you can detect that. (p. 143)

VERBAL PLAY

Many researchers into African American speech, including Labov, have made a very strong case for the verbal agility of its speakers. Very little research has been done on such skills among whites, and the little that has been done (Schatzman and Strauss 1972; Bernstein 1971; Bereiter and Engelmann 1966) has compared lower and working class whites with the middle-class. Since such studies use the middle-class as their norms, naturally the lower class whites have come out badly. In contrast, African American oral activities have been studied for their own sake, without measuring them against the yardstick of middle-class skills. The thrust of the literature, therefore, has clearly been that African Americans are superior to comparable whites in oral ability, and, because there is so little research into white speech activities and so much on Black, of necessity this text will seem to be perpetrating the same misconception. Both whites and blacks with little formal education argue about weighty matters like politics, religion, and life in general as well as engage in verbal play. Different ethnic groups may engage in different kinds of verbal performance, but skillful verbal jousting exists for them in one form or another. Verbal play may consist of any or all of the following:

▶being quick on the uptake
▶verbal thrusting such as joking insults
▶making a joke out of something another has just said
▶conning others by telling outrageous lies with a straight face
▶dueling verbally in boasting contests, riddles
      (Dundes, Leach and Ozkok 1972)

▶joketelling
▶song writing
▶storytelling
▶making up rhymes of various kinds

Certainly, the educated do the same things, but among them such activities appear to be more a matter of individual taste than of social obligation.

Punning as Play

The following dialogues show a punning game very prevalent among working class white males in Rhode Island. A student of mine, Jean

CHAPTER 6

Shields, collected the examples in 1 below from Len, an unskilled kitchen worker in a cafeteria. I collected the samples in 2 from three White males with education ranging from eighth grade to high school. Their occupations were carpenter, carpenter's assistant, and delivery truck driver. Len, an urban dweller, is ethnically Irish, and those in 4, from rural New England villages, were all descendants of the original English settlers. For both groups, the oral sparring is typical unplanned speech behavior.

1. *Jean*: I have a date tonight.
   Len: Last night I had a date with a fig.

   (a day later)
   Jean: I used your line about a date with a fig on my linguistics test.
   Len: Oh, lines. I've got a lot of 'em. (points to his face).

   (during inconsequential chatting about Len's family:
   Jean: What's the difference between your coat and his?
   Len: Oh, well, the blue jacket means he has big hours and the tan ones mean we got little hours.
   Jean: What are little and big hours?
   Len: Little hours are four hours a day, and bigger ones are eight hours.
   Jean: I gotta go—you're a peach.
   Len: I may be a peach on the outside, but I'm a nut on the inside.

2. *Pete*: [to me] You still studying schizophrenia?
   Charley: Schizophrenia? That's in the genes, isn't it?
   Ed: I got something in my jeans once.
   Pete: Pig ripped my jeans last night.
   Dave: The pig in the field or the pig you was out with last night.
   [continues for two hours nonstop]

Len is so intent on making his every utterance colorful that he uses *big* and *little* to describe the number of hours men work rather than *more* and *less*. This works because in some contexts *big* and *little* mean *more* and *less*, as in "give me more cake" when it means 'give me a bigger piece of cake.' Such unusual usages, so long as they fit the topic at hand, are the heart of creative language use.

The game in 1 and 2 consists of making a pun out of another person's statement. For the English if one can also include an insult to the conversationalist whose words are being punned, that is even better. The resulting conversations are like those familiar to viewers of American sitcoms like *Roseanne* and *The Golden Girls*. The difference is that these speakers do not have anyone writing their material. The speakers in 2 are old friends who hunt, snowmobile, and play pool together regularly. During their weekly pool games, the bantering never ceases, and no one is immune. There is never apology or hurt feelings. The activity is understood for the game it is. Unlike the verbal sparring of African Americans described in the next section, there is never overt judgment on any statement, beyond general laughter, although some members of the groups are acknowledged to be more skillful talkers than others. It is interesting to note that on shows featuring African Americans like *In Living Color* when someone makes a telling pun or other remark, the audience gives a "Whoo-ooo" which acts as an evaluation such as, "He zinged you" whereas in other sitcoms, laughter is the usual response. This parallels the responses given to such activities in both cultures.

In the Appalachian mountains there is a tradition of song-making among descendants of the original Scots-Irish and English settlers. Any devotee of American folk music is familiar with one version of this song-making, the talking blues. Black rap songs may have been influenced by this tradition. The Talking Blues are spoken, but with a strong rhythm, usually accompanied by a guitar or banjo. The Appalachians write songs about many topics: love, death, hard times. If asked about an event such as a mining disaster, an Appalachian might answer, "I've written a song about that." and proceed to sing it. One can see such a sequence in the documentary *Harlan County, U.S.A.* Those not "into" that kind of music often find it tuneless at first, more of a chant than a song. Both the Appalachian song-making and Talking Blues have always reminded me of the epic poetry chanted by the minstrels of early Europe. Often accompanied by a stringed instrument, this poetry told of the history of the people, its hard times and good times.

In different parts of the country and in different ethnic groups, undoubtedly many other kinds of verbal activities can be found. The situations that call them forth, however, may differ from group to group.

The Original Rap

Although it has largely been ignored in whites, the gaming aspect of speech and the concern with rhetoric has been well studied in African

American culture. Claudia Mitchell-Kernan (1972) gives an example of a young man **rapping** to her. Note that this original usage of the term *rapping* differs considerably from that activity today. Sitting on a park bench, she was approached by three young men, one of whom started a conversation.

3. M: Mama you sho is fine.
   M-K: That ain' no way to talk to your mother.

The conversation continued. Mitchell-Kernan told the man what she was doing. He immediately adjusted his style.

M: Baby, you a real scholar. I can tell you want to learn. Now if
   you'll just cooperate a li'l bit, I'll show you what a good
   teacher I am. But first, we got to get into my area of
   expertise.
M-K:I may be wrong , but seems to me we already in your area
   of expertise.
[general laughter]
M: You ain' so bad yourself, girl. I ain't heard you stutter yet.
   You a li'l fixated on your subject though. I want to help a
   sweet thang like you all I can. I figure all that book learnin'
   you got must mean you been neglecting other areas of your
   education.
2nd.Man: Talk dat talk. (gloss: ole)
M-K: Why don't you let me point out where I can best use your
   help.
M: Are you sure you in the best position to know?
[laughter]
   I'ma leave you alone, girl. Ask me what you want to know.
   Tempus fugit, baby.
[more laughter]
         (pp. 170-171)

This man used the grammar and words of what is often termed BE, Black English, which is spoken at least sometimes by African Americans, ethnic blacks, regardless of their education and social class. Both Mitchell-Kernan, a respected scholar and the man in the park, apparently uneducated, use recognizable features of BE. There are middle-class blacks who have the values and live the lives of the middle-class, but who also retain features of African American culture. When we speak of BE we can include those who are bidialectal, speaking both the middle-class speech of the region in which they live, and, at other times, speaking BE. Although some people rank BE as being nonstandard, it actually is simply an ethnic variety of speech. Its origins and history are quite different from those of other dialects. (See Chapter 8).

The young man's rap to Mitchell-Kernan is a typical ethnic black activity between men and women. Even though he probably has not received much formal education, he uses the jargon of scholarship: *expertise, fixated*, and the Latin *tempus fugit*. Mitchell-Kernan herself did not present M's credentials. However, having been raised in a mixed African American and white lower and working class neighborhood, and having taught such students both in public school and an Upward Bound program, I can vouch that even virtual illiterates often have amazingly erudite vocabularies, as well as a facility with words that puts many a scholar to shame. Typically those in the lower classes are more familiar with upper class speech than the upper classes are with the lower. Actually, it makes very little difference whether or not M is educated. Mitchell-Kernan's aim was to show the characteristic black ethnic skill with language. It is not likely that M realized that he was going to meet a female scholar while strolling through the park that day. His innuendos based upon scholarly speech had to be made up on the spot. Mitchell-Kernan comments

> By his code selection...the speaker indicates that he is parodying a *tête a tête* and not attempting to engage the speaker in anything other than conversation.

She apparently means that despite the sexual double meanings, M's display is actually a verbal one and is not necessarily intended as a real invitation. Notice that once the young man has demonstrated his virtuosity, it is he who ends it.

In the encounter just presented, once the young man finds out that Mitchell-Kernan is a scholar, he adjusts his rap toward scholarly language. The adjustment is significant. For successful rapping, it is not enough merely to make innuendos; they must be made in language appropriate to the person being spoken to. Like the dialogues in 1 and 2 above the rapper takes what the other conversationalist says and builds on it.

M does this, for instance, by offering to be Mitchell-Kernan's teacher. The "other areas of your education" imply sexual ones, especially since she is a "sweet thang." When the man says, "I ain't heard you stutter yet," he is complimenting Mitchell-Kernan's quick comebacks. The "talk dat talk" from M's friend is an African American congratulatory comment when a speaker uses language both colorful and appropriate to the social context. That the juxtaposition of scholarly and street language is deliberate and intended for humor is shown by both that comment and the laughter at "*Tempus fugit*, baby."

The term *rapping* originally indicated such displays of verbal skill, often but not always entailing the use of ordinary language in such a way that it took on a sexual double meaning, a use we saw also above with white rural males. Although the term *rap* could also be used for rapid witty exchanges of other kinds, today it is most associated with rap songs, which are also displays of verbal skill.

SPEECH ACTIVITIES AND SOCIAL PRESSURES

Rap songs are, of course, the most prominent African American verbal activity today. However, they actually derive from a long tradition in the African American community, one well worth examining. Indeed, one cannot truly understand rap without understanding where it comes from and what social conditions produced its forebears and now rap itself.

M's quick allusions to sex, above, are seen in other ghetto speech activities as well. Polite fictions about sex are stripped away again and again in black oral performances. The pinnacle of these performances occurred in *toasts*[3], although they are rarely if ever recited today. These were poems recited on street corners and in bars. The name *toast* in and of itself is a parody of the polite and laudatory practise of toasting at weddings, testimonials and the like.

The toasts were, actually, epic poems. Admittedly, most people would not think of epic poetry when they first hear black toasts. The ubiquitous profanity and taboo subjects so shock middle-class listeners that most cannot appreciate the skill it took to compose them. Although they now belong to the realm of esoterica, examining toasts is a valuable lesson in the ways language activities mirror social realities and fulfill the need for ego satisfaction. The toasts—and other oral displays—are not braked by any coyness in language or topic. In fact, one suspects that taboos are deliberately woven throughout. Although they offend sensibilities, profanity and taboo subjects are an integral part of any sociology of language as they reflect social conditions and attitudes. This is true for all people, not just African Americans. We are using that group for our examples, because their productions have been well collected, African Americans have raised speech performances to a high art, and, for the young, their speech and music have become the ones to copy today. Because the message of the songs is as important as the form of the music itself, its influence on all of American society is considerable.

The original toasts are actually oral epics like *The Iliad* or *Beowulf:* long poems, originally meant to be spoken, that recount of magnificent deeds of a hero. The hero is a model epitomizing the way men are supposed to be. The epic not only entertains and thrills, but teaches. Examining epic poems, then, reveals cultural attitudes.

The hero of the toasts is often a pimp or lawbreaker. He is just about always a misogynist. Even if he is not, he is overtly antisentimental and tough. Gambling, drinking, procuring, prostitution, and the treachery of women are common themes. These were the facts of life to the anonymous composers of *The Fall, The Signifying Monkey, The Sinking of the Titanic,* and other tales of the Black folkheroes Shine and Stagolee. The attitudes found in the toasts presented below have not changed very much, as an examination of the lyrics of current rap songs show.

Epic poetry sets its scenes in war. There heroes can exhibit the traits that society expects of its men. The battlegrounds of the Black epics are the slums of the large cities, as in these opening lines from one version of *The Fall:*

4. It was Saturday night, the jungle was bright
    As the game stalked their prey;
    And the cold was crime on the neon line
    Where crime begun, where daughter fought son
    And your mom lied awoke, with her heart almost broke
    As they loaded that train to hell
    Where blood was shed for the sake of some bread
    And winos were rolled for their port.

    Where the addicts prowl, where the tiger growl
    And search for their lethal blow,
    Where the winos crump for that can heat rump
    You'll find their graves in the snow;
    Where girls of vice sell love for a price
    And even the law's corrup'
    But keep on tryin' as you go down cryin'
    Say man it's a bitters cup.
    (quoted in Labov et al. 1968. p. 56)

This stark and graphic opener leads into a tale of a pimp who exploited a whore shamelessly, ending with his arrest:

5. Now as I sit in my 6 by 6 cell in the county jail
    Watchin' the sun rise in the east,
    The morning chills give slumber to the slumbering beast

    Farewell to the nights, and the neon lights,
    Farewell to one and all
    Farewell to the game, may it still be the same
    When I finish doing this fall.
            (p. 58)

In "Honky Tonk Bud," the hero is convicted of a narcotics charge. Before sentence is passed, he tells the judge:

6. He said, "I'm not cryin' 'cause the agen was lyin'
    And left you all with a notion
    That I was a big deal in the narcotics fiel'
    I hope the fag cops a promotion.
    It's all the same; it's all in the game.
    I dug when I sat down to play.
    That you take all odds, deal all low cards.
    It's the dues the dope fiend must pay.
            (p. 58)

"The game" is the way things are. Labov et al point out that the toasts do not claim that the game pays off in any way. The satisfaction comes from playing with dignity, and, according to the rules. The rules dictate that one never complains about what happens. Justice is not expected, nor is injustice bemoaned. Heroism consists of great courage as it does in the middle-class world, but, in the toasts, the courage consists partly of being willing to face the penalties of crime.

Certainly, these are poems of despair. Achilles had a battlefield with potential honor. Beowulf could become a bonafide hero by killing Grendel. These were heroes to their entire people. African Americans in the slums often saw no way to become the kinds of heroes general American society set up[4], at least not before the 1960's and the first glimmerings of the Civil Rights movement. This does not mean all black males sought their honor in playing the game of drugs and pimps. Most Blacks did not and do not. But the message was the same to all: "You keep on tryin' as you go down cryin'. You take all odds" and you don't complain.

The toasts taught other lessons as well. Clearly, throughout, no sympathy is to be shown, no self-pity, no pity for others. This is well-illustrated in *The Sinking of the Titanic* when Shine, the hero, starts swimming across the Atlantic away from the disaster. He encounters several doomed passengers who plead with him to save them. Despite the rewards they promise, he rebuffs them all harshly and coldly. Finally, he meets a crying baby.

7. Shine said, "Baby, baby, please don't cry.
   All little m—s got a time to die.
   You got eight little fingers and two little thumbs
   And your black ass goes when the wagon comes."

Labov et al (1968, p. 60) compare this to Achilles' speech in the *Iliad*.

8. Ay friend thou too must die: why lamentest thou?
   Petroklos too is dead, who was better far than thou.
   See thou not also what manner of man am I might and
   goodliness?
   Yet over me too hang death and forceful fate.

However, Achilles says this to another adult, not a helpless babe. What can this mean, and why is it in the toast? Certainly, blacks love their babies as others do. Clearly, Shine shows some feeling for the baby, "Please don't cry." In fact, the baby is the only one of the doomed to whom Shine uses politeness markers. To the others he is brutal. We have ample evidence from this toast and others such as *The Fall* that pity for others is to be squelched at all costs. Many verses in *The Fall* are devoted to first establishing that the prostitute served her man fantastically well. When she becomes ill, however, he throws her out and, again, several verses recount the particular heartlessness with which he does so, such as:

8. You had your run. Now you done...
   I can't make no swag off some swayback nag.
   Whose thoroughbred days are past.
   Why I'd look damn silly puttin' a cripple filly.
   On a track that's way too fast.
             (p. 57)

My interpretation of such passages is that they are intended to underscore an important message to the urban slum dweller. It is not good in that life to have too much pity for others. In a world as harsh as that pictured in these toasts, the only way to survive is to cut off compassion. The passage from the *Iliad* had the same message for the ancient Greek youths: In war one must not be compassionate. In essence, the world of toasts is a world always at war. Just as Shine's swimming the ocean to safety is a tremendous exaggeration, so is his encounter with the baby. It is the message "be dispassionate" carried to the point of hyperbole.

African American storytelling is suffused with tales that teach people not to trust, not to pity. This theme has even been grafted onto stories originally from Africa, such as the talking animal genre like the "Bre'r Rabbit" stories. The difference is that in Africa, these stories were used to teach children to beware of antisocial creatures who disrupted friendship. In America, these were changed so that they taught instead that everyone must look out for him- or herself. Thus are the realities of society mirrored in speech activities.

The attitude toward women in the toasts goes beyond mere lack of pity. It is actively hostile. In one toast, Stagolee casually shoots women at the slightest provocation. In another, Shine makes the cruelest fun at the romantic notions of two young girls, telling them in the bluntest of terms that the sexual act itself, not love or romance, is all there is to relations between men and women.

In *The Fall*, the whore is called a "sex machine," and in an extended metaphor, is likened to a racehorse. A general bitter vindictiveness characterizes all dealings of men with women in the toasts, a vindictiveness matched by the cruel insults hurled at women in verbal games like ranking (see below) long played by black male adolescents (and now by whites as well). In movies as recent as *Boyz in the Hood*, black adolescents typically address girls as *ho, hooch,* and *bitch.* When one girl protests being called a ho, Doughboy sarcastically answers, "Sorry, bitch." Perusing the lyrics to rap songs confirms this misogynistic attitude. Labov et al. (p. 62) point out that the hostility revealed in all such verbal activity makes it especially difficult for women teachers to deal with male members of this culture.

The pimp as hero in the toasts and on the streets is another expression of this hostility. Again, the reason is perhaps to be found in social values and condition. African American culture is, after all, American. In our society, as indeed in most, men are supposed to dominate women. Until recently this has meant that men should make more money than their wives and even control, any earnings their wives bring in. During the years when the toasts were being composed, the ideal was that a man should be able to earn enough so that his wife didn't have to work. That was a particular point of pride during my growing-up years. It must be emphasized that most African Americans have been raised in families with wage-earning fathers. Still, for many years now, a much higher percentage of African Americans than other ethnic groups have come from families in which males often were not the principal wage earners. Fathers in such families were absent much or all of the time, or dependent on mothers, or both. Such men suffered greatly in self-esteem. Yet, in the grim urban neighborhoods of large Northern cities, there were no alternatives. There were few jobs for men of color, and those that were available were usually at the lowest end of the economic scale. It was easier for women to get jobs. If nothing else, they could usually find jobs as domestics. It must be emphasized that having an education or specialized training did not often improve the lot of African Americans until long after the civil rights movement of the 1960s. Even with education, it was very difficult for African Americans to be hired as anything except laborers until relatively recently. Prestigious jobs such as teaching and nursing were open to African American women long before equally prestigious ones were available for men. For some men, the way to dominate women as well as to make a great deal of money was to pimp. Pimping is the rawest exploitation of women as sex objects, of women being subservient to men. (See Chapter 10.) Pimping is a way, a very depraved way, to be sure, of achieving the American ideals of making money and dominating women.

Spike Lee in his book *By Any Means Necessary* angrily speaks of seventies' **blaxploitation** movies like *Superfly,* charging that the unflattering portrait of a drug-dealing, drug-using mysogynist "hero" was a pandering to white tastes. Actually, these movies come straight out of the tradition begun by the toasts. These were among the first movies written and directed by blacks. Like the toasts and other ghetto speech activities, they had a real "in your face" attitude towards whites. For the first time, blacks could publicly express the disdain they had for white society, and the anger they felt toward that society. They overtly blamed whites for the plight of blacks, including the fact that drug dealing and crime were the only avenues "the man" had left open for people of color. The directors of these films, like Melvin van Peebles and Gordon Parks, Jr., stressed that there were few legal options for the intelligent person of color in the United States. They also portrayed white society and government as hopelessly corrupt and hypocritical, and attacked every middle-class value. For instance, in *Superfly,* the "hero" is named "Priest" and he regularly is shown snorting cocaine from a cross he wears around his neck. Given the traditional intense commitment to religion by African Americans, this is hardly a just portrait, but justice wasn't the point. Letting whitey know how blacks felt was. Twenty years later, black directors like Spike Lee and

John Singleton, while still blaming white society, offer very different messages. These directors are antidrug, anticrime, antipimp, and proeducation. While some characters in their movies, like Doughboy, may be misogynistic, some women are also portrayed very positively by younger black directors in movies like *Jungle Fever* and *Boyz in the Hood*. Leading women in these movies are intelligent, articulate, beautiful, honorable, and capable. But American society has changed in many ways in 20 years, both in attitudes towards women and towards people of color, and this change is evidenced in movies. Unfortunately, the lyrics of rap songs, which are closer to the art of the ghetto culture, still advocate a violent lifestyle which deprecates women.

STREET POETRY AS ART

Perhaps a defense is in order of the proposition that the toasts parallel the great epics of the past. It is very easy to look at the topics of the toasts: the profanity, the lawbreaking, the nonstandard speech forms, and dismiss them as being unworthy of scholarly attention. However, examining such productions tell us a good deal about the lives of the people who composed and recited them. It tells us how they saw the world they lived in and why they held certain attitudes. Granting all that, still, why call the toasts poetry? Yes, they had heroes of a sort. They told their listeners how life should be lived: stoically, unromantically, unpityingly. This makes them epics, but does it make them poetry? Without any philosophical haggling about Art and what it is, we can see that the toasts made use of all the devices of poetry and did so skillfully. Poetry manipulates language while expressing even ordinary meanings (Keyser 1976). Often this manipulation makes us see old things in new ways.

Rhyme is a frequent, but not a necessary, feature of poetry. If it is used, in order to detect rhymes, poetry must be read in the dialect in which it was composed. For instance, in order to appreciate the skillful rhyming in the toasts, the reader must realize that the following sets of words rhyme in BE[5]: *odds, cards; cell, jail; deal, field (fiel')*. It is not easy in any dialect to find rhyming words that can fit in the rhythm of a poem as well as give the poet's desired meaning. Still hundreds of lines of toasts and other African American oral activities manage perfect rhyme, many highly clever and unusual. This feat is all the more impressive when we consider the intricate rhyming scheme of the toasts. The basic scheme of many toasts consists of a long line divided in two, with internal rhyme, as in:

She tricked with the <u>Greeks</u>, the Arabs, and <u>freaks</u>
…
She tricked with the <u>Jews</u>, Apaches, and <u>Sioux</u>
                    (from *The Fall*)

He said, "I'm not <u>cryin'</u> 'cause the agent was <u>lyin'</u>
…
That I was a big <u>deal</u> in the narcotics <u>fiel'</u>.
                    (from "Honky Tonk Bud")

These long lines form sequences with short lines that rhyme with each other as in:

…To her they were all the <u>same</u>
She tricked with the Greeks, Arabs, and freaks
And breeds I cannot <u>name</u>
She tricked with the Jews, Apaches, and Sioux.

and

He said, "I'm not cryin' 'cause the agent was lyin'
And left you all with a <u>notion</u>
That I was a big deal in the narcotics fiel'
I hope the fag cops a <u>promotion</u>."

Another very important feature of poetry is figurative language such as metaphor. The image of addicts as vicious felines is reinforced both by the metaphor of people as jungle animals (as the game stalked their prey …Where the addicts prowl…) and is tied together by the rhyme of *prowl* and *growl* and *prowl*. The metaphor of the city streets as a jungle in which game stalks prey sets the moral tone as well as the physical aura of *The Fall*. "And the cold was crime on the neon line" emphasizes the misery and ugliness of the streets. Jungles can be warm and beautiful as well as vicious and unlawful, but these lines make it clear that only the latter meanings are to be taken. Images of heat are followed by images of cold throughout *The Fall*. The winos have canned heat such as sterno, but still die in the snow. Even at the end the sun rises, but it is the morning chills that put the slumbering beast to rest. The word *slumbering* itself is one that even in Standard English (SE) is literary, even poetic. This is another instance of the supposedly unlettered being familiar with the language of books. Throughout, this toast shows skillful use of language, all bringing to us vividly, as only poetry can do, the terror and the feel of the city jungle, the contemptuous feeling for women, the bravery and resignation of the heroes.

The Blues

Erickson (1984) shows that conversations are characterized by a **rhapsody** which "stitches" utterances to each other. This is achieved partially by shared knowledge both about the world and about the rules for discourse in a given culture. Disjointed sentences are transformed into a coherent conversation by such shared knowledge. This applies as well to art forms including popular songs.

Jarrett (1984) describes the blues and demonstrates that they make sense only to an audience that knows the rules for the genre. The same audience would know if a verse could even belong to that genre. What strikes an outsider as incoherent and meaningless may be perfectly coherent to members of the culture itself. If we analyze what the audience knows and expects, we see that is what makes for cohesion (p. 156). Jarrett suggests that the **genre** by itself is a pragmatic device "which constitutes a kind of signal with which to orient an addressee (p. 160)." The blues are songs of complaint, but not just any old complaint. Both in the verse structure and in permissible topics, there are powerful constraints on the bluesman in the guise of a narrator, who is presented by the singer-composer of the song.

This narrator sings only of what one person can subjectively know (p. 167) so that the singer is, in effect, commenting on life. It is for this reason, I think, that the ordering of the Blues is not temporal. That is, there is no "first this happened, then that" (p. 163).[6] The Bluesman is not interested in nature; therefore, a song which sang of someone's going out to look at the moon would not be acceptable to the Blues (p. 161) audience. The Bluesman, however, is knowledgeable about women, booze, and preachers. The form that these comments are encased in is a stanza with the first two lines repeated and the third one as a comment which rhymes with the other two, as in

Baby you so beautiful, you know you're gonna die someday
Honey, you know you beautiful, you gonna die someday
All I want's a little loving, before you pass away.
     (p. 160)
This is highly reminiscent of the humorous wordplay of sexual invitation that we saw with Claudia Mitchell-Kernan. Notice the wheedling

logic, the implication of 'c'mon baby, what's a little sex among friends?' (my interpretation, not Jarrett's).

Jarrett shows what an audience has to know to interpret the blues correctly. He claims that Hispanic and white listeners experience such lyrics as incoherent, but African Americans, understanding their conventions, have no difficulty with them.

> 11. Oh, I wish I had me a heaven of my own Great God Amighty
>   Yeah, a heaven of my own
>   Well, I'd give all my women a long, long happy home
>   Oh, I have religion on this very day
>   Oh, I have religion on this very day.
>   But the womens and the whiskey they would not let me pray.
>   (p. 162)[7]

Jarrett explains that in order to understand such lyrics, one has to be aware that there is a long tradition of teasing preachers for being hypocrites. He points out the satire in many Blues lyrics, including this one, in that they incorporate regular calls heard in very serious church services, such as "Great God amighty," "Lord have mercy," and "amen' (p. 165). We see virtual parody of church in

> Oh, I'm gonna preach these blues and choose my seat and set
>   down
> Oh, I'm gonna preach these blues now and choose my seat and
>   set down
> When the spirit comes sisters, I want you to jump straight up
>   and down.

As with M's rap to Mitchell-Kernan, skillful *double entrendres* abound.

The currently popular rap songs are very much in the tradition of toasting and the Blues. In them, too, one might find references to preachers, as in *Yvette* in which L.L. Cool Jay raps, "The preacher says that you are God." to the promiscuous girl of the title. Rap songs also owe a great deal to the dozens and to sounding. Noticing the continuity of themes, rhyme, and beat, one of my students, Crystal Jones, examined the tradition that has produced rap songs. She calls the raps "toasts set to music," noting that they "insult all women, talk a lot about sex and drugs." Like toasts, rap songs make extensive use of internal clever and even improbable rhyme.

There appears to be no change in the kinds of insults thrown at women in rap. Often, they graphically delineate the depths of what we could term *sluthood*.[8] Ms. Jones quoting from Jackson (1974, p. 4) notes that "sexual relations in the toasts were invariably affectionless" with the female existing "as a device for exercise and articulation of female options."

Interestingly, one ghetto speech activity has for decades centered specifically on insulting women. This was and is such an important activity that it has had many names over the years. *Sounding, chopping, ragging, ranking, cutting, woofing, giving s___, joning, giving S* and *giving J* are some of the local or older terms for the same activity: competitive insulting between African American males (Abrahams 1974), an activity now engaged in by white males as well. Amongst my students, the term *ranking* is now most common, although many report that their parents called it *sounding,* and one African American colleague says it was called *crowing* in her Kansas neighborhood. Changing the names of the activity so often is a way of showing how important and up to date it is. Two more recent terms for this are *dissin'* and *illin',* although these last two can refer to any kind of negative commenting about a person. In this text, the term *ranking* will be used, although in your locale, it might have an alternate name.

Ranking arose from an earlier competition called "playing the dozens," rhymed couplets with four strong beats per long line. These beats are boldfaced below. In my childhood neighborhood, one heard young men being "put in the dozens" with:

> I **don't** play the **dozens**, I **don't** play the **game**
> But the **way** I had your **mother** is a **god** damn **shame**.

This started a round of such couplets, all insulting an opponent's mother, implying that she was promiscuous. By the early 1960s, perhaps because both the structure and topic of the dozens proved too limiting, they had given way to ranking, such as

> Your mother's like a doorknob, a turn for everyone.
> Your mother is like McDonald's, fun for all ages.

The opener "your mother" is so prevalent in these, that, in anger, a boy could insult another by simply saying, "your mother!" When employed as a verbal dueling, however, ranking always involved unrhymed one-line similes followed by a "kicker". This, like the structure of toasts, blues, and rap songs, was an almost invariant structure that had to be conformed to. Early rap songs, those of the mid-1980s, such as *Yvette* by L.L. Cool Jay, showed a similar structure with a strict rhyme scheme and the addition of a chorus (Chaika 1989, pp. 161–162). This has been largely abandoned, and although rhyme is still utilized, it doesn't have to occur at set intervals as before and there is no necessary length of lines. Rather, current rap utilizes series of phrases, some of which rhyme, all chanted to the strong rap beat. Instead of regular choruses, some of them repeat phrases internally two or three times, but there seems to be no rule for this. There are few overt linguistic transitions between the phrases. It is up to the hearer to make the connections. Although, on the surface, the lyrics seem to ramble, on closer inspection it can be seen that they are subordinated to a topic or theme. These have also changed. Instead of female relatives, we now find topics like anger at the police, exhortations to make something of one's life, lectures against eating swine, admonitions about AIDS, and advice about how to deal with faithless partners.

Even ranking did not confine itself to mothers and sisters. Although they were prime targets, actually two other general themes could be ranked on: poverty and physical attributes of the opponent and his family. Again, these don't seem prevalent in current rap music. Ranking often took the form of a verbal duel between two boys. Onlookers overtly commented on the quality of each sound, much as onlookers to the early dialogic rapping between a man and a woman commented "talk dat talk" or "rap city baby." The more original the ranking, the higher it was graded. As with the white repartee mentioned earlier, ranking that elaborates on an opponent's previous statement was considered better than an unrelated one. For street kids, ranking and other verbal displays were—and are—often major determinants of social status.

Although far more data have been gathered on non-middle-class blacks' speech, what little has been gathered suggests that similar attitudes toward middle-class values may occur among non-middle-class whites. There is verbal dueling, for instance, which deals wholly with taboo topics, including those rarely if ever heard from blacks. As with black ritual insulting, what is said in the dueling is not necessarily true. Rather, each person tries to build upon a previous remark either by introducing a taboo subject or by insulting another person, preferably with his or her own words. Puns are not necessarily a feature of such exchanges. The repartee can be between men and women and the entire subject matter of the discourse deals with subjects that are especially taboo in middle-class speech. Although the topics are taboo, taboo words are not necessarily used.

CHAPTER 6

A sample of such dialogue, gathered by a student, Cynthia Marousis, in an urban coffee shop after midnight, started with a male customer's asking a waitress if she was married. When she responded, "Yeah," he asked, "How's your lover?" The assumption, pretended as much as real, that she was immoral enough to have a lover started an entire sequence of exchanges about menstruation, incontinence, oral sex, and homosexuality (not repeated here). The waitress commented, "My husband's good, but my lover's not doing good. He's got the rag on." This comment about her lover shows that the object is to raise a taboo subject somehow. It makes no difference how absurd, impossible, or bizarre the rejoinder is, just so long as the taboo subject is raised. Assuredly, such exchanges are displays of verbal skill, especially one-upmanship. The topics chosen indicated real hostility toward middle-class values.

EGO-BOOSTING IN SPEECH ACTIVITIES

The men who created toasts could gain ego satisfaction from both their creation and their performance. As we have seen, African Americans overtly praise and encourage someone who is giving a good display of speech. With the toasts. men could fantasize as they boasted about the great exploits of their heroes. Similarly, African American men exchange boasts about their prowess in fighting and other street activities. Smitherman (1984, p. 104) reports that the term for this is "sellin' woof" (wolf).

In a study of white barflies, a student of mine, Robert Walling, found patterns of conversation also designed, in his words, to "reinforce and stabilize egos." Their pattern was simple. The conversation started with criticism of current government, society, or sports figures. This, apparently, served as a way of establishing the man's superiority over those in power. An unfavorable comparison of the present to the past was then made. This is not surprising since they always claimed that their glories were in the past. Finally, the barfly gave a sketch of his past life and, if he was a father, his children's fate. These sketches proved to be untrue, though not wholly so. There was always some germ of truth in these tales. Unlike African American street youths, these older white men do not claim fantastic exploits. They only upgrade the past a few notches. The bars they frequent are in stable neighborhoods. Most of the men are lifelong residents, and the bartenders and other patrons could all verify the truth of each tale. Walling found no difficulty in getting the men to talk. Indeed, as soon as they saw a new face, they accosted him and insisted on telling him their tales.

One man who many years ago had driven a city bus for ten months until he was fired for drunkenness claimed:

> I was a bus driver and a damn good one too. My wife used to work at the Outlet [a local department store] and now my two boys drive truck for them.

The bartender confirmed that his boys were doing no such thing, nor as their father also claimed, was it likely that they could have gone to college. Another oldster who had been a janitor at an elegant hotel claimed:

> I worked at the Biltmore. You name it and I did it. There wasn't much in that place that I couldn't do. That used to be the best hotel in southern New England. All the big shots who came to Providence stayed at the Biltmore. [shows autographs from Jack Benny and Jack Dempsey[9].] Pretty impressive, huh? I talked to those two for about an hour apiece. Ya, they were great guys. I still remember what Demps told me, "You got to fight to win in this world." I'll never forget those words and that was almost forty years ago...When I had my big job with the Biltmore I never complained once.

Note the use of a pseudo-nickname, Demps, to indicate familiarity or intimacy with the great fighter. For these men, part of the reason for going to bars seems to be to have a chance to tell their stories, to present themselves as worthwhile people.

Most people apparently use language somehow to boost their own sense of worth, to gain status and maintain their egos. Erickson (1984, p. 145) confirms this. He dissects an ordinary conversation, showing that an African American speaker and his audience "were doing" the conversation together. The speaker was able to display his skill and to persuade the others, but the conversation, which Erickson aptly described "call and response," allowed a strong manifestation of solidarity between the interactors. Although the principal speaker was able to establish how good a talker he was, this wasn't done at the expense of anyone present. His superiority was achieved "by collaboration with, rather than at the expense of less...creative and assertive members of the audience." Thus, says Erickson, "soul" is achieved (p. 145). Notice that the boasting of the bar flies reported on by Walling are not done at anybody's expense.

CHAPTER 6

RITUAL INSULTING

Casual, rough talk can also be very revealing of social attitudes and conditions. Labov (1972) has termed activities like ranking "ritual insults." Unlike true insults, ritual insults do not evoke anger or denial. Instead they evoke other insults, laughter, or, occasionally, a change of subject. Although probably all human societies have ritual insulting activities, some seem to indulge only sporadically. Others, such as American urban black youth have codified the activity. It is virtually an everyday business, and one important in determining social rank.

The frequency of ritual insulting changes throughout one's lifetime. There are times and situations when one is very likely to indulge in ritual insulting. Adolescence seems to call forth a good deal of play insulting. Examples are easily gathered from athletic teams, cafeterias, and schoolyards in the United States as well as other countries (e.g., Dundes et al., 1972). Brothers and sisters often tease each other playfully but with a barb. College students tell me that insulting often reaches a peak in the dorms during exams. Some husbands and wives playfully insult each other. More rarely, and only in some really relaxed family situations, do children "bust up" their parents. In earlier times, when children had to be far more formal with their parents than today, playful insulting was unthinkable. Ritual insulting seems most acceptable when the participants are of equal or near social status, and it occurs most frequently at times of stress, such as adolescence in general and exams in particular. The business of living together as a family can create small tensions. Thus siblings, college roommates, or spouses insult each other jokingly, whereas casual acquaintances are not as likely to. When we see an entire cultural group regularly engaging in ritual insulting, we have good reason to suspect that they are under special strain.

The topics of all ritual insults, including ranking, seem to be constrained (Labov 1972). To overstep the bounds leads into genuine insulting. The limits shield participants from inadvertent hurt. However insulting ranking may be, for instance, they are calculated not to bruise egos. To the contrary, the activity of ritual insulting provides ego-boosting for boys to whom the ordinary ego satisfactions are denied. The street kid who may never make it into college or a prestigious job, who cannot participate in the American dream of upward mobility, can get daily proof of his intelligence and wit by these verbal duels. Abrahams (1974) says that verbal jousts are a safe arena in which to seek success and to exercise aggressiveness.

Labov et al. (1968, pp. 101–102) convincingly demonstrate that mention of a true incident is not taken as part of the game; it is not heard as ritual insulting. Rather, it brings forth angry denials. For instance, although poverty itself may be sounded on, to mention something showing someone's actual poverty is taken as a grave insult. It is all right to say that the cockroaches in Junior's house are so bold they pull a gun on you, but it is not all right to tell about the chair that broke when you sat on it. Labov et al. reported that when one boy mentioned that, the other hotly responded, "You's a damned liar, 'n you was eatin' in my house, right?" In that community, remarking that someone ate at someone's house implies hunger, a real need for food. Thus it is a true insult.

The reader may recall that asking for food is difficult for Americans in general. With all the profanity and vulgar images that the boys proved capable of in the Harlem study, one of the worst insults that Labov et al. collected was "Yeah, but you sure be eatin'." It proved easy to determine true from ritual insults. The true ones were not only highly plausible events, but the boy sounded on angrily justified what was said. Telling the truth about one boy's father, that he stuttered and had gray hair, evoked heated denials, even tears.

Nonetheless a germ of truth exists in ritual insulting. Poverty is ranked on; so are physical attributes like fatness or black African facial features. Although they have some foundation in fact, the sounds are saved from truth by being so fantastic that they could not possibly be true. Perhaps for this reason, bizarre and absurd imagery abounds in sounding. For example, the following was collected from two college students by another student, David Aldrich. It is an excellent example of earthy, even raw language that in reality serves both social and psychological purposes for the speakers. As casual as it is, it follows the rules of the game.

Craig: Man, if I was a chick, I wouldn't kiss you with my dog's lips.
Greg: With the size of your lips, you'd drown her for sure.
Craig: I may not be the best kisser, but man, I'm hung like a baseball bat and swing it like Willie Mays.
Greg: Well, you got your chance tonight. Baby, I got my goggles on and I'm ready to do some heavy divin'.
Craig: Just call me Jacques Cousteau.

The germ of truth here is that Craig's lips are characteristic of black Africans. So are Greg's. However, the very absurdity of the image allows it to remain in the realm of joking. Also, lip size is a permissible topic for sounds among African Americans. Notice how deftly Craig turns Greg's ritual insult into a boast about his other physical attributes. In verbal dueling and one-upmanship, one can best one's opponent by taking another's insult and using it to lead into a self-glorification. Greg then shows his own skill by turning the sexual reference into a metaphor for deep-sea diving. Craig's "Call me Jacques Cousteau" is a way of saying that he is the best 'deep-sea diver of them all'.

Comparing onelf to a famous historical figure or a modern celebrity is quite usual as a way of boasting in the African American community. Although this exchange is undeniably vulgar, as are many insulting rounds, it still is the subtle comment that wins the game. The entire discourse takes a good deal of wit and skill.

Labov found a good deal of ranking on shared physical characteristics of African Americans. This does not necessarily indicate self-hatred as some suppose. I think, rather, that there is a larger principle of social behavior. It sems to me that things which are involuntary, short of deformity, can often be joked about. This seems to be true in many different cultures, although which topics are to be excluded are specific to the culture. Among most Americans, teasing about freckles, red hair, and short stature is permissible, so that a short red-headed boy of my acquaintance was nicknamed "Strawberry Shortcake." If he were a genuine midget, his height couldn't be mentioned. Similarly, if a normal person trips, someone might joke, "Whatsa matter, forget your crutches?" But the same statement to a paraplegic would be outrageous.

Labov et al.'s samples of sounding do include those about poverty, but they were all impossible exaggerations. They were collected on the streets of Harlem from boys who were really poor. Note the difference in sounding on poverty initiated by Craig, an African American college student, and to Bill, his white roommate as they were playing cards:

> *Craig*: Hey, man, you got another trump card just as sure as a bear s—s in the woods.
> *Bill*: I sure as hell don't got no trump card, just as sure as your mother s—s on the floor.
> *Craig*: Well, Mr. Cool, at least we got a floor to s— on. They don't let you s— on the welfare office floor.
> *Bill*: You're pretty bad with the mouth. How about the cards?

It is all right for Craig to tease Bill by implying that his family is on welfare because it is neither true nor likely. To a genuinely poor person in an inner city neighborhood, this would be a true insult. A variant of the "your mother" insult was collected in the same dorm between white students:

Al: I can read 350 words a minute.
Bob: S— you can't even turn the pages that fast.
Al: I turned your mother that fast.

In 1973 in my first sociolinguistic classes, white males unanimously agreed with great vehemence that any slur on their mothers' or sisters' characters would be a grave insult. The question is why did African Americans develop such a game, and why, later, did whites start to imitate it? Some have posited that the dozens were devised as a way of turning aggressions inward. They see such gaming as a result of oppression by whites. Those with a Freudian bent explained it as the need for African American youth in female dominated homes to cut the Oedipal bond. As with glorification of pimping, put-downs for women give black males the opportunity to assert their virility. This does not explain why middle-class suburban white elementary schoolboys glory in "your mother" jokes, however; nor do these explanations elucidate why middle-class blacks from intact homes also do. Then, too, why did whites borrow ranking when they did, rather than, for instance, in 1941?

It would be comforting to mothers to be able to say that such joking is innocent enough, just a way for adolescent boys to get things off their chests, but then it would have to be explained why it isn't fathers who get ranked on, or other male relatives or friends, or any of the host of possible topics that could serve as ritual insults. In Turkey, for instance, adolescent males often insult each other ritually by creating riddles that imply that the other is homosexual. It is hard to escape the conclusion that the devaluing of mothers is part and parcel of a more general devaluing of women in our entire society. (See Chapter 10.)

We have already seen that ritual insulting provides two benefits to a social group: lessening of tensions and ego-boosting by besting others in competition, or at least by getting a good line or two in. It can also be used as a regulatory mechanism in conjunction with another activity. Examining such an occurrence is in itself a study in the sensitivity of language use to social needs.

The Verbal Game and the Real One

In African American neighborhoods games of pickup basketball are prevalent. They constitute a very important activity for the youths of the community. Since there is no referee at such games, the players have to keep score and generally regulate the game by themselves. Such a situation is potentially explosive: unsupervised boys playing a competitive game with no one to judge what is foul or out of bounds and scores kept only in the heads of individual players. Allan Baker, himself at the time a member of the basketball team, shows how the activity of sounding and general verbal gaming is used to regulate the score. The exchange below occurred during a dispute about a score in a game played in a college gym between black male college students from several Northern cities. Baker was watching, taking down the exchange under the guise of doing his homework. A dispute was started when B called a foul on A. Because pickup games are rough, fouls are not usually called. Baker says that the person who does call one can expect to be sounded on. Therefore, A says that B plays like a girl[10]:

A: Look man, you play like my sister at your best.
B: S—. Your sister is better than me. She can dunk on Wilt! [Chamberlain]

B's response is typical, and, for the moment, gives him the advantage, since he turns A's words back into an insult about A's sister. This exchange allows both players to shed their irritation with each other—B because he has a foul committed on him and A because the foul is, in his eyes, unjustly called. Dissipating anger by verbal exchange works because both boys understand the ritual nature of the insults. Then came the following sequence:

A: Look man, you cheatin'.
B: Your a—, I don't have to cheat-ya to beat-ya.
A: I know we got more points than that.
B: This ain't the welfare building, we don't give s— away here, sucker.
A: You ain't givin' us nothin', we takin' it sucker.
B: You ain't no d— gorilla cool.
A: Look man, we got ten baskets.
C: Now I know you jumped out of your tree, fool! You can't count to no f—n' ten!
D: Look, man, give them ten and let's get it on. S—, we been arguin' all night. Other people wanna play.
B: I ain't givin' them no ten, no way.
D: OK, man! Let's start back at eight, tie score, all right?

A: H—, yea. I just ain't gonna get beat out no points.

B: Man, ain't nobody tryin' to beatcha. You always cryin'. You got over this time, but I'm going to bust your a—.

A: Sure, man, you jus' keep talkin' that Jeff Davis s—.

During a pickup game, each team keeps its own score. Although a running patter accompanies the game, whenever one team falls behind, one of its members starts insulting the opposition. The point is to con the other team into thinking the losers have more points than they do. Allan Baker comments, "This is not to say that blacks thrive on cheating, but rather that if the opportunity presents itself and debate occurs, the advantage goes to the most verbal." The technique that A uses is typical. He lures the other side into debate, thereby stalling the game. Baker points out that A sets the other side up by naming a ridiculous number of points, here ten baskets. In order to get the game going again, the opponents have to give A's team some points. Baker, sitting on the sidelines, had been keeping score. In actuality, A's had only five baskets, and B's had ten. A's ploy resulted not only in his team's getting more points but B's giving some up! Mr. Baker presented these data to me 20 years ago. In 1992, the movie *White Men Can't Jump* opened with an analogous dispute which was resolved in the same way by the same kind of ritual insulting.

The reason that such ploys are so successful is the shared cultural behavior of the participants. They know and understand that if an insult has been given, it must be answered and that this will go on until one side can claim victory. The only way to stop the round before then is to at least partly accede to the opponent's demands. Even the team which is actually ahead knows that they will have to give a little as well. In this particular round, some of the insults are quite blunt. "You cheatin'" is a bald accusation. Baker emphasizes that because the participants are all friends, they do not become angry at such insults. Within the context of the athletic contest, the insults are taken as ritual ones. The verbal requirements of the insulting contest take precedence over the game for these players. The entire sequence can be taken as a subcategory of ranking, one used to gain an advantage in a usually nonverbal activity. Baker comments that although none of these boys were professional players, they were all what he calls "professional talkers." Also, he notes that the verbal game is as important as the basketball game in pickup games.

Because ritual insulting can go on concurrently with the game, it has a strong regulatory function. It allows disputes over scoring to be settled on another plane by utilizing the well-known rules for ritual insulting. Here we see a beautiful example of what is probably a universal phenomenon, ritual insulting, as it is adapted to a specific social situation. Verbal sparring takes the place of a referee and scorekeeper.

The apparently mundane matter of how people insult each other in a community is a highly complicated set of interrelated behaviors. They reflect general social conditions as well as the requirements of particular social situations.

Chapter 6 Notes

1   This is clearly an arguable question. as those from educated homes may carry an especially severe load of shame because of their poor reading skills. Financially, they may not be so badly off, but finances are not the only yardstick by which to measure a disability.

2   It has also occurred to me that the big truths of epic poetry had to be said again and again lest people forget. If they were in ordinary, straightforward language, people would soon get tired of hearing them. By putting these truths in figurative and unusual language, people are more likely to listen. Also, people are forced to interpret figurative language. This, too, aids recall. Then, too, having the enjoyment of music and chanting as part of the human baggage makes it more likely that people will want to sing, and when they do, they are reiterating the messages of songs and poetry on their own. Notice that in the toasts, the message of bravely accepting what comes one's way is reiterated, as is the message of untrustworthy officials, but they are saved from being boring by the many different ways they are encoded.

3   Younger African Americans and even somewhat older middle-class ones are largely unaware of these toasts, or, at best, recall a snatch or two from *The Signifying Monkey*, or vaguely recall Shine, the hero. In the movie *House Party*, however, the protagonist's father plays a recording by Domitian of *The Signifying Monkey*. Fortunately, folklorists have preserved many of these toasts before they were forgotten.

4   Even in World War II, most Blacks were relegated to janitorial and other personal service capacities. The Army camps were segregated, and Blacks were given little battlefield operation. This in a war which stressed human rights as its motivation.

5   Other dialects rhyme some or all of these pairs. For instance, in my dialect, *odds* and *cards* rhyme, but not the other pairs here.

6   This effectively rules out "Frankie and Johnny" as being a genuine Blues song, since it is temporal, recounting what seems to be an actual event.

7   ("Preachin' the Blues". Recorded on *The Legendary Son House: Father of Folk Blues*. Columbia CS 9217)

8   I am very aware of the sexist meaning of *slut*. It is my coining, but a coining made while being most aware that female sexual habits are judged quite differently from male's. Ms. Jones is not responsible for this term nor for my comparison with dozens and ranking, although, as indicated, she noted the parallels with toasts.

9   Jack Benny was a well-known comedian and Jack Dempsey, a well-known prizefighter.

10   Note the inherent sexism in using the word *girl* for an insult. This is not confined to the African American culture.

Exercises

1. Find some recent articles on problems in teaching American children to read. What do these articles claim are the causes of illiteracy? Considering material presented in this chapter, what questions do you think should be asked that the articles didn't address?

2. Examine the lyrics of a rap song of your choice. What topics and attitudes are like the verses of the toasts? What has changed?

3. Examine the structure of a selection of rap songs. Do they show evidence of strict form? In what ways are they structured like toasts, blues, or ritual insults? In what ways are they different?

4. Jarrett says that one recognizes immediately that a song does not belong to the genre of the Blues if it contains references to nature. Analyze the lyrics of your favorite kind of music (rap, rock, punk, heavy metal, etc.) and note what topics are never mentioned. What are the usual topics of these songs? You may instead want to compare two groups, such as Bruce Springsteen and U2.

5. Collect some ritual insults amongst your friends. What topics are permissible? What topics are not? That is, what insults are taken as true insults. What reactions do you get from ritual insults? How do these differ from reactions to true insults?

6. Do you find different terms in use for what we have called *ranking,*
dissin' and *illin*? If you are in an environment which includes students
from many different regions, poll them to see what terms they use for
ritual insults.

7. Listen to some comic monologue on TV, tapes, or at a live performance
and count the derogatory jokes about females. How many of these
concern a female's sexual activities? What other characteristics of
females are joked on. Are there similarly derogatory jokes about any
other segment of society, such as all males, the Chinese, Native
Americans, or fathers?

8. What kinds of boasting activities can you collect from your peers? What
is permissible to boast about? Do you find any ego-boosting, tale-
telling (such as the stories of the bar flies discussed in this chapter), or
are the boasts fantastic, like those of Craig in this chapter? Who seems
to boast? How is this boasting evaluated by others in your group? To
what degree does the locale or social situation determine the degree
to which boasting is positively valued?

References

Abrahams, R. (1974). Black talking in the streets. In Explorations in the
Ethnography of Speaking. (R. Bauman, & J. Sherzer, Eds.). (pp.
240–262). New York: Cambridge University Press.

Bereiter, C., & Engelmann, S. (1966). *Teaching Disadvantaged Children in
the Preschool.* Englewood, NJ: Prentice Hall.

Bernstein, B. (1971). *Theoretical Studies toward a Sociology of Language.*
(Vol. 1). Class, Codes, and Control. London: Routledge & Kegan Paul.

Bodine, A. (1975). Androcentrism in prescriptive grammar: Singular "they";
sex indefinite "he"; and "he or she.". *Language in Society, 4,* 129–146.

Chaika, E. (1989). *Language the Social Mirror, 2nd.* Ed. Boston: Heinle &
Heinle Publishers.

Dundes, A., Leach, J., & Ozkok, B. (1972). The strategy of Turkish boy's
dueling rhymes. In *Directions in Sociolinguistics* (J. Gumperz & D.
Hymes, Eds). (pp. 180–209). New York: Holt, Rinehart, and Winston.

Erickson, F. (1984). Rhetoric, anecdote, and rhapsody: Coherence strategies in a conversation among Black American adolescents. In D.
Tannen (Ed.), *Coherence in Spoken and Written Discourse* (pp.
81–154). Norwood, N.J.: Ablex Publishing Corp.

Gelb, I. J. (1963). *A Study of Writing: A Discussion of the General Principles Governing the Use and Evolution of Writing* [Revised Edition]. Chicago: University of Chicago Press.

Gumperz, J., Kaltman, H., & O'Connor, M. C. (1984). Cohesion in spoken and written discourse: Ethnic style and the transition to literacy. In D. Tannen (Ed.), *Coherence in Spoken and Written Discourse* (pp. 3–19). Norwood, N.J.: Ablex Publishing.

Heath, S. B. (1983). *Ways with Words.* New York: Cambridge University Press.

Jackson, B. (1974). *Get your Ass in the Water and Swim Like Me.* Cambridge, Mass.: Harvard University Press.

Jarrett, D. (1984). Pragmatic coherence in an oral formulaic tradition. In D. Tannen (Ed.), *Coherence in Spoken and Written Discourse* (pp. 155–171). Norwood, N.J.: Ablex Publishing Co.

Keyser, S. (1976). Wallace Stevens: Form and meaning in four poems. *College English, 37,* 578–598.

Labov, W. (1972). Rules for ritual insults. In *Language in the Inner City* (pp. 297–353). Philadelphia: University of Pennsylvania Press.

Labov, W., Cohen, P., Robins, C., & Lewis, J. (1968). *A Study of the English of Negro and Puerto Rican Speakers in New York City.* Philadelphia: U.S. Regional Survey.

Michaels, S., & Collins, J. (1984). Oral discourse styles: Classroom interaction and the acquisition of literacy. In D. Tannen (Ed.), *Coherence in Spoken and Written Discourse* (pp. 219–244). Norwood, N.J.: Ablex Publishing.

Mitchell-Kernan, C. (1972). Signifying and marking: Two Afro-American speech acts. In *Directions in Sociolinguistics* (J. Gumperz & D. Hymes, Eds). (pp. 161–179). New York: Holt, Rinehart, and Winston.

Ong, W. J. (1982). *Orality and Literacy: The Technologizing of the Word.* New York: Methuen & Co.

Schatzman, L., & Strauss, A. (1972). Social class and modes of communication. In S. Muscovici (Ed.), *The Psychosociology of Language* (pp. 206–221). Chicago: Markham.

Scinto, L. F. M. (1986). *Written Language and Psychological development.* New York: Academic Press.

Scollon, R., & Scollon, S. (1984). Cooking it up and boiling it down: Abstracts in Athabaskan children's story retellings. In D. Tannen (Ed.), *Coherence in Spoken and Written Discourse* (pp. 173–197). Norwood, N.J.: Ablex Publishing.

Scollon, R., & Scollon, S. B. K. (1981). *Narrative Literacy and Face in Interethnic Communication.* Norwood, N.J.: Ablex.

Scribner, S., & Cole, H. (1981). *The Psychology of Literacy*. Cambridge, Mass: Harvard University Press.

Smitherman, G. (1984). Black language as power. In *Language and Power* (C. Kramrae, M. Schulz, & W. M. O'Barr, Eds). (pp. 101–115). Beverly Hills: Sage Publications.

Tannen, D. (1980). A comparative analysis of oral narrative strategies. In W. Chafe (Ed.), *The Pear Stories*. Norwood, N.J.: Ablex Publishing.

Tannen, D. (1982). The oral/literate continuum in discourse. In D. Tannen (Ed.), *Spoken and Written Language: Exploring Orality and Literacy*. Norwood, N.J.: Ablex Publishing.

Chapter 7
Field Methods

Conclusions are only as good as the field methods they are based on. Field methods include laboratory experiments as well as observations recorded in the field, in the natural surroundings of the people whose speech is being studied. Sociolinguistic testing can be especially troublesome because one has to control very carefully to ensure that subjects are not responding to a factor other than the one being investigated. Measuring results statistically is often crucial. Earlier sociolinguistic studies did not bother with statistics, but it has been found that certain conclusions were not warranted after later scholars did measure them.

RECIPES FOR DISCOVERY

The lot of a social scientist would be considerably eased—and the literature on the social sciences considerably reduced—if it were easy to devise investigative techniques to find out what one wants to know, and be sure that one is getting the information one is seeking. However, humans are nothing if not complex, not to mention perverse, and they will react to the wrong thing, or misunderstand your question, or try to second-guess you and so not give a truthful response, or find ambiguities you never intended in the task you set up. A good deal of the time spent studying the social sciences, especially psychology, sociology, and linguistics, all of which are part and parcel of sociolinguistics, is spent trying to determine the flaws in the studies which are giving the conclusions.

Part of being a good researcher is being an inventive, ingenious designer of foolproof experiments. Unfortunately, nobody is that all of the time. All researchers have had the disheartening experience of carrying out what they think is a brilliant study and then having a commentator point out the fatal flaws in it which invalidate all the conclusions. There is no way to avoid this. It is not possible to give recipes for foolproof experiments. Well, perhaps, one could write a manual with a bunch of set techniques, but this would hardly advance knowledge, for the essence of study is to find out new things, and to find out new things, one must do new things, create new protocols, think of new and different ways to get at an understanding of how and why people act and react as they do.

What we can do is to give some general information about the different kinds of studies possible, what they are good for. We can point out some common pitfalls. We can discuss studies which have been done and show how their results may be interpreted differently from the way the researcher did. We can raise questions about what was done, who was chosen to participate in the studies, whether enough people were tested, even whether the conditions of the testing might have inhibited the subjects. To this end, in every chapter I have included descriptions of studies as well as their results, sometimes criticizing them, sometimes not as the case seems warranted to me. Of course, you, the reader, may notice something I didn't, and you should always be reading with an eye to critiquing the studies on which conclusions are based. Sometimes the studies themselves seem fine, but others find that the conclusions don't hold when they study different populations. Such situations are also included in this book, especially in the next two chapters. The problem then becomes one of trying to reconcile the differences in results.

Beyond such presentation, this chapter gives an overview of some considerations in field methods, and elsewhere in the text I cite scholarly studies, such as using information from the dictionary or other sources as an aid to discovery. The one thing that I always find unacceptable is a conclusion based solely on anecdotes. The fact that three of my friends say that their little girls talk more than their little boys does not suffice to prove that girls talk more than boys. The fact that Nancy's husband buries his head in a paper when he comes home from work and refuses to talk doesn't mean that all husbands do. Anecdotes might provide the springboard for a formal study of an issue, but they never are proof in their own right. They may be used as examples to illustrate a point, but there has to be independently gathered corroborating evidence. People often have a great many "commonsensical" notions about human behavior which, when investigated, turn out to be wrong. It is just such notions that lead to stereotyping and misunderstandings.

SOCIOLINGUISTICS AND FIELD METHODS

Field methods constitute the various ways we can collect information about members of society: individuals or groups. They include laboratory experiments, naturalistic observations of both daily and unusual activities, questions put to people, surveys of the research of others to glean new or more exhaustive information, and analysis of a culture's output: newspapers, TV shows, movies, music, and art.

In sociolinguistics, as in all scholarly research, what you get depends on how you go about getting it. That is, one's results are dependent upon the field methods one uses. In turn, one's methods must conform to what we have discovered about the normal speaking practises of those being investigated. For those groups for which no data or outdated data are available, any research must be preceded by periods of observation to learn the politeness routines, the conditions under which people speak, what their body motions mean, etc. Indeed, all of the factors we have discussed in kinesics and pragmatics, style, and discourse must be considered when devising a study. Given the incredible complexity of language and its ubiquitousness, devising valid field methods is especially difficult when one delves into language use and its import for society. All too often, language is the one variable that is ignored in all nonlinguistic research, despite the fact that virtually all investigation in the social sciences depends on language use, both by the researchers and by those being researched. That is, language use is almost always a variable which must be accounted for in one's results, but, unless the object of the investigation is language use itself, it is often ignored.

Almost any social variable can affect the kinds of linguistic output one can get. For instance, an investigator cannot use the same methods in a bilingual community as in a monolingual one. As we have seen, typically, bilinguals select which of their languages to use according to the social situation. Some will use one language only in the home, or only if relatives are present, finding it impossible to speak it to strangers. Others will find it impossible to speak anything but English unless they are speaking to someone of their own ethnic group. Others are insulted that the researcher makes no effort to speak their language, resenting having to speak English for tests or interviews. Still others will not use one of their languages if the researcher speaks it with a strong accent. To some degree, Americans find this when they go abroad. Even if they do speak the language of the country they are visiting, they may find that natives will slip into English as soon as they hear an American accent. All of this is complicated by *diglossia* situations (Chapter 9), in which members of a culture use different languages for different social purposes. Then the researcher must first ascertain what the proper language for a formal interview is, or the usual language selected for more casual interactions. If testing is to be administered in schools, then the language associated with formal schooling must be chosen. If an investigator uses the wrong language for the situation, the data gathered will be inaccurate.

Amongst monolinguals, close attention must be paid to the dialect or register selected in the testing situation. Monolinguals are as constrained in their speech output by the demands of the social situation as bilinguals are in their selection of language. For both groups, moreover, the social situation itself must be one conducive to eliciting speech. If a child is plucked out of a classroom, taken into a cubicle with a formally dressed adult who then picks up a toy and asks, "What's this?" the result may well be that the child feels intimidated, afraid that there's a catch somewhere, and so refuse to answer. After all, why would an adult ask such a silly question in such a foreboding atmosphere? William Labov pointed this out in his critiques of studies of inner-city children done in the 1950s by researchers like Bereiter and Engelmann. They claimed, on the basis of such interviewing techniques, that African American children were 'nonverbal.' In contrast, William Labov had an assistant dressed in casual clothes, sit on the floor with a group of such children, and start playing verbal games with them, games they were well-practiced in. Under these circumstances, the same children who mumbled and stumbled with Bereiter and Engelmann's testing, proved themselves to have excellent verbal facility.

By carefully investigating the speech behaviors of African Americans, Labov noted that their verbal interactions consisted of a great deal of verbal jousting, and that the way to elicit speech data from this population was to allow them to compete with each other. Of course, this technique wouldn't work so well with children of other cultures who, for instance, have been trained not to interrupt each other, or that it is impolite to contradict someone. Since speaking practices vary so greatly amongst different cultural groups, these must always be accounted for in any investigation.

To get valid data from interviews, one must conduct them so that subjects are put at ease, unless one is specifically investigating behaviors associated with nervousness or hostility. If subjects are to be at ease, then the investigator must conform to their culture. If members of the culture are most comfortable talking in competition with peers, then there must be group interviews. If the subjects are children, and their culture does not allow easy conversation between adults and children, then the adult must dress informally, use the children's usual dialect, and even get down on the floor, ready to play. If not, the children may well respond to all questions with silence or an "I don't know" even if they do know. If members of a culture are uncomfortable talking to someone who is wearing a shirt or tie, then no shirt and tie should be worn.

I find it best not to use hand-held microphones at all. Many speakers clutch them, face them directly, and earnestly talk into them. Casual, everyday speech is very difficult to elicit and record under such circumstances. The results are equally poor if the interviewer keeps shoving the microphone in the subject's face, TV newsman-style. Even those who are at ease with microphones can cause problems with a hand mike. They forget themselves, start their usual gestures while talking, waving the mike back and forth to the detriment of the recording. A microphone that attaches around the neck is best. Alternatively, a good tape recorder with a built-in mike can be placed judiciously near the subject(s). For some kinds of studies, very expensive, supersensitive equipment is essential for picking up such things as fine differences in pronunciation, length of hesitation and voice onset times between speakers.

One cannot just go out and interview or test people. One must first find out something about the way they interact and the conditions under which they are likely to talk or to carry out the task you assign.

Finding Out What You Want to Know

The biggest problem with field methods is devising a test or experiment that tells you what you want to know. Often, despite the most careful planning, once a study is completed, results can be interpreted quite differently from what was originally intended. Experimental subjects may not have reacted as expected; they may have reacted to the wrong cue or been influenced by a speech feature other than the one being studied.

For instance, having subjects evaluate tape recordings of other speakers is a common methodology used for many purposes. If it is important to know how Americans feel about the pronunciation [ə] instead of [r] in words like *other* and *teacher,* a tape of someone who uses the [ə] a great deal would be played and then a tape of a strong [r] pronouncer. Subjects would be asked to rank each speaker on personal qualities such as intelligence, confidence, sincerity, educational traits, and any other traits pertinent to the particular investigation. The investigator could not use just any two speakers as special care would have to be taken to ensure that the only difference between the two speakers was the use of [ə] instead of [r]. If one speaker pronounced the *th* in *other* as [d] and a second pronounced it as [ð], the subject might rate the speakers on the difference between those sounds, not on the way [r] was pronounced. Or, if one of the taped speakers used an [ɔ] in *talk* and the other used an [a], those might be the crucial sounds in the evaluations.

Even if the investigator controls carefully for pronunciation, there is still another problem. If one of the taped speakers has a raspy voice and the other a smooth one, or if one is nasal and the other is not, or if there is any other difference in voice quality, then the reaction might be to that difference, not to any particular feature of speech. Even differences in loudness or tempo, one speaking more rapidly than the other, may cause differences in reaction. In other words, there are so many possible qualities of speech to which subjects can react, that it might prove difficult to prove exactly what influences ratings. This does not mean that evaluations of voices are not good. They are exceedingly valuable sources of information if they are set up correctly. The importance of good field methods cannot be overstressed for what is found depends on how it was sought. The results that get analyzed depend wholly on the field methods used to collect them. Because of the richness of language data, triviality in testing is always a problem. It is easy to devise careful experiments that elicit speech because speech can be elicited in so many ways, but still one can end up with trivial or fragmented data with little, if any, relation to normal functioning. For instance, one can ask subjects to memorize lists of words and recite them backward. Undoubtedly, people will differ in their ability to perform this task, but the relation of such performance to actual speech and memory is obscure. Word association tests, for another example, may tell us a lot about people's associations to given words, but they do not tell us how people select words in a sentence. Normal discourse is not produced by uttering words that are associated with each other. It is produced by selecting words that fit the intended meaning.

Unfortunately, it is not always immediately apparent that a given procedure is going to yield trivial results. The best that can be done is to ask questions like:

▶What aspect of behavior am I testing for?
▶Does this task tap the skills needed for that behavior?
▶What could my subjects be responding to besides what I want them to?
▶What factors could be influencing my results besides those I intended?

If an experiment does not work out as hoped or an investigation yields nothing of interest, that, too, is part of the process of discovery. It happens to everyone or just about everyone at one time or another.

Matched Guise Testing

Often, in sociolinguistic studies, one intends to test for one thing, but ends up getting a reaction to another. For instance, if one wants to find out how prestigious a certain speech variety is, one might simply play tapes of people speaking that way, and have them fill out a rating questionnaire asking how educated, brave, honest, sincere, or whatever the speaker is. One would always include samples of speakers with other dialects as well. If one uses both male and female voices, however, the responses on the questionnaire may reflect the subject's feelings about men and women, not the speech variety itself. One can avoid this simply by having only people of the same sex on the tape. Even here, a problem arises. Perhaps the subject is responding not to the speech variety per se, but to the voice quality of the speaker. That is, a speaker might be downgraded because a subject found his or her voice grating, or a subject might be upgraded because he or she has such a mellifluous voice. In either event, we still haven't found out if the speaker's dialect itself is favored or not.

Wallace Lambert and his cohorts (e.g., in Lambert, Giles, and Picard 1975) avoided the pitfalls of reactions to taped voices by using the **matched guise** technique. They found people who could command two languages or dialects[1] equally well, and had them read passages in each guise. Subjects, not realizing that they were evaluating the same person, rated each. The reaction, then, could be safely taken to be to the given language or dialect, not to other aspects of voice quality. Matched guise testing has proven fruitful in a variety of experimental procedures. For instance, in Great Britain, Bourhis (cited in Giles and Powesland 1975, p. 104) had an announcement made over a loudspeaker in a theater asking patrons to fill out a survey questionnaire. On successive nights, the announcement alternated between a nonstandard dialect and *received pronunciation* (known as RP), the standard dialect of British English, the one learned in school. On the nights that RP was used, more people filled out the forms, and they wrote longer answers. It had already been established that people will write at greater length at the request of someone whose accent they admire (Giles, Baker, and Fielding 1975). It is not always possible to find a bilingual or bidialectal speaker equally proficient in both varieties under consideration. Actors and actresses can be used, but with extreme caution. Although they fancy that they are giving accurate renditions of dialects or accents, usually they are using stylized stage dialects that do not conform to the genuine one. Every Bostonian knows that the mailman Cliff on the TV comedy *Cheers* doesn't have a true Boston accent.

Testing for Voice Quality

Sometimes one wants to test voice quality itself. For instance, it is useful to find out if members of a society find high-pitched voices weak, graceful, charming, honest, or whatever, or if they find raspy voices commanding, irritating, sexy, masculine, convincing, or dishonest. Again tapes can be used with subjects filling out questionnaires, but now one deliberately wants speakers with different voice quality. Here, again, the sex of the speaker is important. A high voice might be attractive in a woman,[2] but not in a man. Conversely, a deep voice in a woman might be downgraded but valued highly in a man, especially if the deep voice is associated with power or authority. Notice that in this kind of testing, one can ask questions designed to find out how weak, strong, dominant, submissive, honest, or dishonest the voice quality is, and that these judgments will differ according to the gender of the speaker. It is probably better not to ask directly, "Is this the voice of an honest person?" Rather, ask questions like, "Would you choose this speaker as a member of a team?" "What occupation would you find this person suitable for: manager, salesman...?" One can also ask subjects to choose speakers for different tasks from an array of speakers on a tape.

One problem in determining reaction to voice quality (or to dialect features, for that matter) is that the meaning (semantic content) of what is being said might affect the subject's judgment. One obvious way to control for this is to have several speakers read the identical passage. Unfortunately, this bores listeners so much that they may start to tune out the readers. Another is to have each read paraphrases of one passage or to have each read successive paragraphs from one article or speech. That way, at least style and topic are limited. Another technique is to mask words by passing recorded speech through an acoustic filter that obliterates the higher frequencies of sound necessary for word recognition but leaves voice qualities like nasality, deepness, tremulousness, or breathiness (Abercrombie 1967; Kramer 1963; Laver 1968). Scherer (1973) has used a Moog synthesizer to approximate certain aspects of voice quality. If such sophisticated equipment is not readily available, the effect of content to reaction to voice quality or other features of dialect can be lessened by having actors and actresses portray emotions while reciting numbers.

Observation and Participant Observation

In the social sciences, there is always a temptation to rely on haphazard personal observations. Some scholars do this a great deal, citing their intuitions about various matters. Others criticize insights offered from intuition. Actually, everyone uses hunches. It is a hunch that makes one want to investigate some aspect of behavior. Even a pioneer like Labov (1963, 1966) who insisted upon intricate methodologies had hunches about what to test for. Later researchers like Shuy et al. (1967), Trudgill (1972), and Milroy (1980) could draw upon Labov's pioneering work, but they also had to have some intuitions about what to test for in each community they investigated. Moreover, analysis of data, no matter how those data are gathered, depends to a great extent on a scholar's intuition and insight. Especially when examining broad aspects of human behavior, it is rare that data inexorably lead just to one conclusion. Interpretation is not only important, but without it, much data are just a random collection of facts. For example, in a study of African American street gangs in Harlem, a research team headed by Labov (Labov, Cohen, Robins, & Lewis, 1968) found that the boys within a gang all spoke somewhat differently. While that was true, it certainly was not interesting in itself. Indeed, linguists had long spoken of individual **idiolects**, as opposed to **dialects**. The latter are speech patterns shared by people within a regional or social group, whereas features of idiolects are not so shared. They are idiosyncratic, individual variations in speech. What made Labov et al.'s study so valuable was that they had charted the friendship network of their subjects on graphs called **sociograms**. When the speech features of the boys were correlated with the sociograms, the variation in speech among the gang was seen to mirror social position within the group. It must have been a hunch that led them to use sociograms in the first place, a hunch based upon Labov's earlier correlations of speech with social facts. Some of the most interesting and valuable works about human behavior have had their impetus from intuition. The works of scholars like Erving Goffman and Harvey Sacks come immediately to mind. There is nothing wrong with hunches or intuitions, so long as a careful attempt is made to verify them.

Observation, both participant and nonparticipant, is vital to the social scientist. A participant observation is one in which the researcher takes part in the action, saying or doing something and then observing the reactions. An excellent example of this is Tannen's analyses of a Thanksgiving dinner with some friends (Tannen 1984). Nonparticipant observation is just looking, noting, and analyzing what is seen and heard in a situation. Because speech behavior is so complex and so inextricably dependent on context for its meaning, much behavior can be understood only through observation. Researchers like Goffman, Sacks, and Birdwhistell, all concerned with discourse and/or body motion in natural circumstances, rely heavily on nonparticipant observation.

Certainly, there must be some controls. Just going out into the streets and listening randomly is not likely to yield verifiable insights. First, the researcher has to define a problem, the object of the investigation. Then, likely spots for observation must be determined. Not only must one choose locales that have the right people doing the right things, but one must consider such ordinary matters as where one is going to sit or stand. Will there be a place for unobtrusive listening and looking? In a participant observation, is there a place to start the interactions naturally so that subjects do not get suspicious? One must also make sure there is not so much noise or movement that confusion could result.

Sometimes the researcher can manipulate a situation under observation without actually participating in it. A student who wished to investigate whether the presence of women affected male speech invited friends to his house to watch a football game. While viewing the game, they commented loudly with a great deal of profanity, as was usual. The investigator had invited two females to drop in at the start of the game before there had been too much beer drinking. As the girls walked in, although the viewers did not acknowledge their presence, the comments instantly became devoid of offensive words. The following week, the experiment was repeated, but with the girls showing up after the viewers had drunk a great deal of beer. This time the profanity did not cease in the presence of the females. In essence, this was an observation, but one done in which conditions were controlled. The investigator did not actually participate, for he did not interact with the viewers beyond greeting them and saying good-bye. What he demonstrated was that, even in these liberated days, men feel inhibited about swearing in front of women, an inhibition, like so many others, lessened by alcohol.

A classic participant observation is Labov's (1966, pp. 63–89) famous department store survey. Checking on his intuition that [r]-full pronunciation was becoming a sign of middle- and upper class- speech in New York City, Labov visited three department stores: Saks Fifth Avenue, Macy's, and the now-defunct Klein's. Saks caters to the wealthy. Macy's is a solid middle-class store, and Klein's, in an unfashionable neighborhood, was a low-priced store aimed at the blue collar and lower classes, although, like Macy's, people of all classes shopped there. Starting on the first floor of each store, Labov asked a sales clerk to direct him to a department he knew to be on the fourth floor. He called this the **casual** style. He then asked the question a second time to obtain a careful repetition. He called this the **emphatic** style. When he reached the fourth floor, he asked, "Excuse me, what floor is this?" On both floors, sales clerks had to answer "Fourth floor." These words have the [r] in the two positions that it is not pronounced in so-called [r]-less speech: before a consonant and at the end of words. As he had predicted, Labov found almost no [r]'s in Klein's, somewhat more in Macy's, and the most in Saks. In the exclusive upstairs salons of Saks, there were even more incidences of [r]'s than on the first floor, which looks more like any other department store and has somewhat less-expensive goods. This study yielded a great deal of significant data in a short time. It had the advantage that the speech of the employees being analyzed was wholly unself-conscious and natural.

This survey is an example of an ingenious investigation, but it also illustrates some real dangers of observation. Since he did not ask any of the salesclerks where they came from, it might be that those who were [r]-full were not native New York City speakers. New York has long been a mecca for people around the country. Also, there is no check on what Labov actually heard. We have to take his word for the fact that he heard what he said he did. Yet, linguists, especially, know all too well that people hear what they expect to hear. There are various degrees of sharpness in pronouncing [r], as Labov himself noted. Often, listeners fail to hear a lightly constricted [r]. The greatest pitfall in all science is that an investigator finds what he or she sets out to find. There is simply an all-too-human tendency not to notice what is not relevant to one's purpose and to think that one has seen or heard what is. Labov himself admits this problem with the department store survey, and he did follow it up with other experiments that studied the same feature of speech, using careful and highly innovative methodologies.

Verifying Results

One can lessen the problem of personal bias in a study such as Labov's department store study in two ways. First, get a partner. At least there will be one other pair of ears or set of eyes to verify what is going on. Second, in these days of tiny recorders, tapings are possible if one adheres to ethical standards, as noted below.

Tape recordings and videos of your studies certainly enhance verifiability. The advent of good tape recorders has made the dialect worker's lot simpler than the older method of transcription as the consultant spoke, but tape recorders are not panaceas. For one thing, especially recordings made in the field, as opposed to a lab, prove to be fuzzy when played back. Environmental noises, hissing, and buzzing may intrude. One finds that the subject's voice fades in and out, or comes out as an indistinct mumble, often in crucial places. Also, even experienced phoneticians may have problems determining exactly which sounds were uttered. Certain sounds come through as almost identical on tape. For instance, it is sometimes difficult to distinguish between [f], [s], and [θ].

Even with the clearest of recordings on the best of equipment, transcription can be difficult if an investigator has to determine very fine differences in pronunciation. Since fine differences are sometimes socially significant, it is essential that transcription be accurate. There are literally hundreds of potentially important pieces of information in every interview, from fine variations in pronunciations to grammatical choices to the very organization of a narrative. All must be noted, categorized, and correlated with other factors. Giving an interview often takes hours, and it can take days to extract all of the data from each interview. Consequently, sample size must be limited.

Virtually any study of body motion, facial expression, or the like demands photographs or videotapings. Their value needs no explication.

Replicability and Variation

In order for any study to be valid, it must be **replicable**. This means that someone else can do the study exactly as the original researcher has and come up with comparable results. Years ago, there was some flurry about a book which purported to show that plants can understand language, a book presenting an impressive list of experiments which "verified" this proposition. The only problem was that nobody was ever able to replicate any of these experiments.

One can also do a study and change one of its **variables** and get a result accounted for by the variation. For instance, Wallace Chafe and his cohorts studied the ways people speaking different languages and coming from different cultures narrate a movie they had just seen (Chafe, 1980). They all saw the same movie. The variables here, then, were the differences in language and culture, not the movie. I adapted this study to a population of diagnosed schizophrenics (Chaika and Alexander 1986; Chaika 1990), with a matched normal population as **controls**. The variable in my study, then, was the schizophrenia. The normals performed like other Americans in the Chafe et al. study. Therefore, differences in features of the narrations could be related to the fact of schizophrenia.[3]

It was not that normals made no errors and schizophrenics did. Both populations had glitches in their narratives, but the schizophrenics did certain things the normals didn't. For instance, normals would break a sentence off in the middle, give a comment, and then resume, as in:

▶and then she—**her father came home from work, whatever—**
she asked her father for money.

In contrast, when the schizophrenics broke a sentence off in the middle, they never resumed it, as in:

▶he was blamed **for** and I didn't think that was fair the way they did that either.

▶and asks if she can **have** then goes to the ice-cream place...

Sampling

The purpose of the investigation helps determine sample size and composition. If one wishes to contrast two attitudes in a community, a much smaller sample is needed than if one wishes to delineate general social stratification. Ten to 20 speakers from each social group in the community is generally considered a sufficient number, especially if long and varied interviews are given. Fortunately, there are statistical measures that allow one to extrapolate from small samples (Woods, Fletcher, and Hughes 1986, pp.101–110).

Finding speakers to observe or interview is a problem in itself. Using any given source might skew the distribution of members in a sample so that it is not representative of the population at large. School enrollment lists skew toward the younger population, those with children in school as well as the pupils themselves. Voting lists do not give names of those who are unregistered, often the poorest or lower classes. Telephone books do not give names of people with unlisted numbers. If, as Anshen (1978) thinks, these are the rich, then they will be underrepresented in the sample.

However one chooses from a population, one is sampling randomly within each group in the community. One can also do **quasi-random** sampling (Butler 1985, p. 3). This is done by selecting the first person—or unit, if people aren't the targets—randomly, then choosing the others at equal intervals, say every twentieth. Rarely can one study every single person within any group, unless one is studying, as Labov et al. (1968) did, a relatively small gang. This means that within each group there is random sampling. Understanding this is important when analyzing results statistically.

In order to come to valid conclusions, there must be an adequately representative sampling of the **target population**, the population under consideration (Woods, Fletcher, and Hughes 1986 p.49). For sociolinguistics, adequacy depends upon distribution as well as numbers if you are comparing or describing more than one group. Even within what you think is one group, say urban blacks or women or Jews, you have to consider that there might be age and/or educational differences, or differences according to length of residency, or some other factor. Therefore, rarely is it sufficient simply to have a percentage of a total population of a city or town, or even a neighborhood, unless those locales are remarkably homogeneous in the above factors.

Usually, the investigator first groups the population on such factors as age, sex, ethnic origin, race and social class, even gangs and club membership, if these seem potentially important. Investigation may show that some of the groups are not significantly different, but speakers still have to be chosen from every possible group at the outset of the sampling. Otherwise, significance or lack of it cannot be proven.

Generally speaking, the larger the sample tested, the more valid the results. However, the analysis of sociolinguistic data is exceptionally time-consuming as one gets so many hundreds, even thousands, of potentially valuable data from each subject. Every variation in pronunciation, grammar, word choice, voice quality, and body motion, all may have to be recorded and tabulated.

One good place to start is the sociology department of a nearby college or university to see if a general sociological survey of the area has been made recently. This not only points to the probable significant groupings in the community but is a source of subjects as well.[4]

Too often, in the United States just about all studies of standard versus nonstandard dialects and, more recently, studies of literacy versus illiteracy, have really been studies of SE, used both by blacks and whites as opposed to the black vernacular, rather than studying other kinds of nonstandard speech as well. This is a faulty and even dangerous practice, confusing issues of race and standard speech, which may be very separate factors in one's results. Since middle-class African American speech is largely ignored, readers can get the impression that African Americans are all nonstandard speakers and perhaps are also illiterates. This is certainly not true. (See Chapters 6, 8, and 9). Other issues influencing results of such studies are that, feeling antagonistic to middle-class teachers, children of color may not have learned the skills that they were taught. Or, middle-class teachers with a low evaluation of persons of color in inner-city schools, may not bother pushing for skills. This is not to say that either of these is necessarily the case. The thing is we don't know. Readers must beware of studies which equate nonstandard speech with members of one race and standard with members of another. Unfortunately, some of our richest studies of standard dialects and literacy have confounded the issues because of such an equation.

In reporting the results of any investigation, it is essential to state explicitly what population was tested, how it was selected, what methodology and techniques were used, and how the data were extracted and analyzed. This information is all potentially pertinent to the results obtained and to their analysis.

Statistics

We also have to show that our results didn't happen by chance. For this, we have to use **statistical tests**. Some people think we can make statistics say whatever we want them to. Unfortunately for researchers, this is simply not true. Nor is it true that, as the old saw goes, "There are lies, damned lies, and statistics." It is true, however, that there are several kinds of statistical tests which can be applied, each for somewhat varying purposes. It is not unusual for a student, scholar or researcher to be criticized because she or he didn't do a given test, one that would give a different result. One of the reasons that scholars give papers at meetings and publish in journals is so that their analyses can be subjected to such checks. Thus, scholarship improves.

It is, of course, not possible in a text such as this to present enough material so that readers can actually learn how to apply statistical measures. It is useful, however, especially for those who have not had a course in it, to explain the purpose of statistics and, very generally, what they mean and why they must be used. That is the intent of the following discussion.

The purpose of statistical analysis in the social sciences is simple enough: to see if differences in scores, or other facts, between two or more groups occur because of the random variation that one would get in any population. If the results couldn't happen by chance, then we have a **significant difference**. This term should only be used for results which have been subjected to tests of **probability** (Anshen 1978; Butler 1985; Woods, Fletcher, and Hughes,1986). In order to have a significant difference, the probability of our results occurring by chance has to be less than one in 20, written as $p=<.05$. That is the highest our p score can be. If $p<.01$ (one in a hundred) or $p<.O1$ (one in a thousand), it is even better.

Labov did not use statistics in his dialect studies. He said that it was not necessary to use statistics when "results are repetitive" (Labov, 1969). Lawrence Davis (1982) shows that this is not true. Davis analyzed Labov's results in the department store survey and found that some of the differences were not significant. For instance, he found that there was not a significant difference between employees at Macy's and Klein's when they pronounced *fourth* emphatically, but there was a significant difference in the casual pronunciation between Saks and Macy's when pronouncing *floor*. However, this is mighty slim evidence that [r]-dropping increases the lower the class, especially when we recall that Labov sampled a population, salesclerks, without knowing anything about their backgrounds. He assumed what social class people belong to on the basis of the feature he had already decided was lower class. This is a classic example of circular reasoning.

You are already familiar with one kind of measure used in statistics: the **mean**, the technical term for *average*. By itself, however, the mean can be very misleading. For instance, we know that nobody pronounces a sound in only one way all of the time. Rather, pronunciation varies. Labov (1966) showed that people from all classes sometimes pronounced the [θ] more like *t* in words like *throw, thing*, and *death,* but that the variation correlated with feelings of identity with different social groups. Characteristically, each pronounced it a different percent of the time. Suppose I wish to replicate Labov's study. I find that two different groups, X and Y, make the *t* for [θ] a mean of 12 times out of a possible 24. If, however, this was distributed so that X pronounced [θ] 24 times, and Y never pronounced it at all then these two groups are heterogeneous and probably shouldn't even be compared. In other words, they form two distinctly different groups. If, however, I find that X pronounces the [θ] fifteen times and Y does so nine times, I still have an average of 12, but it means something quite different. The two groups are comparable and [θ] is a speech variable for both groups (which it isn't if one group never pronounces it and the other always does).

However, we still don't know if the difference between X and Y has occurred by chance. In order to know this, we have to see how closely the scores cluster around the mean. Thus we find the **standard deviation**.

What this tells us is:

If the deviation from the mean is very large compared to the standard deviation, then we conclude that there is a **significant difference** between the populations. If the difference between the means is small compared to the standard deviation, then we conclude that the difference is due to chance.

Where did chance come in? Recall that the members of the two groups were selected at random (by chance) as representatives of each group. When you take random samples from any group, you will observe random differences among sample means. The question is, is the difference in your study one of those random differences or is the difference greater than can be accounted for by random chance?

Richard Lambe (classroom lecture)

ETHICS

Finally, it is not ethical to make people unwitting guinea pigs. With few exceptions, if people are to take part in an experiment, no matter how innocuous, their consent must be obtained. The subjects have to be told exactly what is required of them and, as much as possible without wrecking the procedure, the purpose of the study. Under no condition should someone's performance be ridiculed or criticized in any way. At no time and for no reason should an investigator identify subjects or report their individual performances. If a subject tells the investigator something about his or her life, or makes any comment on a subject beyond the testing situation, that information cannot be used in any way without express consent of the subject. Hidden tape recorders and bugging devices should not be used unless subjects are told about them, preferably beforehand, and then the content of the tapes cannot be used without **informed consent**. This term means that the person taped, interviewed, or otherwise made a subject must give consent, knowing that results of his or her performance will be included in the general results of the study. It is far better to inform subjects that they are being investigated, get their consent, and get them accustomed to the presence of a tape recorder. One has to have very strong reasons for any other procedure. If one wishes natural dialogue, one can contact a club or other groups and ask their consent to record meetings, or one can invite friends to one's home, letting them know a tape is being made and why. The tape recorder can be placed in full view, and as the interaction gets under way, people simply forget about it.

It does not take much reading in sociolinguistics to come across studies done by hidden tape recorders. This is done only in studies of anonymous people in which semantic content is not reported in print or orally, and then only if the data cannot reasonably be obtained in any other way. In the Zimmerman and West study described above the hidden tape recorder was justified in order to achieve the kinds of insights into male-female relations they were investigating.

Soskin and John (1963), seeking to analyze naturally occurring data, got permission to tape a young married couple all day long while they were on vacation. This yielded highly natural data of male-female interaction without resorting to deception, but such a procedure is extremely time-consuming. Moreover, it does not allow adequate sampling. The interactions of one couple are hardly enough to come to any conclusions about male-female interactions generally. The time needed to transcribe and extract data for each couple is horrendous. Think, for instance, of how often even the quietest of us speaks in a day. Then, too, this procedure tells us only about intimate relationships. What about non-intimate ones?

It must be emphasized that science is not an excuse for immorality. People are always entitled to privacy. Hidden recording devices are uncomfortably close to eavesdropping. Before moving in close enough to record, the investigator should make sure the conversation is not private or intimate in any way. Only public transactions qualify, such as greetings and chitchat, conversations on buses, or on benches at malls. If a conversation is loud enough for everyone around to hear easily and no attempt is being made to mask the content, it can justifiably be considered public. The same limitations hold for any other method of preserving conversation, such as writing it down as one hears it. Even if one jots down only selected features of a conversation, such as the number of pauses or interruptions, there should be no eavesdropping on private interactions without prior consent.

Chapter 7 Notes

[1]   These are what most laypersons think of as "an accent", but, as we shall see, it also involves grammar and words as well.

[2]   It must be stressed that a deep voice in a woman might still be higher than a high voice in a man. Often, a man's voice, even if high, will still be heard as lower than a woman's.

[3]   Actually, the Chafe movie was too long and potentially threatening to this schizophrenic population, as would be the paraphernalia of a movie. Therefore, I devised a shorter sequence on videotape, but the task itself was the same.

[4]   The technical term for subjects in a dialect investigation used to be **informants**, but this term nowadays has unfortunate connotations of 'stool pigeon'. Some researchers use the term *consultant* instead, as I did in the first edition of this book. That term, however, has connotations of formal expertise on the part of speakers under investigation. Whereas in one sense this is valid, (that is, people do

have competence in speaking like members of their own social groups), they are not consultants in the sense of a doctor or scholar called upon to consult. Hence, falling back on the term *subject* seems to be the most accurate and least insulting strategy.

Exercises

1. Suppose you wanted to discover how people ranked your accent—or that of an acquaintance. How would you go about setting up a study to do this? What uses might such a study have? How would you design your study so that it could be used for these uses?

2. How would you go about getting a sample of subjects? From what populations would you choose your subjects? How is this population related to the purpose of your study?

3. You want to find out whether or not males are more likely than females to try to solve problems rather than to sympathize with someone's problem, or to find out if males are more competitive in their speech than females. How would you set up a study to investigate any such problem? What pitfalls would you anticipate and how would you try to avoid them?

4. Take a five-minute tape recording of anybody speaking. Try to transcribe it. How long does it take? Have someone else check your transcription. Do they find you have transcribed something wrong? Or differently from how they would? Were there any portions of the tape you couldn't transcribe? What does this experience tell you about dealing with large amounts of oral language in a study?

5. Make up an informed consent form that you might use in a study of your own. Also make up a questionnaire that asks for background information.

CHAPTER 7

References

Abercrombie, D. (1967). *Elements of General Phonetics*. Chicago: Aldine.

Anshen, F. (1978). *Statistics for Linguists*. Rowley, Mass: Newbury House Publishers.

Bereiter, C. & Engelmann, S. (1966). *Teaching Disadvantaged Children in the Preschool*. Englewood, N.J.: Prentice Hall.

Butler, C. (1985). *Statistics in Linguistics*. New York: Basil Blackwell, Inc.

Chafe, W. (Ed.). (1980). *The Pear Stories* (Vol. III). Advances in discourse processes. Norwood, N.J.: Ablex Publishing Co.

Chaika, E., & Alexander, P. (1986). The ice cream stories: A study in normal and psychotic narrations. *Discourse Processes, 9,* 305–328.

Chaika, E. (1990). *Understanding psychotic speech: Beyond Freud and Chomsky*. Springfield, IL: Charles C. Thomas, Publisher.

Davis, L. M. (1982). American social dialectology: A statistical appraisal. *American Speech, 57,* 83–94.

Giles, H., Baker, S., & Fielding, G. (1975). Communication length as a behavioural index of accent prejudice. *International Journal of the Sociology of Language, 6,* 73–81.

Giles, H., & Powesland, P. (1975). *Speech Style and Social Evaluation*. New York: Academic Press.

Kramer, E. (1963). Judgment of personal characteristics and emotions from non-verbal properties of speech. *Psychological Bulletin, 60,* 408–420.

Labov, W. (1969). Contraction, delection, and inherent variability of the English copula. *Language, 45,* 715–762.

Labov, W. (1963). The social motivation of a sound change. *Word, 19,* 273–309.

Labov, W. (1966). *The Social Stratification of English in New York City*. Washington, DC: Center for Applied Linguistics.

Labov, W., Cohen, P., Robins, C., & Lewis, J. (1968). *A Study of the English of Negro and Puerto Rican Speakers in New York City*. Philadelphia: U.S. Regional Survey.

Lambert, W., Giles, H., & Picard., D. (1975). Language attitudes in a French American community. *International Journal of the Sociology of Language, 4,* 127–152.

Laver, J. (1968). Voice quality and indexical information. *British Journal of Disorders of Communication, 3,* 43–54.

Milroy, L. (1980). *Language and Social Networks*. Baltimore: University Park Press.

Scherer, K. (1973). Acoustic concomitants of emotional dimensions: Judging affect from synthesized tone sequences. In S. Weitz (Ed.), *Nonverbal Communication* (2nd ed.). (pp. 249–253). New York: Oxford University.

Shuy, R., Wolfran, W., & Riley, W. (1967). *Linguistic Correlates of Social Stratification in Detroit Speech*. Washington, DC: HEW.

Soskin, W. F., & John, V. (1963). The study of spontaneous talk. In R. G. M. Barker (Ed.), *The Stream of Behavior*. New York: Appleton-Century-Crofts.

Tannen, D. (1979, October). When is an overlap not an interruption? [Talk]. First Delaware Symposium of Language Studies.

Tannen, D. (1984). *Conversational Style*. Norwood, N.J.: Ablex.

Trudgill, P. (1972). Sex, covert prestige, and linguistic change in the urban British English of Norwich. *Language in Society, 1*. 179–195.

Woods, A., Fletcher, P., & Hughes. A. (1986). *Statistics in Language Studies*. New York: Cambridge University Press.

Zimmerman, D. H., & West. C. (1975). Sex roles, interruptions, and silences in conversation. In *Language and Sex: Difference and Dominance* (B. Thorne & N. Henley, Eds). (pp. 105–129). Rowley, Mass: Newbury House.

Chapter 8

Everybody Speaks a Dialect

E very variety of a language is a dialect, even the standard. There is
no sharp dividing line between dialects and languages, although
considering a speech variety a separate language rather than a
dialect can have important political and social consequences. The identity
on projects is bound up with one's speech; hence people are concerned
with using language properly. Unfortunately, those who set themselves up
as experts rely on their own personal prejudices more than on scientific
studies of how people actually react to various speech forms.
Consequently, there is little agreement among the experts. The original
dialect studies were focused on creating linguistic geographies, finding out
how people of each region spoke. Americans increasingly want to sound
as if they don't have a regional accent, but there is no General American.
There is even great variety in regional and ethnic accents. People use ethnic accents to reaffirm their identity. Dialects differ in their lexicon, syntax,
and pronunciation, but all are equally rule-governed. People often misinterpret what speakers of other dialects actually mean. Despite the
onslaught of the media, regional, social, and ethnic dialect differences
remain strong in America, although educated speakers are sounding more
and more alike, at least when they are speaking carefully.

LANGUAGE VERSUS DIALECT

Dialect is the technical name for what Americans usually think of as
an accent. Strictly speaking, *accent* refers only to differences in pronunciation between one variety of a language and another. Dialect refers to all
the differences between varieties of a language, those in pronunciation,
word usage, and syntax. Often, as indicated in Chapter 4, there are paralinguistic differences between dialects: timbre, tempo, and the like, as well
as kinesic differences. These are usually ignored in traditional dialect studies, but that does not mean they are unimportant. To the contrary, they
are often vital in rendering a dialect and in perceiving it. However, only
the linguistic differences—the phonology, lexicon, and syntax—will be
considered in this chapter. In themselves, they are complex, and analyzing
them serves to illustrate the important points about dialects and how and
why they are used in social groups.

No sharp demarcation exists between language and dialect. As a rule of thumb, if two varieties of speech are mutually intelligible, they are considered dialects. If they are not, they are considered separate languages. In actual practice, the situation is far more complicated. There are dialects of one language which are not mutually comprehensible and separate languages that are. The fact that we can't establish an airtight difference between dialect and language might seem a bit of the usual academic nitpicking about definitions, but anything dealing with language has consequences for speakers. For instance, Smitherman (1984) as an expert witness in a class action suit against the city of Ann Arbor, Michigan, argued that Black English is a separate language, not merely a dialect of English, and that schools must take this into account in educating African American students. The Equal Educational Opportunity Act decrees that states must not "...fail[ure] to overcome language barriers that impede equal participation by its students in its instructional programs." The judge ruled that English, being a dialect, did not count as a language barrier, so that children who speak it are not being denied educational opportunity by a system which doesn't recognize it. Smitherman contends that Black English should be considered a separate language on the grounds of structural and sociolinguistic differences between it and other varieties of English. If it is, then schools would have to adjust their methods to African American speakers as they supposedly do for speakers of other languages like Spanish or Portuguese.

Certainly, the test of mutual intelligibility does not hold up when considering any number of languages, including English. And, often when people think they understand another's dialect, they are misunderstanding it. Smitherman (p. 103), for instance, shows how non-African Americans misunderstood Muhammad Ali's assertion that

There are two bad white men in the world. The Russian white man and the American white man. They are the two baddest men in the history of the world.

Smitherman points out that *bad* in the Websterian tradition means 'evil, wicked..' but in Black English it means 'powerful, omnipotent, spiritually or physically tough, outstanding, wonderful, and with emphasis, very good.'

Today, partially because so many languages have become far flung all over the world, often at least one of its dialects is likely to be understood by all speakers of that language. Some of the other dialects, however, may be understood by relatively few speakers, or at least not by all.

In Barbados, as elsewhere in the Caribbean, one dialect of English spoken primarily by blacks is called "talking bad" or "speaking broken" (Chaika 1982; Abrahams 1972). American and British visitors usually can't understand it at all, although they have no problem with standard Barbados English. However, natives to whom I have spoken, black and white, say that "bad talk" just sounds like another kind of English to them.

It is not only English that has such problems. In Italy, for instance, bordering dialects are mutually comprehensible, but those farther apart become increasingly less comprehensible to them, so speakers of rural dialects from the south of Italy often cannot be understood by those from the north. Rodney Delasanta, a native speaker of a northern dialect of Italian, says he could not understand bus drivers in Naples, even though he asked only for directions. His parents, one from the eastern border of Italy, and the other from the western, could not understand each other's native dialect.

Political boundaries, in themselves, often determine whether two speech varieties will be considered different languages or not. For instance, some varieties of Swedish, Norwegian, and Danish are mutually comprehensible, but they are considered different languages because they are separated by national borders. To show just how similar these are, Yvonne Sandstroem, a native speaker of Swedish, remarked to me that Scandinavian Airlines hires stewards and stewardesses from all three countries. They all speak their own native tongue and do not have to translate for the other Scandinavians on board.

Conversely, the so-called dialects of Chinese are as different as French from Italian, but because of national and ethnic feelings, they are not considered separate languages. Sometimes ethnic and social factors determine whether or not two varieties of speech are considered separate languages. A Norwegian scholar once complained to me that when Norwegian speakers appear on Swedish television, subtitles are used, but in Norway they are not used when Swedes are on Norwegian television. To say the least, the Swedes annoyed him. It's like saying that Norwegian isn't "good enough" to be considered mutually comprehensible with Swedish, although, in fact, it is. A similar situation can occur across generations. The Yiddish[1] dialects which were spoken by Jews of Eastern Europe are mutually comprehensible with many varieties of modern German. Both Germans and Jews regard Yiddish and German as separate languages, however. This is a direct reflection of the separate religious and cultural affinities of Yiddish and German speakers.

Social factors can even determine whether or not speech is comprehensible at all. In Africa, the Kalabari are a powerful and important people, but the Nembe who speak a closely related language are not. There seems to be no linguistic reason for the two speech varieties not to be mutually comprehensible. Yet the Kalabari claim that they do not understand the Nembe, and all communication between the two must be in Kalabari or Pidgin English.

A similar situation with dialects occurs in the United States. In public schools, standard-speaking teachers confronted with nonstandard-speaking youngsters often claim difficulty in understanding them. The teachers complain that the students' speech is deficient or broken. However, it has been shown time and again that dialects perceived as nonstandard are as systematically rule-governed as standard ones. Standard speakers don't perceive this because of their attitudes toward those who speak the nonstandard.

Another example of the fuzzy border between language and dialect is given by Trudgill (1983a, pp. 57–58). Although we consider a change in pronunciation to be confined to a language, spreading from one dialect to others, Trudgill shows how a dialect feature, the uvular [r],[2] has spread across national boundaries since its origin supposedly in Paris in the seventeenth century. It hit Copenhagen by 1780, and has spread to Germany and even northwest Italy (p. 56). What one would normally think of as spreading of a dialect feature has spread from one language to another.

Standard Dialects

One reason for the emergence of standard dialects, dialects that do not belong to any particular region, is the need for a speech variety that all people ruled by one national government can understand. As this need has grown in modern technological societies, the more widespread has been the development of national standards. Fairclough (1989) claims that a standard dialect is also a means of a certain class, those who have mastered it, to maintain power, as well as to be gatekeepers, declining to admit non-standard speakers to those positions which lead to power.

In modern countries, typically, there is a standard dialect which can be understood by just about all speakers. Because it is also based upon the speech of the educated, which in most countries concurs most closely with the written language (or perhaps most accurately, the written system is made to coincide with the standard), people often assume that the standard is the "true" language not realizing that it, too, is a dialect. Many people think that dialects are substandard, even defective. In fact, any variety of a language is technically a dialect, even the educated standard. Everyone speaks a dialect. Everyone has an "accent," except perhaps in those languages with so few speakers that there are no varieties at all. The dialect that becomes standard is an accident of history. It has nothing to do with intrinsic worth of the standard. All dialects are inherently equal, just as all languages are, although they aren't socially equal. Some dialects command more respect and power in some situations than others do.

Labov's studies have shown that all speakers in a community share the same standards, even if they don't use them. The evidence is quite clear that even nonstandard speakers would usually look askew at physicians or teachers who did not command at least some features of the standard. It is not at all clear that one has to command the standard perfectly, however. Again, Labov shows that people who use standard pronunciations as little as 30 percent of the time perceive themselves to use them all of the time. (See Chapter 9).

A British scholar might deliver a scientific paper in British RP (the "received pronunciation" spoken by the educated British), but not in Cockney, although that might be better in a brawl. A Brooklyn accent does not seem appropriate for lecturing college classes but it could be very convincing if one were running for political office in a working-class neighborhood. Television commercials often gear the speech variety to the product being sold: *Shake and Bake* and a Southern accent; *Poland Springs* mineral water and a Maine accent; four-wheel drives and a Texas accent. The accent suitable for a given purpose is related to the generally held image of people who speak that way. Often dialects are as stereotyped as the people themselves.

Frequently, because we associate certain kinds of speech with activities, a dialect will take on a vocabulary especially efficient for those activities. Hence, educated dialects have developed a tremendous number of scientific and other learned words. These differ from jargon only in that they are used by more diverse groups in broader social situations. Other dialects could as easily include the same words, but they do not because they are not used for the purposes that demand the particular expression.

Much of the ensuing discussion will be devoted to showing that nonstandard speech is as intelligent and complete as standard. Effective education and politics depend upon such understanding. This does not mean that I or linguists in general think that in speech anything and everything is all right. Even if one recognizes that all dialects are equally complete for their users' purposes, one can still recognize that educated dialects are necessary for many kinds of social functioning. James Sledd (1972) once forcefully condemned attempts to teach standard varieties of American English in school as: the "linguistics of White supremacy." In my opinion, such a view ignores the functions of dialect and the realities of social interaction.

It is necessary for students to be able to command educated varieties of speech if they wish to be able to hold certain kinds of jobs. However, any attempt to teach a standard dialect to a nonstandard speaker must take in to account why people speak as they do. It must also take into account why there are different dialects of a language and what conditions favor dialect learning.

Proper Speech

A good measure of the importance of speech variety is the anxiety it evokes. In the United States, because there is no one acknowledged standard as there are in countries like England, Italy, and France, the anxiety at times almost borders on hysteria. Proper speech is pursued with what can only be called religious fervor. Witness this advertisement for Fowler's *Modern English Usage*: "The most practiced writer will only too often find himself convicted of sin when he dips into Fowler." Clifton Fadiman, a respected scholar, author, and editor, wrote of Fowler that "it is the final arbiter of our language" and "it shows me how bad a writer I am, and encourages me to do better." The equation of grammar choice with sin, with being bad, makes it appear that *Modern English Usage* is on a par with the Old Testament. New Testament status has to be reserved for Nicholson's *American English Usage*, which is based upon Fowler's.

For most Americans, however, the dictionary is the final arbiter of correctness. Fowler and Nicholson are reserved for the select few whose sins are too subtle for Webster's. In 1961, *Webster's Third* unabridged edition innovated. Rather than acting as prescriber of "correct" usage and condemning "substandard" usage, it just listed how words are actually pronounced and used in American English. It lacked convenient labels like "vulgar," "preferred," and "slang." Dr. Max. Rafferty, then superintendent of schools for the State of California, said:

> If a dictionary doesn't exist to set standards and maintain them, what possible use can it have? ...when I go to a dictionary I want to know what's right. I already know what folks are saying. What I want to know is what they should be saying.
> (Pyles 1972, p. 167)

The intensity of concern about proper language forms is startling. One would think that any form short of profanity is proper so long as it's comprehensible. Why can an advertisement promising to convict writers of sin sell a book? The ad for Fowler's reads like a call to that old time religion, not a reference book. Why should an exceptionally literate writer feel that Fowler had the right and competence to show him that he is bad? That word *bad* in itself in the context that Fadiman uses it has a strangely moralistic ring. Dr. Rafferty, an outspoken man, was certainly not one to be swayed by mere public opinion. Why, then, was he willing to take the word about his use of words from a dictionary? The answers to these questions are found when we consider the role of dialects in social functioning.

Over the years, many have warned, wailed, and predicted direly that the language is decaying. No matter that people are understanding each other with perfect ease, and no matter that there is no evidence at any time in history that a language can decay so that speakers no longer can understand each other. John Simons and Edwin Newman, neither of whom are scholars, have had great success castigating the educated for their writing. The fans of their books, respectively, *Paradigms Lost* and *Strictly Speaking*, object, "But they're trying to save the language from decay." They are far from alone in their concern.

Often such self-appointed arbiters of language have very little understanding of how English or any other language really works. They have never considered language objectively. For instance, one can find commentators railing that English is in a state of decay because it "confuses" nouns and verbs. That is, nouns are being used as verbs and vice versa. Jean Safford, a Pulitzer prize winner, excoriated a writer for "Her hair *haloed* her head."

The problem with her reasoning is that English has always done this. Surely even the most careful writers use words like *love, group, kill, hunt,* even *man* or *police* both as nouns and verbs, and for that matter, as adjectives. The practice is not confined to English. Most and probably all languages allow words to cross part-of-speech boundaries in some way. If a language did not allow slipping across boundaries, many of the meanings one wished to convey would need at least two distinct roots: one for a noun, another for a verb. It is much more economical to use the same root as a noun, a verb, and/or an adjective simply by changing the grammatical signal slightly. This may be done by changing suffixes, prefixes, or other syntax markers such as sentence position or *the* before a noun. To give an English example, there is no confusion in interpretation of *love* or *group* in any of the following:

The *love* I had for him is gone. (noun)
I *love* candy. (verb)
That was quite a *love* tap. (adjective).
That's a good *group*. (noun)
Let's *group* them this way. (verb)
It's a *group* project. (adjective)

Great poets often demonstrate their artistry by using old words in new ways, helping us to make new connections by just such violations of part-of-speech boundaries. Think of Shakespeare's "But me no buts" or Dylan Thomas's "the cargoed apples" or "the sweethearting cribs."

It does make sense to suppose that changes in the language could lead to its decay, except that all language is always in a state of change. That is what makes it such a delicate social instrument. In the past 1000 years, English has changed so that its earliest writings have to be studied as if they were written in a foreign language. At no time has such natural change led to a breakdown in communicability, at least among those living at about the same time and in the same regions. Someone who does not understand a new coinage can always ask the speaker who uttered it to paraphrase it. It takes centuries of change before incomprehensibility sets in.

Many historians of the language have taken special delight in poking fun at the preachers of the doctrine of correctness and their followers. This is easy to do, especially since many of the supposed sins of language are among the oldest forms in English and have been found in the best of English writers: Chaucer, Milton, Shakespeare. Worse, there is no justification in the history of the language for many of the rules prescribed by those who would save our speech. They were made up out of whole cloth by self-styled educators like Bishop Robert Lowth in the eighteenth century or self-appointed experts who have never examined language objectively. Such criticism of the purists miss the mark, though, for historical jusification has nothing to do with what should or should not be considered correct.

Neither, apparently, does it make much difference who is telling us what is or is not all right. Who was Fowler that he could condemn speakers of verbal sin? Who are writers of dictionaries? Why are they privy to divine revelation denied the rest of us? Scholars like Thomas Pyles, W. Nelson Francis, Elizabeth Traugott, who are authorities on the history of English, are far less likely to be heeded than prophets like Fowler, Nicholson, Safford, or Newman. Who ever asks the qualifications of an arbiter of language?

What is perhaps most puzzling of all is that people who unquestioningly accept the authority of such arbiters are often precisely those who have been the best trained in questioning what they read, examining all arguments for flaws, or accepting nothing without empirical proof. All this training flees when they hear a lecturer or a writer criticize middle-class usage, prophesying doom and decay. Even the best-educated leap into the lap of the saviors of language. It is they who equate language with sin, who want to be told how to talk, who seek some authority who will tell them what is correct, and, even better, what is incorrect. Others may not notice if you use phrases correctly, but they will notice if you do not. For an educated person publicly to commit a grammar error is profoundly humiliating, like being caught slobbering over food. The heretic few, mostly linguists, who scoff at the doomsayers and linguistic saviors are themselves scoffed at.

Since those who delve into dictionaries, flock to Fowler, and kneel to Newman are clearly among the best and brightest, they cannot be dismissed as unintelligent. For that matter, both Newman and Safford, like most who plead for correct speech, are highly intelligent, perceptive, and literate. Newman is correct, I think, in his judgments about the clumsiness of academic and government writers, but this is not necessarily indicative of mind mold. Language is patently an emotional issue, not wholly an intellectual one. As we shall see in this chapter and the next, the concern with keeping language pristine, if in fact it ever was pristine, stems from social psychological needs. More is at stake in the forms of the language one uses than communicating per se.

Dialect and Identity

Dialect studies show that how one speaks is inextricably bound up with one's identity. Who one is, how one may be treated, and how one may treat others are all proclaimed in one's speech. In earlier times, in stable societies, people in a community knew one another and knew where everyone belonged on the social scale. Where there is little social mobility all one needs to know to assess another's social rank is what family the person belongs to. In many cultures, there are other indicators as well: clothing, hairstyles, jewelry, dwelling place, automobile. Today none of these is exclusive to any one social class. The son of a janitor might be a college president. An eighth grade graduate may own a home next door to a high-ranking business executive with two master's degrees. Even occupation fails as a guide. Your local wood-carver might hold a Ph.D., and the driver of your cab might be an expert on Jane Austen. Nowadays, rich or poor, lawyer, doctor, plumber, or ditch digger all wear the same sorts of clothes, can afford the same gold chains, and style their hair the same ways. The differences between individuals have less to do with money than with other attitudes, such as identifying with punks or preppies. Because of the homogeneity of other aspects of culture, speech is likely to be the most reliable determiner of social class or ethnic group.

This is a matter of great concern to the educated middle class, which above all wishes to be identified as educated. Its members' being recognized as those to be listened to hinges strongly on language. When people say they want to know the right way to speak, they do not mean the right way to communicate their ideas but, rather, the right way to announce that those ideas are to be respected. To some degree, perhaps, people who fear innovation and change in language may really fear that they will no longer know the rules. That is not as petty as it may sound. Not to know social rules is a serious busines to eminently social creatures such as human beings.

When we speak of talking "properly," we are not talking about some objective standard which can be shown to be superior to any other. Rather, what is considered proper is quite arbitrary and depends on who is speaking, the history of a region, and many other accidental and historical facts. Still, unlike many linguists, I do not put *properly* in between quotations, because in terms of social class, speaking properly for that class is exceedingly important.

The rebels among us might ask, isn't it irrational to dread not speaking right or being caught in a solecism (a mistake)? Using incorrect—that is, nonstandard—forms can have consequences that strike right at the heart of middle-class privilege. One field method used to test this out has been the matched guise technique, in which a speaker who commands both the standard and a nonstandard dialect equally well records the same speech in each of his or her guises. In one such study, in which on alternate nights, British movie-goers were asked to fill out a survey questionnaire, people who were asked to do so in standard dialect were not only more likely to fill out the form, but wrote more information than those who received the same request in nonstandard speech. By having the same speaker in both instances, the investigators were assured that it was dialect that people were responding to, not voice quality.

Crowl and MacGinitie (mentioned in Giles and Powesland 1975, p. 91) had six white and six black[3] speakers read identical answers to two questions. The blacks spoke in ethnic Black dialect, which is thought of as nonstandard (hereafter called BE as opposed to AE for Appalachian nonstandard dialect and NE for other white nonstandard varieties.) Many scholars believe that BE is unique in its origins and should not be lumped with "white" nonstandard dialects. The Whites spoke one of the educated standard American dialects hereafter termed SE.[4] Although exactly the same answers were read, the judges consistently rated the SE answers as better. It is not what is said but how it is said that counts. Intuitively you probably knew that. Imagine a philosophy professor lecturing, "To tell you da trut' da problem of good 'n evil ain't gone away." as opposed to "A consideration of the problem of good and evil entails a realization that definitive answers may well be impossible." Although both statements mean the same thing, the second one sounds more authoritative, even more intelligent. Notice that the nonstandard utterance is just as intelligent, in fact, as the one in standard dialect, but listeners are more likely to rate the second as sounding more intelligent than the first. One can be brilliant and say brilliant things in nonstandard dialects, but whether or not people will take one seriously in intellectual matters is another matter.

Speech variety may also influence how willing people are to help. Gaertner and Bickman (1971) had both black and white callers telephone 540 black and white subjects, pretending to get the wrong number. Callers told each subject that they were stranded and had used their last dime. Then they requested that the subject call another number to send help. At this number there was a confederate of the caller who recorded which subjects had responded to the caller's request for aid. Black subjects helped black and white callers equally. Whites helped blacks less frequently than they helped whites. This, of course, might also be explained on the basis of racial prejudice; however, it does show that the dialect used does in and of itself, affect how others treat you.

Giles, Baker, and Fielding (1975) developed an experiment to test the effect of nonstandard English (NE) that did not entail racial differences. Theirs was based upon SE in its British RP form and the NE of Birmingham, England. They used a matched guise technique, having had a male speaker who was equally proficient in both dialects address two groups of high school students. The students had to write letters of recommendation stating their opinion of this speaker as a suitable candidate to lecture high school students about the nature of university studies. The students also had to evaluate him on traditional rating scales. Giles et al. based this experiment on earlier findings that subjects write longer letters about someone they like than about someone they don't like. Also, it had previously been demonstrated that subjects speak more when they are conversing with someone they like.

Giles et al. figured that if more students wrote letters for the fake candidate and wrote longer opinions when he was speaking in one guise than in the other, that would constitute proof that the dialect alone caused him to be rated differently. What happened was that the high school students to whom the speaker had used SE wrote a whopping 82 percent more about him than those who heard him talk in NE. Finally, 13 out of 18 found him "well-spoken" when he spoke as a standard speaker, but only 2 out of 28 who heard him speak nonstandard described him that way.

It must be emphasized that the task in the experiment by Giles et al. is one in which standard speech is considered suitable. One expects educated speech from a man lecturing students about preparation for the university. NS speakers are typically judged higher than SE speakers on some traits, such as being humorous, hardworking, sincere, and being more trustworthy in a fight (Lambert, Giles, and Picard 1975). Bernstein (1971) points out that the selection of an NE dialect, what he calls "restricted code," is a way of indicating bonding, but an SE dialect exhibits status. There is strong evidence that the "in" group of African American urban youth prefer those who speak BE. Those who didn't actually used to be called "lames," and were treated like outsiders (Labov 1972).

Regional nonstandard dialects have survived the massive onslaught of the media and the general mobility of people from one region to another in the United States. Therefore, it is clear that nonstandard dialects have a value for their speakers. Furthermore, the very fact that SE speakers adopt nonstandard forms from time to time suggests that even they value it positively for some purposes.

TRADITIONAL DIALECT STUDIES

Traditional dialect studies concentrate on fine points of pronunciation and lexical differences in different regions. In the older American studies the only syntax investigated were those items that are most closely related to word choice, such as *you-all* or the selection of *dived, dove,* or *div* as one of the dialectal variants for the past tense of *dive*. With a few exceptions, such studies did not analyze dialects as interrelated complex systems as has been done more recently. (See sections 7–10). This is probably because traditional dialect studies were best at eliciting single words from informants, not entire sentences, much less discourses.

They were concerned with linguistic geography[5], the regional distribution of differences in speech (McIntosh 1952; Bloomfield 1965; Francis 1983). They were also interested in basilects, the "older, indigenous, 'pure' form of speech" (Francis 1983, p. 72). These concerns are far from dead, although more recent work focuses on social as well as geographical concerns (e.g. Trudgill 1983b).

Since the earlier investigators were scholars thoroughly trained in the history of language, they were also very interested in the spread of words and sounds from one region to another because of cultural influence or migration. By cultural influence they usually meant finding out when and why words were borrowed from other languages or dialects. In the United States, it has been possible to map the migrations of settlers as they moved westward. For instance, Carver (1987, p. 210) shows that about half of the words which define the West come from the Upper Midwest[6], "showing a close linguistic connection" between these regions. Carver (p. 217) also shows that there is a "wavelike pattern spreading west and northwestward from a core area in Arkansas, east Texas, and northern Louisiana", but these fade as we move toward western Texas and northern Missouri, and fade even more by the time one gets to California. Carver points out that settlement in California is "still too new to have created relatively uniform speech areas," and one can find words there from most of the original eastern and midland settlements in the West, including California. In general in the West, so much of the population comes from somewhere else that it is difficult to find dialect divisions (p. 219). Carver also notes that the West is still going through a process of dialect mixing and leveling. After this, comes the formation of new dialects (p. 220).

Carver explains that the conditions of settling the eastern seaboard and midland areas in the United States were very different from the settlement in the West (p. 20). He thinks of this primarily in geographic terms, the close settlement in the East as opposed to the more isolated settlements in the Southwest.

Linguists in North America began the painstaking work for an atlas in 1931. Raven McDavid, Jr. (1958, pp. 480–533) as principal field-worker for this project, entitled *The Linguistic Atlas of the United States and Canada*, explains its purpose as follows:

> Thus, the American Atlas seeks to record data illustrating the social differences, the dimension of time, and the process of language and dialect mixture that has been going on everywhere since the New World was settled.

As with the European studies upon which it was based, the American linguistic atlas was concerned with the differences in speech between educated and uneducated speakers. To this end, field-workers trained to transcribe speech selected at least two speakers from each area: an older uneducated one and a younger, usually middle-aged one who had at least a high school diploma. The field-workers asked for information from questionnaires prepared for the atlas survey, such as the names of certain activities or items, noting the word choice itself as well as the pronunciation used. The three examples below are typical atlas questions, still pertinent today. The words in parentheses are some of the answers one might expect:

▶What do you call the place to which children run in a tag game? (goal, guwl, base, home, den)
▶Someone who won't change his mind is _____? (bullheaded, contrary, sot)
▶A large, open metal container for scrub water is a _____? (pail, bucket)
    (Shuy 1967)

The questionnaires listed 520 to 850 items. All responses had to be transcribed carefully in the International Phonetic Alphabet (IPA). Great care had to be taken to ensure that all the field workers were using the same symbols for the same sounds. As Francis (1983 p.93) put it, the field-workers had to be "recording machines." In the days before sensitive tape recorders, this was much more difficult than it is today. Then the transcriber had to be able to discriminate fine phonetic differences on the spot. Recordings were available and were employed, but these were primitive by modern standards. A well-trained fieldworker could be more sensitive.

After the painstaking work of collecting the data, they had to be sorted and classified. Maps showing both pronunciation and word choice had to be prepared. It took years to complete the investigation of each area and even longer for the publication of results. The *Linguistic Atlas of New England,* known informally as *LANE,* was begun in 1931, but was not completed until 1943. By 1949, the project of charting a complete map of all of America and Canada was abandoned. It simply was not feasible (Carver 1987, p. 3). Kurath (1949) published *A Word Geography of the Eastern United States.* In 1961 Kurath and McDavid published *The Pronunciation of English in the Atlantic States.* The fieldwork was completed for New England, the Midland South Atlantic states to the northeast tip of Florida, the North Central States, and the upper Midwest (O'Cain 1979). Of these, the only atlas other than LANE to be published in book form is Harold Allen's *Linguistic Atlas of the Upper Midwest* (Carver 1987, p. 3). E. Bagby Atwood's impressive work *The Regional Vocabulary of Texas* has been important in understanding the dialects of both the southern Delta and the Southwest. Carver (1987, p. 3) reports that 300 interviews in California and Nevada were completed in 1959, but the rest of Washington, Oregon, and Idaho in the Pacific Northwest have been done spottily. Moreover, most of these materials are still in archives but have been summarized by Reed and Reed. David Reed directed the work in California and Nevada, and Carroll Reed started the work in the Pacific Northwest. Additionally, we are indebted to researchers like Timothy Frazer who has done extensive recent work in Illinois and surrounding areas, as well as others who have done fieldwork and published articles on smaller areas, including parts of cities.

Reputedly, British dialect specialists often could tell what town someone came from just by listening to them speak for a moment. As can be seen by this thumbnail sketch of dialect studies, this is not possible to do in the United States and Canada. Our information is still woefully incomplete, and, considering both the sheer size of this country and the rapidly changing social scene that characterizes it, it is doubtful if we will ever have a complete and up-to-date dialect geography.

In rapidly changing countries as large as the United States or Canada, the first part of an Atlas investigation is outdated long before the last is completed. The original plan was logical enough: start with the areas of first settlement and move westward as migration did. In 1931, the East Coast seemed entrenched as the cultural and educational center of the country. It was hard to foresee that influence would start flowing West to East with important consequences for linguistic geography.

DARE, the Dictionary of American Regional English under the aegis of its editor, Frederic G. Cassidy, covers just about the entire country.[7] This was possible because of its concentration on words alone, not pronunciations. From 1965–70, 82 field-workers "netted some two-and-one-half million individual responses" (Carver, p. 5). Since *LANE* was started in 1930, *DARE,* by going over the same region, was able to chart the changes over those years of dynamic change.

Carver himself took the *DARE* data and with the help of computers, created dialect maps of the United States from them. His maps concentrate on the migration and spread of words, not the words themselves. Together, they give us a comprehensive overview of this country. Timothy Frazer (personal communication) says that comparison of maps based on the atlas studies and the *DARE* field records shows a remarkable consistency in the distribution of words and phrases.

CRITICISMS OF THE ATLAS INVESTIGATIONS

More recent investigators have roundly criticized the kind of traditional study represented by the atlas efforts. A prime criticism is that people in interview situations use their most careful speech, what they think is correct, not what they ordinarily use. McDavid (1979) objects that some of the field-workers did manage to get casual style from interviewees. However, there was no regular attempt to get more than one style from them. As will be shown, formal style is as necessary to a sociolinguistic investigation as casual style is. Comparing both styles for any given speaker reveals crucial sociological information. Such comparisons are missing in earlier studies. However, the atlas studies were not intended to be sociolinguistic.

Also, the atlas studies investigated the speech of the descendants of the original settlers. They were not at all interested in variations in an area according to ethnic or racial mixes. But, again, that wasn't their original purpose. They were more interested in the linguistic history of each area. They were intended to show the spread of dialects, focal centers, and their area of influence. That they did.

Trudgill (1983b p. 33) complains also that no attempt was made in *LANE* to correlate the New England data with the regions of Britain with which it shares certain features such as the so-called intrusive *r* in phrases like "saw-r-it" for *saw it*, and "Martha-r-is" for *Martha is*. Given the excellent dialect geographies done in England, this is a bit surprising, but given the ready availability of *LANE,* this could be done even now. In fact, the atlas studies should prove excellent for such purposes as locating where settlers came from. For this, they are far superior than the newer sociolinguistic studies, but again, these have a different purpose.

An example will suffice to show the limitations and yet the need for speech geographies. Linguistic geography shows that the working class in eastern New England and New York City share the same /r/ rules as speakers of southern British dialects. That tells us a great deal about the history of the dialects and their range, but it does not tell us anything about the social worth of the /r/ rules in the different countries and the social purposes for which they are used.

Another limitation is well exemplified by Carver's (1987) recent and fascinating study of what has happened to the words plotted in *LANE* (as well as those used in studies of other regions). Citing *DARE,* he (p. 25) says that *orts,* meaning 'garbage' "was at one time known in...northeastern Massachusetts"; in the 1960's it still survived in the vocabulary of [two informants]," one in Bar Harbor, Maine and the other a native of New Bedford, Massachusetts. He does not include southern New England, including Rhode Island. Actually, the word is still well known in that state amongst the descendants of the original settlers. They may not be likely to use it, but they remember when they did use it and they recall their grandparents and parents having done so as well. Either the original atlas did not show the full range of the word, or the follow-up failed to interview the descendants of those who participated in the original studies. Linguistic geographies are useful for comparative purposes only insofar as their original findings and follow-up studies are accurate.

Still, atlases have their place. They show us what we might start looking for and give a historical framework for interpretations of linguistic differences. The dialect geographers did tremendously careful, detailed work. Whatever shortcomings their work had are attributable to the twin states of technology and of knowledge about language use at the time. It is no accident, I think, that sociolinguistics was born after the advent of modern portable tape decks. Most important, linguistic geography suggests where the investigators of social dialects should begin their work, and also gives them an idea of what to look for. One can't just go into a city or town and decide randomly what to look for. Simply listening to people speaking in the street doesn't tell you much, as you don't know their backgrounds, nor does it tell you about the things that have changed or are in the process of change. As we shall see, the changes themselves are crucial for a solid sociolinguistic study.

We have to bear in mind also that the original dialect geographies were done in Europe, in societies that were far more stable than any are now. The disruptions of World War II and its aftermath, combined with the rapid population growth all over America, caused a myriad of changes in American society, changes that couldn't have been foreseen in the 1930s when Kurath started his work. When Labov investigated Martha's Vineyard, it was a Martha's Vineyard already affected by the decline of farming and fishing following World War II.

THE MYTH OF GENERAL AMERICAN

A particularly persistent myth is that there is a dialect which is General American or there is a way of speaking which is accent free. This is not, however, true, nor apparently, has it ever been. Van Riper (1986) demonstrates that the term "General American" changed drastically with each new dialect study. That is, originally it was assumed to be a variety of English that was neither southern nor New England, but as other areas were investigated, its domain was variously considered to be

> ...westward to the Rocky Mountains or the Pacific Coast from the Connecticut River, from the Hudson River, from New England, from parts of New York City, from New Jersey, or from Ohio. It has even been given territory as far northeast as Maine.
> (Van Riper, p. 123)

Most of these domains were a result of happy ignorance on the part of researchers. They had not bothered with gathering comprehensive data (p. 131). Certainly, at least since 1940, we have known that there is a dialect boundary separating the Northern and Midland areas in the Great Lakes and Ohio valley regions, an area formerly thought to be General American. Moreover, the Middle Atlantic states and Western Pennsylvania have been shown to be separate dialect areas, as have Texas, Oklahoma, California, Nevada, and the Pacific Northwest. Timothy Frazer tells me that one cannot go twenty miles in any direction in Illinois without encountering dialect differences, which, indeed, one finds right within the boundaries of the city of Chicago itself, but in states like Indiana, one hears distinct differences in different regions, with some sounding more like—but not identical to—some southern dialects. As close as Milwaukee and Chicago are in distance, their dialects are as different as Boston's is from Providence's, which is considerable—despite their proximity. Van Riper concludes that so-called General American is actually a professional dialect taught in schools that train announcers, although one certainly can find differences in pronunciation between different TV and radio announcers. One thing is certain and that is that pronouncing /r/ wherever it occurs in spelling is now associated with General American speech, but vowel sounds differ considerably from dialect to dialect. Certainly, the common Midwestern pronunciation of [æ] in words like *Barry* and *happy* is not perceived as accent free by many Americans. There may be more of a standard Canadian English (Avis 1986), but, again, there is insufficient dialect investigation to back up this claim (Pringle 1986).

I am often asked, "What is the right way to speak?" or "Which region has the best speech?" In England, one knows that RP is the right speech. This is a social-class dialect, not a regional one. In that country, anyone with education, regardless of regional origin, speaks RP at least some of the time, and the regional dialects are all considered nonstandard to some degree. The United States, being a considerably larger and more culturally diverse country and one without the traditional sharp class divisions of England, has always had several regional standards in speech. One can sound educated in any of the regional standards. There have always been educated varieties of New England, Southern, Midwestern, Southwestern, or Northwestern speech. However, standards even within these areas have been changing a great deal since World War II and the consequent social and migratory upheavals that followed.

The Myth of Regional Dialects

Not only is there no one General American dialect, but there is really no one Southern, New England, Midwestern, California or other statewide or region-wide dialect. Each region is characterized by several interrelated dialects. It is not the case that each dialect is sharply split off from all the others. Rather, dialects are alike in some features and different in others. The more closely related, the more features alike, of course, but differences remain even within one region. Furthermore, regional words and pronunciations do not stop at the same boundaries.

A dialect map shows **isoglosses** and **isophones**. The isoglosses are lines showing the outward limit of a certain word usage, and the isophones are lines showing the outward limit of pronunciation. Actually, there will usually be scattered usage on either side of the lines.

In the days before the internal combustion engine, geographic obstacles like mountains or rivers created dialect boundaries as did trade routes like the old United States Route 44. This is true in all countries. For instance, in the United States the Appalachian Mountains created dialect boundaries between the coastal South and the mountain areas, and the Connecticut River is a major line between eastern and western New England. What people regard as the southern /r/-less accent is actually the coastal one, and what people REGARD as the New England /r/-less accent is actually eastern New England only and, even there, it is rapidly changing.

It is certainly possible to distinguish an educated speaker from Milwaukee from a Chicago or Boston one, even though all of them now pronounce their /r/'s. The differences lie in vowel pronunciations, tempo, intonation, and the like. Similarly, despite the fact that visiting Easterners are completely /r/-full, often Californians know within seconds that they come from "back East."

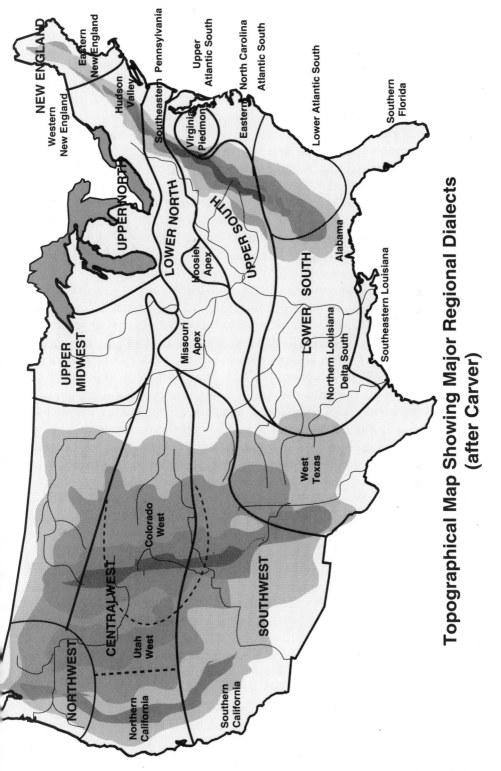

Topographical Map Showing Major Regional Dialects
(after Carver)

CHAPTER 8

DEVELOPMENT OF AN AMERICAN STANDARD

Since World War II, migration from birthplace has become so common that regional loyalties have been weakened. As we have seen, this is partially because social networks have also been weakened. This seems especially true for people most likely to move: the educated middle class who go where their jobs take them. More and more, at least on the East Coast, educated speech is losing its regional qualities. Many middle-class speakers seem almost aggressively pleased if they can claim, "No one can tell where I come from." Although this is truer of speakers about 50 and younger, occasionally informants as old as seventy make this boast. When East Coast middle-class speakers are asked to participate in a dialect study, they frequently respond, "Yes, but I don't have a [name of locale] accent."

The converse is that many Northeast and Southeast educated speakers are convinced that whatever they learned in childhood is not "General American." Throughout the formerly /r/-less dialect areas of the East Coast, both North and South, the /r/ is increasingly pronounced in words like *park* and *car,* especially amongst educated speakers. Many younger speakers, those in their thirties or younger, be they from Lexington, Massachusetts or Atlanta, Georgia consistently pronounce the /r/ wherever it occurs in spelling. At universities like Brown, Harvard, and Yale, with students from all over the country, it is often impossible to distinguish regional variations, even among freshmen. One can contrast Ted Kennedy's increased /r/-pronouncing in such words with the complete lack of /r/ before consonants in his late brothers' speech. Their children, the Kennedy cousins, seem all to be consistently /r/-full, even those like Patrick who was raised in Massachusetts and is now a Rhode Island state senator. Labov noted this change towards /r/-full speech in New York City as far back as the 1960s. Educated people all over the country are sounding more and more alike, although regional differences, particularly in vowels, persist.

As part of the myth that there is a General American dialect out there somewhere in the great Midwest, people associate /r/-full speech with being American. As we shall see, with some modification, so do British linguists, even those who are specialists in dialects like James Milroy (1984, p. 54) and J. C. Wells (1982, p. 473), although one would expect them to know differently. After World War II, America rose as a world power and Great Britain declined. In national terms, so did eastern New England. Southern dialects, the other /r/-less ones, had largely lost their prestige in the aftermath of the Civil War. No longer was /r/-lessness associated with power in America, nor, with the phenomenal growth of the great midwestern and western universities was the East any longer considered the repository of learning and culture. And, large cities drastically changed their sociological mix requiring new variables. The /r/-full pronunciation prevalent in most areas of the States and Canada already was a natural candidate for new prestige marking in formerly /r/-less areas. Thus, although the educated /r/-less accents are far from dead in America, the encroachment of a new /r/-pronouncing standard is evident up and down the eastern seaboard. This is the flip side of SE speakers switching into BE or NE in informal situations. A given pronunciation becomes associated with a given trait; it becomes copied when the image associated with that trait is projected.

It appears as if in time, the British situation may develop in the United States, with regional dialects being preserved mostly in ethnic, blue-collar and lower-class speech. Labov (1987) has shown that the African American vernacular in the inner city of Philadelphia is actually becoming more divergent from standard speech than before. He feels that this indicates a continuing and severe alienation of the younger African American population. Bailey and Maynor (1989) confirm Labov's findings among African American youth in Texas. They compared three age groups of African American rural lower-class speakers, including some old enough to have been slaves, finding that the actual grammar of teens and preteens diverge more from White speech. Bailey and Maynor caution that this finding does not indicate that race relations were better for older speakers than they were for younger. Indeed, more African Americans command standard dialects than before. However, the divergence among rural Texan lower-class youth from the standard indicates, as in Philadelphia, a disturbing separation of these speakers from the mainstream. Spears (1987) has a different take on this, however. He points out that the increasing divergence in BE dialects is not necessarily due to "increasing social isolation of black people" (p. 49). Spears says that this is an INDEPENDENT CULTURAL DEVELOPMENT (caps his), not a divergence, and that it shows that black communities are vital with a thriving cultural life of their own. In other words, we should not be looking at such a development as a feeling of isolation from whites, so much as a bonding between African Americans. Moreover, he points out (p. 51) that much of what is being labelled as a divergence has been around in BE and just not noticed before. This view of BE as a bonding signal explains also why working-class regional and other ethnic dialects are surviving in America.

Those who are primarily concerned with giving off an image of being educated are more and more modifying regionalisms at least in some situations; hence, the development of a national standard. It is dangerous to make any predictions with certainty, however. Sturtevant, in 1921, predicted that the entire country would speak like eastern New England within a generation or two, which indicates how prestigious that dialect was then. Then came World War II and changes that reversed the trend. These changes in American society, and even some in international politics, have changed the dialect patterns of this country.

Dialect overlaps with style of speech to announce the relative social status of participants in an interaction. Dialects can be used deliberately by speakers as a way of marking style, as when middle-class males in a macho mood adopt non-middle-class forms. Dialects differ from each other in the same ways as styles: phonologically, lexically, and syntactically. There are variant ways of pronouncing the same sound, of naming the same thing, and of creating sentences that mean the same thing, just as there are for styles. Like stylistic markers, dialectal ones are perceived independently of linguistic message, and the information the markers provide often is backgrounded in normal interaction. Some dialect messages, especially those that only give information about regional origin, can be overtly commented on. Those that give social class information, however, usually are not. You might say upon meeting a doctor or lawyer, "Oh, you're from Chicago!" but you would hardly comment, "Oh, you're educated" or "Despite your education you were raised in a working-class neighborhood."

Although some dialects are used as styles as well, most stylistic markers in American English don't overlap with dialect. For instance, recall the /t/+/y/ as an indication of formality, anger, and authority, as in "won't you" instead of [č] as in "woncha." Although precise enunciation signals formality, it is not a feature of any dialect in this country, even the most aristocratic. All dialects of American English regularly use [č] for /t/+/y/.

STATUS-MARKING IN WRITTEN LANGUAGE

For people in authority—scholars and bureaucrats, doctors and lawyers—written language can be made to serve the same function as dialect markers. Edwin Newman in *Strictly Speaking* is correct that much government and scholarly writing is overblown and unwieldy. It is not because English is decaying as he asserts, however. Such inflated writing is a signal that the author is educated. An idea expressed directly and in the simplest possible terms just does not sound cerebral enough to many writers. For instance, consider from a sociology article:

> Showing that will involve us in indicating the important sense in
> which this paper is necessarily a study in the methodology and

relevance of members' activities of categorizing members.
(Sacks 1972, p. 92)

This means:

Showing that will indicate that this paper is a study in how and why members of society categorize each other.

A second example from the same page is:

It seems the simplest way to show the generality of the categorization problem is by showing that no uncategorized population may be specified such that only one categorization device is available for categorizing the population's personnel.

In other words:

The simplest way to show the scope of the problem of categorizing is to show that no group can be categorized in only one way.

A part of becoming educated is learning to handle such overblown language.

Samuel Keyser's (1976) comment, that poems say quite ordinary things in unusual and artistic ways, can be applied to scholarly and government writing as well, except that *learned* has to be substituted for *artistic*. The educator who writes or speaks of *positive* rather than of *praising* is really letting readers (or listeners) know that he or she has had special courses in education that included scientific consideration of ordinary behaviors. It is not only English that is replete with scholarese and bureaucratese. It is the bane of modern industrialized societies. Any reader who has had to suffer through courses that included eighteenth or nineteenth century essays knows that the problem is not all that modern. The overblown Latinate writing of the twentieth century results from overblown Latinate writing of the past.

One reason such writing seems to be so prevalent today is, undoubtedly, that, with the advent of typewriters, word processors, and cheap and easy copying devices, more writing is being done today and more rapidly, hence more carelessly, than in earlier times. Another reason and perhaps the prime one is that the need for signaling status in sentence structure and word choice is tremendous in a world in which almost everyone can write.

This is not a defense of such writing, only an explanation. It is easy to accuse writers of being obscure because they want to hide their ideas or lack of them in a barrage of verbosity. That may well be true. What may be equally true is the principle that Bales uncovered (Chapter 4): He who speaks the most is considered smartest, no matter what his ideas. Apparently, obscure but plentiful phrasing and the spreading of semantic content over as many words as possible are equated with intelligence. If people are hard to understand but not bizarre or obviously incoherent, others may assume that they are hard to understand because they are brilliant.

PHONOLOGICAL VARIATIONS

Phonological variants in dialects are more diffuse than are those that operate stylistically. That is, in dialects, phonological variants occur in large sets of words, not limited environments like the [t] + [y] becoming [č] at word boundaries. In Chicago and other Great Lakes cities like Buffalo, Milwaukee, and Detroit[8], for instance, the *a* in words like *back, tag, Barry, that* and *sad* is pronounced [ɨ], whereas most Southerners and eastern New Englanders pronounce it as [æ]. Timothy Frazer tells me that much of the lower Midwest, including downstate Illinois, and the plains states also have the [æ]. In Great Lakes cities and other areas in which the [æ] is pronounced [I], people frequently pronounce the *o* in *John* or *not* as [æ], which is the sound used in *that* in other dialects. That is, they pronounce the vowel in *bad* with their tongues higher than people in other regions do, and they pronounce the *o* as well with their tongues fronted. The entire vowel grid is affected when one vowel starts to be raised—or lowered. Other vowels then follow suit.

Another consistent regional marker is the collapsing of [e] and [I] before nasals, so that in the South and the southern parts of some Midwestern states like Indiana *penny* is pronounced [pIni] 'pinny' and *meant* and *mint* are pronounced alike. Many speakers of this region who have lost all other regional vowel differences still retain this pronunciation. This doesn't mean that these speakers are more careless than anyone else. The rule is that every dialect has its own **homonyms**. That is, every dialect pronounces certain sets of words alike, but distinguishes between others. For instance, in Rhode Island, *cot* and *caught* are pronounced differently, but in Boston they are pronounced the same. In Los Angeles[9], *Barry* and *beery* are pronounced alike, but in Boston they are different. Similarly *walk* and *wok* are alike in many regions, but in New York City and Providence, they are pronounced differently. In most of the United States just about every word spelled with <or> like *orange, corridor*, and

Florida are pronounced [ɔ], but in New York and Providence, the first vowel is pronounced [a]. In Boise, the first syllable of *hurry* is pronounced with the vowel of *her,* but, again in eastern New England, two separate vowels are used. Some regions pronounce *Mary, merry,* and *marry* alike and some pronounce each with a separate vowel so that *merry Christmas* does not sound like *Mary Christmas.* Still others pronounce two alike and one different, so that *Mary* and *merry* are homonyms, but *marry* is not.

Yet, despite these differences in vowel sounds, speakers in America usually have no difficulty in perceiving which word others are saying. When my Milwaukee friend says [bɨk], I know that she means the same thing as my [bæk]. When a newscaster speaks of a [tɚnəmInt] "ternamint' for my [tɔrnamInt] "tornamint", I still understand it as *tournament.* Similarly, the Los Angeles /a/'ah' in *talk, walk, saw* and the like corresponds to the New York City and Southern British /ɔ/'aw'. 'Ah' and 'aw' are different ways of pronouncing the same sound in those two dialects. Generally speaking, the differences between dialects of American English are differences in the pronunciation of vowels. No two dialects have quite the same vowel systems.

Consonants, which seem more crucial to identifying spoken words, show fewer dialectal differences than vowels do. There is one major difference in consonants between most British and American dialects. Both American and British English aspirate the /t/ at the start of words like *toy.* However, the /t/ and /d/ in between vowels is pronounced differently in each dialect. Virtually all American dialects pronounce the [t] and [d] between vowels the same way, as a light [d]-like sound. Thus, *latter* and *ladder* are pronounced the same as are *better* and *bedder.* Many British dialects still make a clear distinction between the [d] and [t] in this position, so these pairs are not homonyms for them. Furthermore, the Britons hold the [d] in *bedding* and both hold and even aspirate the [t] in *betting.* The pun advertising water beds as "off track bedding" would not work in British newspapers as it does in American.

DIALECT DIFFERENCE IS RULE DIFFERENCE

An accent is what someone else has. Usually, you do not notice how others speak unless the others pronounce words differently from the way you do, or use different terms for things or different syntax. Your own speech seems natural; other kinds may sound cute or quaint or harsh or ugly. They may even sound as if their speakers are making mistakes.

For instance, speakers of the /r/-full dialects often accuse those of the misnamed less dialects of putting /r/'s where they don't belong as well as leaving them out where they do belong. The term /r/-*less dialects* is a misnomer because they do have /r/ at the start of a word, as in *ran,* and, for most such dialects, between vowel, as in *marry.*

Is dropping a kind of carelessness? As we have seen dropping /r/'s is not a random occurrence. One can describe where they will occur and where they will not. The American /r/-less dialects share rules for /r/ with the British /r/-less dialects. Both /r/-full and /r/-dropping Americans today are likely to judge /r/-dropping as being wrong. Yet, they do not perceive the British /r/-dropping, especially that in RP, as being wrong; nor do they perceive the /r/-dropping in older movies as necessarily being wrong. For instance, who would accuse Katherine Hepburn of careless speech? Or Lauren Bacall? Or Humphrey Bogart? I have never heard of any Americans today claiming that they cannot understand the speech in old movies. Certainly, everyone understands the adult characters in the *Wizard of Oz,* all of whom were /r/-droppers. However, I hear[10] from older Rhode Island and Massachusetts speakers, those with very educated /r/-less speech, that in recent years when visiting California, Oregon, and even Ohio, people say they don't understand them.

One person reported that someone actually said to him, "This is English?" Clearly, it is not only the Nembe and the Kalahari who selectively understand. And it is not only speech associated with low educational speech which is not understood. Indeed, it seems as if the same pronunciations will be understood in some circumstances, such as in a movie or an interview with Queen Elizabeth, but not in others, such as interacting with a visitor to a distant state. One of my students admitted that she had no difficulty understanding a British speaker who spoke of the [makIt], 'market,' but when she first heard a New Englander say it, she didn't understand what the person was saying.

Since educated, upper-class, even aristocratic British, Australian, South African, and older East Coast American speakers drop /r/'s, then neither carelessness nor ignorance can account for it. In fact, when one examines actual speech of /r/-droppers, one finds very definite rules for when and when not to pronounce that sound. In sum, if the /r/ occurs before a consonant, it is not pronounced, as in [pʰak], 'park.' Also if a word final /r/ occurs at the end of a sentence or in a word by itself, it is not pronounced, as in [kʰa:], 'car.' These dropping rules are actually similar to the elision rules in French in which final consonants of words are dropped.

Some, but not all /r/-dropping English speakers also put an /r/ in "where it doesn't belong." Again, examining when this happens, we see that these are not random occurrences. Rather, they occur in expressions like *saw it,* [s rIt] and *sofa is* [sofərIz]. This so-called intrusive /r/ occurs only when the speaker is going from a mid back or central vowel to a front one. This is a result of the fact that instead of making an /r/ by retroflexing the tip of the tongue, those from /r/-dropping regions often make the sound by humping the back of their tongue upward and making the tongue tense.[11] Thus, the so-called intrusive /r/ is actually a glide caused as the tongue is moving from the back to the front of the mouth. Similarly, those Midwestern and Northwest Pacific Coast speakers who have an intrusive /r/ in *wash* [wɔrš] do not do so randomly. These speakers habitually start to enunciate their vowels at the same time that they are curling their tongues back to make /r/ as in words like *hurry, so* that they automatically retroflex their tongues while making the vowel in words like *wash*. That is, in saying *hurry,* they make the *u* and *r* in the same tongue motion, and in saying *wash*, they make the /ɔ/ and /r/ together, by analogy.

LEXICAL VARIATION

There are small differences in lexicon from dialect to dialect. Since these differences involve the names of commonly used items, misunderstandings can and do occur, even in this land of television and national advertising. In Almacs, a Rhode Island supermarket, a male customer just ahead of me in the checkout line asked the boy packing groceries to place a large bag of dog food in a "sack." The boy looked puzzled, then said dubiously, "I'll have to ask the manager." The customer reddened angrily. I intervened, hastily explaining that, as in many other regions, groceries are placed in *bags. Sacks* are made of cloth. The customer, from Oregon, said, "I never heard of such a thing," and the boy had never heard of *sack* for *bag*. Usage of these words varies considerably all over the country. Some regions reverse the usage just mentioned, so that *bag* means 'a cloth container,' as in *burlap bag,* but *sack* is made of paper. Tuscaloosa County uses the two words interchangeably. For the item made from burlap, Alaska uses *gunnysack,* and Honolulu, Hawaii has one group which call it a "gunnysack," but the other calls it "burlap bag."

The upset over the use of *sack* for *bag,* discussed above, is not as unusual as one might think. At O'Hare Airport in Chicago, a thirsty woman with a strong Boston accent asked an attendant where the bubbler was. The attendant kept saying, "What?" to which the traveler, raising her voice, kept answering "The bubbler!" Given the proximity of Chicago to Milwaukee, one would have thought that the attendant would be familiar with *bubbler* for a public drinking facility. That term is also used in Wisconsin. And, given the fact that only parts of Boston use the term *bubbler,* one would have thought that the traveler would have dredged up *fountain* in her moment of need.

Even so, the traveler seemed unaware that most of the country calls it a "fountain," "drinking fountain," or "water fountain". To those who call it a *bubbler,* a fountain is one of the big, gushing water decorations in parks or in front of buildings. *Water fountain* seems redundant, at least nowadays, but at one time there were soda fountains in drugstores where coke and ice cream sodas were dispensed.

Mike Kenny, a writer for the *Boston Globe* expressed surprise to me that an ex-governer of Massachusetts, Dukakis, on the campaign trail for a Presidential nomination somewhere in the West, remarked that "They don't know what a frappe is." Kenny was surprised that, in this day and age, one would expect everyone to know that the "general American" term is *milkshake.* I countered with an even more narrow provincialism. As I disembarked a plane from Los Angeles to Rhode Island, I noticed a very excited young man joining three male friends who had come to pick him up. As I was passing by, I heard him saying in a high, buoyant voice, "C'n you believe it! They don't know what a cabinet is, and they never heard of coffee milk!!!" (A *cabinet* is a *milkshake,* and *coffee milk* is lowfat milk with coffee syrup in it, a drink not known outside of Rhode Island.)

I was married to my husband for 25 years before I discovered that he said "rubber band" for what I term *elastic* and what some speakers call *gum band.* He is from New York City and I am a native New Englander. Similarly, as an eastern New Englander, I go *down cellar* and *down city* rather than *down the cellar* and *downtown,* and wash up with a *face cloth* rather than a *wash cloth.* As a child, I separated *swill* from *trash* or *rubbish,* although nowadays it is all *garbage. Swill* survives only in the sense of "swill it down," an uncouth pouring of drink down one's throat. I always was fascinated with *fireflies,* but visitors from the South insisted they were *lightnin' bugs.* Similarly, my husband's *dragonflies* were my *darning needles.*

How does someone live in America and not realize that they are using highly local words for things? After all, we do all go to the same movies and watch the same television shows. I suspect it's just another instance in which we extract meaning from what we hear without really noticing the form, unless the form is something which is overtly stigmatized. Certainly, milkshakes and bags are mentioned in the media, although water fountains may not be.

Other terms for common items that still cause confusion across regions are *soda, soda pop, pop, soft drink,* and *tonic.* In parts of the Midwest and Far West, if one orders soda, one is served an ice cream soda. On the East Coast, if one orders pop, one is likely to be greeted with "Huh?" There except for Boston and vicinity the term is *soda*. *Tonic* is peculiar to the Boston area and northward up the coast. In New York City and environs, the bottled stuff is soda, but a drink made at a soda fountain with chocolate syrup, milk, and soda water is an egg cream which has neither egg nor cream in it.

There are also regional differences in the name of the drink made from ice cream, syrup, and milk beaten together. Most of the country calls this a milkshake or shake. Other terms are *frappe, velvet,* and *cabinet* in Massachusetts, Maine, and Rhode Island respectively. Because of national fast-food chains, *shake* has moved into those areas as well. Often, Rhode Island customers often order cabinets[12] at the *creamery* (ice cream parlor), but a shake at a fast-food place. Since the fast-food shakes typically contain gelatinous thickeners, whereas cabinets are only milk, syrup, and ice cream, the two drinks are not alike. Moreover *shake* in Rhode Island and parts of Massachusetts refers to milk and syrup beaten together with no ice cream. With the advent of Massaschusetts chains into Rhode Island, *frappe* is creeping into Rhode Island. To my amusement, on Independence Day, 1993, I saw a sign advertising "Cabinets (frappes)" in Bristol, Rhode Island, a town frequented by tourists from all over America. The owners seemed blissfully unaware that most Americans would have no idea what either one was, although, clearly, the word *frappe* was intended to define *cabinet*. Although Massachusetts *frappe* is crossing state borders, there is no sign of the *tonic* doing so.

Chocolate bits on ice cream are *sprinkles* in New York, but *jimmies* in parts of New England, *ants* in others, and *shots* elsewhere. A huge sandwich on a roll is a *submarine* or *sub, hero, grinder, hoagie,* or *poor boy,* depending on where you eat it. Local terms are retained even in regions close to each other both geographically and culturally. The persistent differences in regionalisms between Rhode Island and eastern Massachusetts are of note because not only are the states adjacent to each other, but many people commute to work on both sides of the border. Rhode Island, parts of Connecticut and western Massachusetts all speak of grinders, but Boston and vicinity order subs. It is not unusual to hear a Rhode Islander order a grinder in a Boston based chain that advertises subs.

It is not only foodstuffs that retain local terms. Some regions call stockings what others call hose. The latter, common in the Midwest, is often not comprehended in the East, where *hose* refers to the long snaky thing used to water a garden. The newer *panty hose* is used alongside *stockings* for many East Coast women. They put on their stockings, even when their stockings are panty hose. Others distinguish between them.

CHAPTER 8

Stockings are what you wear with garters, but panty hose don't need them. In a store, however, customers will distinguish between the two if they want to purchase some, as in "Where are the panty hose?" When I was growing up, we put on our "stockings" every day, referring to what today are called socks. In current dialect investigation, I have found that *stockings* for *socks* survives primarily in educated African American native Rhode Island males.

In building, Northwesterners put *shakes* on the side of homes, but Northeasterners put on *shingles,* referring to the same item: wood squares, usually made of cedar. There are variations on this theme all over the country, with some also putting shakes on their roofs, whether or not they are wood, and others putting shingles on if they are not wood. Yet others use shingles for both siding and roofs, wood or not. Others put shakes on the side, and shingles on the roof. As with *bag* versus *sack,* the material used may affect the word, so that cedar shakes can be used for either roofs or sides, but asphalt ones will be shingles. Size and shape play a part as well. Formerly, areas that only called them shingles now call large cedar ones shakes, but smaller ones are still shingles.

In mobile societies words from one dialect may conflict with words from others. When conflict occurs, two things can happen. Either one term drops out or each word starts to refer to slightly different aspects of the thing originally designated. English *shirt* and *skirt* are old examples of this, originally having been British dialect variants for the same article. In the United States, the hardware on a sink from which one gets water is called a *faucet, tap,* or *spigot.* In areas where two or three of the terms compete, people will assign a slightly different meaning to each, so that *faucet* may become what's on the inside of the house and *spigot* is on the outside. Others, even in the same region, may assign the meanings differently, so the faucet may be inside or out, and the spigot is what's on a beer keg. In southeastern New England, *tap* can refer to a barroom and the thing on the beer keg is the *tap.*

A number of vocabulary differences distinguish American and British English. The British have *lift, hire, lorry* where Americans say *elevator, rent, truck,* respectively. One British term, *bunk* meaning 'escape' or 'leave someplace without telling others' occurs in southern New England in the meaning of 'stay out of school with no excuse,' although younger speakers increasingly don't use it except in the expression "National Bunk Day" (when, putatively, everyone bunks school). In Philadelphia, that would be to *bag* school, and in other places it would be *play hooky* or simply to *cut* school.

Despite the invasion of television and the general mobility of Americans, regionalisms survive. This is an attestation to the supremacy of the function of social marking in dialect and is further proof that language usage is not simply imitation.

Trudgill believes that people change the words they use under the influence of television, but not grammar and sound. That depends. In many places on the northeastern seaboard, the pronunciation of the first vowel in *Florida, horrible, Morris, forest,* and *orange* has always been [a] "ah," but in people twenty-five or younger, under the influence of catfood, orange juice commercials and pop stars, increasingly that vowel is [ɔ] "aw" as it is in the Midwest and Far West.

English is too widely spoken a language, and there are far too many dialect differences in word choice for anything approximating a comprehensive discussion here. The purpose here is to illustrate principles and, of course, to whet the reader's appetite for more.

SYNTACTIC VARIATION

Dialects differ in syntax as well as phonology and lexicon. Americans are generally familiar with the well-known signposts of uneducated dialects such as double negatives and lack of agreement in number of subject and verb. The dialect markers that signal social class distinctions often occur on common constructions of the type that crop up frequently in conversation. This is another manifestation of what we have seen with both style and dialect-marking, that the markers must appear early on in an interaction, or else they would not be reliable as cues to identity and mood (Chaika 1973).

Syntactic markers center on marginal constructions, grammar rules that are relics of bygone days. This is the counterpart of marked sounds being used as phonological markers. Consider the major differences between educated and uneducated American dialects. The educated ones use the forms of *be (am, is, are, was,* and *were)* that agree with the subject of the sentence in which they appear. These different forms for one verb are a relic of the **inflections** used long ago when verbs agreed in person and number in present tense and in number in the past tense. Besides the inflected *be*, the only other survival of that system is the *-s* that marks the present tense third person singular, as in the singular *he goes* as opposed to the plural *they go*.

Be usage is a particularly effective marker of social class in both American and British English because it is hard to talk for very long without one of its forms cropping up. It is quickly evident whether or not a speaker uses the correct form of *be*; hence, whether or not the speaker is middle-class is quickly established. This is because almost none of the nonstandard varieties of English uses the inflected forms of *be* in the standard way. Some speakers say, "I is"; others say, "I be", "You is", "You was", or "You be". Some do not say *be* at all, as in "He good". These are differences in *be* usage from one nonstandard dialect to another, but all seem to differ from the standard varieties of English, whether British or American. In this respect, the standard educated varieties of English are alike.

Similarly, although all educated dialects still use the -s number agreement marker in the present singular, nonstandard speakers often omit it there, saying, "He go", "He don't". Some varieties of nonstandard English do use the -*s* agreement marker, but not necessarily on the third person singular. Rather, they say, "We sits", "You sits", and /or "They sits", but "He sit". Many speakers, educated and not, use what I call a "narrative -s" in the singular, as in "Then I sits myself down and...."

Verb inflections work beautifully as signals because they stand out in the stream of speech in English, which has long since shed the large system of inflection and agreement its words once had to use. The very fact that the *be* forms, relics of the old system of inflections, no longer fit the general grammar of English means that people will notice how they are used in speech. That these relics remain suggests to me, at least, that they may have survived because they are so useful as social class markers.

Another social class marker that is a relic of an earlier stage of the language is the retention of now irregularly formed past tense of certain verbs. Here sometimes the older form is now nonstandard, while the newer regularized one is standard. Appalachian *holp* was the original past tense of *help*. In fact, *helped* originally must have been the kind of kiddie error we saw in Chapter 1, like *sitted* for *sat*. *Have went*, which is today nonstandard, reflects the original past participle of *went* as in "She wends her way." *Wend* used to have the past tense *went*, thus "She went her way," and the past participle *went* as well, just as today we have *spend, spent, (have) spent*. For some reason the present tense of *wend* was replaced by *go*, and the old participle of *go, gone*, was retained, resulting in the **paradigm** (set of forms) *go, went, gone*. When the paradigms of two words are collapsed (coalesced) this way, the process is called **suppletion**. This process typically affects common words in the language. We see another example in the paradigm *good, better, best*. The *good* clearly comes from an originally different set than *better* and *best*. The speaker who says, "have went" is just using the old participle form of *wend*, although it is not clear whether this is a survival in that speaker's dialect or just a new formation on the model of *spend, spent, (have) spent*.

Negatives also have to be used frequently in conversation. They are, by their nature, not part of large sets so that they too stand out in the stream of speech. Negation in English has become a social marker and, by extension, a stylistic one as well. Double negation as in "I didn't do nothing" signals the working and lower classes, but "I didn't do anything" signals the educated middle class. Double negation sometimes is affected by educated speakers as a marker of casual, informal style as they attempt to emulate the naturalness and informality they presume to be characteristic of formally less-educated classes. Therefore, speech forms readily identifiable as belonging to the blue-collar and working classes, especially double negatives in the United States, have become stylistic as well. Again, as it happens, the blue-collar and lower-class practice is the older one in English, and the educated *anything* is the newer.

Some regional grammatical differences are unrelated to social class. These are more subtle, not necessarily concentrated in constructions that have to be used a great deal. People are often unaware that these differences exist, just as they are often unaware of lexical differences.

Prepositions

Prepositional differences offer a good example. Prepositions have a habit of slipping and sliding around over the years. Often prespositions in themselves have little meaning, and the selection of one over the other has little consequence for meaning. Old English prayed to God "on heaven" rather than "in heaven." Today, *in* and *on* vary regionally. New York City and environs wait on line instead of the more common *in line*. In the South *wait on* means what northerners do by *wait for,* although sometimes I hear northern-lovers of jazz and blues say "wait on" for *wait for.* In the North, *wait on* refers to serving another person.[13] In Pennsylvania and parts of the South one might hear *sick on his stomach* or *sick in his stomach*. More commonly in the South one hears *sick at his stomach* as opposed to the usual Northern *sick to his stomach.* Appalachians speak of *at the wintertime,* rather than *in.* Rural Down East Maine says *to home* for *at home.* The Midlands tell time with *quarter till* instead of *quarter to* or *quarter of.* Some speakers in New York City, parts of Wisconsin, and Pennsylvania *stay by* someone when they visit rather than *stay with,* perhaps because of the influence of German and Yiddish in those areas.

Because choice of preposition is determined by arbitrary grammar rules rather than by selection on the basis of meaning alone, much preposition use is considered syntactic. Prepositions in many European languages have replaced old endings on nouns that tell how the noun is being used in a given sentence. For instance, in English, the surviving inflectional suffix on nouns, the possessive 's is also paraphrasable by using the preposition *of*.

Anymore speakers

Many dialects use *anymore* only if it is preceded by a negative, as in:

I *don't* see him *anymore*.
He *hardly* comes here *anymore*.
If he comes here *anymore*, I'll throw him out.

Note that the negative can reside in the meaning of words like *hardly* and *if*.

In some parts of West Virginia, Pennsylvania, Delaware, New York, Ohio, Kentucky, Indiana, and South Carolina (Parker 1985) *anymore* appears affirmatively as well, as in:

Things are getting busier for me *anymore*.
That's what plane travel is like *anymore*.
You really talk a lot *anymore*.
Most people get married around the age of twenty *anymore*.

Speakers unfamilar with this affirmative *anymore* often aren't too sure of what it means. They are likely to assume that it has some relationship to *still*. Actually, it means 'nowadays.'

Even more subtle syntactic differences occur. An educated Detroit speaker says "that squirrel is keeping on getting into my bird feeder." Eastern New Englanders tell me that they would say only "keeps on getting." British RP allows "wanting to" do something, which sounds odd to many Americans. Possibly because of the influence of Italian, Yiddish and other European languages, one hears "We are married for five years" in New York City speakers, whereas it is, "We have been married" for other regions.

Might could and Fixin' To

In English,[14] we can use a **modal auxiliary**[15] with the base form of a verb for a variety of meanings:

I *can* do that.
He *may* do that.
I *will* see to it.
Mary *could* study harder.
Max *might* go.

However, many, if not most, English speakers would not say

*I *can might* do that.
*Jane *may should* go.
*You *might could* see him.

That is, most dialects do not allow two modal auxiliaries to be used in the same phrase. Still, there are large numbers of speakers in the American South and South Midlands who regularly use double and even triple modals like those above. DiPaolo (1989) has collected a plethora of such usages in East and West Texas. She shows that such usages are not random. The two modals cannot occur in just any order. For instance, she found that *may can* is used, but *can may* is not (p. 198). Di Paolo suggests that these are frequently used as hedging so as to sound tentative, hence, pragmatically, they can occur as politeness forms, for instance, a salesclerk in a fabric store suggested to a customer who wanted to redesign a shirt:

You *might* still *could* keep the cuff the way it is.

followed by:

You *might could* keep the cuffs...

We have already seen (Chapter 3) that all varieties of English make verbs more polite by use of modals rather than, as the Japanese do, for instance, by using a set of honorific endings on the verb. Therefore, it is not surprising to see those dialects which use double modals, do so also as politeness markers or ways of making statements seem more tentative.

Another Southernism is the use of *fixin' to* as an auxiliary verb. This is quite different from the use of *fix* as a main verb, as in:

I'm going to *fix* dinner.
I have to *fix* the car.

in which *fix* means 'make' and 'repair' respectively. Ching (1987) reports that in those dialects, there are a variety of meanings for the auxiliary use of *fixin' to*, although all include the meanings of 'immediacy, priority, definiteness, certainty, and preparatory activity' (p. 338). Additionally, there seems to be a meaning of 'delay' in all the usages he reports. He gives as examples of proper usage of this auxiliary:

> I'm *fixin' to* take care of it [cleaning up a spill].
> I'm *fixin' to* get to work [on homework].
> I'm *fixin' to* wash the dishes.

But, he discovered (p. 338) most respondents to a survey said they could not use this form in sentences like:

> *I'm fixin' to leave in the next five years.
> *I'm fixin' to lose weight one of these days.

Perhaps Ching's most interesting finding is that people assigned different meanings to *fixin' to* depending upon the situation in which it was said, and the relative social status of the speakers. For instance, when a maid said to a faculty member, "I'm fixin to take care of it." it was interpreted as her finishing her task at hand, and then immediately going to clean up the spill. A faculty member has the social right, in that situation, to ask a maid to clean up, and she has the social duty to do so as soon as possible, whereas a student's telling her advisor "I'm fixin' to get to work" doesn't necessarily carry the meaning of finishing another activity and immediately doing the homework. He also found, by asking people to choose meanings of several statements, that Southerners disagreed on many of the usages. For instances, 67 said one can't say, "I'm fixin' to lose weight one of these days" but 37 said one can. Similarly, 57 respondents said that they would say, "I'm fixin' to have a baby' [upon discovering she is pregnant]" but 46 said they wouldn't expect to phrase it that way.

Troike (1989) noted that there is an added meaning to *fixin' to*. It signals that the speaker is already aware of the situation, so the maid who said, "I'm fixin' to take care of it" is also indicating that she is aware that the job needs doing. Ching (1989) verified this amongst his students who told him that the only way one can use *fixin' to* in the first person without prior awareness is in a joke, but in the third person it can be used without a notion of prior awareness, as in

It's fixin' to rain [speaker looks out of window].
He's fixin' to get hit [when speaker sees car out of control and
ready to collide with another].

The intricacies of the meaning of syntactic forms, and the difficulties of nonnative speakers in using them accurately are well illustrated by this example.

BLACK ETHNIC SPEECH

Despite American folk beliefs, there is no one Black English. All African Americans do not speak the same way. Many speak the regional standard, and their speech is indistinguishable from whites in those areas. Others command two dialects, one the white regional and one of those subsumed under the common term *Black English*, henceforth, BE.[16] (See Chapter 9 for its origins). The term BE is commonly applied to dialects spoken by African Americans all over the United States and Canada. Despite the many differences in these dialects, some features are acknowledged to be markers of BE; that is, they occur widely or universally in those dialects.

In pronunciation, historically, BE has clearly been influenced by white southern coastal /r/-less dialects (Mufwene & Gilman 1987). Exceptions to this occurred in at least one African American population in the North, the Olney Street neighborhood of Providence, which was settled by freed or runaway slaves during the Colonial and Federal periods. Many of their ancestors were among the slaves brought to New England who never did get to the South, or who escaped when slavery was abolished early on in the Northeast. My dialect investigations into this community shows no southernisms. One of my informants proudly told me, "We talk like the Old English." Certainly, their speech is a clear variant of Rhode Island English. Most Americans hearing tapes of these speakers do not identify them as African American. In the 1950s and 1960s, however, the migration from the South, and the identification of southern-based BE with black ethnicity brought more traditional BE speech to this area. However, many of the descendants of these Rhode Island African Americans still do not use such speech or do so rarely.

What we might call canonical BE, what most people are referring to when they speak of the BE vernacular, is quite traditionally southern in pronunciation. *Time* is pronounced [ta:m], *hard* is [ha:d], *aunt* is [a:nt], not [ænt], and /ɛ/ and /I/ are merged before nasals even in northern cities like Chicago. As with other /r/-less speakers, younger African Americans are beginning to pronounce the pre-consonantal /r/ at least some of the time (Myhill 1988), although a quick course in rap music shows these dialects are still essentially /r/-less. Another feature of BE is the dropping of final consonants, so that *field* rhymes with *wheel*, and *whore* has become *ho*. We saw this in Chapter 6 as a significant source of rhyming in BE speech.

All varieties of American English do simplify final consonant clusters. Everyone usually says, "roas' beef" for instance, dropping the final consonant when the next word begins with a consonant, but the /t/ on *roast* is retained in "roast in the oven" where the next word begins with a vowel. Many BE speakers are likely to drop this final /t/ as well, saying "roas' in the oven." We don't notice that we simplify the consonant cluster in "roas' beef." However, we will notice if someone does it where we wouldn't. Since many non-BE speakers don't simplify the final cluster if the next word begins with a vowel, they notice that BE speakers do. The non-BE speakers then think that BE speakers "drop sounds." One result of this general final consonant dropping in BE is that the plural of words like *desk* and *test* becomes "desses" and "tesses." This is because when the final consonant is omitted, the word then ends in *-s*: "des" and "tes." Words that end in *-s* form a plural by adding *-es*.

The syntax of BE verbs has long been acknowledged to differ from most white varieties of American English. A major difference is the existence in BE of a **durative** versus a **non-durative** aspect in the verb system. This is the contrast of "He be bad" with "He bad." The first means 'he is always bad' (durative), whereas the second means 'he is being bad right now.' As has been often remarked upon, other varieties of English express the durative by adding an adverb like *always*. Richardson (1991) comments that:

Them boys be beating up girls

has no ready counterpart in what she calls SAE (standard American English), noting that the use of the invariant *be* here means both 'habitual' and frequent behavior. Her study of African American and white teenagers in East Palo Alto showed that BE speakers use the *be* to express habitual behavior, using fewer adverbials than whites. White speakers "mark habituality semantically" (p. 301). It is not a part of their syntactic system as it is for BE speakers. Since white speakers do not have this form, not surprisingly, they do not contrast it by leaving out the **copula** (a form of *be*) as do BE speakers when expressing a non-durative or nonhabitual circumstance. (e.g., He all right.) This difference in dialects carries over to questions as well. In BE, a question like "*Do* babes *be* willin'?" means "Are babes *always* willing?" The lack of an *-s* agreement marker on *do* is another feature of BE. However, Bernstein (1988) found that southern blacks over the age of forty-nine use an inflected form of the durative copula *bees*. She found no instance of this in white speech. BE also uses *ain't* as an auxiliary in the sense of *didn't*, as in "I ain't do nothin'." Nonstandard white varieties also use *ain't*, but in the sense of *isn't*.

An especially interesting use of *be* as an auxiliary verb occurs in emphatic expressions like "You be sat there" after a conditional, as in "if you don't do something, you'll be sat there" '(you'll just be sitting there forever.)' Two other auxiliaries which were part of BE, *done* meaning 'action completed in past' and *been*, 'action completed in past and definitely over' have been supposedly disappearing in BE (Wolfram and Fasold 1974, p. 152) especially in northern cities. Yet, one can still hear these in current rap songs or in conversations as in "I *been* settled the score," meaning, "I have already settled the score once and for all." Recently, an African American neighbor of mine told me, "We *been* had those dogs since they were puppies." and Erica White, a Providence native, told me that she and her friends say things like, "Girl, I *been* had those shoes..." to emphasize, 'I've had those shoes a long time.' Apparently, the reports of the demise of the BE *been* auxiliary have been premature, although, in this region at least, it seems to be used also to mean 'event starting in the distant past and continued till now.'

One future marker in BE is *I'ma*. This can combine with the durative, as in "I'ma be workin' in a office" meaning 'I'll be working steadily doing office work.' Another example, from a rap, is "I'ma be somebody..." This seems to add a feature of determination on the future, which is not surprising. *Will* in all varieties of English combines the meaning of determination with futurity.

Spears (p. 51) notes two other grammatical features of BE. One is what he terms the "semi-auxiliary *come*" used in a negative sense, as in "She come callin' me, come yellin' in my phone." He glosses this as 'She had the nerve to call me and to yell in my phone.' He also notes that, although BE often doesn't use the third person singular agreement marker *-s* (as in *she comes*), it does use an *-s* to indicate that a narrative is being related which took place in the past, as in "Jackie COMES out of the hospital," meaning that she came out of the hospital. Actually, this usage occurs in other dialects as well under the same circumstances when someone is relating a string of events, as in "First, Jackie comes out of the hospital, then she gets into her car, turns on the motor, and crashes the car into the gate." This is all to be taken as past action. Only if such forms are used by an announcer doing an on-the-spot will this present tense be interpreted as a cotemporaneous event.

This brings us to the question of the uniqueness of BE, especially in the South. Some scholars have claimed that there is no difference between BE and other southern dialects matched for socioeconomic status, e.g., McDavid and Davis (1972), and others insist that it is a separate language (Dillard 1973; Smitherman 1984). Given the history of African Americans in the South, it would seem odd if there were no mutual effect on the speech of both races. Nor can we forget the generations during which African American women were charged with the care of white children. The slave term *mammy* is but a variant of *mama,* and even after emancipation, African American women continued in their child-caring role. Of course, BE speech forms have long been a source for northern whites as well (Spears 1987).

Fasold (1986) investigated this matter in the South and found eight features exclusive to BE . One difference is that in single syllable words or on stressed syllables, BE speakers often pronounce a final *-d* as a glottal stop followed by a [t], so that *bed* is pronounced [bɛʔt] (Fasold 1986, p. 453). A second is the omission of the -s agreement marker in phrases like *he walks* and *he kisses.* One study in Mississippi found that BE speakers omitted this 87 percent of the time, while others only did 15 percent (p.454). Not surprisingly, the parallel omissions of the plural and possessive markers are also prominent features of BE (pp. 457).

The remote aspect *been,* as in "You won't get your dues that you been paid," although it has been found in Newfoundland speech as well, is, in the United States, a BE marker. Other speakers[17] seem never to use it. Here it means that the dues have long since been paid. Two other major features of BE, which have already been discussed are the dropping of the final consonant in a cluster, resulting in plurals like "desses" from "des" *(desk),* and the omission of the copula. This is not to say that all BE speakers always speak this way. It seems to be the case that if someone does, it is a BE speaker, but not all BE speakers do all of these things.

Chapter 8 Notes

1 Yiddish is the term for the many dialects of German spoken exclusively by the Jews of Eastern Europe as a result both of their enforced isolation from Christians and of their being persecuted for centuries. Because of these factors, they developed into an ethnic group with its own language. As these factors have disappeared, Jews in America

and Israel no longer speak it, and it is largely dying out. It survives almost entirely amongst the very old. Do not confuse Yiddish with Hebrew. The latter is the language of Jewish prayer and the Bible. A modern version of Hebrew is spoken in Israel.

2   This is the [r] associated with German and French as opposed to the American retroflex or Italian trill.

3   In reporting on these studies, I am using the terms for race and ethnicity that the original researchers did. Usually, as is the practice in this book, I prefer the term African American to refer to American blacks.

4   This is not to say that all blacks speak nonstandard English or that only whites speak standard. Apparently these researchers preferred for their example of nonstandard speech to record blacks speaking that way. By no means can one always tell if someone is black by hearing a tape recording of their speech. Many blacks speak indistinguishably from whites and many blacks command both standard and ethnic black dialects, switching between them as they wish.

5   Robert DiPietro informed that the Italian Atlas studies do give information about sentence structures and the contexts in which they appear.

6   Western Wisconsin, northwestern Illinois, Iowa, and southern Minnesota.

7   So far, only the first volume is out.

8   This is hardly a definitive list. I have heard Montana speakers do the same. Even within those cities, there may be enclaves in which the [æ] occurs and others in which the [æ] is now [I].

9   Actually, many places in the United States and Canada use this pronunciation. In this discussion, when I mention the name of a city or state, I am not implying that this locale is the only place where one finds this pronunciation or homonyms.

10 I hear this at the many talks I give each year at meetings of local historical societies, libraries, and other such groups.

11 If the tongue is not made tense, then a [ə] results. An English /r/ is actually the vowel [ə], but with the tongue tightened.

12 I am often asked where Rhode Island got this unusual (when referring to a drink) word. It's actually an example of *metonymy*. The early blenders were housed in small wooden cabinets, so people referred to the cabinet for the thing it made. This is like saying, "The baby wants his bottle" when it's not the bottle the baby wants but what's in it. Rhode Islanders are very aware that others find the word strange, and middle-class blacks and whites, and Rhode Islanders who have lived elsewhere will sometimes deny knowing the term or will use the generic shake when asked in a dialect interview for the term for a

mixture of milk, ice cream and syrup. At the end of an interview, if I casually say, "Have you ever heard of someone drinking a cabinet?" this always elicits a "Oh, yes…" sort of answer followed by an apology like "I haven't had one in years…I forgot." Interestingly, my younger (now in late teens or twenties) informants are not so self-conscious about this term, and freely use it, although they are aware that it is called milk shake elsewhere.

13 However, some young northerners have adopted the southern *wait on* for *for* because of country music and blues, jazz, and rock and roll in which the *on* is used.

14 This is true in the other Germanic languages as well: German, Dutch, and Scandinavian.

15 The full set of modal auxiliaries in English is: *can, could, may, might, must, shall, should, will,* and *would,* with *need* and *dare* surviving primarily in the negative:

> You *need* not *go.*
>
> I *dare* not *go.*

16 Although generally I feel that *African American* is the proper term for Americans who had African ancestors, the term Black English is and has been so prevalent, it is best to use it. The student wishing further research into this subject will almost certainly find it indexed under *Black English* and referred to in that way.

17 This is Fasold's claim. However, as we have just seen, the use of the *been*-auxiliary, which is supposedly disappearing, is alive and well. It is just that the dialecticians haven't met up with the speakers who are using it. It may be that there is an undiscovered group of non-BE speakers in the United States who use the *been*-auxiliary as well.

Exercises

1. Listen to a song or view a movie or television sequence in which a dialect of English unfamiliar to you is spoken. What problems do you find in understanding? What seems to be the difference between this dialect and your own?

2. Make up a list of words which you think have dialectal variants. Make up a definition for each word. Then poll your friends to see what they call them. For instance, "What do you call the square of toweling that you wash yourself with?" Alternatively, ask people if they know what a *facecloth* or *hoagie* (or any other dialectal variant) refers to.

3. Ask several people what kind of "accent" they have. How many say something like "General American" or "Vanilla English"? Ask them where they were raised. Can you detect differences in their speech? Who is likely to say that they have an accent? Where were they raised?

4. Ask those who said they have a General American accent in Exercise 3 how they would pronounce the following pairs:

talk	tock
orange	coffee
cot	caught
sense	cents
tournament	turn
hurry	her
right	ride

(Add any items you think will be pronounced differently by your participants.) Do all of the General American speakers pronounce these the same way?

5. Look in three or four college writing handbooks (Harcourt-Brace, Prentice-Hall, etc.), books on advice to writers, or books commenting about how to use English (like Fowler, Newman, John Simons) for advice on using the phrase *in regard to*. Do all of your sources agree? Take any of the alternatives any of them suggest (e.g., *as regards, with regards to, regarding*) and look those up. Do the sources agree? What can you conclude about the validity of such pronouncements? If you wished to express the thought encoded in any of these, how would you do so, based upon your researches?

6. Watch television commercials that feature speakers using regional or ethnic dialects. What are they advertising? What features of the dialect do they seem to be using so that you will identify it as such? If you are familiar with the dialect in question, how accurate is the actor's representation of it?

References

Abrahams, R. D. (1972). The training of the man of words in talking sweet. *Language in Society, 1,* 15–30.

CHAPTER 8

Allen, H. (1973–6). *The Linguistic Atlas of the Upper Midwest, 1–3*. Minneapolis: University of Minnesota Press.

Atwood, E. B. (1962). *The Regional Vocabulary of Texas*. Austin: University of Texas Press.

Avis, W. S. (1986). The contemporary context of Canadian English. In *Dialect and Language Variation* (H. B. &. L. Allen, Michael D., Eds) (pp. 212–216). New York: Academic Press.

Bailey, G., & Maynor, N. (1989, Spring). The divergence controversy. *American Speech, 64* (1), 12–39.

Bates, E., & Benigni, L. (1975). Rules of address in Italy: A sociological survey. *Language in Society, 4*, 271–288.

Bernstein, B. (1971). *Theoretical Studies toward a Sociology of Language* (Vol. 1) Class, Codes, and Control. London: Routledge & Kegan Paul.

Bernstein, C. (1988, Summer). A variant of the 'invariant' be. *American Speech, 63* (2), 119–124.

Bloomfield, L. (1965). *Language History from Language*. (H. Hoyer, Ed,). New York: Holt, Rinehart, Winston. Bloomfield.

Carver, C. M. (1987). *American Regional Dialects*. Ann Arbor: The University of Michigan Press.

Cassidy, F. G. (Ed.). (1985). *Dictionary of American Regional English*. Cambridge, Mass.: Harvard University Press.

Chaika, E. (1973). Hi! How are you? Paper delivered at the Linguistic Society of America 48th Annual meeting. San Diego, Calif. (ERIC Documents).

Chaika, E. (1982). *Language the Social Mirror, 1st ed*. Rowley, Mass: Newbury House.

Ching, M. K. (1987). How fixed is fixin' to? *American Speech, 62* (4), 332–345.

Ching, M. (1989, Summer). Marvin Ching Replies. *American Speech, 64* (2), 164–165.

Dillard, J. (1973). *Black English: Its History and Usage in the United States*. New York: Random House.

DiPaolo, M. (1989, Fall). Double models as single lexical items. *American Speech, 64* (3), 195–224.

Fairclough, N. (1989). *Language and Power*. Language in Social Life Series. New York: Longman.

Fasold, R. W. (1986). The relation between black and white speech in the South. In *Dialect and Language Variation* (H. B. Allen & M. D. Linn, Eds) (pp. 446–473.). Orlando: Academic Press.

Francis, W. N. (1983). *Dialectology: An Introduction*. New York: Longman Group, Ltd.

Gaertner, S. L., & Bickman, L. (1971). Effects of race on the elicitation of helping behaviour; The wrong number technique. *Journal of Personality and Social Psychology, 20,* 218–222.

Giles, H., Baker, S., & Fielding, G. (1975). Communication length as a behavioural index of accent prejudice. *International Journal of the Sociology of Language, 6,* 73–81.

Giles, H., & Powesland, P. (1975). *Speech Style and Social Evaluation.* New York: Academic Press.

Kurath, H. (1949 Reprinted 1966). *A Word Geography of the Eastern United States.* Ann Arbor: The University of Michigan Press.

Kurath, H., & McDavid, R. J. (1961). *The Pronunciation of English in the Atlantic States.* Ann Arbor: University of Michigan Press.

Labov, W. (1987, Spring). Are Black and White Vernaculars Diverging? *American Speech, 62* (1), 5–12.

Labov, W. (1972). The linguistic consequences of being a lame. In *Language in the Inner City* (pp. 255–292). Philadelphia: University of Pennsylvania Press.

Labov, W. (1963). The social motivation of a sound change. *Word, 19,* 273–309.

Lambert, W., Giles, H., & Picard., D. (1975). Language attitudes in a French American community. *International Journal of the Sociology of Language, 4,* 127–152.

McDavid, R. (1958). The dialects of American English. In *The Structure of American English* (W. N. Francis.) New York: The Ronald Press.

McDavid, R. (1979, Winter). Review of Language in the Inner City and Sociolinguistic Patterns by William Labov. *American Speech,* pp. 292–304.

McDavid, R. I. Jr., & Davis, L. M. (1972). The dialects of Negro Americans. In M. E. Smite (Ed.), *Studies in Honor of George L. Trager* (pp. 303–312). The Hague: Mouton.

McIntosh, A. (1952). *An Introduction to a Survey of Scottish Dialects.* University of Edinburgh: T. Nelson.

Milroy, J. (1984). Sociolinguistic methodology and the identification of speakers' voices in legal proceedings. In P. Trudgill (Ed.), *Applied Sociolinguistics* (pp. 51–71). New York: Academic Press.

Mufwene, S. S., & Gilman, C. (1987, Summer). How African is Gullah and Why? *American Speech,* 62(2), 120–139.

Myhill, J. (1988, Fall). Postvocalic /r/ as an index of integration into the BE V community. *American Speech,* 63(3), 203–213.

O'Cain, R. (1979). Linguistic atlas of New England. *American Speech,* 54, 242–278.

Parker, F. (1975). A Comment on Anymore. *American Speech, 3–4,* 305–310.

Pringle, I. (1986). The concept of dialect and the study of Canadian English. In *Dialect and Language Variation* (H. B. Allen & M. D. Linn, Eds.) (pp. 217–236). New York: Academic Press.

Pyles, T. (1972). English usage: The views of the literati. In D. Shores (Ed.), *Contemporary English: Change and Variation* (pp. 160–169). New York: J.B. Lippincott.

Richardson, C. (1991, Fall). Habitual structures among blacks and whites in the 1990's. *American Speech,* 66(3), 292–302.

Sacks, H. (1972). An initial investigation of the usability of conversational data for doing sociology. In D. Sudnow (Ed.), *Studies in Social Interaction.* New York: The Free Press.

Shuy, R. (1967) *Discovering American Dialects.* Champaign, Ill. NCTE.

Sledd, J. (1972). Bi-dialectism: The linguistics of white supremacy. In D. Shores (Ed.), *Contemporary English: Change and Variation* (pp. 319–330). New York: Lippincott.

Smitherman, G. (1984). Black language as power. In *Language and Power* (C. Kramrae, M. Schulz, & W. M. O'Barr, Eds.) (pp. 101–115). Beverly Hills: Sage Publications.

Spears, A. K. (1987, Spring). Are black and white vernaculars diverging, VI. *American Speech,* 62(1), 48–80.

Troike, R. C. (1989, Summer). Fixin' To. *American Speech,* 64(2), 163–165.

Trudgill, P. (1983a). Linguistic change and diffusion. In *On Dialect: Social and Geographical Perspectives* (pp. 52–87). New York: New York University Press.

Trudgill, P. (1983b). Sociolinguistics and dialectolology: Geolinguistics and English rural dialects. In *On Dialect: Social and Geographical Perspectives* (pp. 31–52). New York: New York University Press.

Van Riper, W. (1986). General American: An ambiguity. In *Dialect and Language Variation* (H. B. Allen & M. D. Linn, Eds.) (pp. 123–135). New York: Academic Press.

Wells, J. C. (1982). *Accents of English, 1–3.* New York: Cambridge University Press.

Wolfram, W., & Fasold, R. (1974). *The Study of Social Dialects in American English.* Englewood, N. J.: Prentice Hall.

Chapter 9

Speech Communities

S tudies of speech communities reveal the social stratification, social networks, and relevant social groupings. Various careful field methods relying upon eliciting speech in a variety of conditions is essential for such research. People within one community do not necessarily speak the same way. Moreover, people may belong to several speech communities simultaneously, with consequences for changing their speech behaviors. Sociolinguistic studies reveal that each community has different values and these are reflected in different social markers in speech. There is no universal marker that one can expect to find in all communities. Bilinguals may switch their languages according to the social situation, just as monolinguals switch their styles. Attitudes toward different groups are readily discovered by examining whose dialects they copy as well as by asking people to evaluate their own and others' speech. Even such matters as the singing of songs and telling of jokes reveal social attitudes. The deaf show the same kinds of variability in their manual languages as the hearing do in oral ones. Dialects have many origins, which affect their present form. Some dialects are a result of creolizing of African and European languages. The course of decreolization is affected by social factors.

WHAT CONSTITUTES A SPEECH COMMUNITY

Unavoidably, our discussion of dialects implied that some are more valued than others for different purposes. There is no universally correct dialect for all segments of society or for all situations. Moreover, what one community values, another might deplore. There are no abstract entities which will be admired or disliked by all communities of speakers. The operative word here is *community*. Each community has its own standards. Saying this, one might think that it is easy to define what a speech community is. One definition is that a speech community is a group of speakers who share a set of norms about the use of a language or languages (Gumperz 1971). Romaine (1982) notes that

    ...in different speech communities, social and linguistic factors are linked not only in different ways but to different degrees so that the imbrication of social and linguistic structure in a given speech community is a matter for investigation and cannot be taken as fact. (p. 13)

Labov's early work (discussed below) uncovered a very straightforward variation in speech behaviors allied to social stratification within a community. However, Leslie Milroy (discussed below) in a very different setting, found that her data didn't admit of such a clearly stratified community. Rather, she found that

> sociolinguistic structure is woven in a complex way throughout the community with different phonological elements being associated with various social groups. (quoted by Romaine, p. 14)

Romaine argues that speech communities can be quite messy. All of its members may not use the rules of language the same way. Moreover, the varieties of a dialect cannot be considered simply a falling away from the rules of the standard. Moreover, people belong to several speech communities at the same time: occupational, regional, social, ethnic, foreign language(s), age, race, gender, education, common disabilities or illnesses, and perhaps even others...And these interact in highly variable ways for each speaker. Moreover, any individual in a community for whatever reason may have his or her own set of rules. As we have seen, we each learn our language(s) by ourselves, so individual variation is inevitable. Moreover, different members of a speech community may have had very different experiences. Some may have gone into the service where they met people of many different dialects, thus changing their own perceptions. Others may have gone to schools in different regions. Still others, for whatever reason, may have decided to emulate the speech of a particular hero or actor or whatever. Finally, clearly, the more people interact with each other, the more alike they sound. In turn, this may be affected by community standards. For instance, a speaker from New Haven, Connecticut, 60 years ago might have tried to emulate Katherine Hepburn even though she was not of the same social group or community. However, 60 years ago, /r/-less speech was considered correct in many parts of America. For that matter, British upper class speech was considered very fine. Today, /r/-less speech in America is generally frowned upon, and Katherine Hepburn's accent seems affected, so a woman who wished to sound like an admired actress would have to pick someone like Jane Fonda or Kim Basinger to emulate. Then again, the person who wanted to sound affected and "different" might decide on those grounds to imitate Hepburn.

Clearly, both factors operate: Individual motivation and community standards, be they nationwide, region-wide, state-wide, city-wide, or even village-wide (Dorian 1982). For individual variation to have its desired effect, however, the individual must consider the community standards. It does no good not to talk like a "good ol' boy" if one doesn't know what speech features are associated with good ol' boys. Moreover, it is hard to account for language change unless we consider both individual variation and social standards. Labov's work, presented below, is undoubtedly a simplification of the true complexity of the communities he studied. However, it seems to me that he does show some methodologies for getting at general community standards. In contrast, Milroy's study of Belfast, also presented below, shows the greater complexity caused by individual circumstances and concerns.

DIFFERENT DIALECTS, SAME REGION

Whereas older dialect studies concentrated on relatively large areas, trying to find uniformity in speech, recent studies by sociolinguists have concentrated on smaller areas, and within those areas have interviewed more informants from more social groups than the older ones did. William Labov pioneered far more in-depth investigation. His inspiration, in part, appears to have been a small study by John Fischer (1958), who investigated schoolchildren's alternating the suffixes *-in'* and *-ing* as in *runnin'* or *running.* Each child was found to use both pronunciations, but the percentage of times each was employed varied according to how genteel or rough the child was or wanted to appear to be.

In the early 1960s, Labov (1963) noticed that there was a great deal of variation in pronunciation of various sounds on Martha's Vineyard, an island off the coast of Massachusetts which had become a playground for Bostonians. The native dialect was originally quite different from Boston's. The original settlers, apparently unlike the Southern British who settled Boston, were strong /r/-pronouncers. Being an island, Martha's Vineyard had not generally succumbed to Boston speech. Labov noticed that native Vineyarders pronounced the /r/ before a consonant, but that there was variation both in how sharply the /r/ was pronounced and how often.

He also noticed that the vowel sounds usually spelled <i> and <ou>, as in *right* and *house,* were tenser and made more toward the center of the mouth than their Boston counterparts. The Vineyarders used an [ʌi] in *right* and an [ʌu] in *house* at least some of the time. To some degree Americans from many regions regularly produce these vowels before the sounds /p/, /f/,/t/, /č/, /š/, /s/ and /k/. You can test your own speech by contrasting *right* with *ride* and *louse* with *lousy*. If you have used different vowels for the first member of each set, chances are the one in *right* and the one in *louse* are at least close to the tense central vowels that Labov noticed Vineyarders using. The fact that many other American dialects in New England and elsewhere have those vowels shows that these are not peculiar to the Vineyard. The point is that Boston, the nearest large city to the island, does not pronounce those vowels quite that way, nor, at that time, did most Bostonians articulate the pre-consonantal /r/. In other words, both in vowel and /r/-pronouncing, some Vineyarders differed from Boston, despite the heavy concentration of Bostonians who summered at the Vineyard.

Wanting to know who spoke with a Vineyard flavor as opposed to a Boston one and why, Labov conducted a survey that asked subjects to read passages that were loaded with words calling for the /r/'s and the diphthongs [ʌi] and [ʌu]. He also asked questions loaded so that the answers had to contain words with those sounds. Like Fischer, he found that it was not a case of using a pronunciation or not. All the Vineyarders tested varied somewhat in these sounds. What turned out to be significant was the percentage of times each person used the Vineyard sound as opposed to Boston's. Most amazing was the correlation between Vineyard pronunciation and the attitudes of the speaker. Labov found that old-line Yankees who felt that the island belonged to them, pronounced the /r/ most frequently and used the tensed Vineyard vowel in words like *right* and *house*.

As the traditional livelihoods of farming and fishing declined, more and more of the descendants of the original settlers found that they either had to cater to tourists from Boston or leave the island. Those who had decided to stay, often in the face of financial hardship, signaled their loyalty to the island by a strong Vineyard flavor to their speech. The Gay Head Indians, who also felt that the island belonged to them, but who did not have quite the assurance of the Yankees, used the Vineyard pronunciation just a little less. Third- and fourth-generation Portuguese made the Vineyard-flavored sounds just a little less often than the Indians. These Portuguese were well assimilated into the island, and felt a part of it, but had even less assurance that they really belonged than the Indians did. The first-generation Portuguese did not use the Vineyard pronunciations at all. Not surprisingly, they showed overtly that they were unsure of themselves and their place on the island.

The pronunciation of high school students was a direct reflection of their career plans. If they were going to leave the island, they talked like

Bostonians. If not, they spoke like Vineyarders. Two important results of this study were:

►Each social group used a key pronunciation a certain percentage of the time.
►Attitude can be precisely correlated with fine points of pronunciation.

Phonological variables, different ways of pronouncing the same sound, were shown to be a potent tool for sociological investigation.

The Variability of Variables

In his later New York City study, Labov (1966) proved even more conclusively that examination of phonological variables is a remarkably exact way of analyzing a community's social organization. Furthermore, it reveals attitudes unerringly, attitudes that people often would never admit to having. New York City, being sociologically more complex than Martha's Vineyard, has more phonological variables. Labov investigated the following:

►Whether or not /r/ was pronounced before a consonant.
►Whether the /θ/ in words like *thing* was pronounced as [t] or [θ].
►Whether the /ð/ in words like *the* was pronounced as [d] or [ð].
►How high the front of the tongue is when pronouncing the [æ] in words like *bad* or *dance*.[1]
►How high the back of the tongue is when pronouncing the [ɔ] in *more* and *coffee*.

Just because a feature is sociologically significant in one region, it does not follow that it will be in another. In both Martha's Vineyard and New York City /r/-pronouncing is important, but it signifies quite different things in each place. The raised [æ] sound, disvalued in New York City, is quite normal for most of northern America and much of Canada. Educated speakers in the Great Lakes cities like Chicago, Buffalo, Cleveland, and Detroit may show far more raising than any New Yorker. However, in those cities, that raised /æ/ sound does not mark social class. In the Midwest the person who pronounces *bad* as [bɨd], *that* as [ðɨt], and *happy* as [hɨpi] is showing a regional, not a social pronunciation.

Similarly, using a [ɔ] for the first vowel in *more* and *coffee* may not denote lower class speech outside of New York City. It appears in the speech of those with impeccable ancestry and schooling, even one Harvard Ph.D. of my acquaintance.

Substituting [t] or [f] for [θ] and [d] or [v] for [ð] marks social class throughout the English-speaking world. For centuries saying [də] for *the* and [tro] for *throw* has marked an adult speaker of English as uneducated, as has pronouncing *mouth* as [mʌᵘf] and *mother* as [mʌvʌ]. This does not mean that there is anything intrinsically wrong with [t], [d], [f] or [v]. They are all just fine in other words, those in which we feel they belong, as in *time, dime, fine* and *vine.*

Swedish, which like English, once had [θ] and [ð] has long since converted, so that the Swedish counterpart to *that there* is "dat dere" for all speakers, and it sounds right to even the most educated Swede. Those sounds are not social class markers in Swedish as they are in English. The two sounds spelled <th> in English fit all the requirements for social class markers. They are marked sounds, appearing in few of the world's languages. When they do appear, as in Swedish, they have a tendency later to disappear. In English, these sounds have disappeared in most dialects. Although they appear in only a few words even in the dialects that have retained them, those few words must be used frequently. One can barely complete one sentence in English without having to use *the.* The sounds are rare enough to stand out and cannot be avoided even in casual conversation. Like agreement markers, they may have survived mainly because of their utility in social class marking. This does not mean that all marked sounds that survive do so only because they are social markers. The reverse may well be true, that the marked sounds which survive become social markers. However, it is remarkable how frequently social class markers are either marked sounds or irregular relic forms in English (Chaika 1973). If the same is found to be true in a wide variety of languages, then we can claim that markedness is a major factor in social marking.

Eliciting Styles

Elaborating on the methods he pioneered in Martha's Vineyard, Labov elicited speech in all styles from formal to casual. The pronunciation that people use in formal styles indicates what they think is correct in formal situations. If the same pronunciation is typical of a particular group or social class, we know that the group is admired, the **point of reference** for the society being investigated. Copying the speech of another group for other purposes, as when being supercasual or recounting a fight (Labov 1964), reveals points of reference for those situations as well.

Everyday, casual speech reveals an individual's true feelings of social identity. Labov (1966) proved this by correlating pronunciations that occurred only in casual speech with a person's membership in ethnic and social classes.

Labov elicited the most careful, formal style by asking people to read lists of words that contain the variables suspected of being important in a community. He found it especially fruitful to include **minimal pairs**, pairs of words that differ by just one sound, especially a socially significant one. For his New York study, Labov included pairs like *guard* and *god* because he felt that the /r/ was socially significant, as many New York City speakers did not pronounce it in casual speech, although they did pronounce it in the reading task. Labov regarded this as proof that the /r/ before consonants has become the prestige pronunciation in New York City. Whether or not someone attempted to pronounce it in the reading task depended strongly on the person's social class. This in itself is significant.

It is not to be supposed, however, that one can uncover prestige pronunciations this way in all societies. Milroy (1980, pp.100-101) found that her subjects in Belfast did not try to use prestige pronunciations in reading tests. Every community is likely to have its own standards for styles, just as it has its own socially significant variables.

Labov used another reading task as well, one that yielded a slightly less careful style. As in Martha's Vineyard, he asked subjects to read passages loaded with **variables**, sounds that are articulated in more than one way by different groups in the community. The passages formed a story, with each paragraph concentrating on one phonological variable. For instance, one was about chocolate milk and coffee cake around four o'clock. This tested for [ɔ]. For [r]-lessness, he used a passage with words like *over, far,* and *corner.* The passage testing for [æ] was awash with terms like *past, can't* and *past.* And, another passage tested for [θ] and [ð] with shibboleths like *thing* and *this.*

One warning to the reader who wishes to use such reading passages. Many subjects get "tipped off" to what you are after very soon, and either become so tongue-tied that they stumble over every key word or they turn it into a joke.

Besides the reading task, Labov also noticed responses to questions in an interview. The pronunciations in the responses were usually careful, but not as careful as those elicited in reading. He found that it is possible to elicit informal and casual speech in an interview, however, by asking informants to describe games that they played when they were children and to recall childhood rhymes. The rhymes often work only in casual style with nonprestigious pronunciations. Both the rhythms and pronunciations of prestigious pronunciations ruin such rhymes as in the jump rope rhyme:

Cinderella dressed in yellow
Went downtown to get some mustard
On the way her girdle busted.
How many people got disgusted.
1, 2, 3,...

The only way this works is if the [r] in *mustard* is left out so that it rhymes with *busted* and *disgusted*.

Labov also found that even when the disvalued pronunciations were not important to the rhyme scheme, subjects still resorted to them. For instance, in:

I won't go to Macy's any more, more, more.
There's a big fat policeman at the door, door, door.
He takes you by the collar.
And makes you pay a dollar.
I won't go to Macy's any more, more, more.

Labov found that informants pronounced *more* and *door* with a vowel close to [u] as in [muwə] even though [ɔ] would have fit as well.

Similarly, the pronunciation "podada" for *potato* was already gone in ordinary speech when I was growing up, but most people my age who grew up in Providence use that pronunciation in "one podada, two podada, three podada, maw *(more)*." Apparently pronunciation in childhood rhymes can preserve relic pronunciations.

Sometimes other questions, such as those dealing with sports or hobbies, will yield unself-conscious speech in an interview. Labov asked about TV shows, fights, and personal aspirations. He even asked questions about others in the same social group, such as, "Is there one guy everyone listens to? How come?" In order to get casual unself-conscious speech samples, interviewers must induce consultants to lose themselves in a topic.

To achieve this end, Labov relied most heavily on a "danger-of-death" episode. Informants were asked to relate a personal experience in which they had felt themselves to be in danger of death. While recounting the episode, people became progressively less formal, lapsing into their normal, everyday speech. In my own dialect collecting, I have found that many informants are daunted by being asked to share their danger-of-death experiences. Many simply say they have never had one. Consequently, I ask them for any unusual or funny anecdote: danger-of-death, a time that they were surprised, or excited, or the like.

Shuy, Wolfram, and Riley (1967), in their Detroit investigation, relied on a variety of questions, being careful to pick cues up from their informants about what they were interested in. I have also discovered that terms like *story* or *anecdote* make the informant insecure. They seem to think that they will be judged on their ability to recount a tale. Instead, then, I ask them to tell me about an experience they've had. There is no instantly magical way of doing a dialect or sociolinguistic study. The community's value systems and social structure finally determine what methodology will yield the information an investigator is looking for.

Speech Studies and Other Sociological Measures

Since he had at his disposal the results of a previous sociological study, Labov was able to correlate his findings with information about social class, occupation, education, income, and personal aspirations. If a preexisting study is not available, however, a researcher determines the social status of consultants by using the *Index of Status Characteristics (ISC),* a common sociological measure that divides populations according to occupation, education, income, and residence. These criteria have repeatedly been found to be important in uncovering the division of communities into social groups. Since language is social behavior, the *ISC* is useful in deciding which groups to study to uncover dialect differences within a community or society.

Labov found in his New York City study (1966) that use of variables within a community not only reveals its social stratification, but it also reveals changing patterns of stratification. Each social division that he found was characterized by distinctive pronunciation of at least one phonological variable. Although each group varied in the utilization of variables according to formality or lack of it, Labov found no overlap between groups in their total behavior.

He found that older speakers used pronunciations associated with belonging to different ethnic groups. Jews could be identified by the pronunciation of [ɔ] in words like *coffee* and *more.* Italians signalled their ethnicity by the height of their tongues as they pronounced the vowel [æ] in words like *gas* and *dance.*

Significantly, younger speakers, those aged twenty to thirty-nine at the time of the study, did not show differences according to ethnic identification. This finding mirrored the changing social stratification of New York

City. By the time of Labov's study the older loyalties to ethnic groups like Jews, Italians, and Irish was giving way. The new divisions were rich or poor, white or black or Puerto Rican, educated or uneducated. The key sounds had shifted to [ð] and [θ] as in *this* and *thing,* and enunciating the [r] wherever it was spelled.

The oldest informants in New York City made no attempt to pronounce preconsonantal /r/ even in the reading lists. Labov surmised that they did not consider it necessarily correct or upper class. Younger educated speakers clearly did. They made a maximum effort to articulate all /r/'s on the word list and reading passage tasks, but pronounced it less often in casual speech. The percentage of times /r/ was pronounced in all contexts varied according to social class, but the higher the social class, the more /r/'s in every context.

The lower class produced no preconsonantal /r/'s in casual speech, or almost none. Although they did produce more in formal tasks than in the casual, they still pronounced it the least number of times overall. One interesting exception to this rigid social class differentiation in the use of /r/ was the lower middle class. They actually out-/r/-ed the upper middle class in the most formal styles. The lower middle class **hypercorrected.** This is typical of lower-middle-class behavior. That class is often extra careful to be correct. They do not have the assurance of the middle and upper classes, who feel they are the ones to set the standards. Unlike the poorest classes, however, members of the lower middle class believe that it is possible for them or their children to move upward. The lower classes do not attempt to pronounce the variables that signal middle class-hood, as it is not likely that they will have a chance to become middle-class.

Since the oldest speakers did not try to pronounce /r/ wherever it occurs in spelling, even in the most formal task, Labov concluded that variable was a relatively new one in New York City. Articulation of /r/ as a prestige factor apparently emerged shortly after World War II. At that time, the social stratification of New York City began to show changes as the flight to the suburbs began. Also a good number of children and grandchildren of immigrants began to "make it" during those years. Labov noted that /r/ more than any other feature correlated with earned status.

When social class became more important than ethnic group, the ethnic vowels leveled off, and /r/-pronouncing became the new badge of those who wanted to proclaim high status. What is ironical is that in older New York City speech, /r/-lessness was considered upper class. However, once all classes were /r/-less, or because they all were, that sound could no longer serve as a status marker. Such a situation is common in the history of languages and is an important cause of language change.

Timothy Frazer (1983) investigated a similar phenomenon, but in a rural area in Illinois. As has happened virtually worldwide, the poorer farmers with small holdings have abandoned the land, selling it or leaving it to those who can afford both larger holdings and the expensive machinery that goes with modern agribusiness. What has happened is that a rural, nonprestigious pronunciation has become more frequent and invaded nonrural settings as well. This is noteworthy because, historically, pronunciations have gone in the opposite direction, from the town to the farm. The sound is the diphthong in words like *cow* and *town*. Formerly, this was pronounced as [a^u][2], but now is changing to [æ^u]. The latter pronunciation is common in many areas of the United States, including Pennsylvania, New York, California, and the Great Lakes cities. It is like the Australian [æ^u] except that Americans don't hold the [æ] quite as long as Australians do.

This new pronunciation in Illinois apparently started with women, but took a generation for men to adopt. Labov has well documented the phenomenon that sound change often starts with women, and women of all classes are more likely to try to use prestige factors than are men. There have been many explanations of this finding in American dialect change, all revolving around the notion that women are more socially sensitive than men. But one possibility has not been mentioned, so far as I can tell. That possibility is that women who use nonstandard forms will, of course, be pegged as lower class. For women, to be lower class is also to be more sexually available, what might be called the "Mae West Factor." A woman speaks like a man at her own risk, and, as we've seen, even standard-speaking men will lapse into nonstandard speech when trying to appear macho, as this connotes sexual aggressiveness. Women have to try to be more correct in their speech unless, of course, they wish to be "Mae Wests".

VARIABLE RULES

People categorize each other according to the phonological variables they use. If they did not, there would be no reason for the systematic way that variants of sounds are pronounced in a community and their tight correlation with social facts. Labov's New York City study, even more than his Martha's Vineyard one, showed that it is the percentage of times that someone uses a variable in each context that reflects social class. It is not a case of uttering a particular sound as opposed to not uttering it at all. Virtually all speakers occasionally used disvalued pronunciations, and all occasionally used valued ones.

Why are social differences so often indicated by frequency of usage rather than by absolutely different pronunciations between groups? Why is the middle class in New York City, for instance, marked out from the upper middle by using a smaller percentage of /r/'s? If the upper middle class is delimited by /r/, why isn't the middle class designated by another sound, say /l/, and the lower middle by yet another, say /m/?

Any answer is purely speculative, but it seems to me that this phenomenon is related to what we saw in development of jargons. Old material in the language is frequently made to do new duty. Human beings are already geared to handle flexibility, matching what they hear to the social context and deriving meaning accordingly. Variables in pronunciation fit into regular decoding strategies, demanding no new techniques.

Marking social groups by percentage of times that a feature is used may well be more efficient than having separate markers for each group. In a complex speech community, there would have to be a great many markers floating around, one for each group. Instead of having to listen for five or six markers, noting frequency of usage in order to categorize people correctly, residents would have to listen for as many separate markers as there are separate groups. Add to this the burden of recognition of regional markers, attitude markers, and purely stylistic markers, and the whole becomes so complex that efficiency in social functioning could well be impaired. In order for social interaction to proceed smoothly, categorization of all sorts has to be swift. Perhaps this is why dialect markers themselves are sometimes used stylistically, as when middle class youths lapse into BE on appropriate social occasions.

Obviously people do not attend conventions to decide how to use speech socially or what markers to adopt. In fact, pronouncements by experts who have tried to legislate speech have rarely, if ever, been successful. Any teacher who has struggled valiantly with trying to get youngsters to speak "correctly" knows how little such efforts help. Yet, patently, people do change their speech patterns. What does make them do so?

Rarely are people wholly conscious of all that they are actually doing with speech, much less why. All of these signaling behaviors seem to be inborn in humankind as is speech itself (Lenneberg 1967). Social markers on language are not products of formal instruction. We may speculate about the origins of such behavior, but the results are clear. In Martha's Vineyard, when a need to signal allegiance to the island became important, sounds already in the dialect began to function as markers of that attitude. In New York City, when it became important to signal social class, /r/-pronouncing developed for that purpose. Stewart (1972) says that in Appalachia, where age is especially important to social groupings, children signal that they are not yet adult by using infantile pronunciations long after children in less age-graded societies. The research of the past two decades has confirmed that as societies change, speech behavior becomes modified to reflect the new situations.

NETWORK THEORY

Milroy (1980) found that Labov-like studies, which neatly correlate social stratification with pronunciation, did not work in her study of the Belfast working-class. She cites the case of two middle-aged women, neither of whom went to school beyond the legal leaving age, both unskilled workers married to unskilled workers, and both satisfied with "the warmth and friendliness" of their neighborhood. Yet, the speech of one consistently evinces more vernacular pronunciations than the other does. Milroy says that "Any attempt to explain the consistency of the difference...in terms of some kind of social status index would, therefore, be inappropriate" (p. 132). In other words, Labovian studies do not necessarily account for individual variation. Considering that Labov's aim was to find what was common to members of each group, not to account for **idiolects**, he really can't be faulted. He did an admirable job of what he set out to do, and, in the process, changed linguistics, dialectology, and sociology forever. But, of course, there remained even finer-grained analyses.

Gumperz (1982) claims that "ethnic identity does not show a one-to-one relationship to language" (p. 39). Even members of one family may differ in their speech because of differences in their social networks. These show the relationship between members of a community, who they converse with and for what purposes. Milroy's studies differ from Gumperz' in that she utilizes sophisticated statistical analysis to bolster her claims. She (p. 174) claims that the concept of social network as contributing to both language change and language maintenance can be applied everywhere, and is less ethnocentric than are studies of caste or class (p. 174). More recently, Salami (1991) has also found that social networks, area of residence, education, gender, and ethnic background all contribute to pronunciation differences among Yoruba speakers in Ile-Ife, Nigeria.

Basically, what one does in such a study is plot the network structure of individuals in a group, here members of the working class in Belfast. Milroy made friends with the people she was investigating, visiting their homes regularly, virtually becoming part of their neighborhood, indeed part of their network in the status of "friend of friend" (p. 174). Thus, she was a participant observer. This was how she was able to plot the social networks of the people.

The concept of networks actually comes from anthropological investigations. This concept works well in working-class neighborhoods, because they foster social relations much like that of people in close-knit villages in, to us, culturally and physically remote places. Specifically, the working class maintains a **dense** network of **multiplex** relations within a territory (p. 174). *Density* here refers to the frequency with which the same people talk to each other and socialize. Working-class neighborhoods typically foster dense networks in which people live, work, marry, and converse with each other. Moreover, network relationships of such people are **multiplex**. That is, people are bound to each other in more than one capacity, as neighbors, relatives, and co-workers (pp. 21, 135, 140). In contrast, the middle class typically has **uniplex** networks which are not dense. Whether dealing with shopkeepers, coworkers or going out for an evening with friends, the middle-class relationships are more compartmentalized. Relationships are more likely to revolve around one function.

What Gumperz, Milroy, and others have found is that dense, multiplex relations foster the retention of vernacular, nonstandard pronunciations. Such relations are based more on solidarity than on power. Differences within the group can be explained by individual differences in the network. In other words, people talk like those with whom they communicate. In far less rigorous terms, this actually is what early dialectologists and linguists thought. Leonard Bloomfield in his monumental work *Language* in 1933, a work long considered hopelessly out of date, gave as the explanation for dialect change "density of communication and relative prestige of social groups" (p. 345).

The work on social networks does not necessarily invalidate Labov. Dense, multiplex communities are characterized by a lack of change. There is little social mobility. However, the middle class, which has networks which are both less dense and uniplex, signal their social class in their speech. Perhaps, it is for this reason that in modern nations the educated professionals and executives talk more like each other than like others from their region. Standard dialects are one result of social mobility and weaker, less permanent social networks.

HOW PEOPLE EVALUATE SPEECH

The same ways that sociolinguists use to ascertain how people evaluate voice quality can be used to discover how they evaluate various pronunciations. Labov created a tape from the recorded interviews, one which included all of the variables. Then he asked the participants in the study to listen to the tape, pretending that they were personnel managers interviewing job candidates for a large corporation. They were given a rating form on which to indicate which job would be suitable for each speaker on the tape. The jobs listed ranged from TV personality to factory worker.

The results matched those of the original interviews; hence confirmed those results: the variables rated as appropriate for the highest-ranking jobs were exactly the ones people tended toward in the formal reading tasks. Significantly, no matter how they themselves regularly talked, everyone rated speakers on the tapes the same way. Just because someone habitually says "dese" for *these* does not mean that he or she has values in speech much different from those who use the standard pronunciation. Labov found that, even more than others, speakers who used a stigmatized pronunciation the most are likely to downgrade speakers on the tape who used the same pronunciation. What we dislike most about ourselves is what we so often dislike the most in others.

Labov also found that people don't always talk the way they think they do. In fact, one sure way to get people angry is to tell them they are using a particular pronunciation that they criticize in others. Labov played a tape with different pronunciations of seven key words: *card, chocolate, pass, thing, then, her,* and *hurt.* Each word was pronounced four different ways and subjects were asked to circle the number that correlated with their own pronunciation. In most instances, people reported themselves as using prestigious pronunciations even if they really used them no more than 30 percent of the time.

Labov's New Yorkers monitored their own speech according to the community's standards of higher-class features. However, the way they actually talked correlated with their social class or ethnic group. In other words, people talk according to their feelings of identity without realizing it.

This has not proven to be a universal finding, however. Trudgill (1972) found that in Norwich, England, people claimed they used fewer prestige pronunciations than they did. This must be because the working-class pronunciation has its own "prestige." We have to disabuse ourselves of the notion that elevated social class is what constitutes prestige for everyone.

Rebels in a Speech Community

Nobody is immune to the community's values. Even tough street kids who rebel against established institutions in every way can show a surprising concern with correct speech. In the Harlem study, Labov et al (1968) got some unexpected results from a subjective reaction test. Because African American youths respond best in competitive situations, the test was given to the whole gang at once in the form of a **vernacular correction test**. An African American field-worker read sentences to the group, having asked them to correct the sentences to make them conform to the boys' usual way of saying them. If the sentences were correct according to the BE dialect they spoke, the boys were to make no correction. When reading the following examples, remember that the entire exchange was performed out loud so that all could hear and verify the truth of the responses. One sentence read to the boys was:

That's Nick boy.

One feature of BE is that it does not ordinarily use the possessive 's. Even so, Boot, one of the toughest, roughest members of the group, one who spoke virtually pure BE, shouted out three forms using this possessive marker:

That's Mr. Nick's son. That's Nick's son right there. Do you know that's Nick's son?

Later, the field-worker gave:

She a real stab bitch.

Again, Boot was on his toes with a response:

She a real [laughs]— she **is** a real stab bitch.

That *is* was important. Boot started to affirm the BE version, then caught himself and inserted standard *is*. Although, as we have already seen, BE doesn't use it in such a sentence, Boot again reported himself as using the standard form. Then the worker asked, "What does *stab* mean?" Boot answered, "She bad." He left out the *is* when caught off guard. Boot talked BE but reported himself as using the "correct" form. That he knew the community's standards is shown by his response to the field-worker's sentence. The worker also gave the BE form of a question:

Interviewer. Why he do that?
Boot. Why did he do that, man?
Interviewer. Don't people say "Why he do that?"

Boot: Some people that don't speak correc' English do. Calvin little brother do.

Here he failed to use the very possessive that he reports himself as using in the second exchange. Note, too, that in each instance, he zeros in on the very constructions that SE considers correct. He knows just where BE differs and what forms have to be supplied.

Positive Attitudes in Dialect Copying

With the advent of the 1960s and the accompanying questioning of middle-class values and new admiration of naturalness, nonstandard dialects took on new value for American youth. This was reflected in the increased use of BE and other nonstandard dialects in popular songs, even those sung by SE speakers. Today many middle-class SE speakers sing with overtones of BE and AE (Appalachian) dialects. Bob Dylan and James Taylor come to mind. Compare them with Frank Sinatra who was one of the most popular teen idols ever at the start of his career in the early forties and who has always rendered song lyrics in SE with an occasional "ain't" for liveliness. Whites have been borrowing from African American music at least since the twenties, but usually by "converting" the style to make it more palatable to a general audience.

The converse of today's singing dialects was found in the forties and fifties with many African American singers such as Lena Horne, Nat King Cole, and Johnny Mathis singing in SE. This was essential if their music was to be accepted by mainstream white America.[3] Some, like Sam Cooke, switched from BE to SE in different songs. Harry Bellafonte sweetened up black Caribbean songs, which appealed greatly to mainstream America. Charley Pride, an African American singer who prefers country and western to traditional black music, sings in a dialect completely indistinguishable from other Nashville performers. One has to see him to realize that he is a person of color. One cannot hear it.

Peter Trudgill (1983) examined the pronunciations of British rock singers from the late fifties Cliff Richards through the Beatles, to 1978 and 1979 albums from rockers like Dire Straits *(Dire Straits)* and Supertramp *(Breakfast in America)*. It's very evident that when you hear British rock stars interviewed, they sound much more British than when they sing. Why? Obviously because they want to. Americans have been exporting pop music since the 1920s, but this escalated with fifties rock 'n roll. Americans were the rock scene and British singers wanted to sound like them.

Just as Americans have stereotypes of British speech, stereotypes which don't take into account dialectal differences in Great Britain, so do the British have stereotypes of American pronunciation. They characterize all American speech as:

▶Pronouncing /r/ in words like *car, girl, bachelor,* and *park.*
▶Pronouncing words like *can't, aunt,* and *dance* with [æ] rather than the British [a:].
▶Converting both the /d/ and /t/ in between vowels to [D] so that *bedding* and *betting* are homonymns.
▶Pronouncing the vowel in words like *life* and *my* like [a:] as in American southern and BE dialects.
▶Pronouncing the vowel in *love* and *done* with the American [ʌ] rather than British [U].
▶Pronouncing the vowel in *body* and *top* as [a] rather than [o].

In addition, they use Americanisms like *guy* instead of *chap* or *bloke* and *call* for *phone* or *ring.* Obviously, they do this because "it is appropriate to sound like an American when performing what is predominantly an American activity" (p. 144). The African American origin of rock leads the British to try to imitate BE, just as white Americans have done. This is shown by the borrowing of specifically BE (and Southern) features like dropping *is,* "He livin' there still" (Beatles *White Album*) and "My woman she gone" (Dire Straits *Dire Straits*), dropping the -*s* on verbs, as in "She make me cry" (Stranglers *Rattus Norvegicus*) and "Here come old flat top" (Beatles *Abbey Road*), and using *ain't* as *there isn't,* as in "Ain't nothin' new in my life today" (Supertramp *Breakfast in America*). Despite this general dialect copying, the British singers do have /r/-less rhymes, as in the Beatles rhyme of *Rita* and *metre* in *Sergeant Pepper.*

As in any dialect copying, the rock singers hypercorrect. This happens because the copiers don't really know the details of the dialect they are trying to imitate. For instance, they know that Americans put /r/'s in where the British don't[4], so sometimes they pronounce them where they never occur and never have, as in Cliff Richards repeatedly singing [ər] for the article *a* ([ə]) in "you'll be **uhr** bachelor boy," the Kinks singing "**Mar** and **Par**" for *Ma* and *Pa* in *Sunny Afternoon,* and Paul McCartney in *Till There was You* warbling "I never **sawr** them at all." Because these errors are repeated, Trudgill feels that they arise from ignorance, not from slips of the tongue in the heat of encoding (p. 153). Of course, Americans would make similar mistakes if the tables were turned.

Trudgill also shows that as British groups made their mark and began writing more and more of their own music, there was a decline in the total number of their Americanisms. Of the myth that the Beatles, for instance, began to sound more Liverpudlian, Trudgill says that their early records used both more American and more Liverpool features than in their later ones. Punk rockers singing on British themes use fewer Americanisms and more British "low-prestige south of England" pronunciations. Trudgill feels that this is because of their conflicting identities. It seems to me that this could be because both sets of dialect features are associated with denial of middle-class standards, freedom (from middle-class mores) and naturalness (by their definition, not possible with middle-class mores).[5]

Negative Attitudes in Dialect Copying

Not all copying is so benign. Negative attitudes can also be revealed by dialect copying. Labov (1964, p.492) cites the example of an African American, Mr. McSorley, who spoke SE in a "quiet, pleasant, and cultivated manner." There were no traces of BE in his normal speech, and on tape nobody could identify him as being Black. However, in the danger-of-death episode, Mr. McSorley recounted a frightening expeience he had had as a guard at a YMCA when he had to investigate a man who was threatening others with a gun. In imitating this gunman, Mr. McSorley used BE. When asked what the man's background was, Mr. McSorley answered, "I don't know. Some kind of Hungarian I think." Labov explains, "In this incident, we see a process of unconscious substitution taking place in accordance with the value system of the speaker." For this speaker, rough, uncultured speech was associated with BE.

A similar kind of dialect copying is often heard in ethnic jokes. If these are about Jews, joke tellers frequently lapse into a pseudo-Yiddish accent. If they are about Italians, a supposed Mafia accent ensues, complete with rough voice and "dese, dems," and "doses." Although the telling of the joke itself is sufficient for showing the jokester's prejudices, the dialect copying underscores the teller's feelings that Jews and Italians are foreign, not like "real Americans," and that the Italians are not only rough and coarse but uneducated.

THE VALUE OF A SOCIOLINGUISTIC SURVEY

Sociolinguistic surveys are especially valuable for determining social stratification of a community for three reasons. First, a tremendous amount of pertinent information is obtained in every interview, as much as 400–500 pieces. Therefore, only 10 to 20 representatives of a given group need be interviewed to obtain reliable data. Second, subjects do not usually know what is being looked for if it is looked for skillfully, even if they are told that it is a language survey. The purpose need not be hidden from them.

Labov found that subjects' unconscious use of phonological variables was more consistent with their social and ethnic group than were their answers to any single question on the original sociological survey that he used for selecting subjects. People asked directly what their attitudes or feelings are often give the answer they think is correct or say what they think the investigator wants to hear. Of course, they do the same in language surveys as well, but the very lie contains valuable information about social attitudes. It reveals what is considered the prestige speech and the points of reference in the community. Frequently, for example, lower-class white boys live in open hostility with African American youths, engaging in urban guerrilla warfare with them. The whites express open disdain and even hatred for the African Americans. Yet when discussing fights, the same white youths frequently lapse unconsciously into BE (Labov 1964, p. 493). In their fieldwork my own students have frequently gathered samples of white youth lapsing unconsciously into BE when discussing sports, especially basketball and football. When discussing nonclassical music—jazz, blues, bluegrass—SE speakers often replace SE with BE expressions. Much American slang, dead and alive, like "real cool, man," "groovy"or "jammin'" seems to have entered SE by such borrowing.

HIDDEN ATTITUDES IN DIALECT EVALUATION

Although few northern college students would seriously venture to claim that southerners are stupid, lazy, and intolerant, when asked to evaluate a tape recording of a woman speaker with a strong Alabama accent, they consistently peg her as having those traits. The woman in question is in fact a practicing medical doctor, comes from a definitely upper-middle-class family and is most tolerant.[6]

Feminism has made enough strides so that college students would not claim that women are more emotional and less intellectual than men. Yet their true feelings surface when they are asked to evaluate a man and a woman with the same regional accents, reading from the same speech. In such a test, the two read different paragraphs, but the paragraphs are matched for various speech features. The woman is consistently rated by listeners as less intelligent, more emotional, and less logical than the man.

If subjects are asked to check off the character traits of speakers they hear on tape, clear pictures of stereotypes often emerge. We discover what speech and what groups are associated with intelligence or toughness, with sincerity, honesty, humor, diligence, or laziness and even general attractiveness. Lambert, Giles, and Picard (1975) studied attitudes toward French Canadians, both in Canada and in Maine. They found that in the St. John's Valley in Maine, both those who were not ethnically Canadian French and those who were, evaluated French speakers favorably; in contrast, Quebec French Canadians were inclined toward self-deprecation, mirroring the prejudice of those who are not French. The authors explain that the explanation for the difference in self-evaluation between the two Franco-American populations is explicable by the attitudes of those in power. In Canada, there is considerable demeaning of the French. In Maine, there seems to be none or little.[7] Carranza and Ryan (1975) found that in Chicago, Mexican-American adolescents assigned Spanish speakers the same social rank as non-Hispanics did. Both groups evaluated the Spanish speakers lower in status than English speakers. Whether or not they are conscious of it, people do take society's evaluation of their own group.

HYPERCORRECTION

It is easy to make fun of people who make mistakes because they are trying too hard to be correct. For example, one hears schoolteachers ridiculing parents who say things like:

We wants the best for our children. They tries hard, but that
Mr. S. he give them bad grades.

He don't belongs with them.
        (Labov et al. 1968)

In both of these, the speakers seemed to have formulated their own rule. Knowing that -s marks the plural on nouns, they assumed that it also marks the plural verb rather than the singular. This is certainly a logical assumption even if it is not correct from the viewpoint of standard speakers.

Some speakers are not sure which person gets the agreement marker, so they put it on the wrong ones, as in the paradigm:

I trusts my friend.
You trusts my friend.

He trust my friend.
We trusts my friend.
They trusts my friend.

Virtually all BE speakers do realize that the -s goes on the present tense. The important thing to remember is that the very fact that a speaker is hypercorrecting means that a person does perceive social norms. Moreover, it means that he or she wishes to be well-thought-of by educated speakers.

We have already seen that BE drops final consonants where other varieties do not. Such dropping may result in conflict. In reading classes, for instance, if a child pronounces *cold* as "col'," the teacher might say that the word was not read correctly, thus baffling the child who has indeed read it correctly for his or her dialect. Worse yet, because BE speakers frequently do not pronounce the final consonant that indicates past tense, saying "kick" for *kicked* or "love" for *loved,* other speakers have assumed that BE is lacking in verb tense. This became a political issue when researchers like Bereiter and Engelman and Deutsch concluded that BE speakers are therefore verbally deprived and that their speech is too defective for its speakers to learn to do well in school, a claim hotly disputed by linguists. Many languages, such as the various forms of Chinese, do quite well intellectually without a past tense in their grammar. However, BE speakers do use a past tense, especially in the irregular verbs so that one hears:

I lef' it
We play ball yesterday

With irregular verbs like *leave—left,* the past tense is preserved even though the /t/ is dropped, but with *play,* it is not. BE speakers often seem to be aware that such consonant (or "past tense") dropping is stigmatized by middle-class speakers. Therefore, in careful speech, they may hypercorrect by adding an extra past tense ending as in:

I loveded it.
But it did tasted like chicken.

Lest we chuckle, we should be reminded that standard English bears traces of the same kind of hypercorrection. The modern-day plural *children* actually has two plural endings on it. At one time in English, there were several ways to form a plural. Originally, the plural of *child* was *childer.* Other nouns had other endings, such as *-en.* Still others changed their vowels internally, as they still do, such as *foot—feet*. And others used -*s*. Gradually, more and more nouns switched to using the -*s* ending until the only survival of -*er* as a plural was on *childer*. Since -*en* was already an unusual plural by that time, surviving only in *oxen, brethren* and *kine*[8], speakers endeavoring to be correct put both plurals, the -*er* and the other irregular plural ending, -*en,* on *child*. The hypercorrect double ending on *children* remains to this day.

There is another hypercorrection rampant in educated varieties of English today:

Between you and I...
He gave it to Jake and I.
He saw Mary and I...

In all of these, *I* should be *me*. The system of signaling subject versus object pronouns has been dying out for centuries in English. The old *ye/you* distinction was moribund for Shakespeare. The original object of *it* was *him,* but this died out shortly after *ye*. NE speakers often got rid of the rest of the alternations, uttering sentences like "Him and me went." Even SE speakers followed a general rule of using the object form after intransitive verbs, as in "It's me." Generations of schoolteachers railed against such barbarisms, stressing "He and I went," and "It's I." Since the old subject/object alternation is not really a part of the language anymore, speakers who did not quite understand why the *I, we, she, he,* or *they* was preferred began to hypercorrect by putting those forms in even where *me, us, her, him,* and *them* are correct.

Perhaps because so many doctors, lawyers, teachers, and businessmen in this country rose up from the lower middle-class whose native dialect actually included "him and me went," the hypercorrections above have become widespread. Even children whose parents don't hypercorrect seem to be learning the "between you and I" form from their peers. In a generation or two, I suspect, that "between you and I" will be ordinary standard English.

It can easily be seen that the fate of a hypercorrection depends upon who is doing it. That, in general, is true of speech. Errors are what the socially disvalued or the politically disenfranchised make.

VARIABLES AS A SIGN OF GROUP MEMBERSHIP

The way people speak tells us where they come from and who they are. It also tells us who they are not. There used to be a term in BE for a person who doesn't belong, a *lame*. Although it is not so current now, the original metaphor is still apt. The person who doesn't use the membership markers of the community operates somewhat on the outside, like a lame person. The term did not denote a true outsider, but a person who should belong but didn't. A lame might be an African American youth who rejected the street life and attempted to be middle class or it could be a rough, tough BE speaker who simply prefers to go it alone. Females could be lames as well, as seen in one line of *The Fall* "Girl you ain't no lame, you know the game." Labov (1972) claims that lames in Harlem literally did not sound like gang members. Both by the percentage of times certain pronunciations were used and also by using other pronunciations entirely, lames were differentiated from gang members. For instance, lames, but not gang members, occasionally pronounced the ending *-ing,* as [In] not [In]. Lames also used the verb *be (am, is, are)* more than twice as frequently as gang members in sentences of the "he (is) good" variety. These findings accord with social network theory as well. Gang members talk more with each other than with the lames. Wolfram (1969) found a high correlation between the isolation of African Americans and their retention of a BE dialect in Detroit.

DIGLOSSIA

Some countries normally have what Ferguson (1959) termed **diglossia**. This refers to "two or more languages (or varieties of a language) in a speech community [which] are allocated to different social functions." (Saville-Troike 1982, p. 56). Ferguson, discussing Arabic, originally conceived of diglossia as a switching from a vernacular to a higher form of the same language associated with a "glorious tradition" such as religion and art. However, it soon became clear that diglossic situations can involve different languages. Before the demise of the Latin mass in Catholicism, for instance, Latin was in a diglossic relationship with other European, Asian, and even African languages. Prerevolutionary Russians of noble birth spoke French to their peers in Russia, especially on social occasions but spoke Russian to their servants or in everyday activity. The term *lingua franca* itself refers to a general European diglossia in which the upper classes could command French on formal occasions, including political activities like treaty making. In Paraguay, the Indians speak Guarani for intimacy and other matters relating to solidarity, but Spanish for education, religion, government, and high culture (Rubin 1985). Spanish for them is clearly the HL (high language).

Reserving one language—or one form—for purposes such as religion, law, and education, makes those activities special. Typically, in such instances, the language used for higher functions has a long tradition associated with erudition and sanctity. Religions typically depend upon dead languages and archaic dialects, a form of speech no longer used for daily business for their scriptures and prayers. Sanskrit, Hebrew, and Latin are examples of dead languages so used. The dead language separates religion from mundane activity and, since it is ancient, it has an aura of purity about it that spoken languages ordinarily lack. Religions that do not have dead languages often use archaic forms for the same purposes, such as English *thou art* and *he leadeth*.

An interesting example of diglossia occurs in the American deaf community. Manual languages of the deaf show the same kinds of divisions into dialects and languages that oral languages do. Moreover, there are different styles in each deaf language. Many of the deaf are, in essence, bilingual or even multilingual, with one of their languages being oral English. Although some deaf are virtually balanced bilinguals in spoken and manual language, others show varying degrees of competence in spoken language. In other words, just like bilinguals of two or more spoken languages, degrees of competency vary in each language. A person deaf from infancy or early childhood may be a native speaker of ASL as may a hearing person whose parents are deaf and regular users of ASL. Lucas and Valli (1989, p. 11) explain:

> ASL is the visual-gestural language used by members of the deaf community in the United States. It is a natural language with an autonomous grammar that is quite distinct from the grammar of English. **It is also quite distinct from artificially developed systems that attempt to encode English and can include the use of speech, ASL signs and invented signs used to represent English morphemes** (emphasis mine).

Besides true ASL and signed English, there is *contact signing* (p. 15), "an interface between deaf signers and hearing speakers..." labeled Pidgin Sign English (PSE). Besides this, there is finger spelling of actual English words, so that the deaf resources for communication range from ASL on one extreme and a continuum to English on the other, with Signed English, contact signing, and finger spelling in between. Researchers consider this a diglossia situation with the H language (superposed or high variety) being English.

Lucas and Valli studied the varieties of sign that ASL speakers chose in interacting with both a deaf and a hearing interviewer. They were testing out the twin assumptions that native ASL speakers would always use ASL with other deaf people, but use contact sign or signed English with hearing people. The deaf can detect an "accent" in sign, just as hearing speakers can detect one in oral language. That is, one who has not learned ASL in childhood will, like any other bilingual speaker, have different degrees of competency in it, but will usually be distinguishable from a native speaker.

Contrary to expectation, Lucas and Valli found that the deaf didn't always use ASL with deaf interviewers, although most used either signed English or contact signing with hearing ones. Three of the informants did use ASL with the hearing interviewers, contrary to the widely held belief that deaf native signers automatically switch away from ASL with the hearing. Another surprising finding was that although the deaf interviewer consistently used ASL, some actually used contact sign or Signed English with the deaf interviewer, despite the fact that they knew ASL natively.

The decision to use contact signing or Signed English with another deaf person appears to have been motivated by the formality of the interview situation, including the presence of a video camera. In other words, some deaf chose the more H (English) part of the continuum in the presence of cameras in a formal interview, despite mutual knowledge of ASL. This argues for a diglossic situation. However, two deaf persons used ASL throughout, even with the hearing interviewer and despite the taping. Apparently, for them, the desire to establish their identity as a "bona fide member of the deaf community" superseded considerations of formality (p. 24). The researchers conclude that "Different sociolinguistic factors motivate the language choices of different individuals." Because the deaf did not always choose the more H varieties in all formal situations, this indicates that there isn't a classic diglossic situation in this community. However, this finding may be mitigated by recalling that, currently, the issue of the validity of being deaf, of belonging to the deaf culture, is a big one. Like other minorities, the deaf are insisting on their right to be themselves, to their own culture. This may be the reason some deaf persons do not bother with the H language, which is associated with the hearing culture, even in formal situations. That is, this shows an awareness of the diglossic situation, but a conscious refusal to conform to it. It is like the African American who refuses to speak in a non-BE dialect even in a formal situation.

LANGUAGE CHOICE AND SOCIAL BONDING

We have seen that one reason for maintaining a language is the need for solidarity. Shifting between two languages is yet a way to show camaraderie. Fishman (1970) presents a long dialogue between a Hispanic employer and secretary. He shows that the man used English to dictate a business letter and the woman responded in English. As soon as the dictation was done, however, conversation moved to the topic of a coming Puerto Rican parade. Concurrent with the topic shift came a shift in language. The switch into a second, shared language symbolizes the values associated with a cultural activity such as the Puerto Rican parade, itself an affirmation of group loyalty.

This is an excellent example of what Gumperz (1982, pp. 55–99) terms **code-switching**. He defines this as

> ...the juxtaposition within the same speech exchange of passages of speech belonging to two different grammatical systems or subsystems.

This definition includes changing languages according to topic of conversation within the same social situation. This can occur with dialects as well.

Gumperz and Hernando-Chavez (1972) show code-switching between Mexican Americans:

Woman: Well, I'm glad that I met you, okay?
Man: Andale, pues, and do come again, mmm?...Con ellos dos. With each other. La senora trabaja en la caneria orita, you know? She was...con Francine jugaba...with my little girl.

Gumperz and Hernando-Chavez point out that this kind of switching is not necessarily related to differences or setting, factors that often determine style shifting within a language. Rather, lapsing into Spanish signifies more warmth. It is akin to using a more casual, intimate style within a language.

Sometimes a language switch is used for emphasis, as in "I say Lupe, no hombre, don't believe that." A Yiddish parallel is "I'll give you nothing, gor nisht."[9] The change from one language to another, in itself, has meaning. No matter what else such a switch means, it reinforces bonds between speakers. Such switching can obviously be done only between those who speak the same languages. It may be done in the presence of nonspeakers as a way of excluding them, a phenomenon that we have seen in the use of specialized jargons. (See Chapter 5).

Sometimes a foreign language phrase will be thrown out to see if a stranger really belongs or is "one of us." Italians, for instance, often interject a "kabeesh?" meaning 'understand?' Or Jews ask "Fershteyst?" African American "dig?" for 'understand' has been traced to West African *dega,* which apparently was once used the same way. Throwing out a word like this can be done by people who have no real knowledge of their ancestral tongue, commanding only a few words or phrases. Paradoxically it can also be used by those of other backgrounds as a way of saying, 'Even though I am not of your group, I still feel warmth for it.' or even 'Just because I am not one of you, don't think you can put one on over me.' All of these messages can be made across dialects as well with someone deliberately throwing out a word or pronunciation in another's dialect. It is also heard stylistically, as when someone raises or lowers style either to achieve more intimacy or to sound tougher or more in the know.

Switching to a second language when talking about cultural or home affairs in also a way of reinforcing that the cultural heritage belongs to the country that speaks that language. Susan Ervin-Tripp (1967) found that Japanese-born wives of Americans often slipped into Japanese when talking about domestic concerns. It may also be that the person is used to discussing certain matters in one language rather than another, and the grammar and vocabulary in the more familiar language are therefore more accessible than in the second language. It may also be that use of the first language is associated with warmth and love. For this reason, in many families the ethnic language may be all but forgotten except for words and phrases spoken to babies, usually in games or just terms of endearment.

THE ORIGINS OF AMERICAN DIALECTS

Our knowledge of speech communities helps cast light on the origin of American dialects. Some linguists have claimed that the first settlers were /r/-pronouncing but that in the nineteenth century East Coast speakers began dropping the /r/ out of admiration for the British upper classes whose dialects had dropped it. Surprisingly, even in so recent a work as Wells' *Accents of English*, vol. 3, this scenario is portrayed (p. 470). Supposedly, the Easterners became /r/-droppers because they had more contact with the British than those who lived further inland. They offer no explanation of the fact that Philadelphia, also on the Eastern seaboard, is and was /r/-full. As it happens, there is evidence that the original settlers brought the /r/-dropping with them. Even if there was no actual evidence, however, our knowledge of sociolinguistics tells us that this must be the case, for there is no other way that so much of the East Coast would have adopted /r/-dropping rules after independence from Great Britain.

Study after study has confirmed that people speak like those with whom they wish to be identified and those with whom they interact. There is no reason to suppose that early Americans, striving for their own nationality, were likely to adopt innovations in British speech. Even if a few wealthy families did remain in contact with Britain, this wouldn't have affected the speech of the large working-class, artisan, and farming populations. Similarly, it is not likely that the upper and middle classes copied the /r/-lessness of Cockney sailors visiting coastal towns as some have posited. For one thing, the /r/-dropping rules are too complex to have been borrowed from casual contact with a few people. The prevalence of /r/-less speech up and down the East Coast by speakers of all classes also argues strongly that the original settlers were already /r/-less, except for the settlers of Pennsylvania. After the local dialects had been established, later immigrants conformed to what was already there. The reason that the speech of other areas, such as Pennsylvania, the Appalachian Mountain regions, and western New England (west of the Connecticut River) are /r/-full is that the settlers of those areas were in fact British /r/-full speakers. For instance, the Quakers who settled Philadelphia came from northern England which was strongly /r/-full (Williams 1975).

Although our knowledge of how people speak and why tells us that the above scenario is correct, it still is nice to have some concrete proof that there were British /r/-droppers before and during the initial colonization of these shores. There is such evidence, much of it derived from examining rhymes, puns, or spelling errors. Schlauch (1959) points out that the Pastons, a married couple who kindly left us some of their fifteenth century correspondence, made spelling errors that showed that the /r/ was already being dropped. For example, they spelled *answer* as <arnswer>. We know from older manuscripts that the word never had an <r> after the <a>. It originally was *andswer*, with the *and* from the same Indo-European root as in Latin *anti-* 'against, and *swer*, the ancestor of *swear.*' Originally *andswer* meant 'to swear against, to rebut a legal argument.' Why, then, would a writer suddenly insert an <r> where it never existed before, and where it still is not pronounced? That would happen if the /r/ after an /a/, as in *park*, was no longer being pronounced, so that the spelling <ar> indicated the pronunciation of "ah," as it still does for /r/-less speakers today. The /a/ in *answer* originally was pronounced as [a] as it still is in much British speech today. The misspelling <arnswer> was a logical way to indicate [ansər] to people who had already lost the preconsonantal /r/. Similarly, /r/-less speaking children today might often misspell words like *socks* as <sarks> because the <ar> indicates [a].[10] The Pastons were writing well before colonization of the New World by the British.

Kökeritz (1953) pointed out that Shakespeare rhymed *John* with *forsworn, death* with *earth,* and *dyrst degree* with *high'st degree.* He also made a pun of *food* with *ford.* Such rhyming and punning show that Shakespeare, and by implication, his audience, was familiar with /r/-less pronunciation, although he himself was probably /r/-full. Shakespeare was writing just before and at the time of original colonization of America.

On the other side of the Atlantic, colonists were keeping records. Often they spelled the way they pronounced words as people still do today. These spellings provide us with definite clues as to articulation, as do sporadic misspellings today. For instance, in contemporary America one occasionally sees a misspelling <ornge> for *orange.* This only occurs from strong /r/ pronouncers who leave out the vowel after the /r/ in *orange* just as the <sarks> misspelling comes from /r/-less speakers.

Celia Millward (1975) delved into colonial records and found convincing evidence that the Eastern New England /r/-dropping rules were in Colonial times the same as they are today. She investigated spelling errors as evidence of pronunciation. She found

1.	*Misspelling*	*Word Intended*
	brothe	brother
	therefo	therefore
	administe	administer
	furthe	further

These show that the writers did not pronounce the /r/ at the end of a word.

2.	Mach	March
	Osbon	Osborne
	orchad	orchard
	Sanphod	Sanford

These show that the writers dropped /r/ before consonants.

3.	piller	pillow
	Marthere	Martha

These show the /r/-glide on words ending in /ə/.

The reader may have noticed that some <r>'s that would not be pronounced by /r/-less speakers today do occur in the spellings. Does this mean that the /r/-dropping was more sporadic than it would be today? Probably not, for there is no reason to suppose that the colonial record keepers always spelled everything phonetically. Although spelling was not as standardized as it is today, there were spelling conventions. Literate people were familar with spellings of words that represented pronunciations different from their own. Therefore, the misspellings were not wholly consistent.

Furthermore, as we have just seen, spellings represent different pronunciations to speakers of different dialects. Just as <ar> represents [a] and <or> represents [ɔ] to /r/-less speakers today, to a consistent /r/-dropper the <ar> in *Marthere* and the <or> in *orchard* did not necessarily represent an actual /r/. For them, the <r> was a silent letter indicating how the vowel should be enunciated.

To give a modern example: for /r/-less speakers the donkey's name in *Winnie-the-Pooh* is Eeyore, that is 'ee-aw' (for *heehaw*). He is a cockney donkey, one who drops /h/'s as well as /r/'s. Most Americans miss the point entirely because they do not realize that in Milne's British English, <ore> represents [ɔ]. Neither puns nor rhymes work well in dialects other than the one the writer wrote it.

So strong is the connection between the <ore> for [ɔ], that many /r/-less speakers think they are hearing an /r/ in [ɔ]. For instance, a South African /r/-less speaker complained to me that in London, he was disgusted by the way people put [r]'s in where they don't belong. Thinking he meant the [r]-glide, which he certainly used, I asked him for examples. He said, "Why the [r] they put in *off*!" Bewildered, I asked, "What [r] in *off*?" He proceeded to use a strong [ɔ] for the vowel in *off* with nary a trace of an [r].

The Virginia Tidewater and eastern New England were settled by colonists from the East Midlands and Southeast of England. These settlers were already using [r]-less pronunciation. They also pronounced the so-called broad *a* [a], 'ah' in words like *half, calf, ask, aunt,* and *can't*. The Middle Atlantic states were settled by Quakers from the north of England who were [r]-full. Western New England and the Great Lakes regions were also settled by northern Britishers.

A second source of dialect features in this country is migration from East to West. One can still trace old migration routes on a map that shows dialect features. Marietta, Ohio, for instance, was colonized by New Englanders and until recently speech there contained vocabulary features of the New England dialects, such as *pail* rather than *bucket*. Los Angeles speech shows some features of Oklahoma dialect because of the great migration from that state during the Depression. The strong Los Angeles /aː/ 'ah' in words like *talk* and *law* has been traced to that source. Because of the influence that Los Angeles now has on fashion, entertainment, and trend setting, that pronunciation is also being imported into locations which used to pronounce it [tɔk]. Conversely, words which used to have an [a], as in *Florida* and *orange* (pronounced "Flahrida" and "ahringe") are now being pronounced with the [ɔ] ("Flawrida" "awringe.") In other words, [a]'s and [ɔ]'s s have flip-flopped, each occurring precisely where it didn't used to. These changes, like the [r]-pronouncing changes, show a distinct pattern of West to East influence. Like the changes in Illinois which Frazer documents, these are pronunciations moving into a region even though they were not prestigious for older speakers.

PIDGINS AND CREOLES

A third source of dialect differentiation is creolization. The term *creole* in linguistics does not refer to French nor to cooking. Rather, it is the technical term for the process of a new language's being formed when two —or more—languages mix together to form a new one. The first stage of this process is the formation of a pidgin, a limited speech code typically used for business dealings between people who don't know each others' language and don't want to. Pidgins also arose out of the slavery and near slavery of plantation workers in places as far-flung as Hawaii, Mississippi and the Caribbean (Bickerton 1981). There, the owners and their overseers weren't about to learn the West African, Polynesian, or Oriental tongues of their workers. Indeed, even if they wished to, it would have been impossible to learn them all, for even on the plantations serviced by African slaves, many different tongues were spoken, so slaves had the double handicap of not knowing the masters' language and not necessarily sharing their native one with others. In Hawaii, workers spoke Japanese, one or the other Chinese dialects, or a Polynesian tongue, so again the workers didn't necessarily share language with their cohorts.

Consider the plight of children born on these plantations. There is no native language for them to learn. There is the pidgin based upon a European language, European only because it was they who owned the plantations and businesses. They were a distinct minority, and their language was not really available for the workers or their children to learn. So, by a mysterious process, the children created a full-blown language out of the pidgin. Consequently, there are French, Spanish, Portuguese, and English-based creoles. Bickerton (1981) says that all of these creoles are more like each other in their grammars than they are to the European languages which provided much of their basic vocabulary, despite the fact that the speakers of one creole had no contact with those of others. We have already seen that deaf children denied oral language or a pre-existing sign will make up their own. This is a similar situation. The process is, to me, both wonderful, in the original sense of that word, and mysterious. The details of the characteristics of creole languages are beyond the scope of this book, but Bickerton claims that examining the grammars of creoles provides insights into what the original human language must have been like, hence the title of his book *The Roots of Language*.[11]

The issue of possible creole origins of BE has become a political one, and one which has excited bitter scholarly debate. Some scholars claim that BE is not a nonstandard variety of American English, but an African-English creole. Because of this, some have argued that BE has its own validity, and, even, that schools should not try to modify BE speech. Certainly, BE is as complete, flexible, and intelligent as any other variety of English; however, there still may be good reason for schools to teach what are considered standard forms, such as not using double negatives. Fairclough (1989) demonstrates that the imposition of a standard dialect is one way to maintain power by those who already have it. Those who can learn the standard will have an edge over those who do not. The corollary to this is that the standard should be at least available to all speakers if there is to be equality of opportunity. Not to attempt to teach it at all does speakers a disservice. Whether or not they choose to employ it at least some of the time is ultimately their decision.

Many scholars feel that the substantive difference between BE and other forms of English must be recognized in classrooms, as the differences are a result of various West African tongues mixed with English (Stewart 1968; Turner 1971; Dalby 1971; Smitherman 1984). Certainly, there are similarities in words. To *badmouth* is a direct translation of a Vai expression meaning 'to curse.' BE *dig* 'to understand' seems to be derived from *dega* 'understand.' Words like *goobers, jazz, banjo, jumbo, voodoo,* and *okra* are clearly derived from African languages.

Gullah, spoken on the Sea Islands of Georgia and South Carolina is a distinct Creole. And, if we can believe the literary representations of African American speech in the eighteenth and nineteenth centuries, it was far more different from white than it is today. This seems to be true of mainland southern BE as well. The change from the original Creole toward a less "mixed" variety is called **decreolization** and its development over time during the decreolization process is the long **post-creole continuum**. Those features of BE which are most unique to it, as outlined in Chapter 8, are the present stage in the post-creole continuum. They do not represent a falling away from a standard dialect, nor do they represent a deviation from some ideal. They are developments that started with the original African American creoles, and must be considered as part of that variety of speech. When we speak of BE as part of a post-creole continuum, we recognize that there are variations within BE itself. We are referring to those features which, upon investigation, have been shown to differ from other varieties of speech and that are found in many varieties of BE.

The indubitable decreolization of BE seems to contradict findings that it currently is diverging from other varieties of English. What seems to have happened is that, first, BE became less and less African and more and more like white varieties of English, but it is again diverging. This is part of the post-creole continuum. Geneva Smitherman (1984) points out that when African Americans were first emancipated, they erroneously thought they would assimilate into white society. This, of course, would lead to their speaking a less creolized English. With the continued alienation of many urban African Americans, their speech has been developing more ethnic markers, although these are not necessarily Africanisms.

One apparently clear influence of West African, at least on older BE speech, was the substitution of a [b]-like sound for /v/ in words like *river* and *devil*. West African languages lack a /v/ so the original slaves must have substituted the closest sound in their native speech. Because they were socially and psychologically isolated, many BE speakers kept the *b*-like sound for generations. It is not a feature of most BE dialects today, however. Similarly, the increased tendency in BE to drop final consonants in consonant clusters can be attributed to the lack of such clusters in many of the slaves' original languages. Such simplification is a well-known occurrence in creoles. Also, it is typical of creoles not to use inflectional endings, like the plural[12] or agreement markers. This tendency would be reinforced in English by the fact that these endings often cause consonant clusters[13] which would not have been pronounced by native speakers of African languages.

Some features that have been advanced as evidence for a creole origin for African American speech can also be traced to some British dialect or other. Even if the feature did not appear in slaveowners' dialects, often slaves could have picked them up from overseers. Two good examples are the BE verb forms of durative *be,* meaning 'all the time,' as in "He be good." and the *been,* indicating completed action in the distant past. Much of the claim that African origins of BE cause its difference from other varieties rests upon these two forms. The *be* is supposed to be a translation from West African durative *blan*. Such carryovers are quite usual in bilinguals.

One objection to this interpretation is that there was a durative *be* in Old English, too, and one has been found in Newfoundland white speech. Joseph Williams (1975) believes that it must have submerged into a lower- or lower-middle-class social dialect in England, so it did not appear in writing for many centuries. Then it must have been brought to this continent by such speakers where it surfaced again. He argues, and I believe correctly, that the whites in Newfoundland were not likely to have learned this form from African Americans. His arguments appear to be bolstered by the fact that the *been* meaning 'completed past' has also been found in Newfoundland. Perhaps the slaves learned English from those who spoke the same dialect as that from which Newfoundland English is derived. Or, more likely, the fact that they were already used to a durative in their own languages would have made it natural for them to adopt even a vestigial one still existing in English.

There were Irish overseers and plantation owners whose Irish English could have contained such a survival; through them, it could have been transmitted to the African American population. That population, in turn, could have been receptive to the durative verb forms because they already had them in their native tongues. In other words, the existence of a feature in some form of English does not negate the fact that the same feature may have had a creole origin. The issue of the development of BE speech is clearly a complex one, complicated by the conditions of the original slavery, then the years of social and psychological isolation of African Americans themselves, an isolation attested to by the fact that a distinct BE group of dialects still exists all over the United States (Smitherman 1984). The isolation is probably what is important, not the specific origin of verb forms.

Certainly, there was a major difference in the formation of African American ethnic dialects. When the African slaves were first forced onto these shores, they were often deliberately isolated from others who spoke their own language, possibly as a way of preventing rebellion, and, just as likely, because their owners didn't care if they had anyone to converse with. Thus, their own language was forcibly taken from them, and they had to forge a new one out of African languages and the English they heard on the plantations. There is no question in my mind that there had to have been a creole origin to original African American speech. The question now is, "Does the fact that BE shows evidence of still being in a post-creole continuum mean that it should be considered a separate language?"

As already mentioned, the ardent proponents of the creole theory of the origin of BE insist that BE is a whole different language system that should be recognized as such. Recall that Fasold (1986) was able to find evidence of differences in BE and other varieties of American English, even when he matched populations for socioeconomic factors. He, and others, safely attribute these differences to the creole origins of BE, claiming that this dialect is in the post-creole continuum, although certainly it is closer to "white" Englishes at this point than it is to its creole origins. Still, many scholars want BE recognized as a creole, as a blend of West African and English rather than a derivative of other English dialects, so that it would not be considered nonstandard (Smitherman 1984).

We should, however, make a distinction between the undoubted creole origins of BE and its present status. The very existence of creoles of African and European languages, including English, all over the Caribbean and on the Sea Islands off Georgia where Gullah persisted into this century, argues for such an origin for BE. But this doesn't mean that BE is still a creole. Geneva Smitherman believes that on historical and sociolinguistic grounds, BE should be considered a separate language even though, she admits, it is very much like white varieties of English. This poses a problem, for, as we have seen, many immigrant groups kept the sociolinguistic behaviors of their ethnic groups, and their English has been influenced by their ancestral languages. Do we call these separate languages as well?

One of the proofs that creolists invoke in favor of their claim is that BE is systematically different from other varieties of English. However, all dialects are systematic, hence systematically different from each other. In my opinion, no matter what its origins, BE is now far more like other varieties of English than it is like African languages. However, it certainly should be recognized as an ethnic dialect, not a nonstandard one, and teachers should learn the sociolinguistic rules of the ethnic groups their students belong to and adjust their classrooms accordingly. (See Chapter 11.) It is not unusual for African Americans or anyone else to command more than one dialect or language: one used for status situations, and another for social bonding. Perhaps part of the schools' task is to teach students appropriate times to talk in each of their varieties.

Chapter 9 Notes

1 Labov found that there were five ways of pronouncing this <a>, ranging from the tongue being held low enough to produce a very low [æ] to a high [i].

2 The elocution scene in *Singing in the Rain* in which the teacher is emoting "how, now, brown cow" has the [aw] which once was prestigious in America.

3 However, blues and jazz singers did not modify their BE dialects.

4 The British are often not aware that there are /r/-dropping accents in America, and, since British dialects are /r/-dropping, in order to sound American, the singers try to pronounce /r/'s everywhere.

5 Of course, middle-class mores have undergone a tremendous shifting since the '50's, a shift towards the values espoused in rock 'n roll.

6 During speaking engagements I play recordings of local speakers and have the audience try to classify the speaker's ethnic affiliation, education, and general pleasantness on rating sheets. I was shocked to discover that speakers who sound "unpleasant" are almost unfailingly tagged as being Italian, even though they are not. (Actually, I never use an Italian ethnic speaker in these tapes). This shows the true feelings of my audiences, which, incidentally, always contain a good number of Italian Americans. Members of the audiences themselves have commented on how people's prejudices are revealed by their evaluation of speakers.

7 Things may have changed considerably since this study was done, especially since Canada has become officially bilingual, and the French Canadians have reasserted pride in their ethnicity. However, the principles uncovered in this study are still valid. If a group is stigmatized by society, it will not value its own variety of speech, even as it clings to it as a sign of solidarity.

8 The original plural of *cow*.

9 *gor nisht* like German *gar nicht* means 'nothing at all.'

10 Berlitz guides to foreign languages for English use British and American /r/-less speech as their basis for rendering pronunciation. Consequently, if they wish to indicate the [a] "ah" pronunciation, they do so by using the spelling <ar>. This can cause trouble for /r/-full Americans. For instance, the real pronunciation of Italian *mange* is rendered as "marnge." One wonders what happens to /r/-full Americans in Italy. They have [r]'s all over the place where Italian doesn't.

11 This is not to say that all scholars agree with him, scholars being the feisty lot they are, but he makes a good case for his general thesis, I think.

12 It is certainly not insignificant that many African languages, such as Swahili, use prefixes rather than suffixes for inflections.

13 Many languages do not allow many consonant clusters. A consonant-vowel syllable structure is universal in the world's languages, but consonant clusters are not. Japanese, for instance, doesn't have them, so that the English word *baseball* in Japanese is pronounced "basaboru".

Exercises

1. What "speech communities" do you find in your school, workplace, or place of residence? How would you try to determine what these speech communities are? Which model is better for describing your community, Labov's social stratification model or Milroy's social network one?

2. What variable(s) seem to operate in these communities? How do these seem to relate to national, regional, or ethnic variables?

3. Make up a brief speech evaluation survey and poll your friends to see their attitudes toward some variable pronunciation in use in your community. Which variant does each of these friends use? What does each friend report him- or herself as using?

4. If you are bilingual, or know someone who is, investigate the conditions under which code-switching occurs.

5. If you have access to the papers of an elementary school student, examine these for misspellings caused by dialect. Explain how the misspellings relate to the dialect in question.

6. Can you find evidence of features of creole in the BE of a rap song, or the dialogue of a movie like *Juice* or *Menace II Society*? What features of speech used by characters in these movies differ from non-BE speech of adolescents in the United States?

References

Bickerton, D. (1981). *The Roots of Language*. Ann Arbor: Karoma Publishers.

Bloomfield, L. (1933). *Language*. New York: Holt, Rinehart, Winston, Inc.

Carranza, M. A., & Ryan, E. B. (1975). Evaluative reactions of bilingual Anglo and Mexican American adolescents towards speakers of English and Spanish. *International Journal of the Sociology of Language, 6,* 83–104.

Dalby, D. (1971). Black through white: Patterns of communication in Africa and the new world. In *Black-White Relationships* (W. Wolfram & N. H. Clarke, Eds). (pp. 99–138).

Dorian, N. C. (1982). Defining the speech community to include its working margins. In S. Romaine (Ed.), *Sociolinguistic Variation in Speech Communities.* (pp. 25–33). London: Edward Arnold.

Ervin-Tripp, S. (1967). An Issei learns English. In A. Dil (Ed.), *Language Acquisition and Communicative Choice: Essays by Susan Ervin-Tripp.* Stanford, Calif.: Stanford University Press.

Fairclough, N. (1989). *Language and Power*: New York: Longman.

Fasold, R. W. (1986). The relation between black and white speech in the South. In *Dialect and Language Variation* (H. B. Allen & M. D. Linn, Eds) (pp. 446–473). Orlando: Academic Press.

Ferguson, C. (1959). Diglossia. In A. Dil (Ed.), *Language Structure and Language Use: Essays by Charles Ferguson* (pp. 1–27). Stanford Calif.: Stanford University Press.

Fischer, J. L. (1958). Social influences on the choice of a linguistic variant. *Word, 14,* 47–56.

Fishman, J. (1970). *Sociolinguistics: A Brief Introduction*. Rowley, Mass.: Newbury House Publishers.

Frazer, T. C. (1983). Sound change and social structure in a rural community. *Language in Society, 12,* 313–328.

Gumperz, J. (1982). *Discourse Strategies*. New York: Cambridge University Press.

Gumperz, J. (1971). Social meanings in linguistic structures. In A. Dil (Ed.), *Language in Social Groups: Essays by John Gumperz* (pp. 247–310). Stanford, Calif.: Stanford University.

Gumperz, J. (1982). Social network and language shift. In *Discourse Strategies* (pp. 38–58). New York: Cambridge University Press.

Gumperz, J., & Hernando-Chavez, E. (1972). Bilingualism, bidialectism, and classroom interaction. In *Functions of Language in the Classroom* (C. Cazden, V. P. John, & D. Hymes, Eds). New York: Teacher's College Press.

Kökeritz, H. (1953). *Shakespeare's Pronunciation*. New Haven, Conn.: Yale University Press.

Labov, W. (1972). The linguistic consequences of being a lame. In *Language in the Inner City* (pp. 255–292). Philadelphia: University of Pennsylvania Press.

Labov, W. (1966). *The Social Stratification of English in New York City*. Washington, DC: Center for Applied Linguistics.

Labov, W. (1964). Stages in the acquisition of standard English. In *Readings in American Dialectology* (H. B. Allen & B. N. Underwood, Eds) (pp. 491–493). New York: Appleton-Century-Crofts.

Labov, W., Cohen, P., Robins, C., & Lewis, J. (1968). *A Study of the English of Negro and Puerto Rican Speakers in New York City*. Philadelphia: U.S. Regional Survey.

Lambert, W., Giles, H., & Picard., D. (1975). Language attitudes in a French American community. *International Journal of the Sociology of Language, 4,* 127–152.

Lenneberg, E. (1967). *Biological Origins of Language*. New York: John Wiley and Sons.

Lucas, C., & Valli, C. (1989). Language contact in the American deaf community. In C. Lucas (Ed.), *The Sociolinguistics of the Deaf Community* (pp. 11–40). New York: Academic Press, Inc.

Millward, C. (1975). Language of colonial Rhode Island. *Rhode Island History, 34,* 35–42.

Milroy, L. (1980). *Language and Social Networks*. Baltimore: University Park Press.

Romaine, S. (1982). What is a speech community? In S. Romaine (Ed.), *Sociolinguistic Variation in Speech Communities* (pp. 1–24). London: Edward Arnold.

Rubin, J. (1985). The special relation of Guarani and Spanish in Paraguay. In *Language of Inequality* (N. Wolfson & J. Manes, Eds) (pp. 111–120). The Hague: Mouton.

Salami, L. O. (1991, June). Diffusion and focusing: Phonological variation and social networks in Ile-Ife, Nigeria. *Language in Society, 20(2),* 217–245.

Saville-Troike, M. (1982). *The Ethnography of Communication: An Introduction.* Baltimore: University Park Press.

Schlauch, M. (1959). *The English Language in Modern Times since 1400*. Warsaw: Panstowe Wydaawnictwo Naukowe.

Shuy, R., Wolfram, W., & Riley, W. (1967). *Linguistic Correlates of Social Stratification in Detroit Speech*. Washington, DC: HEW.

Smitherman, G. (1984). Black language as power. In *Language and Power* (C. Kramrae, M. Schulz, & W. M. O'Barr, Eds) (pp. 101–115). Beverly Hills: Sage Publications.

Stewart, W. (1968). Continuity and change in American Negro dialects. In *Readings in American Dialectology* (H. B. Allen & G. N. Underwood, Eds) (pp. 454–467). New York: Appleton-Century-Crofts.

Stewart, W. (1972). Language and communication problems in southern Appalachia. In D. Shores (Ed.), *Contemporary English: Change and Variation* (pp. 107–122). New York: J.B. Lippincott.

Stewart, W. (1967). Sociolinguistic factors in the history of American Negro dialects. In *Readings in American Dialectology* (H. B. Allen & G. Underwood, Eds) (pp. 444–453). New York: Appleton-Century-Crofts.

Trudgill, P. (1983). Acts of conflicting identity: The sociolinguistics of British pop-song pronunciation. In *On Dialect: Social and Geographic Perspectives* (pp. 141–160). New York: New York University Press.

Trudgill, P. (1972). Sex, covert prestige, and lingistic change in the urban British English of Norwich. *Language in Society*. 179–195.

Turner, L. D. (1971). Problems confronting the investigator of Gullah. In *Black-White Speech Relationships* (W. Wolfram & N. H. Clarke, Eds) (pp. 1–15). Washington, DC: Center for Applied Linguistics.

Wells, J. C. (1982). *Accents of English*. (Vols. 1–3). New York: Cambridge University Press.

Williams, J. (1975). *Origins of the English Language*. New York: The Free Press.

Wolfram, W. A. (1969). *A Sociolinguistic Description of Detroit Negro Speech*. Urban Language Series. Washington, DC: Center for Applied Linguistics.

Chapter 10

Gender and Language

A society's attitudes are revealed in its vocabulary and speaking practices. Examination of euphemisms show what members of a
society are uncomfortable with. Words for females in English typically take on meanings of sexual availability and desirability. Once
equivalent, words for males and females diverge in meaning over time so
that the feminine counterpart takes on a trivial meaning. Moreover, words
which indicate strength in women take on negative connotations. These,
combined with an examination of male-female practises in speech show
gender differences in our society.

VOCABULARY AS A MIRROR OF SOCIAL REALITIES

So far as linguists know, all languages are mutually translatable. What
can be said in one language can be said in any other—somehow. All languages are so constructed that new thoughts can be expressed in them.
To be sure, it is easier to express some ideas in one language rather than
another. This is because the vocabulary of each language develops partly
according to the priorities of its culture. The objects, relationships, activities, and ideas important to the culture get coded onto single words which
are often highly specialized to express subtle nuances. Everyone's favorite
example is the Eskimos, to whom snow is a central feature of life. For this
reason, they have anywhere from 8 to 12 distinct words for it, such as one
for the kind to make igloos with and one for snow good for snowshoeing.
European speakers have to deal with snow, but not so extensively as the
Eskimos. Therefore, they have fewer words for it. African languages, spoken where there is no snow, do not have a word for it. Still, they could
describe it, as, for example, white, cold flowers from the sky that turn to
water when they are touched.

People make their language say what they want it to, as we saw with
jargons. If it were possible to say certain things in one language but not
another, then we would have the problem that people who speak one
language could know things that those in another could not. Bilinguals
might have the problem of being able to know something in one
language but not another. In fact, although it may be more difficult to

express a given idea in one language rather than another, there has never been any proof that it is impossible.

This, however, does not mean that there is a one-to-one correspondence between languages. If there were, it would be possible to translate any language into any other by machine. However, this has proven to be a very knotty problem. Machine translations are still extremely limited after three decades or more of intensive research. The major problem is that, although all languages can potentially say the same things, the way they say them is considerably different. Each language carves up the semantic universe (the universe of all things which can possibly be said) differently. Even when two words mean the same thing in two different languages, the entire semantic load of those words differs. For instance, in English *climb* can be used in:

▶Maxine *climbed* the tree.
▶Maxine *climbed* out on a limb
▶Maxine *climbed* out of bed
▶The airplane *climbed* 20,000 feet.
▶Maxine *climbed* to the top of her company.

There is no reason to suppose that in any other language on earth all of these meanings of climb would be combined in one word. In other languages, there might be separate words, each with its own semantic load (the entire complex of meanings of a word.)

Prototype theory and recent theories of metaphor (Lakoff and Johnson 1980; Lakoff 1987; MacLaury 1989) have shown that cultural models underlie the variable meanings of a word such as English *climb*. For instance, in English, the prototype of *climb*[1] consists of:

▶vertical movement
▶use of hands in grasping position
▶use of legs, bent at knee, in sequence[2], climbing is a purposeful activity, not done by accident

It is not necessary that all of these features be present in all usages of *climb,* but all use some combination of them. For instance, "Climbing up in a tree" uses all of these features. "Climbing out on a limb" refers to the prototypical hand and leg movements, but to horizontal motion, rather than vertical. Climbing out of bed uses vertical movement and perhaps leg movement, but not the grasping hands. The airplane's climb is vertical motion without hands or feet. The metaphor for climbing up the corporate ladder depends on the entire picture of climbing, including the prototypical motion of the hands. This last adds a picture of grasping, of ruthlessness, so that the metaphor "climbing to the top of a corporation" indicates a determined person who grasps at opportunity.

In another language *climb* might be conceived of solely as an animate activity, so the equivalent of the word *float* might be used for the airplane rising. In our society, we often treat social structures metaphorically as if they were objects, so that we see corporations as ladders. Therefore, we go up or down them. Hence our metaphor for social or business climbing. In another language, instead of the metaphor for climbing up in the business world, another culture, which conceives of power as being a hidden entity in the center of things, the metaphor for success might be based upon an image of burrowing to the center of something.

Such prototypes help explain why semantic loads of words differ cross-linguistically and why there are often differences in metaphor in different languages.

Sociolinguistic Construction of Reality

For humans, reality is "filtered, apprehended, encoded, codified, and conveyed via some linguistic shape" (Smitherman 1991, p. 117). The words we use for concepts do help form our ideologies, attitudes, and behaviors. This doesn't mean, as Whorf thought, that we are prisoners of language. It does mean that language reflects cultural attitudes, and that we unconsciously adopt those attitudes as we learn the language. Our consciousness can be raised. We can learn to recognize the biases in our language, and we can learn not to use sexist, racist, or otherwise prejudiced speech forms. Two areas in which this is very evident is in gender and race. Besides the prototypes mentioned above, meaning is derived from the breakdown of individual words.

Semantic Features

| HUMAN | MALE | POWER |

Words do not have holistic meaning. Rather, they are composed of features of meaning. For instance, boy is composed of features like [+human, +male, -power]. Features of one word can be transferred onto another, which is one important way we get meaning. Uriel Weinreich (1966) gave an apt example. Pretty has a feature of [+female]. If pretty is used with boy, the [+female] gets transferred so that pretty boy implies a feminine young male. In American culture, this often also implies a tinge of homosexuality. In the Eagles' song "Hotel California," it is sufficient to say that a woman is surrounded by "pretty, pretty boys" to indicate their sexual persuasion. Handsome, which has the feature [+male], when used with woman, implies an older woman, not a 'sex kitten.' This used to mean a woman who is past the prime of her sexual life. Nowadays, it can mean a young woman, but one who is a well-educated career woman, not one who is to be judged primarily on the basis of sexual attractiveness. This change in meaning coincides with the change in the expected roles of women.

Differences in meaning between two dialects or languages are often differences in the way features are attached to words. For example, in England, the features [+car, +top, +front] are attached to *bonnet,* but, in America, to *hood.* In the American South, the verb *favor* includes [+concrete, +appearance] in the sense of "she favors her mother," meaning she looks like her. In the North, it is most likely to be interpreted as meaning 'prefer'.

Even within the same dialect, choice of one word over another can subtly convey an attitude. If our side has to take a *military action,*[3] we *land* on someone else's territory, but if our opponents do, they *invade.* The start of warfare against Iraq in 1991 was announced by our government as "Ladies and gentlemen, the *liberation* of Kuwait has begun." One man's liberation is another's invasion.

Our attitude toward a given activity is conveyed by the choice of synonym. If we don't wish to raise the spectre of all-out war, then we "take military action," we don't "go to war." If we approve of the military landing on another country's shores, then we say it is a *landing* or a *liberation*, but if we don't approve, then it is an invasion. By utilizing synonyms this way, the media and the government and other institutions are able to influence public opinion without people's being aware of it.

Fairclough (1989, p. 50) gives the even more subtle example of how the media systematically build in the perspectives of dominant groups in society by their word choice. For instance, he says, that when industrial disputes are systematically referred to as *trouble* or *disruption* in the media, "that is systematically building the employer's perspective into industrial news coverage." The very term *labor troubles* implies that it is labor causing trouble to management, not the other way around.

Words take on the semantic features of [+good] or [+bad] according to how a particular culture feels about the item designated. If a word marked [+bad] denotes something that must be mentioned in the course of a daily routine, other words are substituted. The substitutes, called **euphemism**, are close in meaning but do not quite mean the "bad" thing. Instead of having the feature [+bad], they are neutral or even pleasant.

One example is the attribute *fat*. The feature [+bad] is firmly attached to *fat* nowadays in America. It is no longer desirable on meat, much less on people. This poses a problem for clothing stores that wish to sell specially cut garments for the obese. These certainly can't be called what they are: clothes for fat folk. Rather, for girls there are *chubbette* or *pretty plus*; for boys, *husky* or *husky plus*; for men, *portly*, *big*; and for women, *women's sizes* (as opposed to *misses* or *junior*), *queen size, full sizes, half-sizes*, and *hard-to-fit*. *Stout* used to be a euphemism, as in *stylish stouts*, but when it ceased being used in the general language in its original senses of 'healthy' and 'brave,' it came too directly to mean 'fat'. One hardly, if ever, sees the term in clothing departments anymore. Similarly, the male *portly* is being replaced by *big* on labels.

Some of the euphemisms for *fat* used to be words meaning 'strong' and 'tough' such as *stout* and *husky*. *Portly* used to mean 'imposing, dignified'. The euphemistic character of *pretty plus* is obvious, as is reference to *half-sizes* instead of the true 'size and a half'.

Even in casual conversation, referring to a person's bulk, people skirt around the word *fat*. Instead they say, "Well, he certainly is big" or "It's hard for a big woman to find clothes." *Plump,* an older, favorable term for *fat* is today pretty much reserved for chickens or pillows. Students in my classes, when asked to rate words for *fat,* typically consider *plump* archaic and humorous. The only word associated with obesity that can be positively evaluated is *jolly*. Even so, this is restricted to Santa Claus, the Jolly Green Giant, and babies who are still allowed to be fat in our society.

Cultures that do—or did—not find fat repugnant treat it differently in their word stock. In both Italian and Yiddish, for instance, the same word can be used for both *fat* and *healthy*. Occasionally, in English, *fat* and *healthy* can be used synonymously, as in *fat profit* and *healthy profit*. The choice of one over the other depends on our feeling about the profit in question: *fat* if we disapprove of or are gloating over the profit, *healthy* if we approve. For instance, a stockbroker would tell you that an investment gives a *healthy* profit, but a reporter in a story about a shady businessman might call it a *fat* one.

Recently, my son was astonished by some African American youths who admiringly called his new shoes "fat." This is a current BE word meaning 'good.' This is part of what Geneva Smitherman calls the semantic inversion of BE, an inversion which explained why earlier BE introduced "bad" for 'good.' Since *fat* generally has a negative connotation, its meaning is inverted to 'good' in this culture.

Euphemism

When a culture frowns upon an activity or situation, typically it creates **euphemisms** to refer to it. Euphemisms usually occur in sets of several words, none meaning exactly the thing being referred to. When one euphemism becomes too directly associated with the disvalued meaning, it is replaced by other euphemisms. This is clearly seen in the euphemisms for the places where Americans urinate and defecate. Even with the supposed lifting of taboos in modern times, American prudishness about voiding remains in full force. Taboos about swearing, sex, and nudity have all weakened, but the bathroom functions still disgust us. One consequence of this is the dearth of public restrooms in America. In England, as one enters a town, there is usually a welcome sign proclaiming *Toilets*, with an arrow pointing the way. When Sigmund Freud visited the United States, he was appalled at the lack of facilities. Anyone who has ever traveled across country with small children still is.

The discomfort Americans have in mentioning elimination is well illustrated in the preceding paragraph. Except for the erudite Latinate *defecate* and *urinate,* there is not one direct polite term for the process under discussion. Nor is there even one direct term for the room where the body functions are performed. *Bathroom* actually means 'the place where one takes a bath.' In England it still means that since, unlike Americans, the

British do not keep the tub and the "hopper" in the same room. *Toilet* originally meant 'getting dressed,' as in the archaic, "She made her toilet," or the survival *toilet water*. It must have been assumed that part of the process of getting dressed was *going*. Of course *restrooms*, another designation of the place to *go* are not for resting. Since we all know that the only place to rest when away from home is a hotel room, we hear *restroom* as a euphemism for the place in which we rest (stop) briefly for unmentionable purposes. How unmentionable these purposes are is seen by the general terms like *facilities* for the place, and *going* for the acts. In many languages use of very general, virtually empty terms, indicates a taboo. In English the word *facilities* usually has to be followed by *for X* as in the *facilities for cooking*. When it occurs alone, as in "I have to use the facilities," it usually means the "loo," to use the British slang for it. Similarly, *going* is normally followed by an adverb of place or manner as in "going to New York" or "going by plane." By itself, it means one is voiding. Compare this with the general *doing it* used without reference to a previously stated act, which means 'fornicating,' another Latinate substitute.

The sheer number of euphemisms for voiding indicates the degree of discomfort Americans have about bodily waste: *powder room, comfort station, head, lav(atory), John, little girls' room, little boys' room, lavette, half-bath, commode*. In a restaurant, one often has to guess if the right room has been found, especially if a coy picture is used on the door. Usually, there are two signs indicating male and female gender: *buoys* and *gulls; knights* and *damsels; his, hers; signor, signorina*.

In contrast there is only one word in English for the place where food is prepared: kitchen. Clearly, that is not a taboo which, when you think of it, is odd in a society which disvalues fat.

Propaganda is a kind of euphemism, on calling unpleasantness by another name. The difference is that propaganda is a euphemism used by governments and other political organizations. The term *ethnic cleansing* was intended as propaganda. It really meant 'massacring a group of people.' The seemingly innocuous word *apartheid*, literally "apart-hood", 'the state of keeping something apart,' really meant 'keeping blacks in Africa in poverty and servitude.' The only 'apart' for them was being herded into special, poverty-ridden townships apart from the white folks. In the United States, all one need to do to justify almost any action is to speak of "freedom" and "rights." The NRA has successfully kept gun-control laws to a minimum on the grounds that they would violate our "freedom" and our "rights", despite the fact that every other free society in the world has strict gun controls, and far fewer murders from shooting. The kicker is that the "rights" are "constitutional," another potent word in American politics. The word itself is used as a justification.

Sometimes propaganda and common euphemisms coincide. A case in point is death, another phenomenon with which our culture is uneasy, and which governments have to discuss. Again, we can tell that English speakers are uncomfortable with death by the number of euphemisms for it. People do not die, they "pass away," "pass on," "go to sleep," "go to the other side," "meet their maker," "go to rest," "go to their final reward," "croak," "kick the bucket," "buy the farm," "buy it," and become "traffic fatalities" not corpses. Also, we "lose" our relatives, as in I recently lost my favorite aunt. Our pets are "put to sleep, put away," or "put down," not killed (except for a cruel outside party.) Gangsters "deep-six, waste," or "off" their victims rather than murder them.

Our uneasiness about mentioning death conflicts with the military's need to talk about it. The military is in an exceptionally difficult position, for if we cannot talk directly of natural death, how can we talk of unnatural death? Yet soldiers must deal both with killing and being killed. Death must be mentioned in their training, but if it were mentioned too directly, soldiers would be too often reminded of their mortality and of the true awfulness of what they are supposed to do.

Robert Sellman, a ROTC student, examined military euphemisms for death in a field manual, *The Combat Training of the Individual Soldier and Patrolling*. He showed that the manual is written in a highly impersonal, distant style which is "designed to negate the psychological impact of killing and destroying." One way this is done throughout is to use the modal auxiliary *may*, as in "A nuclear explosion may cause heavy casualties among your leaders" and "may even completely destroy your unit's chain of command." Nuclear explosions will cause these disasters. There is no "may" about it. By using *may*, the field manual makes it much less certain, much less frightening. Also, referring to "heavy casualties" as a cover term, rather than elucidating with direct words like *the dead, the burned, the wounded*, or *radiation sickness* glosses over the true horror. The stress on the leaders' being destroyed is especially interesting. Nuclear bombs are not selective. Anyone around gets dead. By overtly citing "leaders" and "chain of command" but not actually mentioning enlisted persons or peers, the potential deaths of the ordinary soldiers are backgrounded. It is not so much that the manual lies; it just mentions part of the truth.

Sellman focused on two other terms: *fire for effect* and *engage the enemy*. The first is the command to the artillery to destroy an area with its explosives. Sellman points out that the emptiness of *for effect* matches that in the euphemism *do it*. He feels that this emptiness minimizes the personal involvement of the artillery observer who has to give the command. The second term also does not mean what it says. It means 'fight, shoot, kill.' It says "take part in an activity with the enemy." The soldier has no difficulty extrapolating the meaning, but the meaning is never explicitly given. The reason is simple. If the field manuals were explicit, if they directly reminded soldiers what they were training for, to kill and to be killed, getting soldiers on the battlefield could become more difficult.

Both of these terms illustrate a common factor in euphemism: **circumlocution**, which means spreading meaning over several words rather than using a single one. This weakens meaning and is one way to avoid confronting an unpleasant issue head-on. *Kill* is not only more semantically direct than *fire for effect*, it is more powerful because meaning is concentrated on one word. In the same way, *engage the enemy* is weaker than *fight*. A beautiful example of the semantic weakening by circumlocuting is the United States Army's statement of intent, "the management and application of controlled violence." In other words, *war*.

Sellman also examined the slang terms that soldiers use for death. He notes that these allow soldiers to discuss the unpleasant aspects of their job while still keeping their courage and morale up so that they can function as soldiers. The euphemisms for death are unusually explicit, but they keep soldiers at a remove from the true horror by denying the humanity of the corpse. For instance, *die* is "get iced" or "get waxed." Dead fish are usually put on ice, and mannequins are made of wax. Dog tags are really death tags, used to identify dead soldiers, but who would put them on if they were constantly being reminded of that? Sellman suggests that "Making the dead seem inhuman allows the individual to say it can't happen to him. This is the attitude that the soldier must have in order to throw himself in front of bullets."

Euphemism is also accomplished by **understatement**, using words which have combined semantic features that do not add up to the meaning intended. Saying that children are "nutritionally deficient" when you mean 'starving' is an example. Sellman also gives one from soldier slang: *zap* rather than *kill*. *Zap* can also mean 'strike a blow' that is not fatal.

There are more overtly damning ways of doing propaganda as well. For instance, the November 6, 1987, edition of a South Florida newspaper, *The Sun-Sentinel*, featured a story with an accompanying picture of a handsome, young, tall slender rabbi wearing a prayer shawl who was leading a group in prayer (p. 9e). The headline read "Rabbi planning to **peddle** Judaism over the airways." (Boldface mine) The choice of the word *peddle* not only showed the author's contempt for Judaism, but gave the implication that the rabbi's religious program was for his personal material profit, not for the spiritual well-being of listeners. Since the article also stressed that the rabbi didn't look like one because he was tall and handsome, that message was doubly reinforced. This, too, is how to sway opinion by manipulating word choice.

Metaphor and Idiom

The preceding sections claim that things people are uncomfortable with have many euphemistic names and phrases. These all mean roughly the same thing, although typically they do not mean quite what they say. **Metaphors** and **idioms** are very common as euphemisms, perhaps because they are the embodiment of circumlocution, of not calling a spade a spade.

A metaphor is a word used so that its central meaning cannot be taken. Rather, one must extend its meaning. For instance, *that old bag* in the right context means 'the old, unpleasant, unattractive woman.' The extension of *bag* to mean 'woman' is a metaphor.

Idioms are different from metaphors in that a mere extension of meaning of the words used will not give the intended meaning. The meaning of the idiom is not garnered by an examination of its parts. Rather, the entire group of words has a meaning as if it were one word (Chafe 1968). Frequently, idioms consist of whole parts of sentences, typically a complete predicate. The difference is that it is not the meaning of each word in conjunction with the others that counts in idioms. It is the meaning attached to the whole. For instance,

Idiom	*Literal Word*
put x's foot in x's mouth	verbally blunder
shake a leg	hurry
pull x's leg	deceive teasingly
chew the fat	talk
shoot the breeze	talk
kick the bucket	die
roll in the hay	fornicate
shake the dew off the lily	urinate

Because the actual meaning of idioms is so removed from the meaning of the sum of their parts, idioms are the epitome of beautifully indirect reference. It follows, then, that one way to uncover the attitudes of a people is to examine their idioms and other euphemisms.

CHAPTER 10

At the beginning of this chapter, it was mentioned that a culture has multiple terms denoting items or activities that are important to it. There is a difference between these multiple terms and euphemisms. In euphemism, all the terms mean the same thing. In contrast, multiple terms for culturally important referents all refer to slightly different aspects of the same activity, object or concepts. Consider the synonyms of *talk:*

> *Chatter, gab, prattle, gossip, jabber, nag, babble, clack, jaw, jib-ber-jabber, B.S., shoot the breeze, shoot the s—t, chew the fat*

All of these refer to idle talk or ordinary sociable talking with no intellectual or business purpose. People who talk a lot are:

> *talkative, gabby, wordy, glib, bigmouthed, fatmouthed, full of hot air*

or are:

> *gossips, nags, shrews, chatterboxes, windbags*

Although there is no noun that specifically means 'a person who does not talk a great deal,' there are a number of adjectives to describe such a person:

> *quiet, laconic, reticent, taciturn, reserved, closemouthed*

Recall how many words exist for idle talk. Just about all have the connotation of 'not desirable' and stupid.' Some, like *prattle, babble,* and *chatter* also carry the connotation of 'childish'—and 'feminine.' Besides the feminine *gossip* and *nag* with their connotations of 'nastiness' and 'triviality' the only phrases for idle talk that do not carry bad overtones are those that refer to the casual speech of men, *chew the fat* and *shoot the breeze.* In other words, all words for talking which have semantic features of [-good, -important] also have one of [+female]. Likewise, the adjectives listed above denoting people who talk a lot are not only demeaning but feminine. From the semantic features on these words, it certainly seems that the speech of men is more valued in our society than that of women. Notice that there are few common words to describe someone who does not talk very much and those that do are somewhat literary. In contrast with the words for talking too much, none of these is exclusively feminine.Clearly, talking per se is not a highly valued activity in the general American culture. There is no term in English that is the equivalent of the

Yiddish *shmuesen* 'social talking for the purpose of enjoying each other's company,' a word applied equally to adults of both sexes.

GENDER AND LANGUAGE

The very fact that so many words for unpleasant talk have a semantic feature of [+female] on them, tells us a good deal about how women are valued in this society. The ensuing discussion on gender is not intended to be feminist polemics. Gender is so pervasive and so important a part of society, that when we find clear attitudinal differences in references to each, we are constrained to look into the matter. We cannot overlook the amount and quality of important research that has been done into these differences. Gender-biased language affects everyone, both males and females. Women and their treatment are an inextricable part of society. There is no way to investigate human and cultural behavior without considering women. When we examined speech activities in Chapter 6, virtually all of those discussed were male. The reason is simple. Studying speech and other social behavior has been largely a study of male activities. Yet, all male-centered accounts of society are woefully incomplete and inaccurate. Finally, speech about and by women is a superb example of how language behavior mirrors social attitudes and facts.

Attitudes toward women are clearly revealed in English vocabulary and confirmed by differences in male/female speaking practices. It has already been demonstrated that English vocabulary reflects a disvaluing of talk for its own sake. Moreover, it was shown that most words that mean 'idle talk' in SE are also marked [+female] and/or [+young +trivial -good]. A person who is *gabby, talkative* and *gossipy, a nag, a shrew* or *a chatterbox* must be a woman. What are the male equivalents? There are none. A woman is a nag when she asks for something too often. What is a man? Persistent. A man who is aggressive and ambitious is aggressive and ambitious. He is also a success. A woman who is aggressive and ambitious is a "power bitch." If a woman bests a man in an argument, she is said to castrate him, or to be "a castrating bitch." A man who bests another man or a woman is just being forceful. A woman who complains or criticizes is a shrew or bitch. What are men called who do the same? There is no single word for it. Women gossip. But men? They "shoot the breeze," a far more pleasant and potent activity. Notice there is no favorable term for a woman who is strong, dominant, and intelligent. Such qualities earn women derogatory labels. Our language tells us that women are supposed to be submissive.

An important difference between words marked [+female] and those marked [+male] is, in fact, potency. All the words that refer to women's talk mean 'talk that is inconsequential.' It is not talk of important, valuable issues, or indeed, of issues at all. The equation between women's talk and baby talk is seen in words like *babbling, chattering,* and *gabbing,* all essentially mindless, aimless, speech production. Furthermore, note who babbles: babies, women, the insane, and brooks.

Men may be glib, but this implies expertise in using language persuasively. Glibness does have a negative connotation, but it is still positive in that it denotes a speech trait leading to success and, unlike those ascribed to women, one applied to goals. I can refer to men as "bigmouthed" or "fatmouthed" although many of my students find even these apply to women. "Loudmouthed" seems to describe both genders. Words like these that do refer at least sometimes to men are more potent than those reserved exclusively to women. Someone who is "full of hot air" is not a quiet, retiring type; hence, men may also be so described.

The term *eloquent* is one of the rare ones in SE for one who talks both well and at length. Ostensibly, both men and women can be eloquent, but the *Oxford English Dictionary* (OED) gives as examples of usage recorded over the centuries (hence the unusual spelling and capitalization):

Eloquent speakers are enclined to Ambition.
Her dark eyes—how eloquent.

And, the quality of being eloquent is illustrated by:

His eloquence was irresistibly impressive.
Her tears were her only eloquence.
A Scantling of Jack's great eloquence.

When the female is specified, it is only tears and eyes that give eloquence, not her speech. Under the entry for *nagging* only feminine nouns and pronouns are given as examples.

To complete the picture, the words for male idle talk are all idioms with at least one word that indicates [+power, +activity]: *bulls__t, shoot the breeze, chew the fat.* Not one word for idle trivial talk in English refers exclusively to men, although several refer exclusively to females—-and babies, fools, and the insane. Words for idle talk that are masculine at all are marked for potency and activity. Those that are feminine exclusively have no sense of potency or activity. Clearly, not only is the mainstream attitude toward talk revealed by vocabulary but very different cultural attitudes toward the talk of men and women. Despite the tremendous gains in feminism and the ascent of women in careers like law, as I write this in 1993, these differences have not substantially changed. As we shall see, speech activities mirror this state of affairs.

This lopsidedness when referring to males as opposed to females pervades the entire vocabulary. Robin Lakoff (1975) pointed out that words that were once equivalent terms for males and females have often diverged in meaning over time. Consider the following, for instance:

Master/Mistress. These were once counterparts of each other as shown in the children's rhyme, "Mistress Mary quite contrary. How does your garden grow?" The modern *Mrs.* was originally an abbreviation of *Mistress,* although today they can seldom, if ever, be interchanged. Rare survivals of the original meaning of *mistress* do occur, as in

> The walls are full of pictures of famous people, all of them autographed to the mistress of the house, former movie star Shirley Temple Black.
> (Dubois and Crouch 1975)

Note that this quotation expands on the word *mistress* so that the wrong meaning is not derived. Moreover, the mistress here is that paragon of sweetness and virtue, Shirley Temple. Therefore, the older, nonsexual meaning of *mistress* is forced. The first meaning of *mistress* today—that is, the more common usage—is 'woman kept by a man for sexual purposes.' It is probably not without significance that the surviving pronunciation for the abbreviated spelling, *Mrs.* hides the original derivation from *mistress.*

Sir/Madam. The same fate has befallen *madam:* it too has taken on a sexual meaning. Its older use as a form of address signifying respect does survive, at least in impersonal situations, as when salesclerks address female customers. Even here, it is usually replaced by its short form, *ma'am.* Despite its survival as a politeness marker, "May I help you ma'am?", its primary meaning is 'keeper and procurer of women for men to use for sexual purposes.' In other words a madam is a mistress of a house of ill repute.

Some might object that, after all, *madam* and *ma'am* still do survive as polite forms beside *sir,* and ask what difference it makes that *madam* has also taken on another sexual meaning. The difference is that, over time, terms for females in authority have taken on sexual meaning, but those for men have remained the same. Worse, these terms originally denoting high female position have been demeaned to refer to women with the least admirable feminine sexual behavior. The lofty *mistress* and *madam* have been lowered to provide elevated terms for those held in contempt: whores and procurers. A mistress is one better than the prostitute on the streets or in the houses that are not home, but still, she is a whore. The madam? Well, we do not call a pimp a "sir". Elevated terms for men do not suffer such a fate.

King/Queen. This is also evident in the words for the highest ranking of all in the English-speaking world. A *king* is either a crowned head or a top dog. A woman may be the former and, in her home, the latter. Elsewhere, if she acts like a queen, she is likely to be considered a bitch rather than a top dog.

But *queen* has two other meanings as well, both unfavorable, both sexual. The first, most common today, at least in America is 'male homosexual who acts like a woman.' A female homosexual who acts like a man is not called a king, however. Rather, she becomes a "butch," an older nickname for a tough, lower-class boy. An outcast male who acts like a woman is called a queen, the highest ranking for a woman. A woman who acts like a man becomes a lower-class boy, not even a man, much less a king.

The second use of *queen,* occasionally still found among older working-class men in Eastern New England[4] is for the woman other than his wife with whom he has regular sexual relations. This may come from older *quean* as the <ea> used to be pronounced differently from <ee>. The *Oxford English Dictionary*'s definition of *quean* tells it all:

> A woman, a female, **hence** in disparagement: a bold or ill-behaved woman; a jade; a harlot, strumpet (es. 16–17 c.)

The notation in parentheses means that this usage was most common in the sixteenth and seventeenth centuries. In this definition, note especially the logical connector *hence.* It follows for the writers of that venerable dictionary that a woman who is bold is sexually promiscuous. It also seemed to follow for them that a term for a woman would be demeaned as a matter of course. The latter sense of *quean* eventually won out, so when *quean* began to be pronounced just like *queen* (just as *meat* came to sound like *meet)* then *quean* pretty much died out. Some historians of the language think that this is because of its scurrilous meaning, which conflicted with the fact that England does have a queen. In context, *queen* as a homosexual male causes no confusion.

Gentleman, Lady. This pair shows a curious disparity. *Gentleman* seems to be dying out. It survives in the stock salutation "Ladies and gentlemen." In a fancy restaurant or store one might hear, "This gentleman wishes to order/see ..." And once in a while one sees it on restroom doors. It has been replaced for the most part by *men's* as a designation for clothing departments, stores, and toilets. If not used as gender specification, its meaning seems limited today to 'very polite and honorable,' as in "He's a real gentleman."

The feminine counterpart, "She's a real lady" also survives. Beyond that, some strange things have happened to *lady*. Robin Lakoff (1975) pointed out that unlike the many terms for females that have taken on a sexual connotation, *lady* can connote sexlessness. She gives as examples:

She's my woman, so don't mess with her.
*She's my lady, so don't mess with her.

A perhaps more telling contrast is:

Girl, you're a woman now.
*Girl, you're a lady now.[5]

The first instance refers to the girl's being sexually mature now. The second, if said at all, simply implies that she is now polite. The song from the movie *Saturday Night Fever*, "She's More than a Woman to Me," also shows that *woman* in and of itself implies sexuality. The force of Bob Dylan's song "Lay, Lady, Lay ("upon my big brass bed")" is that ladies are not usually seduceable. *Lady* seems to have become a desexed term for *woman*. This, in itself, is noteworthy. Why do we need such a word for women? There isn't one for men. If *gentleman* ever was a candidate, it certainly is not now, as its usage is becoming more and more restricted. *Lady,* on the other hand, seems to be as alive and well as ever. The expression *lady of the evening* shows that *lady* did start on the path of sexual derogation. However, a need for a term for women that had no sexual implications apparently overrode that natural course.

Lady has had yet another fate. Lakoff points out that it is used in trivial contexts. It is "Women's Strike for Peace", but "Ladies' Garden and Browning Society." There is a "National Organization for Women," but what would you think of "The National Organization for Ladies?" Several years ago a great-uncle of mine was complimenting me on my three sons, and admonished me, "Now don't go joining that ladies' lib." His choice of words gave me his opinion of it. Just as there is no counterpart for the desexed meaning of *lady* in terms for men, there is no counterpart for its meaning of [+trivial].

A third thing has happened to *lady,* this not at all unexpected in the light of other once elevated female terms. Although *lady* is still elevated, or at least genteel, in some contexts, it is insulting if used as an address form without a name. *Lady* followed by either first or last name is still an honorable title in England, as in "Lady Margaret" or "Lady Grey." However, *"Look, lady"* is a rude put-down. In contrast, "Look, sir," its counterpart, is very polite, even in anger. Its other counterpart, "*Look, lord," is not even said. Note also that the rude, equalizing "Hey!" does not co-occur with *sir,* although it does with *lady,* as in "Hey, lady, you dropped your wallet!" There is no equivalent, "*Hey, sir, you dropped your wallet."

Yet the saga of *lady* is not complete. The term "foxy lady," originally from BE, does refer to a sexually desirable, beautiful woman, and this usage is sometimes heard from young men. It is also the name of a club for "exotic dancers" in Providence. Also, besides its trivial connotations, which make it unfit in the title of a serious woman's organization, individual career women, (note, not *career ladies) may be referred to in positive terms, as in "She is one smart lady," although to me, at least, *capable* seems more natural with *woman,* so a capable woman can be a smart lady. As women's roles and men's expectations of women's roles change, and have been changing, terms like *woman* versus *lady* can be expected to change as well. The unmistakable degradations over time of terms for women speaks most strongly of the position of women in our culture.

This proves especially true when we examine terms for men. This does not mean that rude terms for men do not exist. They do, but they are composed of words completely different from the titles used to signify respect for men. Terms for degraded men aren't degradations of elevated terms. Rather, they are completely different: *tramp, bum, stud, thief, pimp, jerk, dope, drip.* Terms we use to address men rudely are not debased versions of higher titles either: *mac, bud, fellah,* and so on. Do *king, gentleman, lord,* or *sir* ever mean 'pimp' or 'stud' or 'cheat' or 'forger?' Yet, sirs, kings, lords, and supposed gentlemen can be all of those things as well.

What is at issue here is not so much meanings per se, but that meanings change in certain ways for terms for women but not for equivalent words for men. Faced with the prospect of a female judge, the United States Supreme Court quietly droppped the *Mr.* from their usual address: *Mr. Justice.* This was done to avoid the presumed awkwardness of having to say "Madam Justice." In itself, this sums up the preceding discussion. One gets the impression as one views the history of words for women that any feminine word that is elevated in meaning will eventually be degraded. It is as if women who achieve high status in our society must somehow be brought down. So far as I can see, these words are as true today as when I first wrote them (Chaika 1982, p. 208).

This is clearly seen again in terms derived from less-elevated masculine ones, such as *majorette* from *major* or *governess* from *governor*. In such words, the female term does not take on an immoral sexual connotation, but, instead, adding the feminine ending makes it applicable to a more trivial or low-ranking function than its male counterpart. In these two examples, the actual role denoted is different, but in some words denoting identical functions the feminine ending often carries the implications of less seriousness, as in *poetess, sculptress, authoress*. Apparently, for this reason, many of the older *-ess* words are rarely used today. Racial terms like *Jewess* or *Negress* sound archaic now. It is not without significance that in earlier times, females of the despised minority groups were designated with the *-ess* endings, much like females of animal species (*lioness, tigress*). There was never, so far as I can tell, *Christianess, *Frenchess, *Italianess, *Caucasioness.

Perhaps most revealing of sexual prejudice are words that change meaning when applied to each gender. Consider, for instance, *tramp, dog, beast, pig,* and *professional* (or *pro.*) A male tramp has no job or home, a female tramp is a loose woman. A loose man is casual; a loose woman is a tramp.[6] If a man is untrustworthy and adventurous, or if he takes sexual advantage of a woman, he is a dog; a woman who is a dog is sexually unattractive, unsuitable for dating. As women are modeling their behavior on men's more and more, some women are beginning to call some men dogs in the sexual sense as well. However, liberated or not, a woman is never called a dog in the sense of 'rogue' or 'rascal' although a man might be. *Beast* shows a similar split in meaning. Of a woman, it means 'even less sexually attractive than a dog.' Of a man it means 'sadistic, brutally strong.' Interestingly, "He's a beast" can be "vaguely attractive" as a former student Nancy Mello remarked.

Surprisingly to me, Mary Lizabeth Gatta (1993), in a phone survey of college students, found that thirteen out of sixteen either think of a female professional as a prostitute or "admitted to being aware of a semantic connection between a woman professional and being a prostitute." Three females said that they would never make that connection, and two males said they always would. Even so, "She's a professional" still[7] carries the implication that sex is her profession for some young people today. "She's a pro" means only that. Furthermore, the expression "world's oldest profession" referring to prostitution is far from archaic.

Looking at the brighter side, despite these rude survivals, still among some younger speakers, *professional* can mean that she has a career such as law, medicine, or academia. Although most of Gatta's informants could get the sexist meaning of this word, still seven-eighths of them also use it to refer to a woman in the learned professions. As society changes, so does its vocabulary.

Earlier we saw that topics with which a society is uncomfortable are referred to with a multiplicity of terms, terms that are highly volatile over time. What are we to make, then, of the multiplicity of terms for females: *dame*, (another originally elevated term), *broad, piece, dish, tomato, chick, filly, bird, fox, tigress, baby, poontang, hag, old bag, prude, slut, squeeze, ho* and more currently, *wench, honey* (as in "she's a fine honey"), *hottie, hoochie mama, hooch, babe*?[8] All of these refer to the sexual attractiveness of women. What is noteworthy is how many of them are no longer current and how many new ones there are. The need to designate women vividly on the basis of their sexuality is so strong that new words are constantly being employed for the same old meanings. Even archaic words like *wench* get called into service again.

In contrast, most of the terms we have for men, good or bad, refer to somewhat different aspects of masculinity except, perhaps, those referring to male incompetence in dealing with life, such as *jerk, drip, dope, nerd, turkey, wimp, douchebag, dweeb,* or *shnook*. Of course, a grave insult is to call a boy or man a "girl." English speakers who are privileged to live near speakers of other languages may have also picked up terms for men such as Italian *gibroni* or *shtoonatz* or Yiddish *shlemiel, putz,* or *shmuck,* all of which refer to general incompetence.

In contrast to the terms for women, there are far fewer favorable terms for sexually attractive men and none specifically for sexually unattractive men. There are, to be sure, terms for sexually attractive males—*hunk* and *stud*—although nowhere near the number of terms for females. Both males and females can currently be called "hot," meaning 'sexually attractive'.

Still, note the difference between *stud* and its counterpart *slut*. Even with the advances women have made in the past two decades, the double standard lives. Still, the lines are clearly drawn, with women being defined by their sexuality and men by what they do besides sex or what kind of persons they are. My students tell me that they can refer to a male as a "male slut" which is about as uncomplimentary as it gets. Notice that, just as calling a male "a girl" is always a grave insult, to use another feminine term—distinguishing it by especially noting the feature [+male]—is extremely insulting. *Slut* alone is always female. *Stud* refers to a handsome male who can get anyone he wants, but the presumption is that he goes for sexually attractive women. A *male slut* is not so attractive and he takes on unattractive women. African American females at Providence College, at least, tell me that they can also refer to some men derisively as *male ho,* or can even say, "He's a ho," which has the same effect as using the word *male*.

There are many terms for men which denote weak or effeminate men: *fag, queer, fairy, wimp, swish, sissy, gutless wonder,* even *girl.* These do not imply lack of sexuality, but sexual preferences not approved by society. Since physical bravery is valued as a masculine trait, words meaning 'coward' often come to be used for homosexuals as well. It is assumed that homosexuals, not being 'manly,' are also not strong nor courageous. It is also assumed that women aren't brave either, hence *sissy* from "sister." Our culture's unease with homosexuality is well-exemplified in the vocabulary.

Why are there so many more sexual or demeaning words for females than for non-homosexual males? One possible answer is that men have the power in our society, hence the right to set standards and to label as they wish (Spender 1985). Anne Bodine (1975) provides what is undoubtedly the clearest example of this view: the rules for pronoun agreement with indefinite pronouns such as *everyone,* and *anybody.* Because English shows no gender marking in the plural, speakers and writers for literally centuries have used plural pronouns and verbs to refer to those indefinites.

▶Will **everyone** who wants pizza raise **their** hands?
▶Does **anybody** want **their** coffee black?

The purists are correct that, semantically, the *their* doesn't agree in number with *everyone* and *anybody,* but to use *his* instead doesn't agree in gender. The indefinite pronouns are not gender-marked. Therefore, either solution, using a plural sex indefinite pronoun or a singular masculine pronoun, is off by one feature. Why, then, has the solution been to make the agreeing pronoun one that is wrong in gender rather than allowing the correctly gender-marked plural? Because, as Bodine shows, males in the British Parliament decreed this, as they felt the female is subsumed under the male.

British Parliament? British Parliament actually concerned itself with a matter of gender, one which would codify inequality of men and women? A history of scholarship, as well as of laws, shows that codification of social inequality has long been a prime mover of both scholarly and legal explanations. Truth is never pure and it is never simple, in scholarship or out. As Gilbert and Mulkay (1984) have so convincingly shown, the findings in even so apparently a value-free and objective area as biochemistry are slanted according to the views of the researchers.

Baron (1986) devotes considerable time to what would be truly hilarious etymologies of words for women offered by reputable scholars, including such venerable names as Jespersen and Skeat. The latter, for instance, whose *Etymological History of the English Language* was long a classic, actually tried to prove that *wife* comes from *wib*, 'tremble,' and Partridge as late as 1959 said that the German word for a woman thus means 'the vibrator' or 'the veiled one.' In 1978, Roger Westcott decided that *wife* must come from a hypothetical Indo-European form *wey* which had seven different meanings: 'turn, twist' (wife as a weaver, hip-swiveler, fickle person); 'drip, flow' (menstruator); 'grow, sprout, gestator';' magic, sorcery' (witch); 'fault, defect' (weaker sex); 'strong, vigorous' ('person of stamina'); and 'wither, wrinkle' (one who both blooms and ages rapidly) (reported in Baron 1986, p. 37). In fact, the *Oxford English Dictionary,* which relies upon the most careful reconstructions of etymologies, says *wife* simply first meant 'woman' in the Germanic languages. The first written usage of it in Old English was in 725, where it was used to translate Latin *femina* 'woman.'

Aside from the improbability of any one Indo-European root developing into so many contrary words in one language, one wonders why Westcott didn't see words like *wise* and *wonderful* as deriving from the hypothetical *wey*. Moreover, for Westcott or any other scholar to derive an origin from Indo-European[9] or any other ancient source, they would have to show regular sound changes that occurred in all words with the given sounds from their origin to today. Words do not change willy-nilly into other words. That is, such scholars would have to show that there was a word *wey* which miraculously grew sounds to produce *witch* and *wib,* and also somehow turned into all of the other words they claim. That is, they would have to show that English and other Germanic languages have words meaning 'drip, flow, strong, fickle, grow, sprout, magic, fault," etc. and that these words today can be traced logically to an older *wey.* Furthermore, they would have to show that some other Indo-European languages, such as the Slavic group, Hindi, or Celtic also had such a strange potpourri of words traceable to one root. These principles of reconstruction were well-known to scholars like Skeat and Westcott. They are the stuff of first year linguistics. Strangely, etymologists have been far less fanciful as to the origins of *man,* and, where they have speculated, it is to suggest that *man* is derived from words meaning *mind* or *hand.* Thus scholarship itself through the ages has been in the service of keeping women in their place.

Even such a scientific endeavor as tracing the history of a language can be skewed to create and maintain superiority. The word *marry,* for instance, does come from Indo-European *mer* or *mor*, which clearly meant either sex, and which appears through the several Indo-European languages as a variety of words meaning 'young man' or 'young woman.' (Baron, 1986 p. 45). *Marry* came into English through French around

1325, and then, as since, it referred to both men and women. As we shall see, in Portuguese, the same root did become specialized for men only, but in the sense of 'husband.' In any event, many commentators, all male, long after the fact, have tried to redefine *marry* so that it makes the woman a passive object and the man the agent. As one man said, "Properly speaking, a man is not married to a woman…nor are a man and a woman married with each other. The woman is married to the man…we do not speak of tying a ship to a boat, but a boat to a ship. And solong as man is the larger, the stronger, the more individually important…it is the woman who is married to the man." (quoted in Baron, p. 46). As recently as 1973, the respected scholar Beveniste stated that men do the marrying and women are just the objects of marriage. This, despite the fact that English has allowed both female and male subjects of *marry* ("Jane married" is as grammatical as "John married" since 1325!)

Robin Lakoff gives a somewhat different analysis. She suggests that the multiplicity of labels is a result of extant taboos, as sex still being somewhat taboo, resulting in men's discomfort with women. This arises because they define women in sexual terms. The multiplicity of terms for women, like those for homosexuals and bathroom functions, indicate both a debasing of and a discomfort with women.

It seems to me that the data are clear. Women are still sex objects to men. If they are not, why do words for women take on sexual connotations over time? Why are elevated terms for women so regularly degraded? Why are there so many terms for sexually desirable women? Why are there words for women who do not put themselves forth sexually, all of them uncomplimentary?

As further proof that this analysis of our vocabulary is on target, consider the sentences,

    a.   You know what SHE needs.
    b.   She needs a good you know what!

This last was once said to me by a Roman Catholic male professor about a nun! Everybody knows by such omissions that what the female "needs" is sex from a male. Notice these are empty sentences, equivalent to the empty phrases *do it* to refer to the sexual act, *go* for bathroom functions, or fire *for effect* for 'kill'. Both (a) and (b) above are empty in that the *she* in both might actually need anything from the universe of needs, but the answer to both is always 'sex.'

English is not the only language to suffer from sexism. Portuguese shows the same disparities. The most insidious thing about a sexist lexico-semantic system is that the attitudes are learned without anyone's ever teaching them overtly (Chaika, 1984). This doesn't mean they can't be changed. They can. It's just that most people in the culture never notice the bias. If we examine Portuguese words for women and men, we find a situation much like English, if not even more so. One is inevitably reminded of Fairclough's assertion that power is wielded by language because we respond to it subconsciously. My informants, Dr. Gilbert Cavaco, Mr. Jose Antonio DaAscensao Battista, and Ms. Maria Guerreiro represent mainland, island, and Brazilian Portuguese. Since Portuguese still has gender marking on nouns and adjectives, it is especially easy to see disparities in words for men and women. The same lexical item takes on different connotations just by using the feminine *-a* instead of the masculine *-o*.

Feminine	Masculine
fodilhona 'wanton woman'	*fodilhão* 'stud'
porca 'slut'[10]	*porco* 'slob'
puta 'whore'	*puto* 'endearment for one's homosexual lover'
rapariga 'whore'	*rapaz* 'boy'
rainha 'snob, know-it-all not chaste'	*rei* 'king'

Note the disparity in phrases as well—*ficar para titia* literally 'become an aunt', means 'old maid.' If he becomes an uncle his sibling had a baby. *Ela é feia mas é boa* is 'she's ugly but she is good in bed anyhow.' There's no masculine counterpart to this either. His ugliness has no direct parallel to bedroom behavior. One male consultant told me that when he visited his mother in Portugal and asked her about his old friends, she commented about women only on their marital status and sexual behavior. She never mentioned male sexual behavior. Of women, she'd say *"vergonhada"* 'she has no shame.' There is no masculine counterpart. *Ela é boa* means 'she is good' which, naturally, can mean she's good you know where, but the masculine for this only means 'he's a good person.' It gets worse. As in English, only women gossip *fofogueira*. Rarely, if ever is a man *fofoqueiro*. Rather he is said to *bater papo* 'shoot the breeze.' In Brazil, a *chata* is a nag. *Chato?* Only if he is a boor, so men don't nag although they can be rude.

Most telling, and most blatant, is the entry in a mainland Portuguese dictionary which lists *sabio* as meaning 'wise man.' However, no feminine counterpart is given. The best a woman can be is *sabichona* 'a woman who presumes (dictionary's word) to know a lot.' This is closer to *sabichão*, 'he is crafty.' As in English, a woman who is smart is uppity. The gender disparity is evinced even further in *pensa em si misma* 'she thinks a lot of herself, is too aggressive.' But if he thinks a lot of himself it means he is genuinely powerful.

Even in the matter of the respectably married, we see a disparity. The title *senhora* 'Mrs.' is as polite as *senhor* 'Mr.' but matters go swiftly downhill from there. A man refers to *minha mulher*, literally 'my woman: the woman I'm sleeping' with or 'my wife.' Women do not refer to their husbands as *meu mulher* 'my man.' She calls him *meu esposo* 'my spouse' or *meu marito* 'my husband.' A feminine version of the polite *marito* doesn't even exist.

How much does other language behavior fit with the social image of women portrayed in English vocabulary? Do other speech behaviors support the view of women as passive, essentially trivial sex objects? Robin Lakoff suggested also that, in many ways, women themselves talk weakly and ineffectually. This prevents them from being taken seriously. Unfortunately, she made no attempt to verify any of her intuitions by experimentation or careful, controlled observations. More recently, it has become clear that the supposedly feminine patterns she delineated are characteristic also of children and of men in subordinate positions (Crosby and Nyquist 1977). Those of inferior status speak in certain ways, and that includes much speech by many women.

Although she has been criticized for relying too much on her intuitions, still Lakoff did break out of the system enough to notice, and then to point the way for subsequent research, and she wasn't far off the mark, either. Briefly, Lakoff claimed that women (and, we now know, subordinates):

▶ Use empty nonforceful adjectives and expletives, such as *charming, divine, darn,* and *shoot.*
▶ Use more hedges in their speech, such as qualifying adjectives with *so* (It's so nice), *I guess,* and *maybe.*
▶ Use tag questions more, thus weakening their statements, as in "Tastes good, doesn't it?"
▶ Use more extreme intonation contours, allowing their voices to fluctuate in pitch more dramatically the way young children do, and end statements on a questioning, rising pitch. When asked, "What time is dinner?" a woman may answer, "At eight?"

One obvious problem with such assertions is that they are tough to prove. They don't lend themselves to laboratory experiments, and they are likely to vary according to social situation and perhaps according to idiosyncracies of particular speakers. They can be investigated by observing interactions between males and females, matched for age and status. Eakins and Eakins (1978), for instance, analyzed male and female speech during faculty meetings. Even more than with dialect investigation, there are so many relevant features in studies of natural interaction that it is very time consuming. Still, some, like Soskin and John (1963) and Pamela Fishman (1978) have braved such studies.

By using evidence from co-occurrence restrictions, we see that Lakoff is correct in her first assertion that the more feminine words do not co-occur with important subjects. It certainly would sound unnatural for someone to say, "Shoot! They vandalized my house" or "The nation's economy has been divine all summer." The real problem with her assertion, however, is that no one seems to use the alleged feminine speech forms much anymore, and that men as well as women use them in some circumstances.

The use of softened expletives, such as *shoot* or *fudge* for their forceful and taboo counterparts may be characteristic of some women, but it is also of some men. In fact, the last *fudge* I heard was from a young man in a supermarket who dropped a jar. He looked normally masculine and was surrounded by a wife and young children which, combined with his being in a public place, may explain the *"Fudge."*

Lakoff was correct in saying that stronger words were specifically masculine—at one time. Men used to have more leeway in using such words, especially in masculine company in informal situations. However, for some years now, in order to signal that they are liberated, many women deliberately have been using taboo words, especially when first meeting other women. It seems to be a badge of liberation. Often this is done only once at the beginning of an acquaintance. The taboo word functions like an address form in that it makes a statement about the speaker that is to be remembered throughout interactions with her.

Kottke and MacLeod (1989) examined the reactions to women therapists and their clients using profanity. One hundred sixty college students listened to tapes of female therapists interacting with both men and women clients. When the therapist herself used profanity, the students were less willing to say that they would go to her for therapy. However, when the client used profanity, the therapist was perceived as being more attractive and more trustworthy than when the client did not. Apparently, it is not all right for women to speak strongly, but it is a measure of their "niceness" if they let others do it.

Another signal of weakness is the use of **hedges**. Eakins and Eakins found that at academic meetings or conferences, there was a tendency for women to use more hedges or disclaimers than men, although they did not collect a significant number of such hedges in their sample. But, then, they were investigating academic women who are used to competing with men intellectually. Considering this, the fact that they found even a trend might be significant. Even these women preceded statements with disclaimers like "I know this sounds silly but...", "This may strike you as odd...". "You're going to think this is stupid, but..." and "Well, I'm not the expert, but..." Such data certainly support Lakoff's premise that women's speech habits weaken their assertions.

Tag questions like *isn't it, aren't you,* and *aren't they* are used by males and females alike in polite chitchat of the *nice day, isn't it?* variety. They are also used for genuine requests for information as in

The factory grosses $15,000, *doesn't it?*

They can also be used after statements, as in

Tastes good, *doesn't it?*
It isn't right the way he's getting pushed around, *is it?*

Dubois and Crouch (1975) roundly criticized Lakoff for her stance on tag questions. They taped a meeting in which all the tag questions were posed by men. The problem is that DuBois and Crouch never specified which kinds of tags the men used. From the few they report, it seems as if they were like legitimate information-seeking tags. Eakins and Eakins found other uses of tags almost exclusively from female faculty. My own students, as a regular assignment, have been asked to count all tags during a family meal or gathering, classifying them as to type. So far, the results have been overwhelming. If one can believe the evidence from tags, women do not trust their own sight, hearing, tastebuds, or judgment, for they continually attach tags to personal statements. Outside of greetings, men rarely do. Furthermore, in many families, there is a difference between generations, with grandmothers using more tags than mothers, and daughters using them least. This also reflects an educational difference. Typically, the younger generations have more formal education than the older. The question of tags should highlight for the student how careful the investigator must be in a study both to classify one's data properly and to gather sufficient amounts of it.

In sum, our vocabulary treats women as trivial sex objects, and our speaking practices show a strong preference for weakness in women's speech. Not surprisingly, our vocabulary treats women's talk as trivial, carping, annoying, and as foolish as a baby's or mental incompetent's. Furthermore, so the myth and language go, women talk a great deal, and their speech is irritating and unpleasant. Even children's storybooks help perpetuate these stereotypes. I have seen even recently published books portray little girls as tattletales, but little boys as helpful informers who alert adults to genuine problems. Little boys and men are shown advising and solving problems, while little girls are shown comforting. This is tantamount to teaching children at a very young age to disvalue female talk. In combination with the vocabulary the child ingests, it is no surprise that the lesson is so well taken.

A man can hardly get a word in edgewise when the "old biddies" or "young chicks" start clucking at their "hen parties." And certainly, the myth implies, women are as assertive as men—so much so that if men are not careful, women (being hens, I guess) will "henpeck" their men, or, worse, "pussywhip" them. Significantly our language has no equivalent terms for masculine domination of women.

The actual evidence in interactions which involve both genders gives quite a different picture. As we already have noted, people are quite blind to the way they really behave as opposed to the way they think they behave. One of the most enduring myths of our society is that women talk more than men do. Virtually all actual investigations of the matter, those not confining themselves to anecdotal information, at least, have shown that men speak more than women. There have been some exceptions, however. O'Barr's study of legal proceedings (Chapter 11) found that women spoke more than men when women were in dominant positions. Aires (quoted in Lucas 1989) found that among white college students, women and men speak the same amount, or women may even speak more. Most recently, Nowell (1989) has shown that ASL female speakers produce more verbiage than males in informal conversation, but that males produce more than females in interview situations. The raw question, "Who speaks more, men or women?" has little meaning in and of itself. There are obviously individual personality differences between the sexes. Moreover, one has to ask who speaks more in what situations, what variables ethnicity, social rank, and profession have on the relative amount of speech produced by each gender, and also whether we are speaking of mixed or same sex-dyads. All of these factors determine who speaks the most. When we look at these together, however, we find some interesting insights into the role of women.

Most studies have found that males dominate females in interactions between the sexes especially in business settings, academia, formal committees, and the like. My own observations have been made at parties amongst educated professional couples and here, too, most men talk more than women, but not all. There is an occasional couple in which the female does dominate the conversation, but often, she is often negatively evaluated by other participants after the party. Topic can also be expected to play a role in verbal production between genders. If the topic is nursery schools, for instance, women might speak more and longer than men. The questions then become: Do women speak of women's concerns in mixed company? Do men? In my own circles, intensive observations of eastern, high-involvement, professional couples sharing dinner show clearly that it is quite usual for men to talk about their business concerns and sports in front of women, but women do not talk of fashion, housekeeping, or even their jobs in front of the men, much less nursery schools. If women in this group persist in trying to discuss such matters, it is not unusual for the men to go off and form their own discussion group. My students who have examined these behaviors report the same phenomenon. Shibamoto (1985) reports that the Japanese also subscribe to the belief that women outtalk men, but actual observation there has shown that middle-class men speak more and longer than women (pp. 97–98). Perhaps the perception that women talk more is because women don't have the same right to talk as men do.

The male control of topics, or rather, the interesting assertion that women are expected to listen to men's concerns, but men are not expected to listen to women's, in and of itself helps explain disparity in amount of verbiage in mixed-sex interactions. Pamela Fishman (1978), for example, found that women raised as many as 62 percent of topics in ordinary household conversations with their husbands. If husbands did not respond to a topic, it was dropped. By contrast, 28 our of 29 topics raised by the husbands in this study got discussed. Even the remaining one was not dropped outright. Fishman claims that the content of the women's topics were indistinguishable from their husbands' but that men have the right to control what is being talked about. Fishman believes that women raise so many topics in an effort to increase their chance of success, because so much of what they say is ignored by men.

Many other female speech tactics can also be seen as ways of getting attention or getting some kind of control over conversation. Men do the same things as women when they want or need some attention and response. What is significant is that in ordinary male/female conversations, women resort to such tactics far more frequently than men do. For instance, women ask three times as many questions as men. Questions force hearers in a speech community to make a response and are therefore powerful controllers of interactions.

Women, like children, very frequently ask, "D'ya know what?" The response to this, "What?" guarantees that the first speaker will be able to elaborate on his or her chosen topic. It is no surprise that those whose right to choose topics is curtailed, women and children, resort to this kind of opening question far more frequently than do men unless men are talking to male superiors. Women also introduce topics with comments like, "This is really interesting!" far more often than men do. Again, this seems to be a ploy to get attention. In some transcripts, it has been found that women use pause fillers like "you know" as much as ten times more than their male co-conversationalists. Women do this the most when men are giving the least response (Fishman 1978).

Certainly another major reason that men have been found to talk more in mixed-gender interaction is that men feel free to interrupt women, but not vice versa. Zimmerman and West found this in California. My own students have found it in Rhode Island. Whether it is between husbands and wives, male and female faculty, and students of all ages, at home, on the street, at parties, at sports events, at concerts, and in restaurants, men interrupt women more than the reverse. In one sample observation, for instance, husband and wife were observed for three hours during a social gathering. The man outtalked his wife, five minutes to every one she spoke. Furthermore, in that period, he interrupted her ten times, whereas she did not interrupt him even once. All participants afterward characterized the man as being very quiet, docile, and good-natured. His wife was considered exceptionally talkative, forceful, and dominating.

Zimmerman and West found in mixed male/female interactions that 96 percent of all interruptions were by men. Women did not object when men butted in, although they did say, "One minute!" "Please let me finish," or "Wait till I'm done" if other women tried to interrupt. One is strongly reminded of the way adults interrupt children. Zimmerman and West comment that the right of females to speak "appears to be casually infringed upon by males." What this means is that both men and women subconsciously concede that men have the right to control conversation, that women may speak only if men wish them to.

Typically men give women very little feedback during conversations. As men talk, women give little murmurs of encouragement, such as "mmhmm, uh huh, yeah," or "oh." Men do not reciprocate. It is very difficult to keep on talking if the other party does not make such sounds. Similarly, women look at men more when they are talking than men look at women. In effect, then, women encourage men to talk, but men do not encourage women to.

Furthermore, silences in conversations are not equally distributed between the sexes. Women are silent when men interrupt, and they remain silent longer after a man's interruption than a man does if he is cut off. Women are also silent if men give them a delayed minimal response. This is the dampening pause, as in:

> *Woman*: [joyfully] Oh, boy! You'll never guess what happened to me today!
> *Man*: [long, long pause] ...What?

The man's delayed response is calculated to convey complete lack of interest. The impression is that the man responded at all only because of the woman's "You'll never guess..." a powerful opener, equivalent to a question in eliciting the response, "What?"

The entire picture that emerges is one of men controlling male/female interaction in every way and not being overly concerned with what females wish to talk about. Females can, by special strategies, force their topics into the conversation, but men break in on the woman with impunity.

Deborah Tannen quips in her best seller *You Just Don't Understand*, that men lecture (report), whereas women seek rapport. Women are cooperative in speech and men are dominant. Women seek to mend feelings and keep relationships viable. Men don't. People who are subordinate in society are most interested in smoothing out personal relationships, keeping peace, and affirming personal bonds. People who are dominant aren't.[11] They are concerned with remaining dominant. Had she investigated nondominant males and dominant females in the workplace, for instance, she might not have found the same differences in speech behaviors. However, even educated women in personal encounters with men act like subordinates.[12]

Thus, male dominance is evinced in many ways when men and women talk together. Men talk more than women in many circumstances. Men interrupt women with startling frequency, more than women interrupt men. The very way that our language labels women's speech suggests that men would encourage women to continue speaking less than women encourage men. That has also been borne out by objective studies. Men even choose the topics of conversation, deciding what will be talked about, and, in fact, in some circumstances, such as dating, it is accepted that it is up to the woman to find out what the man wants to talk about. Teen magazines actually advise girls to deploy such a tactic on dates if they wish to be popular.

Such assertions have been verified by taping conversations between men and women in a variety of naturalistic settings. Zimmerman and West did this in drugstores, coffee shops, and other public places by putting their tape recorder in a knapsack. Others have done the same by putting a recorder in a purse, a shopping bag, or, if using a microrecorder, even in a pocket. Unfortunately, although it might be construed as violating a person's right to privacy, covert taping is the best way to get natural data of frequency of speaking and the like unless one wishes to confine oneself to academic meetings and classrooms and other such limited arenas of talk.

Notice that anecdotal evidence is not valid for such studies. It is not sufficient for someone to say, "I know someone who.." or "My boyfriend always..." Actual observations must be made and recorded. One counts both the number of turns each party takes and the length of each, as well as things such as the number of interruptions, who makes them, and how the interrupted party responds. This last does not have to include personal semantic information. It is sufficient to count how many times the interrupted party protests, ignores the interruption, falls silent, fidgets, or the like. This can be done with worksheets upon which an observer keeps a tally while pretending to do homework or writing a letter.

Given what we already know about male/female speaking rights accorded by custom, one would expect that women give more indirect requests than do men. Eakins and Eakins (1978, p. 47) had students tell each other how to draw an arrangement of squares. Only verbal cues were allowed. They found a decided tendency for males to tell where the lines should be penciled in, but for females to request. They offer as examples:

Man: Next! Put your pencil on the bottom left corner of the square... Draw your line at a 45-degree angle to the left side of the square. Now get this! This line is the top side of a second square...Don't get it off center or you'll blow the whole thing.

Woman: Then I'd like you to construct another box just below the first one, all right? Only this time, try to arrange it so the left point of the first box touches the top of the second box...

Notice that when the man asks for close attention, he gives a bald command, "Now get this!" The woman softens her directions, "…Then I'd like you to …" and "try to arrange it so…"

Maltz and Borker (1982) point out that boys and girls learn to interact differently from early chilhood. In other words, they become socialized differently with regard to talk. Girls do not play as competitively as boys. Girls see friendship as a matter of intimacy, not competition or power. Their relationships are horizontal rather than vertical. By the fifth grade, girls have learned not to deal with disputes by quarreling. Rather, their friendships just break up. Maltz and Borker say that:

> Basically, girls learn to do three things with words: (1) to create and maintain relationships of closeness and equality, (2) to criticize each other in acceptable ways, and (3) to interpret accurately the speech of other girls. (p. 205)

Moreover, girls learn to form friendships through talk: through giving support, letting others speak, acknowledging what others say, and generally creating cooperation through speech.

Boys, on the other hand, use speech to:

> (1) assert [their] position of dominance, (2) attract and maintain an audience, and (3) to assert [themselves] when other speakers have the floor (p. 207)

Interestingly, the finding that boys use speech to gain dominance has been found to be independent of ethnic group or social class (p. 213). These differences determine only the forms of the verbal competition between boys, i.e., whether or not they play the dozens, have boasting competitions, or show off erudite knowledge. Boys learn to gain an audience by becoming good storytellers, jokers, or narrative performers. Again, in all social and ethnic groups, part of this skill resides in learning to deal with mockery, challenges, and side comments about his story, so that he can get to the end of it. Finally, they have to learn to act as audience members, and this they do by asserting themselves and their opinions. Note that this is in contrast to females who form an appreciative, supportive audience. Although such disparities in speaking practices result in male dominance in many situations, it must be noted that female "weak" practices are often socially preferable, less likely to lead to confrontation and hostility. Also, there certainly are low-key, soft-spoken men who do not overpower others in their speech.

The vocabulary of a language, then, indicates what is important to its speakers. It also indicates how certain aspects of culture or society are valued, whether favorably or unfavorably. It tells us what makes speakers uncomfortable and what they feel about the rightful role and behavior of different members of society. In two instances, speech activities of African Americans and women, a strong corroboration was shown between the attitudes revealed in vocabulary and actual behavior. This does not necessarily mean that the vocabulary is shaping behavior or thoughts. The fact that we can think things quite opposed to what our vocabulary encodes is in itself proof that although vocabulary mirrors, it does not shape. Despite what English has always said about women and their speech, with very little encouragement from society, feminists have been able to say that women are as bright as men, and that they should not be defined in terms of their sexual relations to men. Further, they have set out to show that the vocabulary lies. The degree to which men are willing to "buy" the feminine stance is another story. Still, many women have been able to rise above the language system.

Gender and Persuasiveness

More recently, it has been found that the gender of the speaker has a strong influence on their persuasiveness, especially when coupled with the style apparently considered appropriate for that gender (Carli 1990). Carli observed both mixed- and same-sex dyads to see if there were gender differences in the ability to persuade others, using a topic on which they disagreed. Women were more tentative, but only when speaking with men. This was not a disadvantage, as men found tentative women more influential than women who spoke more positively. Women, however, were less impressed by another woman who spoke tentatively. Considering that most women followed the practice of being more tentative with men than with women, apparently most women have learned their lessons well. Men were equally effective with both sexes whether or not their speech was tentative. In a second study, Carli had 120 subjects listen to an audiotape of identical persuasive messages presented by either a man or a woman, in which half of each spoke tentatively. Again, tentative female speakers were more influential with men than with women, and again, assertiveness or lack of it made no difference upon male speakers' persuasiveness. The lesson is, one supposes, that women should not be assertive and direct around men if they wish to get their views adopted. One is inevitably reminded of African Americans before advances in their civil rights when they spoke of "shucking" and "jiving" to the white man in order to be at all effective in their demands. That is, they had to dissemble and pretend to an exaggerated humility in order to hope to get any advantages from whites. One certainly hopes this is not still the case, although, considering the wrath that bluntly-speaking African Americans like Spike Lee call on themselves, one suspects that this pretense is still as advantageous to African American males as it is to women.

BREAKING THE BARRIERS

It is true that the gender disparity in language and interaction is frequently not noticed, even by women in the professions. Part of Robin Lakoff's genius is that she noticed, thereby raising others' consciousness. We so buy into our language system and rules for social interacting that most of us don't even think of the import of what we're doing. But, still, the Robin Lakoffs of the world manage not to be imprisoned by their language.

Examination of a vocabulary can reveal a good deal about a culture. The lexicon of a language is, to a degree, but not wholly, a mirror of its speakers' attitudes and ideas. A mirror reflects. It does not determine; it does not hold prisoners. As Kay and Kempton (1984) point out, Whorf himself could not have thought that we can't break out of our cultural mode, since his works imply that we should do just that.

Chapter 10 Notes

1   George Lakoff is not responsible for all of this analysis, however. I have added the feature of the motions and the metaphor for climbing in a job.
2   That is, one uses first one leg then the other in a crawling-motion.
3   Note that this term is used instead of *attack* in order to make us seem less aggressive.
4   Perhaps elsewhere as well, but modern dialect studies don't seem to mention this.
5   In linguistics, an asterisk (*) in front of a sentence means that native speakers would not be likely to say it because it is semantically or syntactically odd.
6   Some younger people today are surprised when they discover that the sobriquet "the little tramp" is being used for the male comic Charlie

Chaplin. Since little is an adjective associated with women, they erroneously assume that it is a female who is being denigrated by being called "a little tramp."

7   The older the speaker, the more likely that "she's a professional" means 'prostitute' or 'loose woman.'

8   This term has actually been in and out of usage since about 1915 according to the *Random House Dictionary,* 2nd. ed.

9   English, like Latin, Greek, Hindi, Russian, Hittite, and most of the languages of Europe today came from one parent language, which no longer exists, called *Proto-IndoEuropean. The methods of tracing words back to parent languages have been rigorously formulated and tested out over the past 200 years. The earlier scholars who began this work, developed the art of reconstruction so well that they were able to take modern Romance languages, for instance, and figure out what Latin words must have been that gave birth to the different but related words in French, Spanish, Rumanian, Portuguese, and Italian. Then they could verify their reconstructions by going back to Latin texts. George Waterman's *Perspectives in Linguistic,* 2nd ed. is a good beginning treatment of the growth of this knowledge.

10 In Brazil, she, too, can be a slob.

11 Now that there are house husbands, it might be fruitful to examine their speech behavior and their wives' to see if the economically dominant female interrupts her spouse more than he does her.

12 From my sporadic viewing of television talk shows with men and women arguing about some issue, it seems as if women are very willing to interrupt men and vice versa. Again, this points up the need to localize data and speak only about the situations which elicit the data. The same woman who casually infringes on a man's right to speak on Ted Koppel's show, might herself be infringed on by men at a party.

Exercises

1. Examine how girls and boys are portrayed in children's books. Preferably select books for a certain age group and make a table of who does the talking in each, what kind of talking each does (advising, complaining, informing, comforting, rebelling, etc.). How much talking do men, women, girls, and boys do relative to each other? Does your research suggest that children are taught at an early age to value male speech more than female?

2. Given the disparity in the ways that males and females are socialized to speak what problems would you expect to find when females have male bosses, and vice versa. Also, what kinds of problems would occur in mixed gender interviewing situations or committee meetings.

3. Carefully observe and record the number of interruptions in male-male, female-female, and male-female dyads. Do your findings support those in this chapter? What tactics does each gender employ to deal with interruptions? Are there strong gender differences?

4. Observe one group of boys and one of girls talking together (or playing games). Do you find the differences in interactional patterns suggested by Maltz and Borker?

5. Write down all of the words you can find which refer to females either on television shows, movies, or just your own circles. Do your observations verify that women are still defined in terms of their sexuality and their submissiveness?

6. Make up a list of words like *intelligent, hungry,* and *athletic,* which you think might be associated with males rather than females. Ask your cohorts to use a sample sentence with the word. Do they choose female or male subjects, or neither. What can you conclude about the semantic features on words associated with each gender?

7. Examine the front page of a newspaper. How many examples can you find of words being used to color one's attitude, such as using *land* rather than *invade,* or appealing to "constitutional rights?"

References

Baron, D. (1986). *Grammar and Gender.* New Haven: Yale University.

Bodine, A. (1975). Androcentrism in prescriptive grammar: Singular "they"; sex indefinite "he"; and "he or she." *Language in Society, 4,* 129–146.

Carli, L. L. (1990, Nov). Gender, language, and influence. *Journal of Personality and Social Psychology., 59* (5), 941–951.

Chafe, W. (1968). Idiomaticity as an anomaly in the Chomskyan paradigm. *Foundations of Language, 4,* 109–127.

Chaika, E. (1984). The force of linguistic structures on cultural values: Some distinctions as exemplified by the Big Dan rape case. *Interfaces, 11*, 68–74.

Chaika, E. (1982). *Language the Social Mirror*, 1st ed. Rowley, Mass.: Newbury House.

Crosby, F., & Nyquist, L. (1977). The female register: An empirical study of Lakoff's hypotheses. *Language in Society, 6*, 163–189.

DuBois, B., & Crouch, I. (1975). The question of tag questions in women's speech: They don't really use more of them, do they? *Language in Society, 4*, 289–294.

Eakins, B. W., & Eakins, R. G. (1978). *Sex Differences in Human Communication*. Boston: Houghton-Mifflin.

Fairclough, N. (1989). *Language and Power*. New York: Longman.

Fishman, P. (1978). What do couples talk about when they are alone? In *Women's Language and Style* (D. Butturf & E. Epstein, Eds). Akron, OH: University of Akron Press.

Gatta, M.L. (1993). Sexist Language: A comparison of male and female college students. Paper delivered at Women on Women Symposium. (March 27). Providence College. Providence, RI.

Gilbert, G. N., & Mulkay. M. (1984). *Opening Pandora's Box: A Sociological Analysis of Scientists' Discourse*. New York: Cambridge University Press.

Kay, P., & Kempton, E. (1984). What is the Sapir-Whorf hypothesis? *American Anthropologist, 86*, 65–79.

Kottke, J. L., & MacLeod, C. D. (1989, Oct). Use of profanity in the counseling interview. *Psychological Reports, 65* (2), 627–634.

Lakoff, G. (1987). *Women, Fire and Dangerous Things: What Categories Reveal About the Mind*. Chicago: University of Chicago Press.

Lakoff, G. & Johnson, M. (1980). *Metaphors We Live By*. Chicago: University of Chicago Press.

Lakoff, R. (1975). *Language and Woman's Place*. New York: Harper & Row.

Lucas, C. (Ed.). (1989). *The Sociolinguistics of the Deaf Community*. New York: Academic Press.

MacLaury, R. (1989). Zapotec body-part locatives: Prototypes and metaphoric extensions. *International Journal of American Linguistics, 55*, 119–154.

Maltz, D., & Borker, R. (1982). A cultural approach to male-female miscommunication. In J. Gumperz (Ed.), *Language and Social Identity*. (pp. 196–216). Studies in interactional sociolinguistics 2. New York: Cambridge University Press.

Nowell, E. (1989). Conversational features and gender in ASL. *The Sociolinguistics of the Deaf Community.* (C. Lucas, Ed.) (pp. 273–288). Boston: Academic Press.

O'Barr, W. M. (1982) *Linguistic Evidence: Language, Power, and Strategy in the Courtroom.* New York: Academic Press.

Shibamoto, J. (1985). *Japanese Women's Language.* New York: Academic Press.

Smitherman, G. (1991) "What is Africa to me?": Language ideology and African American. *American Speech, 66,* 115–132.

Soskin, W. F., & John, V. (1963). The study of spontaneous talk. In R. G. M. Barker (Ed.), *The Stream of Behavior.* New York: Appleton-Century-Crofts.

Spender, D. (1985). *Man Made Language,* 2nd ed. Boston: Routledge Kegan-Paul.

Weinrich, U. (1966). Explorations in semantic theory. In *Current Trades in Linguistics,* Vol. 3. (T. Sebeok, Ed.) (pp. 395–477). The Hague: Mouton.

Zimmerman, D. H., & West. C. (1975). Sex roles, interruptions, and silences in conversation. In *Language and Sex: Difference and Dominance* (B. Thorne & N. Henley, Eds.) (pp. 105–129). Rowley, Mass: Newbury House.

Chapter 11

Sociolinguistics and the Professions

E very facet of life is affected by language and how it is used. Here, some applications of sociolinguistics to medicine, law, education, and religion are discussed.

APPLICATIONS OF SOCIOLINGUISTICS

The previous chapters have demonstrated the sensitivity with which language usage mirrors social realities. Studies of dialect reveal who individuals think they are, how a community or a country is stratified socially, where allegiances are, and what covert aspirations people may harbor, as shown by hypercorrection. Analysis of conversations show how to understand what people are really saying. Comparison of different styles of interaction sensitize professionals to what their clients and patients are signaling in their speech. Analyzing the relationship between speech activities and cultural conditions leads us not to condemn or belittle groups other than our own. Knowing about the variation in learning styles among cultures aids us in effectively educating everybody, not just the middle class. It is impossible in this chapter to discuss every application of sociolinguistics to the real world. We can, however, show the scope of such application.

LANGUAGE AND MEDICINE

Although most physicians are committed to equal care for all who come to them, often disjunction in their speaking practices and those of their patients lead to real miscommunication. Moreover, unexamined social attitudes can have a strong effect on actual diagnosis and treatment.

First, the setting of the physician's office itself can be a real deterrent to effective communication. The patient is often very well aware of the physician's high status, which makes it difficult to speak up or criticize in any way. The physician, in turn, no matter how concerned may not realize the difficulties caused by both the setting and relative social status of interactants in a medical setting. If we add to this, the fact that many physicians are overworked, hence in a rush, hence not amenable to extended conversation, we have a situation rife with possibilities for resentment. Then, too, most physicians still are male, and their patients female. Since females have been socialized not to interrupt men and not to speak up forcefully, and since males have been socialized not to really listen or encourage females, women are at a tremendous disadvantage in many medical settings.

Sue Fisher (1982) made a disquieting study which resulted in showing that a patient's social class was a prime determinant in the treatments administered when a Pap smear revealed precancerous cells. Using the techniques of sociolinguistic investigation, she blended verbatim linguistic data with ethnographic data and as in other sociolinguistic investigations, found that neither practitioners nor patients overtly verbalized their reasons for decision making. For instance, staff would never say that certain women sounded uneducated or were poor, nor do they say:

> ...that a particular patient has all the children she needs because she is on welfare...They do not say that...asking too many questions, acting too passive or too aggressive, wanting children or not wanting children...contributes to the treatment recommended.
>
> (Fisher, p. 53)

The guidelines physicians are supposed to follow indicate clearly that hysterectomy, the removal of the uterus, rendering a patient sterile, is to be used only as a last resort, or if the patient wishes to be sterilized. What Fisher found, however, was that private patients never received hysterectomies, but seven out of 13 patients at a community clinic did. Clearly, more was at stake here than decisions based upon the patient's incidence of abnormal cells.

One major difference between the two populations was that the private patients saw a gynecologist in his office while they were fully clothed, and had an opportunity to discuss treatment in private. In contrast, the welfare patients were spoken to in the halls in the presence of other patients or in the examining rooms themselves, while sitting undressed. That the former situation calls for more dignity goes without saying. But, this difference in circumstance was not the major reason for the disparity in treatment. What Fisher found, not surprisingly, was that physicians used Presentational strategies when talking to the private patients, discussing the many modes of treatment. However, when speaking to the poor women in the clinic, they used Persuasional strategies, designed to influence them to accept a hysterectomy. Moreover, it was clear that the more educated private patients were able to question the physicians more skillfully than the poorer women. A microanalysis of the medical interviews clearly showed the sociolinguistic influences on treatment decisions.

PSYCHOTHERAPY

Psychotherapy, the talking cure, constitutes a social event organized around an exchange of information. As such, the ordinary rules of discourse come into play. For years, Freud and his followers interpreted the speech of clients in a highly idiosyncratic manner, treating the entire discourse as the linguistic unit, and fitting whatever the client said into a preconceived set of interpretive rules. An instance of this is the case of Carrie which I have reported on extensively elsewhere (Chaika 1982, 1990, pp. 283–286.) One fragment of her speech and its interpretation suffices:

You know what the experiment is geared to find is how vulnerable, I guess, and you know, if you get close to this person and how you feel about it and some pretty basic questions like it may have something to do with psychiatry, I don't. I'm beginning to think psychiatry is rather old-fashioned, you know there are young people on Yonge Street selling books about, I don't even know how to label them, but there are new ways for man coping with the environment and the people in it. And I haven't got into that but, I don't know I, I just, like you have your set ways of doing things and you're in control. You know and you're talking about yourself personally yesterday, you know, and I walked out of here yesterday and I didn't really have any feeling at all. It was kind of like a release. I like people to confide in me, but, like, where is it going? What, it must serve some purpose, I don't have any theories about it. All I know is that I do get involved with people and it usually ends the same way I, I become very angry and you know something, well not always, but I always get taken, I get sucked in, you know, and I, I was just immobilized last night I didn't accomplish anything and here again today. I, I haven't accomplished anything and I think it's your hang-up too, I, I really don't know. But I get involved in, with and when someone tells me I want to help out, and I want also to give something of myself like I'm older than you, like I would like to give you some of my own insights and I, I don't know if it's appropriate what are we talking about? We're just talking about relationships an they're different, you're a man and I'm a woman and I guess I identified a bit with your girlfriend because I've done that with my boyfriend.

Her psychiatrist interpreted this entire stretch of discourse as:

The whole segment can be taken to mean: Do you like me, and if you do, that puts me in an intolerable position. And if you don't, that's unbearable. There seems to be no solution.[1]

Carrie's discourse was produced during an experiment to show that the speech of schizophrenics disintegrates as the patient becomes more intimate with someone. To this end, her therapists had Carrie meet daily with a first-year medical student, a male, to discuss any neutral topics she wished. The medical student himself did not seem to contribute to the conversation. In light of what we now know about normal interactions, this experiment was faulty in several respects. First, it pitted, so to speak, a woman with a long history of schizophrenia against a male authority figure. Second, there was none of the usual give and take of ordinary conversation. Moreover, the experimenters at that time were unaware of the raggedy quality of most unplanned discourse. Not only does Carrie's speech conform well to discourses reported in the linguistic literature, but it shows the kind of nervousness that even a normal person would have in such an unnatural situation. She seems to be rambling on, trying to fill up the silences in approved American/Canadian middle-class practices. These are exacerbated by the fact that women in our society are responsible for carrying the conversational ball until the man wishes to expound on a topic. The medical student never seems to want to expound, leaving Carrie to prattle on. Moreover, she is quite clearly—using normal discourse analysis—telling this authority figure that she doubts that psychotherapy is effective and that this particular experiment is leading to any kind of beneficial outcome for her. Of course, she buries this criticism in a spate of verbiage, but note that she does mention the parallel with these experimental conversations and usual boy-girl relationships. All the maxims of conversations and the social situations that surround them come to bear on the analysis of discourse in a therapeutic situation. After all, that is a social circumstance, and all cultural and linguistic knowledge is not magically suspended during psychotherapy.

Anthony Wooton (1975, p. 70) gives an example from psychotherapy. Psychiatrists typically do not tell patients what to do. Rather, by asking questions, they try to lead the patient into understanding. The problem is that the questions asked and the answers they are supposed to evoke are different from those already learned as part of normal routines. As an example, Wooton gives:

Patient: I'm a nurse, but my husband won't let me work.
Therapist: How old are you.
Patient: Thirty-one this December.
Therapist: What do you mean, he won't let you work?

Here, the patient answers the psychiatrist's first question as if it were bona fide, a real-world question. The psychiatrist was not really asking her age, however, as we can see by his next question. What he meant by that question was 'you are old enough to decide whether or not you wish to work.' His question was aimed at leading her to that conclusion.

Not only may the patient have to learn new discourse routines in order to benefit from the therapeutic situation. The therapist may use modes of questioning different from everyday discourse. This is not surprising, since the aim of psychotherapy is for the psychiatrist to lead the patient into self-discovery. Some patients become very annoyed by the questioning, feeling that the therapist is refusing to tell them anything. In traditional psychoanalysis, it was accepted that there had to be a period during which the patient "fought" the analyst by refusing to dredge up the answers from the murky subconscious. It has occurred to me that this period may be caused by such a very unnatural situation. It is very hard to gain insights into oneself by sustained self-questioning, perhaps because questioning is rarely used that way outside the therapeutic situation. Furthermore, repeated questioning is threatening. In many societies, including our own, it is associated with accusation of wrongdoing and ferreting out the truth of one's guilt. It is used as a technique for teaching, to be sure, but even then it is often done as a way of ferreting out the pupil's lapses in learning. Many therapists now practice more relaxed conversational techniques, finding them far more fruitful. In that quest, a knowledge of speech act theory and other facets of discourse analysis can enhance the therapeutic process.

Gale (1991) expounds on the efficacy of everyday conversational techniques convincingly in regards to family therapy. He calls the use of microanalytical ethnomethodology and conversation analysis as presented here in Chapters 5 and 6, essential to discovering the practices through which interactants produce and interpret their own and others' behaviors. He points out that conversation analysis is not wedded to preconceived meanings, but, rather, is a "detailed examination of how the talk itself is a performative action that helps to both interpret and produce behaviors" (p. 3) and also shows that context is produced as part of the conversation itself. Detailed analysis of discourse in a therapeutic situation is vital to learning about the therapeutic process itself, as well as how the therapist and the patient shape it. For instance, the following discourse was produced in a psychotherapeutic session between a clinically depressed patient and her psychiatrist:

> *Patient*: My brother used to wake me up in the middle of the
>   night to make me type his college papers, and I had to
>   practically rewrite them....
> *Psychiatrist*: (sarcastically) Oooh, and did we get good grades?

A prime consideration in therapy is to create an environment in which the patient or client can speak freely even about matters which are painful or even shameful. This is what the talking cure is about. The psychiatrist's response in this instance had the natural effect of closing off all further revelations by the patient, thus defeating the purpose of the therapeutic situation. Moreover, his response clearly accused the patient of immoral behavior, and certainly showed that he disapproved of her. Certainly, the psychiatrist's response served to make the patient feel bad about herself, although, one supposes, a depressed patient is seeking therapeutic help in order to feel better about herself. The clinical profile of a depressed person indicates that she or he has low self-esteem.

The physician's response presumably was predicated on his interpretation of what the patient meant, and the efficacy of his response can be determined only in relationship to her meaning, which, as we have seen (Chapter 5), includes her intention (See also Chaika 1990, pp. 150–192). As in all discourse analysis, we must start with deducing the patient's intent. It is not likely, although perhaps not impossible, that she was bragging about writing her brother's papers. However, the middle-of-the-night activity she recounts seems as if it must have been quite distasteful. Furthermore, it suggests a good deal of coercion on this woman by her brother, if not the entire family. Why would a daughter not protest such demands made on her unless her family acquiesced in the brother's behavior? She could have been afraid that her parents wouldn't believe her, or that the brother was capable of severe retaliation. The brother's demands certainly revealed a great deal about the woman's unenviable position in her family, a position which probably had great bearing on her current illness. Many questions could have been asked of the patient which could have led to deeper understanding all around. The psychiatrist, by closing off all further discussion with his sarcasm, also missed an excellent opportunity to learn more about the dynamics of the patient's situation, and, ultimately, the roots of her depression. Moreover, there is a very real risk that the patient was left with even more feelings of worthlessness than she brought to the session, a potentially serious matter with clinically depressed patients.

In defense of the therapist, it must be noted that he might have been using what is known as aversive therapy for some reason or other. Whatever else such therapy does, it does not allow many patients to yield up confidences. Perhaps had the therapist been aware of the delicacy of situation necessary for a person to speak, he would have utilized another technique. As we have seen, unless the social conditions are right, people often cannot talk at all, much less honestly and openly.

Gale (1991, p. 33), discussing solution-oriented family therapy, that is therapy focusing on finding new behaviors rather than on the source of the problems, believes, along with other family therapists, that the creative and mindful use of language is the single most influential method for creating contexts to change behavior. These must be based upon our knowledge of how language is used and interpreted. It should be noted that traditional psychotherapy, with its emphasis on finding the source of problems such as depression, has the same dependency on language use and interpretation. One wonders if the older psychoanalytic practice of being in analysis for years and years before any insights could be made into one's condition was not an artifact both of the unnatural situation of having a patient talk at length without feedback from the analyst, as well as from the idiosyncratic nature of psychiatric interpretation. Rather, culture-specific conversation in the therapeutic situation effects more rapid communication and insights. Fortunately, many therapists have come to a similar conclusion.

LANGUAGE AND THE LAW

We have already seen that location is very important in determining what speech activities can go on and what styles will be used. This is underscored greatly when we consider the law, for as soon as one crosses the threshold of a courtroom, one is suddenly in a world of *plaintiffs, negotiable instruments, demurrers, forthwiths, torts, corpus delecti,* and *mens rea.* The court may be called to order by a sheriff or bailiff who says, "Oyea, oyea, oyea" or "Hear ye, hear ye, hear ye," upon which everyone has to stand, as the sheriff continues, "All persons having any business before the honorable Superior Court come and draw near and you shall be heard." In Massachusetts, this is followed by "God save the Commonwealth and this honorable court. Mr. (or Miss/Mrs.) Justice X presiding. You may be seated." We are assailed with archaisms here, "Oyea," "Hear ye," and "God save." The address forms are suitably elevated, "Mr. Justice X" and "the honorable Superior Court."

One needn't enter a courtroom to hear all varieties of legalese. Go to a lawyer and ask him to write you a will. You wish to leave your jewelry to your cousin Tillie, so the lawyer writes: "I hereby grant, give, devise, bequeath, bequest all my jewelry including but not limited to my diamond and emerald earrings, silver and turquoise Indian bracelet, and any other items of adornment customarily worn and used as such which I may have in my possession, under my control, or for which I possess a power of appointment, express or implied to my dear and beloved cousin Tillie Smits if she survives me, or if not to her heirs."[2]

There are those who, uncharitably, blame lawyers for deliberately using obscure speech so people will have to go to them to straighten out the mess that the lawyers have created simply by using such language. Although sorely tempted, I will not pass such a summary judgment. The language of the law qualifies as a jargon. It serves to identify the lawyers (and judges) as being in the know. One of the ways we know a lawyer is a lawyer is the way he handles language pertaining to the legal system. Perhaps some lawyers deliberately do use the jargon to obfuscate and confuse. But it is a gross simplification to say that is a major reason for its existence.

As with other jargons, legalese uses specialized words with specific meaning. For instance, *of course* in lawtalk means 'as a matter of right,' *serve* means 'deliver legal papers,' and *contributory negligence* means 'legally defined specific acts or failure to act so as to injure another party.' All of these terms are used in non-legal settings, but with different meanings. In instances such as these, the legal jargon is more precise than ordinary language. This can be seen as a positive adaptation of jargon. The repetition of words with the same meaning so often seen in legal documents as in "grant, give, devise, and bequeath" above is also an attempt to be precise. However, these violate the maxim of discourse of not saying more than one needs to in the context. Repeating synonyms is confusing as the hearer or reader will assume that there is a special reason for mentioning them all so that he or she tries to figure out why each has been alluded to. What is intended as precision becomes nearly unintelligible.

Another function of legalese, one found also in other learned fields and in religious language, is that it separates the activities of the courtroom apart from everyday activities and does so by using high-flown language. In both religion and the law, archaic language is usual because it removes what is said from the ordinary here and now. The archaic legal "hear ye" has a counterpart in the religious use of *thou* when referring to God. Foreign language words are also typical of legal and religious languages. This, too, has the function of elevating language by making it more remote from the present and everyday activity. Legalese is loaded with lexical items from Latin such as *mens rea, nulla bona,* and *res judicata,* and French *voir dire, chose in action,* and *fee simple.* The last shows the French arrangement of putting the adjective after the noun.[3]

Excessive length of legal sentences, both spoken and written, also obfuscates understanding, but makes the language more serious. Long sentences are a mark of high-level literacy, hence a mark of education. Finegan (1982) discovered that sentences in wills averaged 39.8 words, those in government documents 25.5 words, and those in other kinds of writing, only 19.3 words. In order to comprehend long complex sentences loaded with difficult words, one has to be able to go back and forth, defining words and figuring out what goes with what in what relationship. O'Barr (1982, p. 18), quoting Melinkoff (1963, p.26), shows how a judge charges a jury orally using the rhetorical devices of high-flown writing. Although this makes his utterances clearly solemn and important, it also renders them incomprehensible. The jargon and overuse of synonyms make it impossible to understand. It is difficult to decode even when written:

> You are instructed that contributory negligence in its legal significance is such an act or omission on the part of the plaintiff amounting to a want of ordinary care and prudence as occurring or cooperating with some negligent act of the defendant, was the proximate cause of the collision which resulted in the injuries or damages complained of. It may be described as such negligence on the part of the plaintiff, if found to exist, as helped to produce injury or the damages complained of. It may be described as such negligence on the part of the plaintiff, if found to exist, as helped to produce injury or the damages complained of, and if you find from a preponderance of all the evidence in either of these cases that plaintiff in such case was guilty of any negligence that helped proximately to bring about or produce the injuries of which plaintiff complains, then and in such place the plaintiff cannot recover.

In all fairness, prompted by the large body of research on legal proceedings, law journals have been presenting the case for making the language of the law comprehensible, and individual lawyers and judges have heeded the call.

Because courtrooms are arenas for adversaries, it is extra essential that decorum is maintained, especially in the control of turns of who is going to speak at a given time. If people did not respect the proceedings or feel highly constrained against speaking out of turn or assaulting someone, then there would be too many physical confrontations. As we have seen, social routines often have the result of lessening the chance of direct confrontation. I suspect that much of the formality, high-flown language, and courtroom ritual proceeds from this need. As in religion, ritualized activities accompanied by unusual but high-flown language keep people in line, so to speak.

Juries are selected by a process called *voire dire* ('see say') by lawyers. As pompous as their language be at other times, during the jury selection, lawyers frequently use colloquial, casual language. This is a way of putting the jurors at ease, in the hope that they will reveal their true selves instead of being on their guard. When questioning witnesses for the other side, lawyers may try to make nonstandard varieties of speech appear stupid. Conversely, when expert witnesses for the opposition are called, the lawyer may try to suggest that they are using big words to obscure relatively simple matters.

The outcome of cases is decided largely on the performances of witnesses. Although one would think this depended on what the witness has to say, it often results from how they say it. The trial manuals used by lawyers have an entire mythology about women, giving the lawyer such advice as "Be especially courteous to women," presumably because they are such delicate creatures that they can't be treated normally, i.e., like a man. Worse, we find that "women are contrary witnesses" and "they try to avoid the answers", and "like children, they are prone to exaggeration" and "given to fabrications" (Bailey and Rothblatt quoted in O'Barr p. 34). Needless to say, there is absolutely no evidence for such assertions. O'Barr thinks that female speech styles contribute to this impression. Language may be weak (WL) or powerful (PL). As we have just seen (Chapter 10), Robin Lakoff (1975) speculated that women's speech is weak because they constantly hedge, qualify their statements and, generally give impressions of vagueness and weakness. Here is testiimony from a woman talking about the death of a neighbor:

Q. State whether or not, Mrs. A, you were acquainted with or
   knew the late Mrs. X.
A. Quite well.

Q. What was the nature of your acquaintance with her?
A. Well, we were, uh, very close friends. Uh, she was even sort
of like a mother to me.
                    (O'Barr 1982, p. 66)

We see two characteristics of weak language here, the use of qualifiers
and hedges like *sort of* and *quite,* and the fact that her answers are what
O'Barr calls **fragmented** (F) style. That is, she doesn't completely answer
the question, but has to have the lawyer pull it out of her. An appropriate
answer to the first question would have been "Yes. We were close friends.
She was like a mother to me." If she had answered fully like this, her testimony would be in **narrative** (N) style, and is a sign of strength and
confidence, as is the omission of the hedge words.

However, O'Barr found that there are women who don't speak this
way. For instance, from a female pathologist testifying in the same case
we find a narrative style with no hedges:

Q. And the heart had not been functioning, in other words, had
the heart been stopped, there would have been no blood to
have come from the region.
C. It may leak down, depending on the position of the body
after death. But the presence of blood in the alveoli indicates
that some active respiratory action had to take place.
                    (p. 66)

From a man we see even weaker language than Mrs. A's:

Q. And you observed what?
D. Well, after I heard—I can't really, I can't definitely state
whether the brakes or the lights came first, but I rotated my
head slightly to the right, and looked directly behind Mr. Y, and
I saw the reflections of the lights, and uh, very, very, very
instantaneously after that, I heard a very, very loud explosion—
from my standpoint of view it would have been an implosion
because everything was forced outward like this, like a grenade
thrown into a room. And, uh, it was terrifically loud.
                    (p. 68)

Not only do we see hedging here, but other signs of weakness such as
using empty adjectives like *terrifically,* and repetitions of qualifiers as in

very, very, very. Hypercorrect forms also give messages of WL, but formal ones belong to PL.

Hypercorrect forms:
> 72 hours, rotated, implosion, not cognizant

Formal:
> three days, turned, explosion, not aware

O'Barr found that one's gender per se did not determine weak and strong styles, but one's social position did. Well-educated, professional, middle-class women showed few features of WL, whereas men who were unemployed or in subordinate lower-status jobs did show them. Examining further, O'Barr discovered that upper- and middle-class educated witnesses of both sexes were more likely to use PL, although people who testify a good deal such as policemen, also use PL (pp. 69–70).

To test how style affects the outcome of a trial, O'Barr created four versions of the same testimony, WL and PL by both sexes. He composed juries of undergraduates, law and psychology students who heard the testimony on tape, and evaluated the participants in the mock trial for competence and dynamism. He tested for the way both the lawyer and the witness was perceived. Although all of these jurors were educated, and in a university situation where they are used to intellectual women, they still showed traditional sex biases (p. 81).

Women who gave testimony in PL were believed more than women using WL, and the same was true for men. Clearly, using a powerful style leads to one's being believed. But there is a big "but" here: males were found overall to be more convincing, truthful, and trustworthy. That is, there is a tendency to believe anyone more if they don't use WL, but men are, nevertheless, more believable than women (pp. 71–75).

There are interesting differences between the ratings of "jurors" in law school and the other "jurors" in O'Barr's study. Because women are supposed to be nonassertive, when they do talk in narrative style, the law-school jurors especially took this as evidence that the lawyer holds a high evaluation of the witness, "as demonstrated by the fact that she is permitted to deliver narrative testimony" (p. 81). The other "jurors" rated the female the same in both styles. Female fragmented testimony seems to have been expected, so that wasn't downrated. Legally trained "jurors" were not taken aback by fragmented male style, probably because they expected lawyers to control the situation. However, the other "jurors," those not legally trained, gave particularly low ratings to a male who gave fragmented answers. O'Barr thinks that this was taken as "particularly indicative of the lawyer's negative evaluation of the witness" (p. 81). It is assumed that if the lawyer doesn't allow a male his usual assertiveness, then that male is not to be trusted.

O'Barr also found that witnesses using hypercorrect style were down-rated, but those using formal style were rated as more convincing, intelligent, competent, and qualified (p. 86) than the hypercorrectors. They, apparently, are perceived to be phonies. Drawing upon research in social psychology, O'Barr speculates that the more listeners are like the speakers, as when both come from the working class, the more punitive the listener's evaluation be if the speaker hypercorrects (p. 87). What this means is that if a working class speaker says things like "dire need" or "rotated my head," he or she will be discredited by jurors who share their accent. Although O'Barr didn't tackle the question, I wonder if this would extend to someone who was trying to use upper-class pronunciations.

O'Barr also edited his tapes to create four more experimental situations. In one, he edited out all overlappings of two speakers. In this tape, speakers talk only when the other has stopped. The remaining three contain simultaneous speech, but differ in who dominates: (1) lawyer and witness equally interrupt and persevere by not giving up the floor; (2) the lawyer interrupts and perseveres in three fourths of the turns; and (3) the witness does the same in three fourths of the turns. *Persevere* in this context means 'takes control of the floor, forcing the other to be silent'. The first and most surprising result is that in all conditions of overlapping speech the lawyer is perceived as losing control. The unsurprising corollary is that the witness is perceived as having control in those situations. That is, no matter who is interrupting more, the witness is perceived as being powerful and the lawyer weak.

However, this is not necessarily bad in the eyes of the juror. When the witness dominates by persevering more often, the jurors felt that he or she had a better opportunity to present his or her case. Similarly, the lawyer in this instance is felt to be more intelligent and fair to the witness. The overall finding showed that the "jurors" prefer and evaluate most positively the situation in which there are no hostile exchanges. Hostility in real courtrooms is shown by lawyer and witness interrupting each other. Jurors don't like this, but, if the examining lawyer gives up the floor, he is rated more positively. O'Barr speculates that the lawyer who bullies a witness on the stand will do damage to himself in the eyes of the jury (p. 87–89).

People tend to match their style to that of the co-conversationalist. That's why we can manipulate style to make others change theirs (Chapter 3). This has important consequences for the law. A lawyer can lead a witness into changing style just by speaking faster or slower, by pausing, by enunciating exceptionally clearly, and even by varying the length of utterances, including questions. By using hypercorrect language, the lawyer can lead the witness into doing the same. Since, as we have seen, the style witnesses use colors the jury's evaluations, the lawyer can have quite an impact on the testimony.

Loftus and Palmer (1974) in a deservedly well-known set of experiments showed that the words used by a questioner had profound effects on what a viewer claims to have seen. They showed people films of auto accidents, then asked questions of the participants, changing the verb they used. For instance, "About how fast were the cars going when they *smashed* into each other?" elicited a faster supposed speed than if the verbs *collided, bumped,* or *hit* were used. Also asking "Did you see *the* broken headlight?" elicited more "Yes." responses than if they were asked about *a* broken headlight, although there actually wasn't one. Similarly, during a trial the "object of an abortion" was referred to differently by the prosecution and the defense as a *fetus, person, male child,* or *baby boy* (O'Barr 1982, p. 75). As O'Barr notes (pp. 29, 75), word choice wields enormous power as do grammar choice and style, so that research into their effects has important implications for our entire legal system.(p. 66)

Anne Graffam Walker (1982) has shown yet more subtle biases inherent in the legal system, biases caused by factors that witnesses have little control over as they are unaware of what it is that they are doing. As an experienced court stenographer, she was able to be present at depositions, a legal proceeding in which lawyers are allowed to question hostile witnesses before the trial. She specifically investigated how lawyers evaluate **cospeech**, another word for overlapping and hesitations (1982) of witnesses. Cospeech can occur at different points in the speaker's turn and can have different meaning. It can take the form of a challenge, such as a lawyer's "I'll ask the questions here." This is termed disruptive as it is perceived as trying to take the floor away from the speaker. A more common type occurs when witnesses try to correct the lawyer's misinformation or they don't understand him. They are not trying to get the floor. They want to repair the situation. Lawyers evaluate each kind of cospeech differently. One woman who had a great many overlaps even in the middle of a clause was regarded as 'sweet.' None of her cospeech was disruptive because she only answered questions. Her husband, termed 'a good ole boy' (p. 109) fell into the change rather than challenge category. A third deponent interrupted counsel's turn 36% of the time and the counsel didn't like it or him. Lawyers, on their part, were guilty of "overwhelmingly disruptive cospeech" (p. 104) if the deponent gave an answer like "I don't know."

Walker maintains that in question and answer exchanges "...where issues of truth are important, silence is two-faced." (p. 55). One face is allied to someone's need to collect his or her[4] thoughts, planning what to say next. The other is the hearer's need to attribute motives to a pause. That is, does a pause indicate that the speaker is being dishonest? Or that he or she is slow in formulating an answer? Actually, not all pauses are silent. Some are filled. By "filled," linguists mean those "uh," "hmm," "aah," and throat clearing sounds, which both indicate planning what comes next and that the speaker doesn't want anyone to take the floor from them just because he or she gets a glitch in encoding. Silent pausing before answering a question is interpreted as hesitancy (p. 68).

Walker found that attorneys interpret those who used filled pauses before giving an answer (filled A-pause) to be straightforward and cooperative, wanting to answer questions, responsive to questions, and speaking immediately at the end of every question. Those who used more silent pauses (unfilled A-pause) before answering were judged to be nervous and afraid, recalcitrant, not careful in answering, and not spontaneous (p. 69). Judging this way is called **attribution**.

There was one exception to these judgments. The examining lawyer afterwards, having been asked to comment, said that witness E both gave "excess consideration to her answer" and "shot from the hip" (pp. 70–71). Walker was puzzled because she found no evidence for either conclusion. What she did find was that E spoke faster than the lawyer, 5.3 S/S (syllables per second) to his 4.69 S/S, so actual speed couldn't have given the impression of slowness (the impression of "excess consideration"). However, E did not once use a silent A-pause. That is, she never hesitated before answering. A full 11 of E's answers came so fast they resulted in cospeech. 23 were instantaneous, and only 9 had pause fillers. Walker considers two possible reasons for the lawyer's impression of E. One is that the 9 filled pauses were so in contrast to the rest of her speech that they were specially remembered. The other is that E committed a cardinal sin early in the interview. She interrupted the lawyer. This resulted in her being viewed negatively. If you don't like people, you notice and remember the bad things. Walker's explanation for the attorney's belief that E shot from the hip rests on speed. Like E, Walker speaks rapidly. The lawyer, as indicated above, does not. Consequently, Walker got no feeling that E's responses were precipitous, but the lawyer, a slow speaker, did. Notice that the lawyer got two contrary impressions of E, both related to tempo.

DISCOURSE PRACTICES AND EDUCATION

In order to do well in American (and European) style schools pupils must be willing to answer questions put to them and to otherwise speak out in the classrooms when the teacher wants them to. Philips (1970) showed that the Warm Springs Indians do not feel free to speak up in school because they are not socialized into the kinds of responses that most other Americans are. The Warm Springs Indians feel that to make mistakes publicly is very humiliating. When tribespeople have to learn something, they observe it until they think they know it. When they are ready, they ask others to come watch a demonstration. The idea of learning by humiliation, as in European based societies, is repugnant to them. Scollon and Scollon (1981, p.8) claim that Athabaskans feel that it is dangerous to the spiritual, mental, and psychological health of a child to make him[5] perform in public. They even feel that it is wrong to observe the child in any way that would intervene in his or her activities.

Erickson (1984, pp. 88-90) explains a somewhat different state of affairs in the socialization of black children in Chicago. In the late 1940's and early 1950's, children were taught **controverting routines**. These were ways of teaching a child to make a personal display in "the spotlight of public attention" (p. 88). An adult would say something, such as 'Don't touch the refrigerator' to which the child answered 'I gonna'

> ...and the subsequent interchanges escalating in intensity, with more and more drastic threats uttered by the adult. At the end of the routine an adult...would say admiringly, 'Oo:::h, he so ba:::d[6].

Erickson says that such routines have been recorded amongst black migrant workers and New England Cape Verdean children as recently as 1979. Children socialized to "play argue" this way in the face of an adult command get into a great deal of trouble in school. Although Native American children don't learn to answer back that way, they get into equal amounts of trouble by their inappropriate silence.

Also, many non-middle-class children of color are not socialized to tell adults what they, the children, already know. Shirley Brice Heath (1983) documents this thoroughly in the Piedmont. One New York researcher asked an Afro-American child where he lived. Since she had given him a ride from his house to the park where they were picnicking, he vaguely pointed 'over there'. Then her husband who had not been in the car asked the child. The boy answered with specific directions, complete with the requisite left and rights and numbers of streets to cross.

Stephen Boggs (1972) found that Hawaiian children would not answer questions put to them directly by a teacher. They perceive questions directed at one child as threats. If the teacher asks questions of the group at large, however, pupils answer readily.

Researchers like Deutsch (1967) and Bereiter and Engelmann (1966) claimed that Black children were deficient in language skills. Labov (1972) showed that the methodology these researchers used to test black language skills was guaranteed to produce defective language. Taking a child of color into a room with an adult white tester, then asking the child to identify something so obvious as a toy elicited silence or a scared "I don't know." The child suspected some kind of trap. Why else would this strange adult in this strange environment be asking such a stupid question? Moreover, it has always seemed to me that when someone is summoned, especially in school or at work, the natural inference is that something is wrong. In any event, the threatening nature of this summons was especially strong for black inner-city children as they are more used to interacting with peers than adults. Such children are used to questioning from adults only if the adult patently must know the answer.

Labov showed that one gets very skillful language from these same children by interviewing them in groups and setting up competition with each other. The same kind of children who mumbled and stumbled over Deutsch and Bereiter and Engelmann's testing showed exceptional facility under Labov's testing situation which was designed to duplicate the situations in which these children usually communicate.

In a world relying increasingly on the skills taught in school, it is frustrating not to know how to teach children who haven't been socialized into getting literacy skills. Middle class black and white children are taught to tell adults all sorts of trivia, things that adults certainly know, such as "And what does the doggy say?" and "Where's your nose? And your tootsies?" But not all children receive this kind of training, and those who do not, do notoriously poorly in the typical public school. If children are not socialized this way, what do we do? Even providing pre-schooling for such children does not necessarily solve the problem, for, as the Scollons have shown, literacy skills actually begin in toddlerhood. It must be emphasized that non-middle class parents are usually very anxious for their children to learn in school. In their frustration with the failures of the schools, they may accuse the system of deliberately making things tough for their children. However, we are just beginning to understand what a child needs to become literate, and we are far from knowing what to do for those who don't come from literate homes.

The persistent problem of low IQ scores in non-middle class children may not be caused by culturally biased questions, but by culturally biased testing situations. Inner-city Blacks are socialized into showing off their intellectual skills in oral displays and competition, not by sitting and marking answers with a pencil. Moreover, they are taught to be original both in their speech and their interpretations of others' speech. Robert Aronowitz (1984) demonstrates that such children fail at standardized reading tests because their answers are creative and perceptive, whereas the test-makers prefer "maximally-redundant-minimally-informative..." answers.

DIALECTS AND READING

We have already seen that dialects differ not only in pronunciation but in syntax. Both circumstances can cause problems in teaching reading as well as affect a teacher's evaluation of certain pupils.

The problem with such differing systems is that schoolteachers typically speak one of the regional standard dialects. Even if they started out as non-SE, they usually think that NSE (nonstandard English of any variety), their own original one and everyone else's, are full of mistakes. As we have seen and as could be illustrated many times over, this is not true.

It is not fair to isolate one form from a dialect and then compare it to a different dialect. It is such a practice that leads one to think that the other dialect contains errors. Teachers confronted with speakers of dialects different from their own should listen carefully and try to ascertain the ways the other dialect operates. Then they should try to analyze exactly how it differs from their own accustomed usage.

In the foregoing examples, notice that even when BE and SE use the same forms, they sometimes mean quite different things. An investigator should never assume that the identical forms in two separate dialects mean the same thing or can be used the same way. Remembering this can be crucial in teaching reading. Everyone who reads well translates the printed sentence into his or her own dialect. For instance, recall the great differences between BE and SE in verb tenses. BE speaking children are not likely to come across their own dialect's verb system in reading textbooks. Nor are NSE children of any other group. The teacher can point out to a BE speaking child, for instance, "Oh, this 'I did sing' means 'I really DID do it' not 'I did it yesterday'" or he or she can say 'I will go' is the same as your 'agonna go.'"

Some immediately object with horror. "But isn't that reinforcing undesirable speech habits?" Not really. In fact, the opposite effect is more likely. By nonjudgmentally pointing out to the child that others say things differently, one is helping the child notice the differences between his or her speech and that of others, including the standard. Also such equations give the child a handle on which forms to focus on. Chapter 8 examines the factors that lead to a child's picking up new dialects. Here, note simply that it is impossible to learn to read unless one knows how to relate the printed page to the speech one already has.

Similarly, understanding differences in pronunciation between dialects is essential to teaching reading and spelling. English orthography has a woefully poor fit to all varieties of English. No dialect of English is spoken the way it is spelled. We all had to learn how the written language corresponds to our spoken language. On the one hand, /r/-full speakers learn that <ar> and <or> each stand for two sounds, the vowel + the /r/. On the other hand, /r/-less speakers consider each simply a vowel. For them <ar> is [aː] 'ah' as opposed to the <a>, which is pronounced [æ], in *cat*, and <or> stands for one sound as well, [ɔ] 'aw' as opposed to <o> in *cot*. In each instance what stands for two sounds in one dialect is a digraph, two letters for one sound. Everyone has to learn that the <k> in *knee* is silent as is the <gh> in *weigh*. We also all have to learn that the printed *have* in *they have gone* is really the *'ve* we are accustomed to hearing for the same sentence, which is pronounced "they've gone." In order to learn to read, all speakers must learn the correspondences between his or her dialect and the written one (Labov 1967; Baratz and Shuy 1969.) Early researchers like these did assume that BE and nonstandard speaking students came to school with no clue about reading, but Heath's (1983, pp. 190–235) study shows that such children do, although they don't use their pre-literacy in ways that conform to traditional classrooms. It is up to the school, then, to relate reading both to children's dialects, and also to discover what uses are made of literacy in their culture. Then the teacher can capitalize on what they already know, leading them gently into the requirements of school.

We have already seen that people not only announce who they are by their speech variety but also the positions they may take in society. Blacks overtly recognize this by the label *lame* but it is true of society as a whole. We have also seen that people unhesitatingly assign others to particular job categories according to their taped speech alone. Bowlers, CB'ers, and other jargon users consider only other speakers of the jargon as really belonging, as being "in the know."

One implication of all this is that there can be no equality of opportunity unless all English speakers can handle standard English of the sort necessary to enter higher level jobs or professions—if that is what they want. Labov (1966) tells the tale of a Ph.D. who could never get a university appointment because he never lost his original working class accent, specifically pronouncing /θ/ as [t] and /ð/ as [d]. This is not a singular instance. How trusting would you be of a professor who said "dese" and "ting" for *these* and *thing*? Of course, that can work both ways. A person doing unskilled factory or construction work would be ridiculed for using refined, educated speech. And, we must also admit that being an executive or a professional is not what everyone wants to do, nor can society function only with chiefs.

Public schools traditionally and correctly felt that part of their duty is to introduce students to standard speech. They have done this by giving regular grammar lessons and having teachers correct pronunciation sporadically. None of this helps. As we have seen, children and adults speak like those with whom they identify. If they do not identify with the teacher and the middle class, nothing will make them talk that way, although they get the message about the inferiority of their native speech. They also become convinced that school is not for them.

Since they do not identify with the middle class, many students are not likely to identify with the values of school, that archetypal middle-class institution. Even those who do are often under peer pressure not to conform to the demands of school including "proper" speech. When teachers correct their speech, many such children feel insulted as if they themselves have been attacked. Considering the close connection between speech and identity, such feelings are justified.

Yet once they reach their twenties, some of these pupils will change their minds. They may start to see some value in middle-class ways and want to become better educated or to get higher level jobs. Native Americans, by tribal custom, frequently do not start to prepare for adult roles until their late teens or early twenties (Ohanessian 1972). Black youths frequently make no attempt to adopt middle-class speech until their late teens or early twenties either. In fact, this is true of many adolescent males. The biggest problem for education is that sometimes it is very difficult by that age to begin to use certain sounds and constructions with any consistency (Labov 1966). The sounds hardest to change are just those the most implicated in social class marking, such as the <th> sounds.

There are ways out of this dilemma, ways that do not insult students or get their backs up so that they refuse to learn standard speech forms. Students can be asked to act out natural situations, such as being interviewed for a job, lodging complaints with authority, or impressing a schoolteacher. They should be directed to speak appropriately for the roles. Heath (1983, pp. 317-320) stimulated children to become ethnographers, reporting on the kinds of speech used by different people and for different purposes. As part of a science unit, she had them interview people about farming techniques and, then, write a book about their discoveries. This, of course, enlarged the children's social networks and sensitized them to language differences.

Such technique can be adapted to writing as well. Inner city high school students with reading achievement scores as low as second grade proved able to write coherent newspaper articles for teachers in a college workshop that I guided (Chaika 1978). Students worked in groups, correcting one another's work, with the teacher floating from table to table to give help with mechanics. Teachers are pleased to find that such students show a hefty passive knowledge of standard speech and writing forms when these are not elicited punitively. Other tasks which allow students to practice standard speech include putting on plays in which the characters are middle class, having students write and produce mock TV shows, and even asking them to instruct their classmates. Thus they can all practice educated speech, and, if they ever want to speak that way, the resource will be awaiting them. The school's aim is to allow students to become functionally bidialectal.

APPLICATIONS TO BILINGUAL EDUCATION

Both bilingual education and ordinary foreign language classes share the same concern: to teach people how to communicate effectively in a new language. To this end, it is useful to examine how bilinguals themselves deal with their languages, how they use them, under what circumstances, even how they have learned them, if not in a school situation.

There is still a great deal that we don't know about how bilinguals draw upon their separate languages, but it seems at least likely if not sure that they don't normally simply look for equivalents between their languages as they select one or the other for a given transaction. Yet, as noted above, the traditional classroom focuses on translation.

⋅ Bilinguals often make mistakes in speaking their non-dominant language (if both aren't equivalent for them.) Very fluent bilinguals seem happily unaware that they do small violences to their second language in pronunciation, lexical choice, and syntax. Yet, the traditional classroom stops the student at every error. In the heat of conversation, bilinguals typically don't stop to repeat learned rules as they talk away. Yet, the traditional classroom belabors rules.

But the times are changing. As far back as 1967 when I attempted to dip my toes into Chinese at Brown University, Professors Jimmy Wrenn and David Lattimore taught by having us learn dialogues appropriate for myriad ordinary social interactions. Such an approach had the advantages of making us talk, but the disadvantage was that the dialogues were "canned." We had to memorize them. They weren't necessarily what we wanted to say. In those days, it was assumed that sheer memorization was the best way to learn a new language. There couldn't be too much drilling. This was before the research into language acquisition showed that language learning is an active, creative process.

More recently, Robert DiPietro (1987) has applied his considerable sociolinguistic knowledge to language teaching. He set up scenarios, **frames**, then allowed his students to work out for themselves both what they wanted to say and how they wanted the scenarios to be resolved. For instance, one group of students might be told that they were having a heart attack, and another that they were the doctors. Students were given a chance to rehearse individually what they wanted to do. For instance, one "doctor" may wish to be indirect, and another might want to be blunt and even scold the "patient." Neither group knew how the other was going to behave, so that the students had to figure out the intentions of the other as they would in normal conversations. Each had to change tactics in response with the other. As in real life, students were allowed to make errors, and to repair them. In short, they learned by doing, naturally. In dialogue-based instruction, students may even be allowed to make typical bilingual errors, sacrificing perfection for the sake of fluency and comfort in speaking the foreign language. To show that this method works, DiPietro recorded the students' conversations and edited out the errors. Then he had the students look over the corrected manuscripts, but not memorize them. Subsequently, when the students re-enacted their scenes, they were far more fluent and made fewer errors the second time around, showing that they had actually learned.

LANGUAGE AND RELIGION

We recall that formal uses of language increase the feeling of respect people have for others. This applies as well to religion. Everyday language is not usually suitable for religious purposes as worshipers are supposed to pay special respect to the Deity and to their clergymen. Consequently, many religions use now dead languages to increase their mystery, or, at the very least, archaic formal forms of their present speech. The former is illustrated by the Hebrew in a Jewish service, Classical Arabic in a Moslem one, and the latter by the King James' Bible for Christian English speakers.

An unusual religious discourse activity is "speaking in tongues," known scientifically as **glossolalia**. This is unusual because the utterances aren't in a recognizable language, and, if they were, then activity wouldn't be "speaking in tongues". Nobody has ever been able to prove that the glossolalists are actually speaking another language. In fact, there is little proof that speakers make sounds not native to their own languages. Indeed, one of the primary researchers in the field, William Samarin, says that glossolalia bears no resemblance to any language, living or dead, although the speaker believes it does.[7] He points out that the intonation used in the speaker's "utterances" make them sound like real language, but they always lack the central feature of language: a semantic system tied to specific words and grammar. In the 1940s and 1950s, Danny Kaye and Sid Caesar, two comedians, produced babbling which sounded like foreign languages in their routines, very successfully too, I might add. This is not said to disparage speaking in tongues, just to point out that there are parallels in that language-like sequences can be made, but, of course, for very different purposes. Then again, we have seen that all linguistic production depends on context and intent for its ultimate meaning. It is not unusual for similar or even identical utterances to mean very different things when correlated with intent and context. Magicians also use meaningless sounds as if they are words. Some schizophrenics do, too, but, for them, it doesn't seem deliberate.

Although the speakers themselves do not or cannot explain what they have said, others in the church, either laypersons or ministers, interpret it. Laffal, Monahan, and Richman (1974) had a young minister speak in tongues in response to words they read him, and played the resulting tapes to different audiences. The audiences were willing to ascribe meaning to each portion, but the meaning they derived was not the same as that intended by the speaker.

Speaking in tongues proceeds from religious conviction. The New Testament is the authority for it, taking it to be proof of the Holy Spirit within the speaker. Samarin (1979) says that most think they are speaking a language, either direct speech of the Holy Spirit or as speech inspired by the Holy Spirit. A great difference between glossolalia and ordinary speech is that the glossolalist can't repeat at will what he or she said, nor can he or she paraphrase it. Whereas ordinary speech is decodable by breaking it down into its components of recognized words built up from recognized sounds, glossolalic "speech" gives a meaning independent of such decoding procedures. Moreover, whereas ordinary speech can be decoded by most other speakers of the language, glossolalia typically can be decoded only by another at the meeting where it occurs.

Laffal et al theorize that language produced for social sharing is noncommunicative, as is language used for catharsis. Similarly, Hamby (1980) says that glossolalia is a social phenomenon with a shared meaning. In other words, the fact of speaking in tongues gives its own meaning. One thing all agree upon, however, is that whatever meaning can be construed from glossolalic productions, it is not done by ordinary people using ordinary decoding means. Instead, another member interprets for the speaker.

One heated debate has pivoted on the question of whether or not speakers in tongues are in a state of altered consciousness or not. Felicitas Goodman (1972a, b, c; 1973) is a firm proponent of the altered states theory. She investigated Apostolic congregations in Mexico, the Yucatan, and Indiana, finding that speaking in tongues is accompanied by a hyperaroused trance brought about by rhythmic clapping, music, singing, and praying. There are other physical manifestations, such as twitching, shaking, jumping, even a catatonic-like state. Those affected say they feel heat, floating, pressure, and relief of tension. She was able to tape speech examples. She also claims that, in small congregations, a set of stock syllables develop. She claims that there is a striking agreement across congregations and across cultures in rhythmic patterns and intonation, and even in speakers of different languages (Goodman, 1969). She explains this surprising agreement as occurring because the glossolalic behaviors arise from speakers being in a trance.

Samarin (1972a, b; 1973a, b) vociferously denies this. Rather, he gives a sociolinguistic interpretation. He states that glossolalia is nonsense which is given the form of language by the speaker's intonation and pauses, but that it is not a trance which causes it, but the belief in the Biblical authority for it. To its practitioners it is a symbol of faith and is another "language" in their religious repertoire. It is their beliefs, not a trance, which causes the phenomenon. He goes so far as to declare that all groups of Christians who indulge in such verbal behavior share theological beliefs and criteria for its use and even its form. He may well be correct, but this does not eliminate altered states as one cause of the glossolalia. It is entirely conceivable that people are able to achieve an altered state because of their belief that they can.

Samarin further claims that glossolalia is a religious language, and it can be explained by noting that it is simpler than natural language, and is caused by a general linguistic regression in which speech is produced unconsciously using rules of pronunciation acquired early, but modified somewhat according to the social and religious factors leading to glossolalia. Samarin's description of speaking in tongues makes it appear to be a kind of religious baby-talk sanctioned by a particular religious belief.

Indeed, his description supports such a view. Usually, it utilizes a limited number of sounds, about twelve, and makes use of alliteration and reduplication[8]. He compares glossolalia to other pseudo-languages, such as be-bop talk, magical incantations, and jabberwocky, all of which have purely social functions apart from what we usually think of as communication of information.

In defense of Samarin's views, Spanos and Hewitt (1979) investigated Goodman's trance explanation, as well as speakers' susceptibility to hypnotism, and possible psychopathology of speakers. They found that speakers performed with their eyes open, and evinced none of the trembling, shaking or disorientation as one would expect of those in trances. They also found no indication that the speakers were more easily hypnotized than anyone else, nor was there indication of psychosis. Rather, they shared religious beliefs and experiences with others. Hamby (1980) describes how Catholic Charismatics learn to speak in tongues both from discussing it, and by hearing others do it as well as hearing others' interpretations.

These studies support Samarin, but do not rule out the possibility of trance states such as Goodman posits. Both things can go on simultaneously at least for some speakers. My own research has been with schizophrenics, some of whom also produce glossolalia, but they do not do it in a particular social setting (Chaika, E. 1974; 1977; 1982; and 1990) . For them it is linked to the severity of their illness, and is evidence that they are not "in their right minds". They don't necessarily look as if they are in a trance, nor do they twitch, and, anecdotally, I keep hearing stories of how someone locked in a back ward of a mental hospital in the olden days learned to "speak schizophrenic." A comparison is very much in order of these two glossolalic populations, and, yes, of magicians and their incantations, of bebop singers in the 1940s, of Dr. Seuss and Lewis Carroll and all who love their glossolalia.

Perhaps glossolalia is another way of elevating language, a way of creating a foreign language, so to speak. It is interesting that this phenomenon does not occur in Judaism, which uses archaic Hebrew for worship, nor, apparently, did it occur in Catholicism when masses were in Latin. For solemn functions, the vernacular just won't do.

Chapter 11 Notes

1   The psychiatrist, Dr. Mary Seeman, has long since written to me, telling me she realized that she agrees with interpreting Carrie's speech according to the rules of current discourse analysis. At the time she made her investigation of Carrie, she was using accepted psychoanalytic techniques of interpretation, and sociolinguistic discourse analysis was not yet widely developed or disseminated. This is being presented now only as an example of how to apply sociolinguistics to therapy.

2   Thanks to William Chaika, Esq. for providing this pseudo-will. It is, of course, a parody, but not far off the mark. He assures me that **he** would never word a will thusly, but thousands of lawyers do.

3   This is also true of names for officers of the government such as *surgeon general* and *attorney general*. These mean literally 'general surgeon' and 'general physician'. In other words, the surgeon and attorney for everybody. What has happened, however, is that English speakers have reinterpreted these to equate the *general* with army generals, meaning those of high rank.

4   This *their* is intentional. As argued in Chapter 9, it is no more incorrect than having to use the male pronoun when referring to females and males.

5   Pronoun choice theirs.

6   The colons indicate long, drawn out vowels.

7   One of my students told me he was positive he was speaking Hebrew as he made many guttural sounds while speaking in tongues. He was, however, not able to reproduce his glossolalic state while talking to me, so I couldn't tell whether or not he did. However, he definitely was not able to imitate my renditions of Hebrew words.

8   Repetition of syllables produced consecutively as in "bye-bye," "bow-wow," and "higgly-piggly." It differs from rhyme in that (1) it can be a repetition of the entire syllable, and (2) rhyme has intervening words.

Exercises

1. Find several words with the spelling <ea>. How many pronunciations are there for this combination of letters? Do the same for the <gh> spelling and one other use of letters of your choice. On the basis of this mini-study, do you think it is possible to teach someone how to read who doesn't speak with a standard dialect or a strong regional one different from your own?

2. Find a contract or lease in your home. The statement of credit liability on a bill for a credit card is fine. What elements of legalese do you find on the document you chose.

3. Examine the language of a prayer of your choice. What archaic or unusual words or syntax can you find in it. Translate the prayer into everyday casual speech. What is the effect?

4. If you and a friend are studying the same foreign language, or if you have studied one that you know another friend has also studied, give yourself a topic of conversation and prepare what you want to say about it in the foreign language. Now try conversing with the friend. What difficulties do you find in expressing yourself.

5. Try to talk to a friend as if you are the friend's physician. What features of your speech behavior do you change? How does the friend's behavior to you change?

6. For any of the topics covered in this chapter—or any other sphere of life—suggest other applications of sociolinguistics. For instance, consider the role of sociolinguistic investigation in discovering what kind of talk is persuasive, the best dialect to use, the kinds of kinesics, and how that might be applied to teaching effective pastoral counseling or selling used cars.

References

Aronowitz, R. (1984). Reading tests as texts. In Coherence in Spoken and Written Discourse (D. Tannen, Ed.) (pp. 245–264). Norwood, N.J.: Ablex Publishing Corp.

Baratz, J., & Shuy, R. (Eds). (1969). *Teaching Black Children to Read.* Washington, DC: Center for Applied Linguistics.

Bereiter, C., & Engelmann, S. (1966). *Teaching Disadvantaged Children in the Preschool.* Englewood, NJ: Prentice Hall.

Boggs, S. (1972). The meaning of questions and narratives to Hawaiian children. In *Functions of Language in the Classroom* (C. Cazden, V. John, & D. Hymes, Eds.) (pp. 299–327). New York: Harcourt, Brace, Jovanovich.

Chaika, E. (1974). A linguist looks at "schizophrenic" language. *Brain and Language, 1,* 257–276.

Chaika, E. (1977). Schizophrenic speech, slips of the tongue, and jargonaphasia: A reply to Fromkin and to Lecours and Vaniers-Clement. *Brain and Language, 4,* 464–475.

Chaika, E. (1978). Grammars and teaching. *College English,* 39, 770–783.

Chaika, E. (1982). How shall a discourse be understood? *Discourse Processes,* 4, 71–87.

Chaika, E. (1982). A unified explanation for the diverse structural deviations reported for adult schizophrenics with disrupted speech. *Journal of Communication Disorders,* 15, 167–189.

Chaika, E. (1990). *Understanding Psychotic Speech: Beyond Freud and Chomsky.* Springfield, IL: Charles C Thomas, Publisher.

Deutsch, M., & Associates. (1967). *The Disadvantaged Child.* New York: Basic Books.

DiPietro, R. J. (1987). *Strategic Interaction: Learning Languages Through Scenarios.* New York: Cambridge University Press.

Erickson, F. (1984). Rhetoric, anecdote, and rhapsody: Coherence strategies in a conversation among Black American adolescents. In *Coherence in Spoken and Written Discourse* (D. Tannen Ed.) (pp. 81–154). Norwood, N.J.: Ablex Publishing Corp.

Finegan, E. (1982). Form and function in testament language. In *Linguistics and the Professions.* (R. DiPietro, Ed.) (pp. 113–120). Norwood, N.J.: Ablex Publishing.

Fisher, S. (1982). The decision making context: How doctors and patients communicate. In *Linguistics and the Professions* (R. DiPietro, Ed.) Advances in Discourse Processes. Norwood, NJ: Ablex Publishing.

Gale, J. E. (1991). *Conversation Analysis of Therapeutic Discourse: The Pursuit of a Therapeutic Agenda*. Advances in Discourse Processes, vol. XLI. Norwood, NJ: Ablex Publishing.

Goodman, F. (1969). Phonetic analysis of glossolalia in four cultural settings. *Journal for the Scientific Study of Religion, 8,* 227–239.

Goodman, F. (1972a). Altered mental state vs. "style of discourse:" Reply to Samarin. *Journal for the Scientific Study of Religion, 11,* 297–299.

Goodman, F. (1972b). *Speaking in Tongues: A Cross-Cultural Study of Glossolalia*. Chicago: University of Chicago Press.

Goodman, F. (1972c). Speaking in tongues. *New Society, 22,* 565–566.

Graffam, A. M. (1985). The two faces of silence: The effect of witness hesitancy on lawyers' impressions. In *Perspective on Silence* (D. Tannen & M. Saville-Troike, Eds.) (pp. 55–75). Norwood, N.J.: Ablex Publishing.

Hamby, W. C. (1980). Glossolalia among Catholic charismatics: A symbolic interactionist perspective. Mid-South Sociological Association.

Heath, S. (1983). *Ways with words*. New York: Cambridge University Press.

Labov, W. (1972). The logic of new standard. In *Language in the Inner City* (pp. 201–204). Philadelphia: University of Pennsylvania Press.

Labov, W. (1966). *The Social Stratification of English in New York City*. Washington, DC: Center for Applied Linguistics.

Labov, W. (1967). Some sources of reading problems for Negro speakers of nonstandard English. In *New Directions in Elementary English*. (A. Frazier, Ed.) Champaign, Ill.: NCTE.

Laffal, J., Monahan, J., & Richman, P. (1974). Communication of meaning in glossolalia. *Journal of Social Psychology, 92,* 277–291.

Lakoff, R. (1975). *Language and Woman's Place*. New York: Harper and Row.

Loftus, E., & Palmer, J. (1974). Reconstruction of automobile destruction: An example of interaction between language and memory. *Journal of Verbal Learning and Verbal Behavior, 13,* 585–589.

Mellinkoff, D. (1963). *The Language of the Law*. Boston: Little-Brown.

O'Barr, W. M. (1982). *Linguistic Evidence: Language, Power, and Strategy in the Courtroom*. New York: Academic Press.

Ohanessian, S. (1972). The language problems of American Indian children. In *The Language Education of Minority Children*. (B. Spolsky Ed.) Rowley, Mass.: Newbury House Publishers.

Philips, S. U. (1970). Acquisition of rules for appropriate speech usage. In *Bilingualism and Language: Anthropological, Linguistic, Psychological, and Sociological Aspects*. (J. Alatis Ed.) Monograph series on Languages and Linguistics: Georgetown University Press: Washington, DC.

Samarin, W. J. (1972a). Glossolalia. *Psychology Today*, 6, 48–50.

Samarin, W. J. (1972b). Sociolinguistic vs. neuropsychological explanations for glossolalia: Comment on Goodman's paper. *Journal for Scientific Study of Religion, 11*, 293–296.

Samarin, W. J. (1973a). Glossolalia as regressive speech. *Language and Speech, 16*, 77–89.

Samarin, W. J. (1973b). Variation and variables in religious glossolalia. *Language in Society, 2*, 121–130.

Samarin, W. J. (1979). Making sense of glossolalic nonsense. *Social Research, 46*, 88–105.

Scollon, R., & Scollon, S. B. K. (1981). *Narrative Literacy and Face in Interethnic Communication.* Norwood, N.J.: Ablex.

Spanos, N. P., & Hewitt, E. C. (1979). Glossolalia: A test of the "trance" and psychopathology hypotheses. *Journal of Abnormal Psychology, 88*, 427–434.

Walker, A. G. (1982). Patterns and implications of cospeech in a legal setting. In *Linguistics and the Professions* (R. DiPietro Ed.) (pp. 101–112). Advances in Discourse Processes. Norwood, NJ: Ablex Publishing Corp.

Weir, R. (1962). *Language in the Crib.* The Hague: Mouton.

Wolfram, W., & Johnson, R. (1982). *Phonological analysis: Focus on American English.* Washington, DC: Center for Applied Linguistics.

Wooton, A. (1975). *Dilemmas of Discourse: Controversies about the Sociological Interpretation of Language.* London: Allen and Unwin.

Author Index

Subject Index

SUBJECT INDEX

Russian, 8, 18, 22, 35
Russians, 35

Samoan, 14
sampling, 253
sampling, faulty, 254
schemata, 155
schizophrenia, 160
school, 3
Scots English, 66
Scots Gaelic, 66
scripts, 155
self-monitoring speech, 323
self-regulatory behavior, 131
self-righting mechanism, 192
semantic features, 353
   cultural attitudes in, 354, 355
   dialect differences in, 353
semantic inversion, 355
semantic load, 351
semantic universe, 351
sentences, 15
Serbo-Croation, 22
sermon, 161
sexism
   and speaking practices, 373
sexism in grammar rules, 369
Sicilian, 129
Signed English, 333, 335
significant difference, 255
sign language. See ASL.
silence, 145, 171, 403
   and middle-class practices, 391
   misinterpretation of, 171
silent language, 123
Simons, 268
slander, 153
small group interactions, 141
smiles, 1, 126
   cross-cultural, 126
   kinds of, 126
smiling
   and dominance, 126
   and manipulation, 126

and ratings of competence, 128
categorization on amount of, 127
cross-cultural, 127
cross-cultural misunderstanding, 128
frequency of, 127
regional differences in U.S., 127
snub, 86
social class
   and medical interviews, 389
   speech as marker of, 271
social connotation, 83
social convention, 90
social distance, 86, 87, 88, 104, 106, 108
social interaction, 135
   and oral culture, 208
   and speech acts, 153
   male dominance, 379
social interaction and meaning, 20
social intimacy, 87
socialization
   gender differences in, 381
   in speaking to adults, 403
socialization, cross-cultural
   in talking to adults, 404
social markers, 17, 314
social networks, 321, 332
   and standard dialects, 322
   field methods for, 321
   multiplex, 322
social rules
   conflict with individual, 183
social status
   and speech activities, 203
social stratification, 3, 309
   changing, 317, 318, 319
sociolinguistic investigation, 311
   and other sociological measures, 317
   field methods in, 314, 315, 316, 317
sociolinguistics, 1, 2, 3, 5
   and medicine, 388

and social attitudes, 382
multiple terms in, 360
words for talk, 360
vocabulary differences
cross-cultural, 36
vocabulary for females
sexual connotation, 371
voice
black, 94
breathy and sexuality, 98
voiceprinting, 99
voice quality, 92
voice quality
and bidialectalism, 93
and social groups, 93
different judgments of, 93
voices
breathy, 98
harsh, dominant, 98
metallic, resonant, 98

Walloon, 66
Warm Springs Indian, 177
Warm Springs Native Americans, 136, 144
weak language, 398
Webster's Third, 267
Welsh, 66
Welsh Gaelic, 66
Welsh Gaelic, fate of, 66
West African, 351
Whorf, 54
Whorf hypothesis, 54, 55
Whorfian hypothesis, 54, 55, 352
Wills, 153
women
and prestige pronunciations, 319
word, 1
word choice
as influencing opinion, 354
as opinion, 358, 359
word order, 19

words, 1, 4, 5
words
multiplicity of meaning in, 1, 14,

Yiddish, 56, 57, 61
and association with persecution, 57
Yoruba, 94

Zambians, 126